STAPLE SECURITY

STAPLE SECURITY

BREAD AND WHEAT IN EGYPT

Jessica Barnes

Duke University Press   *Durham and London*   2022

Typeset in Portrait and Trade Gothic by Westchester Publishing Services

Library of Congress Cataloging-in-Publication Data
Names: Barnes, Jessica, [date] author.
Title: Staple security : bread and wheat in Egypt / Jessica Barnes.
Description: Durham : Duke University Press, 2022. | Includes bibliographical
references and index.
Identifiers: LCCN 2021051021 (print)|
LCCN 2021051022 (ebook)
ISBN 9781478015864 (hardcover)
ISBN 9781478018520 (paperback)
ISBN 9781478023111 (ebook)
Subjects: LCSH: Bread—Social aspects—Egypt. | Bread—Government
policy—Egypt. | Bread industry—Subsidies—Egypt. | Wheat trade—Social
aspects—Egypt. | Food security—Egypt. | Food supply—Egypt. | BISAC:
SOCIAL SCIENCE / Anthropology / Cultural & Social | SOCIAL SCIENCE
/ Human Geography
Classification: LCC HD9058.B743 E37 2022 (print) | LCC HD9058.B743
(ebook) | DDC 338.4/766475230962—dc23/eng/20220321
LC record available at https://lccn.loc.gov/2021051021
LC ebook record available at https://lccn.loc.gov/2021051022

Cover art: A woman carries bread after purchasing it at a bakery. Cairo,
Egypt, March 9, 2017. Reuters/Mohamed Abd El Ghany.

Contents

A Note on Transliteration and Units

TRANSLITERATION	I have used a simplified version of the standard system for transliterating Arabic. I represent the letter *ayn* with ' and omit diacritics, long vowels, and initial hamzas.
CURRENCY	The Egyptian currency is the Egyptian pound, EGP. One Egyptian pound is made up of 100 piasters. At the time of writing in December 2021, 1 EGP = $0.06.
LAND AREA	The common unit of area measurement in Egypt is the feddan. One feddan is made up of 24 qirat and is equivalent to 1.04 acres or 0.42 hectares.
GRAIN QUANTITY	Egyptian farmers typically assess grain quantities using a volume measure called the keila, which comes from the scooping implement that was traditionally used for grain. Twelve keila make up an ardab. The weight of a keila of grain is approximately 12 kg; an ardab is thus generally rounded up from 144 kg to 150 kg. Grain traders and policy makers assess grain quantities using the weight measure of the metric ton. One metric ton is 1,000 kg.

GRAIN QUALITY   The Egyptian measure of grain quality is the qirat,
not to be confused with the area measurement.
This is an indicator of purity that is measured
out of 24. Wheat that is 22 qirat, therefore, has
a 92 percent purity level.

On my first trip to the Middle East in 1999, while visiting my sister who was working in Jordan, the meze accompanied by freshly baked bread made almost as much of an impression on me as the exquisite ancient city of Petra. When I returned to the region after college to work for a Palestinian research institute for six months, my favorite spot in Bethlehem was a café where I would chat with friends over large platters of bread cut into strips, deep-fried, and sprinkled with salt and thyme. The following year, as a master's student, I spent a summer doing an internship with an agricultural project in Lebanon's Beqaa Valley. My main memory of those summer days, other than of the mouse that would play around my feet late in the day when the office was quiet, is of the mid-morning snack that my colleagues would pop out to buy—manaqish, a thin bread topped with thyme or cheese, wrapped in paper and hot from the oven. In Syria several years later, I did a summer of preliminary PhD research in Aleppo. It was cherry season and the old woman with whom I lived made wonderful cherry jam; that was a summer of cherries and bread.

So when the political situation in Syria rendered doctoral research there unfeasible and I shifted my research site to Egypt, bread was one of the first things I looked for. I arrived in the village of Warda in Fayoum Governorate in the summer of 2007.[1] At that time, Warda, a village of around three thousand people, did not have many places where you could buy food. The only options were a couple of small fruit and vegetable stands, where women sold produce that they had purchased at the weekly market a few villages away, and several kiosks that sold dry goods like tea, sugar, rice, and pasta alongside small packets of brightly wrapped chips and cookies. Nonetheless, with the few items that I brought with me from Cairo, I was confident that I could manage. With bread, I knew that I would not go hungry.

Not being accustomed to baking my own bread, I set out to find a village bakery. But I could not find one.[2] Loaves of white pita bread, packaged in plastic bags and brought from a bakery in another village, were sometimes available at the fruit and vegetable stands, but these never looked as appetizing as freshly baked bread. Occasionally, when passing through the provincial city, I would buy the government-subsidized baladi bread, but I was put off by its gritty texture and what I found to be a bland taste. When visiting people's homes in Warda, I would sometimes join them for meals served with delicious homemade bread, but this bread was not for sale. I asked around for someone who might be willing to bake for me, but the woman I found said that she would have to bake with 10 kg of flour a time. Even as an avid bread eater, I knew that this would be too much for me to get through. In the end, I managed primarily on the foods that I could buy and bread that was given to me; each time a woman I knew well would bake, she would give me two or three large round loaves, which I would cut in quarters and store in my freezer until I was ready to eat them.

Hence, from the beginning of my fieldwork in Egypt, bread was on my mind. I thought little about its deeper significance, though. My attention was focused on irrigation, the topic of my doctoral research, and everything else seemed peripheral. I noted crowds in front of bakeries and complaints about shortages in the supply of government-subsidized bread, but I did not look into the complexities of the subsidized bread program or think about whether it was being impacted by the global food crisis ongoing at that time. I wrote fieldnotes on farmers' practices of cultivating wheat and storing grain within the home, but I did not ask where the rest of the wheat, sold to traders, went. I observed women clustered around ovens baking bread, but I did not pause to think about what inputs this production was contingent upon.

Shortly after I received my PhD, however, as I was turning my dissertation into my first book, the Egyptian revolution took place. The call of the revolution—for bread, freedom, and social justice ('aish, huriya, 'adala igtima'iya)—reverberated through the media coverage, scholarly work, and political commentaries. The first of this trio of demands, bread, was partly a call for better livelihoods, but it was also a call for the food that constitutes the cornerstone of Egyptian diets. This food was everywhere: in Tahrir Square, in the hands of protestors waved above the crowds; on the front page of newspapers in a widely circulating image of a man wearing a helmet fashioned out of bread; in downtown Cairo graffiti art of a tank facing off against a citizen carrying a tray of loaves on his head. Yet the one place where bread was relatively absent was in the scholarly literature.[3] This led me to reflect back on what I had learned about bread during my earlier period of fieldwork in 2007 and 2008. It also made me wonder about how the story of bread is intertwined with processes of cultivating, trading, and milling the wheat from which that bread is made.

This book is my effort to tell that story. Initially, I thought the book would be about bread shortages, long lines, and protests. But when I began my fieldwork for the book in 2015, I did not find any lines. Instead, I found a government subsidy program that was under reform and introducing electronic ration cards. I discovered ways of handling bread on the street and in the home that had always been there but which I had never noticed before. I learned about the importance of grain storage, something I had thought little about previously. I followed the archival records to trace the transboundary flows of seeds and expertise that have made Egypt's wheat what it is today. I entered the mysterious world of the grain trade and came across a whole new language and way of thinking about wheat. As costs of living rose precipitously after Egypt devalued its currency and removed fuel subsidies (under the conditions of an IMF loan agreement signed in 2016), I observed the significance of cheap bread come into relief. When the coronavirus pandemic hit in early 2020, I read about President al-Sisi's calls to stockpile wheat amid fears of an interruption in global trade flows. I came to appreciate how, to most Egyptians, the prospect of being unable to obtain a decent loaf of bread is an existential threat.

I introduce the concept of *staple security* to explore the ways in which different people endeavor to counter this threat and ensure that they have good bread to eat. Staple security refers to a set of practices that seek to secure the continuous supply of a palatable staple, on a national, household, or individual level, so as to address anxieties about staple absence and meet desires for staple quality. These practices are diverse, ranging from scientists breeding productive and resistant wheat varieties to farmers planting seeds, government agencies procuring huge amounts of grain, bakeries producing subsidized bread, and women warming loaves of bread for a family meal. They are practices that sometimes work in tandem, other times in opposition. In approaching these varied acts as staple security, I depart from the common frame of food security by focusing attention on staple foods specifically and by bringing security—as an affectively charged state of being and a form of action—to the fore.

This book speaks to multiple audiences beyond those interested in Egypt, the Middle East, or the particular case of wheat and bread. To those interested in food, it offers an in-depth theorization of staples. It also offers a nuanced understanding of the nexus between food and security. To scholars of security, the book demonstrates how security extends beyond military domains into lived experience, in the Middle East just as it does elsewhere, and into the realm of food specifically. To anthropologists and geographers interested in environment-society interactions, the book presents a framework for understanding how security is part of the way resources are imagined and managed on both a national and household scale.

The book follows wheat from the seed, through its planting and importation, to its transformation into and consumption as various kinds of bread.[4] At each of these stages, I trace the ways in which different actors work to secure the continuous supply of quality wheat and quality bread. These multiple practices of staple security are underpinned by varied meanings, take place across contrasting temporal and spatial scales, utilize a range of devices, and rely on different measures for gauging success. Some of these acts are in alignment; others run counter to one another. Yet all play a part in shaping whether the Egyptian people have bread to eat each day and what that bread tastes like.

The introduction lays out my argument and introduces wheat farming in Egypt, the process of wheat importation, and the different kinds of bread consumed by Egyptians. I explain what I mean by *staple*, how I use the word *security*, and the value of bringing these words together through the concept of staple security. I end the chapter by outlining my methodology for following Egypt's wheat and bread.

Chapter 1, "Staple Becomings," tells the story of the becoming of wheat and bread in Egypt over the course of the twentieth century and on through today. I start by tracing the history of the development of wheat varieties and the production of a high-yield, disease-resistant crop, showing how this has been tied to concerns about the threat of disease epidemics and the nation running out of food. I then follow the seeds from research stations to the fields, probing the work of seed production, dissemination, and fertilizer-heavy cultivation required to translate these new seeds' promise into reality. The points of tension in this process are revealing of how farmers' security calculations do not always match those of the government. In the second part of the chapter, I shift my focus to the history of Egypt's government-subsidized bread. I show how successive governments have tweaked the price, size, composition, and style of subsidized bread over time in an effort to maintain an unfailing supply of bread that the general public deems acceptable. While these two histories—of a breeding program and a bread subsidy—engage distinct groups of actors and forms of expertise, staple security underscores the necessity of reading them together.

Chapter 2, "Gold of the Land," follows the wheat seeds from their implantation in Egyptian fields to the moment of their harvest. It explores what staple security means to rural households that cultivate wheat, as well as the relationship between those households and the government agencies that claim a national stake in this homegrown staple. I begin by tracing the seasonal cycle of planting and harvesting wheat through Arabic newspapers, analyzing the attention given to wheat as a crop of national significance. I contrast this with how small-scale farmers, who produce the majority of Egypt's wheat, see the seasonal cycle of the crop. The second part of the chapter turns to procuring domestic wheat as the mechanism through which the government moves wheat out of the domain of household bread production and into the domain of national subsidized bread production. I look at the procurement price as a device that the government employs to incentivize farmers to grow wheat and sell their harvest. I then examine the disconnect between this vision and the reality of small-scale farmers, who grow wheat primarily as a crop for household consumption rather than for profit.

In chapter 3, "Grain on the Move," I examine procuring foreign wheat, assessing wheat quality, and storing wheat as practices of staple security. First, building on the discussion of domestic wheat procurement in the previous chapter, I look at the government's procurement of imported wheat, which meets roughly half the country's consumption needs. I explore the factors that shape the government's ability to secure wheat from global markets and the popular and political anxieties that surround the government's procurement process and the question of whether Egypt will be able to access sufficient wheat for its population's bread needs. Second, I look at quality concerns regarding imported wheat, which stem from the threat of contaminated bread to Egyptian people and contaminated grain to Egyptian fields. I use the case of a recent controversy over a fungus called ergot to explore these questions of quality, trust, and security. Third, I look at storage and the role it plays in ensuring that the supply of the staple grain is consistent. I examine the political salience of strategic storage and the government's efforts to expand and improve its storage infrastructure. I also look at how storage itself can pose a threat as a locus of corruption.

Chapter 4, "Subsidized Bread," looks at the widely eaten government-subsidized baladi bread, a foundation of most Egyptians' daily sustenance. Such is the centrality of this food that the possibility that it could run out or become unpalatable is understood as a threat not only to those who depend on it but to the stability of the nation. This chapter, coauthored with my research assistant, Mariam Taher, is about the everyday practices of countering this threat by securing the supply and quality of baladi bread. We begin by looking at bread lines, which are emblematic of scarcity, and the reforms implemented by the

Ministry of Supply in 2014 to reshape production and purchasing practices at bakeries so as to address shortages. While these reforms have ensured, by and large, that there is bread in the bakeries, access to this bread is now mediated by an electronic ration card. We turn to the labor involved in getting one of these smart cards and keeping it working, both of which are preconditions to people being able to buy baladi bread at the subsidized price. The second part of the chapter looks at practices of securing quality baladi bread and at how the 2014 government reforms encouraged competition between bakeries as a way of incentivizing them to produce quality bread. The government's bread specifications and bakers' production practices only shape the quality of baladi bread through to the moment of sale, though, leaving a final stage—between purchase and consumption—during which its quality can shift. The final part of the chapter examines how people handle baladi bread, at the bakery and on the street, and the role these practices play in shaping the taste and texture of the loaves they end up eating.

In chapter 5, "Homemade Bread," I turn from the baladi bread associated with the government to the various homemade breads eaten in Egypt. For those who consider good bread to be bread made within a home, staple security means ensuring a steady supply of such bread. I explore, first, homemade bread in a rural context. Drawing on my work in Warda, I examine the value that rural residents attach to homemade bread. I then discuss the practices they employ to make sure that they have this bread in their homes: sharing labor, accessing the necessary inputs, and handling the loaves to preserve their quality. Second, I look at homemade bread in the city. While the consumption of homemade breads in Cairo is far outweighed by the consumption of baladi bread, the fact that some urban residents choose to buy more expensive homemade breads is revealing of the importance they attach to taste. I examine the tactics that these urban residents use to secure their supply of homemade bread in the city, including identifying street-side vendors through local knowledge networks, making informal arrangements with home bakers, and bringing bread from rural areas. Finally, I look at homemade bread as an object of national concern. I follow narratives of Egypt's bread-baking heritage and the story that some Cairo residents tell of a decline in baking knowledge and bread varieties. I examine the efforts of Cairo elites to sustain Egypt's homemade breads as objects of cultural heritage through crystallizing them in museum exhibits, recording them in encyclopedias, and logging them in online databases.

The conclusion brings together these strands and reflects on the significance of this work. I draw parallels between this case and those of other staple foods around the world, showing how staple security can further understandings of food politics. I examine what this analysis of food and security says about the nexus of other environmental resources and security, calling for a more dynamic approach to resource security—as a mode of practice rather than as an achieved status—and adding nuance to how the resource itself is conceived. I close with a quotidian scene of a family eating a meal with bread, a moment that captures the social, material, and political relations that are produced through the presence and taste of this staple food.

Acknowledgments

In writing this book about Egypt's staples, I drew on a number of staples of my own. People without whom this project would have been incomplete. People who boosted my energy at times when it flagged. And people who were not only present but offered quality feedback, valuable perspectives, and kind support along the way.

I am grateful, first, to all the people in Egypt who shared their time and knowledge with me. I thank my friends in the village I call Warda for introducing me to the world of baking, feeding me many loaves of delicious bread, and teaching me so much over the years. I thank Bianca Longhi and Xavier Puigimarti for their hospitality. I thank the agricultural specialists, grain trade experts, journalists, and development practitioners in Cairo who were generous with their time and patiently answered my many questions, in particular Ahmed Wally, Hesham Hassanein, and Sami Salaheldin.

For the archival component of this work, I thank Lee Hiltzik at the Rockefeller Archive Center in Sleepy Hollow, New York; the staff of the US National Archives in College Park, Maryland; and Fabio Ciccarello at the archive of the Food and Agricultural Organization of the United Nations in Rome for helpfully guiding me through their records.

Two writing groups have been with this project since its infancy. Conversations with the first group—made up of Sophia Stamatopoulou-Robbins, Kali Rubaii, Tessa Farmer, Simone Popperl, and Caterina Scaramelli—played a key role in helping develop my ideas. This lovely group of smart women epitomizes, to me, all the best things about academia; our biannual meetings are highlights of my academic year. The second group, the Critical Ecologies Lab at the University of South Carolina, similarly offered feedback on almost every piece of this book at some point in time. I thank the original members, who helped shape my first grant proposal for this project—Conor Harrison, David Kneas, Josh Grace, and the late Ann Johnson—as well as more recent additions: Tom Lekan, Monica Barra, Meredith DeBoom, Dean Hardy, Magda Stawkowski, and Robert Kopack. This collection of scholars is my source of intellectual inspiration at the University of South Carolina.

Three people generously took the time to read the manuscript in its entirety. Ben Orlove read an early draft, providing detailed feedback and great insights that guided its subsequent development. David Kneas read a later draft, putting his creativity to work in thinking through my data and giving me pages of comments that helped me refine my argument. Liddy Pleasants spent days of the first coronavirus lockdown reading the manuscript, calling me to account for anything that was not absolutely clear and providing many thoughtful line edits.

Several other people gave valuable feedback on parts of the book, including Annie Claus, Amy Zhang, and Jessica Pouchet. I thank Judith Carney for her encouragement and our conversations about staples. I thank Hayden Kantor for his early guidance on the food scholarship.

I am grateful to those who invited me to speak about various parts of this project and for the helpful interactions I had in the process. These include the Center for Middle Eastern Studies, Rutgers University; UCL Anthropocene, University College London; the Middle East Studies Center, University of Pennsylvania; the Department of International and Area Studies, University of Oklahoma; the Sawyer Seminar "Bread and Water: Access, Belonging, and Environmental Justice in the City," Carnegie Mellon University; the Summer School on Materiality, Ghent University; the Department of Geography, University of California Los Angeles; the Department of Geography, Kent State University; and the Development Sociology Seminar Series, Cornell University. I thank, also, participants of the following workshops for their comments on different sections of the book: the workshops on Infrastructures of Daily Life at the University of Southern California, Food in the Global Welfare State at Harvard University, Environmental Temporalities and Expertise in the Middle East at Harvard University, and Climate Change and Capitalism at the University of Oslo.

At the University of South Carolina, I thank my colleagues in the Department of Geography and School of Earth, Ocean, and Environment for their support. In particular, I thank Greg Carbone, Caroline Nagel, Conor Harrison, Meredith DeBoom, Amy Mills, and Susan Lang for their interest in this project. As I continue along my academic path, I am thankful for the ongoing mentorship from Timothy Mitchell, Michael Dove, Paige West, and Andrew Mathews.

I am appreciative of the funding that made this fieldwork possible and gave me the time to write this book: an ACLS Fellowship from the American Council of Learned Societies; a Howard Fellowship from the George A. and Eliza Gardner Howard Foundation; a Rockefeller Grant-in-Aid from the Rockefeller Foundation; and a Peter and Bonnie McCausland Faculty Fellowship, Provost Grant, ASPIRE I Grant, and Walker Institute of International and Area Studies Faculty Research Grant from the University of South Carolina.

I thank my siblings—Toff, Liddy, and Tasha—who never fail to cheer me up and help me put things in perspective. I thank Katie and Sarah for creating a sister network in my time zone. I thank my old friends who have checked in along the way: Beth Willis, Florence Miller, Tara Wigley, Sarah Winchester, Sarah Vogel, Ellie Kingsbury, Katy Bower, and Beth Pillsbury. I thank my friends in Columbia for making Columbia feel like home, in particular Meredith A'Hern and Payal Shah for our morning runs.

At Duke, I thank my editor, Gisela Fosado, for her interest in the project from its early stages, as well as Susan Albury, Ale Mejía, and the production team. Two anonymous reviewers provided detailed and insightful comments, which were extremely helpful in the revision process. I thank Bill Nelson for his figures, Chris Catanese for his copyediting work, and Celia Braves for her index. I thank Ahmed Elabd, Mariam Taher, and Ellen Geerlings for permission to include their photographs, as well as the College of Arts and Sciences at the University of South Carolina for a Book Manuscript Finalization Grant that funded the purchase of three images.

I began this project when I was pregnant with my third child, with two other sons aged five and two. Henry, Oliver, and Oscar have brought endless joy, their boundless enthusiasm and curiosity bringing a smile to even the most difficult of work days. They have also brought endless distractions. With these three bundles of energy in the picture, I could not have completed this book were it not for two things: my research assistant, Mariam Taher, who allowed me to explore dimensions of this topic that I would have been unable to on my own, and all the people who looked after my children while I was researching and writing.

Mariam was a delight to work with—an excellent fieldworker with a great eye for detail, a beautiful writer, a deep thinker, and always reliable. It was a pleasure to cowrite chapter 4, which draws primarily on data that Mariam gathered. The book as a whole is undoubtedly richer for Mariam's input and our many conversations together about this material. I appreciate, too, all the people who shared their thoughts with Mariam—among them the woman we call Fayza and Mariam's father, Adel Taher.

I am fortunate to have a wonderful partner in parenting—my husband, David. A fantastic father and brilliant companion, David brings happiness and laughter to all our lives. I am so grateful for his willingness to step into a single parent role during my research trips and for his ongoing support of my work. Several great nannies also kept our boys amused, engaged, and well exercised. I thank, in particular, Allyson Giroux, whose cheerful spirit sustained our family during the first coronavirus lockdown in spring 2020. Grandparents were the final key ingredient. I thank my in-laws, Ann and John, for always being ready to make a long drive and spend days looking after their grandchildren, somehow invariably managing to magically transform our house into an ordered space in the process. And I thank my parents, who warmly welcomed us into their house in London for the 2020–21 academic year to stay out the coronavirus pandemic, providing hours of childcare and entertainment as I finished revisions on this book, always focusing on the positives as their home descended into a noisy chaos.

STAPLE SECURITY

INTRODUCTION

On the morning of January 25, 2011, Egyptian protestors took to the streets, calling for "bread, freedom, and social justice." The bread that featured in their rallying cries was in part symbolic. *Bread*, in Egyptian colloquial Arabic, is ʿ*aish*, which means life. Alongside the demands for freedom and social justice, bread was a reference to livelihoods, to people's frustrations at their inability to access basic services, get good educations, find jobs, and build decent lives for themselves. But it was also literal. Some protestors carried loaves of bread in their hands, waving them above the crowds. They were calling for bread because bread is a food that most Egyptians eat every day, three times a day.

EATING BREAD, EATING WITH BREAD. *Photograph by Mariam Taher.*

They were calling for bread because the years prior had seen severe shortages in the supply of the widely eaten government-subsidized bread and widespread complaints about quality. To the protestors, these deficiencies were emblematic of the Mubarak regime's shortcomings. The lack of satisfactory bread was not acceptable.

Eight years later, one morning in 2019, Hisham left his apartment in a Cairo neighborhood to get bread. By this time, subsidized bread was no longer in short supply. But its significance had not waned; it was still a central part of daily sustenance for most Egyptian families, especially at a time when other costs of living were escalating. At the bakery that sells subsidized bread, Hisham handed over his ration card and requested twenty loaves of bread for his family of four. These round, flat loaves are made from a mix of domestic and imported wheat, procured by the government from Egyptian farmers and international grain traders, stored in silos, milled, and distributed to bakeries as flour. As the server placed the loaves on the counter, Hisham picked up each one to check it. He handed back a couple of loaves that were slightly burnt and another that had a tear in it, asking for replacements. He then laid the loaves to cool for a few moments on the hood of a car parked nearby, before stacking them carefully in his bag. He took the bread back to his apartment, where his wife prepared breakfast, placing a pile of bread on the table next to bowls of stewed fava beans and pickles. The family began to eat.

Eighty miles away in the village of Warda in Fayoum Governorate, Marwa rose early. She took a large metal bowl and the sack of unrefined flour ground from her family's wheat harvest the previous year. She mixed flour, salt, and yeast, then added water by the cup until it came together into a dough, which she kneaded. Leaving the dough to rise, she and her daughter spread a mat on the floor and covered it with bran. When the dough was ready, she divided it into balls, dipping her hands in oil, taking out a handful and throwing it between her hands a few times, then placing it on the mat and pressing down slightly to form a dome. She lit her gas oven. Picking up the first mound of dough, now enlarged after resting on the mat, she put it on her matrah—a circular wooden implement with a handle. She tossed the matrah gently up and down, expanding the dough until it reached the edges, forming one of the large round loaves that her family prefers to eat. The bread was ready to bake.

These moments are united by bread and, implicitly, by the wheat from which that bread is made. The first is a moment of exception in which bread deficiencies reverberate as a symbol of popular unrest and dissatisfaction with an autocratic regime. The latter two are moments of normality, one in which a man buys bread, the other in which a woman produces it. The monumentality of overthrowing a nearly thirty-year regime stands in stark contrast to the mundanity of feeding a family. Yet they are linked by bread as a staple food.

This book is about bread and wheat in Egypt. It is about the central role they play in Egyptian daily life, the sense of existential threat tied to the possibility of good bread not being available, and the acts designed to ensure that it is. I introduce the notion of *staple security* to describe a set of practices that seek to secure the continuous supply of a palatable staple on a national, household, or individual level, so as to address anxieties about staple absence and meet desires for staple quality. Staple security is not something that a country or individual has or does not have. Rather, staple security is an ongoing process of ensuring not only that people do not run out of bread but also that they are able to eat bread that they find satisfying. People care about the quality of the wheat and they care about the flavor of the bread. There is a taste to security.

Among Egyptians, there is a prevalent sense that they cannot live without bread, even though physiologically this is not necessarily the case. Bread is a central component of the Egyptian diet, eaten at almost every meal, and often used as a vehicle for eating other foods. It is also inexpensive and so, for poor Egyptians, constitutes a major portion of their caloric intake. From an individual perspective, therefore, not having bread is a threat to one's very being. From the perspective of the Egyptian government, on the other hand, not having bread is a threat to the state's very being. Cheap wheat bread has become an expected part of the state's social contract with its people. Violent protests in the past—in 1977, for instance, when the government tried to increase the price of one kind of bread; in 2008, when there were bread shortages; and in 2011, when revolutionaries took up bread as a central part of their call for change—have underscored how people do not sit idly by when their bread expectations are not met. The absence of good bread carries the risk of political instability.[1]

Hence at the national level the link between wheat, bread, and security is clear. Military symbols abound as politicians talk about procurement campaigns to secure the wheat necessary to produce subsidized bread for the masses, build strategic stores of grain to guard against harvest risks, and call on the army to distribute bread in times of shortage. At a household or individual level, the explicit security discourse fades, but the underlying rationale remains.[2] Individuals are just as concerned with securing their supply of good bread as the state is, whether through carefully handling the bread that they buy each day or growing their own wheat to bake bread.

By connecting disparate realms of action—breeding seeds, altering government bread specifications, planting wheat to make homemade bread, building silos to store imported wheat, standing in line to get a ration card, and freezing and heating a loaf of bread—this book reveals the multiple practices that go into securing a quality staple food. It connects the labor of policy makers, who frame security planning as their domain, with the less visible security labors of crop scientists working in experimental fields, women preparing bread for a meal, or men making daily trips to the bakeries. It shows how staple security infuses everyday life.

Wheat in Egypt

The field is a half-feddan in size, roughly half an acre, full of a golden-headed crop.[3] It is bordered by an irrigation ditch on one side, which intermittently feeds the crop with water from the Nile that has traveled here through a network of canals. Across the drainage ditch on the other side of the field is a small patch of Egyptian clover, which the farmer is cultivating as fodder for his livestock, a field of onions, and a cluster of olive trees. Then there is another field of gold. Small fields like this, which dominate the patchwork landscape of Egypt's cultivated land through the winter season, are the source of roughly half the nation's wheat (figure I.1).

Wheat is Egypt's most widely grown winter crop, planted in October through December and harvested in April and May.[4] It is grown primarily on small-scale irrigated farms, characteristic of an agricultural landscape in which almost two thirds (63 percent) of farms are less than 1 feddan in size and 99 percent are less than 10 feddans (McGill et al. 2015: 13).[5] All farmers use modern varieties, some replanting seeds saved from the previous year's harvest, others obtaining certified seeds from the agricultural ministry.[6] The varieties grown are mostly bread wheat (*Triticum aestivum*), although some farmers in the south grow durum (*Triticum turgidum*), which is used in the pasta industry as well as for bread production. In the Nile Delta, the triangle-shaped alluvial plain north of Cairo, many of the farms are mechanized. In the Nile Valley, the narrow strip of cultivated land along the river between the Aswan High Dam and Cairo, much of the sowing and harvesting is still done by hand. Outside the Nile Valley and Delta, wheat is grown on some large-scale, highly mechanized farms in the reclaimed desert lands, but these constitute just a small part (11 percent) of the area in wheat cultivation (map I.1).[7]

Egypt has a long history of wheat cultivation, dating back thousands of years. During the period of Ottoman rule, Egypt was often referred to as the granary of the empire, exporting wheat to other areas under Ottoman rule and to Europe (Richards 1986). In the nineteenth century, cotton eclipsed wheat as the country's most valuable export, the latter increasingly unable to compete

FIGURE I.1. Wheat field, Fayoum. Photograph by the author.

on international markets with grain produced elsewhere. Farmers continued to grow wheat, though, and the cultivated area remained stable through the early decades of the British occupation and into the twentieth century. The flow of wheat in and out of Egypt also continued. Around 1900, Egypt became a net importer of cereals. This was due not to a decline in domestic production but to an increase in demand; population growth and rising living standards led more families to purchase imported flour, which at this stage many saw as being higher in quality (Owen 1969). Over subsequent decades, through the First World War, the depression of the 1930s, and the Second World War, the balance between wheat flowing in and out of the country fluctuated, with shifting government policies that variously permitted and banned exports, taxed and subsidized imports (Scobie 1981).

Government interventions in the wheat sector continued after the formation of the Egyptian Arab Republic in 1953. While wheat remained a widely cultivated winter crop, exports of wheat ceased and imports comprised an increasing proportion of the nation's wheat consumption (Scobie 1981, Kherallah et al. 2000).[8] This was stimulated by the flow of subsidized wheat from the United States after 1954, with the exception of the 1966–74 period, when the

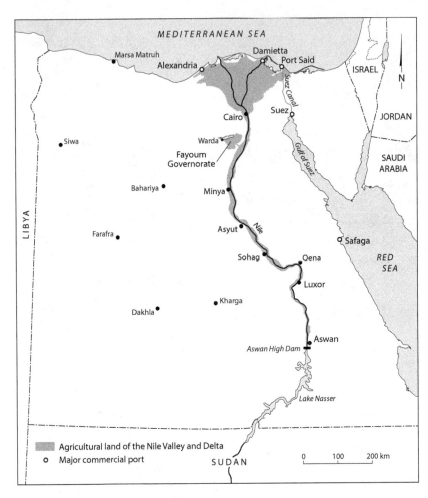

MAP I.1. Egypt. Map by Bill Nelson.

United States suspended this aid (Burns 1985, Dethier and Funk 1987, Mitchell 2002, Iyer 2014). By the mid-1980s, Egypt was producing only a fifth of its wheat. The situation changed with agricultural liberalization in the 1990s, and the partial removal of controls on wheat production and trade (Sadowski 1991, Fletcher 1996). Domestic wheat production rebounded to its current level of meeting about half the country's needs. Today, wheat is grown on 4.3 million small farms (McGill et al. 2015: 6).

The ministry that oversees production of this crop, which the government considers to be a strategic crop (mahsul stratigi), is the Ministry of Agriculture and Land Reclamation (wizarat al-zira'a wa istislah al-aradi). This ministry gathers statistics on cultivated area and production totals and, through its extension program, offers advice on seed choice and fertilization rates. It also has a research wing, the Agricultural Research Center, which occupies a large compound opposite Cairo University in the Giza district of Cairo. On this network of experimental fields, far removed from the clamor of the streets beyond the gates, as well as at several research stations around the country, government scientists are developing new varieties of wheat and managing the production and distribution of seeds to farmers.

At harvest time, when the millions of small farmers around the country cut their wheat, many keep a portion of the harvest for their own use. This wheat they grind in village mills into a coarse flour, which they use to make homemade bread. The remainder they sell, either directly or via a local trader, to one of the three government agencies responsible for domestic wheat procurement. (It is illegal for private companies to purchase Egyptian-grown wheat.) The government-procured wheat is ground into 82 percent extraction flour, meaning that 18 percent of its weight is reduced in the milling process as the grain's germ and bran is removed.[9] This milling is done in both public mills and private mills that have been contracted by the government for this purpose. The 82 percent extraction flour is then used for the production of the government-subsidized baladi bread (figure I.2). Thus the two potential endpoints for the wheat grown in small fields throughout the Nile Valley and Delta are loaves of homemade bread eaten within the home, or loaves of government-subsidized bread, baked and sold at small bakeries scattered around the country's cities and villages. None of the wheat grown in Egypt today is exported. But while no wheat leaves Egypt through its ports, considerable wheat enters Egypt at these points.

Half of Egypt's wheat arrives in the country as grain on bulk carrier cargo ships. Wheat is Egypt's most important agricultural import by far.[10] Global commodity trading firms and regionally specialized traders manage the import process, connecting sellers of wheat (these days, primarily countries around the Black Sea) with buyers within Egypt. About half of this imported wheat is destined for use in the subsidized bread program. This wheat is purchased by the General Authority for Supply Commodities (al-hai'a al-'ama lil-sila' al-tamwiniya), which is part of the Ministry of Supply and Internal Trade (wizarat al-tamwin wa al-tigara al-dakhiliya).[11] It is then distributed to mills for processing into 82 percent extraction flour. The remainder of the imported wheat is bought by the private sector and processed in private industrial mills into a more refined,

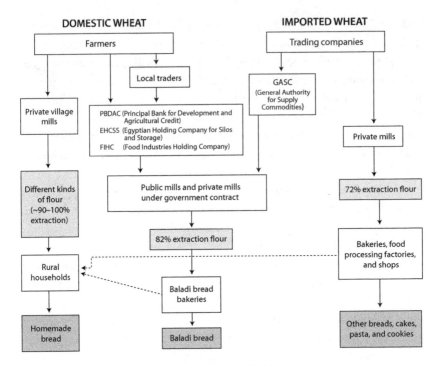

DOMESTIC WHEAT

Farmers

Local traders

Private village mills

PBDAC (Principal Bank for Development and Agricultural Credit)
EHCSS (Egyptian Holding Company for Silos and Storage)
FIHC (Food Industries Holding Company)

Different kinds of flour (~90–100% extraction)

Public mills and private mills under government contract

82% extraction flour

Rural households

Baladi bread bakeries

Homemade bread

Baladi bread

IMPORTED WHEAT

Trading companies

GASC (General Authority for Supply Commodities)

Private mills

72% extraction flour

Bakeries, food processing factories, and shops

Other breads, cakes, pasta, and cookies

FIGURE I.2. Egypt's wheat sector. Figure by Bill Nelson.

Note: The dotted lines indicate relatively small flows of wheat. They represent the fact that women baking in rural homes sometimes add refined flour in small amounts to their homemade bread, and, if they do not have sufficient wheat from their own harvest, they use 82 percent extraction flour as a supplement (see chapter 5). This diagram notably does not include flows of wheat that are illegal but still take place (such as some farmers' sale of wheat to private mills that produce 72 percent flour), nor does it include other parts of the wheat grain and crop (such as the bran or straw), which may be put to a number of different uses.

72 percent extraction flour, which is used in the production of other kinds of bread, as well as in foods like pasta, cakes, and cookies (see figure I.2).

My ethnography focuses on the two ends of this production and consumption process: the cultivation and import of wheat and the baking and eating of bread. I dwell less on intermediary sites, like the ports through which imported wheat passes or the flour mills where grain is transformed into flour, in large part due to my inability to access these politically sensitive sites.[12] Nonetheless, it is important to acknowledge the role that practices taking place in these multiple locales play in shaping the staple that Egyptians eat on a daily basis.

Bread in Egypt

A young girl knocks on my door. "Come," she says. "Come eat dinner." It is an evening in March 2008, and I am living in the village of Warda in Fayoum Governorate. I walk over to my neighbor's house and sit on the floor around a low, round table, joining the male members of the household who are already seated. The mother and her daughters are in the room next door, crouched beside a double gas burner on the floor, finishing their meal preparations. They start bringing in bowls of steaming food and place them on the table. It is a Sunday, market day, and the one day of the week when the family always eats meat and rice.[13] The women place a large dish of rice in the center and several bowls of mulukhiya (a thick broth made from finely chopped jute leaves), potatoes stewed in tomatoes, and salad around the table for the family to eat from communally. One of the girls brings in a pile of homemade bread—large, round, flat loaves, which the women have cut into quarters. She passes a quarter or two to each person. Another girl places a few spoons around the table. The girls squeeze in, finding space between the men. Everyone begins to eat, pulling pieces off the bread in front of them and dipping it in the mulukhiya, or using a fold of the bread to pick up salad or a chunk of potato. The mother selects a piece of chicken for everyone from the large pan at her side, carefully choosing an appropriate part and size for each recipient. As she passes around the meat, each person places their chunk in front of them, on top of their bread.[14]

The cooked dishes being served are special foods, eaten just once a week. Yet despite the meat and rice on the table, bread remains a core component of the meal. It is not just an object of consumption, but a tool for eating. There are spoons, but the family members use them only occasionally—to eat a mouthful of rice or have a spoonful of soup. The rest of the time, they use the bread to dip in or scoop up the other foods. Eating takes on a rhythm. Pull off a piece of bread, look around the table for the next desired item, dip the bread, eat and repeat.[15] The bread acts not only as an implement for conveying food to the mouth but also for holding food. Whereas bread can be placed directly on the table, tablecloth, or serving tray, other foods—like meat or, in more everyday meals, a boiled egg or taʿmiya, the Egyptian version of falafel—cannot; the bread therefore acts as a buffer.[16] Over the course of the meal, the bread plate becomes smaller, as the person eating tears pieces off the edge, and the food on top also becomes smaller, until eventually it is gone and the bread can be eaten in its entirety. Throughout the meal, the mother monitors consumption around the table, keeping an eye on any bowls that might need refilling and passing around bread as people approach the end of theirs. This is part of her

FIGURE I.3. Meal with bread. Photograph by the author.

care for the family, a way of demonstrating bounty at the family level. Those eating should always have bread in front of them.

Many Egyptians, like the family that I lived next to in 2007–8, eat bread three times a day. Sometimes, as in the meal described above, bread is an accompaniment; other times, like breakfast and lunch, it is the main constituent, eaten with just a small amount of cheese, beans, or egg (figure I.3). The prevalence of bread is evident within the home, in the daily meals consumed by family members within most Egyptian households. It is evident, also, outside the home, in small slivers of outdoor space. Walking around Cairo one might see, for instance, a group of policemen on a street corner, sitting on the ground, a bowl of ful (stewed fava beans) between them, using bread to eat from the shared dish; store employees pausing their work to breakfast on some falafel and salad with bread; several female street vendors clustered around a plastic container of food, using bread to scoop it up; a boy sitting at a makeshift table fashioned out of a crate with a loaf of bread, some cheese, a pile of arugula, and a tomato.

Not only do Egyptians eat bread frequently, but they eat bread in quantities that "experts" sometimes describe as excessive.[17] One agricultural specialist working for an international agency in Cairo commented to me that bread consumption in Egypt is "too high." He illustrated his point with some figures.

"In Egypt," he said, "people eat 160 to 190 or 200 kg of bread [per year], possibly more." He talked with confidence, evidently not feeling the need to explain the source of his figures or the basis on which he was judging this level of consumption to be inappropriate. "This contrasts," he said, "with the average worldwide, in the countries where bread is a staple, of 90 kg." A nutritionist I spoke with, who was working on a donor-funded food security project, described her work with rural households on fruit and vegetable production and rearing small animals. When I asked whether they were looking at bread as part of household food security she looked surprised at my question. "We want to *decrease* the amount of bread people are eating," she said. In her view, consumption of a calorie-rich, micronutrient-poor food runs counter to food security objectives. Indeed, one study of nutritional standards in Egypt, which ranks among the countries with the highest rates of obesity (a third of the female adult population is classified as obese), concluded that high bread consumption is tied to overnutrition in both urban and rural areas (Ecker et al. 2016).

Looking at bread through a nutritional lens, however, misses the broader social context of bread consumption and the role it plays in people's daily lives, as I discuss further below. Bread is also not singular, but rather a food that comes in multiple forms. When I arrived in Cairo for my initial fieldwork for this project, I was keen to observe one type of bread in particular: the government-subsidized bread, typically referred to as baladi bread, which costs a mere five piasters for a loaf, less than half of a US cent.[18] On my first walks through the city searching for baladi bread, though, I could not find it. I saw many bakeries, but none that seemed to be selling subsidized bread. I saw many people buying bread, but no one using the ration card that is required to get bread at a subsidized price. I saw bread packaged for sale in grocery stores that was marked as baladi bread, and plastic bags of loaves labeled high-quality baladi bread (khubz baladi fakhir) for sale in news kiosks, but none of these cost just five piasters. I also saw lots of bread that I found difficult to identify. Arranged on tables under road bypasses, being carried on palm-frond trays, balanced on the heads of bicycle delivery men weaving through the traffic—this bread looked like subsidized bread, but it was circulating far from the bakeries that sell such bread.

The bakeries that produce baladi bread are not always easy to locate. Privately owned but licensed by the government, these bakeries are small premises, typically comprising just a couple of rooms in a larger building, with a separate booth or window where sales take place.[19] Some of the production process is now mechanized, like dough mixing and baking; other parts, like the shaping of the loaves, are still done manually. These bakeries are unevenly distributed throughout the city, more common in poorer neighborhoods than affluent ones, sometimes located on narrow alleyways, unmarked by large signs. They are identifiable by the ration cards that are used to complete the purchase at these bakeries alone, which might be clasped in the hands of customers waiting in line or passed over the counter to a vendor who places it in a small, handheld card reader. But cards and card readers are not always highly visible. Thus while baladi bread bakeries are well known to people living in a neighborhood, to visitors they are not readily apparent.

In addition, there are a number of round, flat, pita-style breads in Egypt that are similar to the government-subsidized bread but differ slightly in color, size, and texture (table I.1). Some of these, like siyahi and shami breads, are frequently discussed in policy reports and newspaper articles about Egypt's bread. But whereas in those texts the distinctions appear clear cut—siyahi bread being lighter and less bran-rich than baladi; shami a white bread made from refined flour—in an urban landscape full of breads, these distinctions are far from clear.

This observational challenge is compounded by a linguistic one. There are, in fact, a number of breads that people describe as baladi bread (hence the labeling on the packaged breads I saw for sale during my first visit). The word baladi has national associations—it can mean my country, or belonging to the country—and class connotations: it can be a descriptor for something that is cheap or low-class. Baladi can also mean traditional, rural, or local and so can be used to describe any bread that is perceived as holding one of these characteristics. Any round, flat bread that is relatively dark and has a noticeable bran content may be called baladi bread. For clarity, in this book I reserve the term baladi bread for the government-subsidized bread. This is the most common name for this bread, although there are other terms that people sometimes use, including the literal translation "subsidized bread" (al-ʿaish al-mudaʿam) or "the bread of the [Ministry of] Supply" (ʿaish al-tamwin), after the governmental body that manages the subsidy program.

The apparent lack of baladi bread during my early walks around Cairo was less a reflection of the bread's limited circulation than an outcome of me not knowing where to look. Baladi bread is Egypt's most widely eaten bread by far (figure I.4). Around 70–80 percent of Egyptians have a ration card that entitles them to baladi bread at the five piaster price (the rest of the population has to buy bread at a higher price).[20] These figures do not necessarily reflect consumption patterns—some of those entitled to baladi bread may prefer to bake their own, especially in rural areas, or may choose occasionally to buy other breads. They do, however, speak to this bread's prevalence. Baladi bread is not just a food of the very poor; it is eaten not only by those below the poverty line

TABLE I.1

Breads Commonly Found in Cairo

Baladi bread (ʿaish baladi or ʿaish al-tamwin)	This round, flat bread is made with 82 percent extraction flour. It is made and sold by private bakeries, which are licensed by the government. Egyptians with ration cards are entitled to up to five loaves a day at the price of 0.05EGP/loaf.
Siyahi bread (ʿaish siyahi)	This bread is similar in appearance to baladi bread, but it is made with a more refined 72 percent flour and less bran and so is whiter in color. Despite its name, which means "tourist bread," this bread is readily available from small bakeries around urban areas, as well as from stands in the street, and is widely eaten by Egyptians.
Shami bread (ʿaish shami)	This bread is similar to breads found in countries like Lebanon and Syria (the name means "Levantine bread"). It is a round, flat bread that is distinctly whiter than baladi and siyahi breads. It is made from 72 percent extraction flour. It is sold from bakeries and stands in the street.
Fino bread (ʿaish fino)	This bread, sold from bakeries, is a soft white roll. It is made from a refined flour and has a slightly sweet taste.
Homemade bread (ʿaish beiti)	This is a bread, sold by women on the streets of Cairo, that is homemade rather than produced in a bakery. It is a round, flat bread, larger than baladi bread. Sometimes women mix millet and corn flour into this wheat bread.
Miladin bread (ʿaish miladin)	This is a round, crunchy bread made from drying out siyahi bread. It is sold from bakeries and stands on the street.
Diet bread (ʿaish sin or ʿaish regim)	This is a very dark, round, flat bread. It has a high bran content and is hard. Bakeries sell this bread by weight.
Roqaq	This is a large, round, white bread made from refined flour, often with added milk and sugar. The bread is thin and hard, like a cracker. It is sold from bakeries. Homemade versions are also sold on the street.
Bitau	This is a round, flat bread made with a mix of maize, sorghum, and wheat flour and flavored with fenugreek. It is homemade and sold by the side of the road, usually in a dry form that can be stored; the loaves are then dampened to soften before eating.
Specialty breads	Specialty breads can be found in bakeries in upscale neighborhoods, including various forms of sliced bread (typically called *toast*) and baguettes.

Note: I do not give price indications for the nonsubsidized breads because they fluctuate widely both in time (they have increased considerably since the 2016 currency devaluation) and space (the same bread can sell for different prices in different neighborhoods and depending on who is buying it). As of 2019, most nonsubsidized breads cost around 1EGP a loaf, and subsidized bread bakeries sold baladi bread to those without ration cards for 0.5EGP a loaf. Outside of Cairo there are also regionally specialized breads, such as the ʿaish shamsi found in southern Egypt.

FIGURE I.4. At the bakery, with baladi bread. Photograph by Mariam Taher.

(30 percent of the population) but also by the vulnerable and lower middle classes above it. Nor is it just a food of the cities; it is eaten both in urban areas (where 43 percent of the population lives) and in the countryside.[21] This bread, decent in taste, cheap in price, is something Egyptians expect the state to deliver, perhaps because over the span of most Egyptians' lifetimes, it has always done so.[22] To those who consume it, baladi bread provides about 52 percent of daily calorie requirements and 70 percent of carbohydrate and protein needs, as well as some vitamins and minerals (Hassan-Wassef 2012: 13). To most Egyptians, baladi bread is a staple.

Staple—Security—Staple Security

Staple Foods

Staple foods have long featured in ethnographies of everyday life, from early discussions of millet consumption among the Bemba (Richards 1932) and milk among the Nuer (Evans-Pritchard 1940) to later studies that highlighted the role of potatoes and barley in Highland Ecuador (Weismantel 1988), bananas for the Haya (Weiss 1996), and rice in Japan (Ohnuki-Tierney 1993). Scholars have also probed the question of how various staples—including maize (McCann 2007), rice (Carney 2002), bread (Andrae and Beckman 1985, Head, Atchison, and Gates 2012), potatoes (Earle 2018), milk (Du Puis 2002), and sugar (Mintz 1985)—came to be established in particular places and among particular peoples over time. Yet there has been little recent theorization of the meaning, provisioning, and consumption of staple foods. Here, therefore, I draw together elements from the literature with my own research to identify the core elements of what defines a staple as a type of food.

One day in 2008 I was driving through Fayoum Governorate with a community organizer from the Ministry of Irrigation. It was a time of severe baladi bread shortages, long lines at bakeries, and high flour prices. As was frequently the case during this period, the conversation within the car turned to bread. "I didn't bring bread for my children today," commented the driver. "They won't have anything to eat." His words were striking. For by this he did not mean that his children, literally, would not have anything to eat all day; rather, that without bread, their meals would be incomplete.

This comment captures the first characteristic of a staple. *A staple is a food that defines a meal.* In the absence of the staple, there is a sense that a meal is not a meal or that someone has not properly eaten. Liberians talk about not having eaten unless they have eaten rice (Trapp 2016); some Ghanaians say the same thing about a day without fufu (a thick dough made from cassava and plantains) (Williams-Forson 2010). Moroccans consider bread a food that must be available at every meal (Graf 2018). In Japan, the full-stomach feeling cannot be achieved without rice, no matter what else is consumed (Allison 1991, Ohnuki-Tierney 1993). Although the French are eating less bread than they did in the past, in France there is still a common understanding that a real meal requires bread (Kaplan 2006, Gnaba 2011). In rural Mexico, corn tortillas are a fundamental part of the main meal of the day (Wynne 2015).

As defining features of a meal, staples may be foods that are eaten in the largest quantities, as is suggested by Avieli's (2012: 22) description of the two to three bowls of rice served to adults in a Hoianese meal (a local cuisine within Vietnam), or by the figures of baladi bread constituting over half people's caloric needs. But this is not necessarily the case (Ohnuki-Tierney 1993). Rather, there is something about a staple food, whatever the quantities in which it is consumed, that is central to the experience of feeling satiated. As my neighbor in the village of Warda once said to me, "It's impossible to last a day without bread. Bread is something fundamental [asasi]." Another Egyptian I spoke with, who comes from a wealthier background and lives in Cairo, described himself as being "addicted" to bread. Having developed diabetes, he can no longer eat three to five loaves a day as he used to, but still, he says, "If a day passes and I don't eat a loaf or one and a half loaves, I don't feel right."

The association between staples and meals is evident in linguistic markers. In Rincón Zapotec, for instance, the invitation to eat, "gáuru yht," means, "Let's eat tortillas" (González 2001). In Vietnam, the term for cooked rice (com) is also the word for a meal in general; the Vietnamese refer to the three meals of the day as morning rice, noon rice, and evening rice (Gorman 2019). In the Singida region of Tanzania, the grains with which people make the staple food ugali (a stiff porridge) are referred to simply as food (chakula) (Phillips 2018). Thus a staple is the most foundational of foods. It is a food that should be present in the house and should be present on the table.

At the same time, the everyday significance of a staple is shaped by lines of social difference, including class, ethnicity, gender, and age. The staple food among the poor may not be the same as that among the rich. In Weismantel's (1988) study of Highland Ecuador, for example, she described the staple of the Indigenous as being barley, whereas for white families it was rice. Among the Gadaba ethnic group in India, while both rice and millet are eaten, rice is a higher-status food, associated with lowland peoples (Berger 2018). In Egypt, although bread is eaten across classes, it tends to be less prominent in the diets of those who can easily afford alternative staples like rice or pasta. Across generations and gender, too, there are differences in staple consumption. One young woman who lives in Cairo, for instance, talked about how she does not eat bread with every meal. She ensures that bread is on the table at every meal, however, because otherwise her father, who is accustomed to eating bread three times a day, will ask for it. While this woman tied her limited bread consumption to her personal preferences, I have heard several women, but never any men, talk about limiting their bread consumption so as to keep their weight down (this does not seem to be a prevalent theme, though, unlike in other countries where low-carbohydrate diets have become popular).

Beyond their importance as central items of consumption, staples are also distinct in the ways in which they are typically eaten. *A staple is a vehicle for or accompaniment to other foods*, as opposed to a food that is eaten on its own. In Richards's (1932) classic account, for example, she describes how a satisfactory meal for the Bemba must comprise two elements—a thick millet porridge and a relish of vegetables, meat, or fish. In his study of the Haya in northwestern Tanzania, Weiss (1996) describes a similar pattern of meals comprising a starch staple and vegetable relish. Among the Zapotec in Mexico, a meal consists of maize tortillas alongside beans, soup, or vegetables (González 2001). In southeastern China, an ordinary meal is made up of rice and trimmings (Oxfeld

2017). This is in part a matter of preferred taste pairings, but it is also because the staple may be used as a tool for eating the other foods. Bread may be torn and used to dip in a soup, as was illustrated in the meal I shared with my neighbors; stiff maize porridge formed into a ball and used to scoop up a stew; or a tortilla rolled and used to hold other ingredients. The staple also enables other foods to be stretched further, reducing the burden of obtaining more expensive goods. A small bowl of fermented cheese and some olives can become a meal for six if accompanied by bread.

Hence the staple is often the background food to another more varied part of a meal. But this does not mean that the staple's flavor is unimportant. Staples are highly differentiated by taste. Sometimes these variations derive from the crop variety—as, for example, in the nuanced taste distinctions between different varieties of potatoes (Keleman Saxena 2017) or rice ([Seung-Joon] Lee 2011, Temudo 2011, Avieli 2012). In other cases, the varying tastes and associated preferences stem from how the staple is processed and transformed into food. Among Yucatec Maya women in Mexico, for instance, there is a common "taste hierarchy," which positions home-cooked tortillas made from locally grown and ground corn as preferable to home-prepared tortillas made from purchased dough, which in turn are preferable to tortillas made on tortilla machines (Wynne 2015). In Singida, Tanzania, middle-class and urban residents tend to prefer soft white ugali made from hulled maize kernels, whereas rural residents prefer a coarser, denser ugali made with unhulled maize, which they find more filling (Phillips 2018). In terms of bread, its taste depends not only to the grain from which it is made but the leavening agent that makes it rise and the way in which it is baked. A bread leavened with sourdough starter tastes quite different from one made with instant yeast ([Jessica] Lee 2011). The breads featured in this book, however, are almost all made with wheat from similar varieties and commercially produced instant yeast. The primary source of taste differentiation in Egyptian wheat breads, therefore, is the degree of refinement of the flour that goes into them.

The third characteristic of a staple is that *a staple is a food that carries a deep symbolic resonance*. In Egypt, this is evident in a statement people commonly make about the link between bread and life. Chatting with a Cairo taxi driver, I mention that I am interested in bread. "In Egypt," he responds, "bread is life" (fi Masr, al-khubz 'aish). In an interview with a program officer from an international organization, he tells me, "Very simply, bread is the life of Egyptians. They call it 'aish, which means life." When the Minister of Supply gives a press conference about the subsidized bread program, he notes, "Egypt is the *only* country that calls bread 'aish, because it is the basis of life ('aish) and living (ma'isha)."[23] This repeated statement is in part a reference to the fact that Egypt is the only place in the Arabic-speaking world where the colloquial term for bread is 'aish rather than *khubz*. But it is also a reference to the centrality of bread in Egyptian lives.[24]

While many foods have layers of symbolic meaning, there is something notable about the particular kinds of symbolism associated with foods that are staples. In Russia, for example, the potato is a symbol of survival; grown primarily on small household plots, it is an emblem of the population's hard work (Ries 2009). The tortilla in Mexico has traditionally been seen not only as a filling, cheap, and plentiful food, but one that holds "symbolic weight as an emblem of culture, comfort, and identity" (Gálvez 2018: 74). Sometimes, there is a spiritual dimension to the symbolism. To the Jola people of West Africa, for instance, rice is sacred (Davidson 2015). Bread, too, has sacred associations in both Islam and Christianity, the major religions in the world regions that have the longest histories of bread consumption (Jacob [1944] 2014, Hafez 1994, Kanafani-Zahar 1997, Laudan 2013).[25] In many parts of the world, these religious connotations permeate everyday practices of handling bread, imbuing in those practices a form of deference toward the bread. Such customs range from not wasting bread to picking up any bread that falls to the floor so that it is not stepped on, ensuring that a loaf is never turned upside down, or kissing loaves (Jacob [1944] 2014: 145–46, Hafez 1994, Kanafani-Zahar 1997, Kaplan 1997). Palestinians, for example, often place unwanted bread in outdoor spaces so that it may be reused by others, rather than throwing it away (Stamatopoulou-Robbins 2019, chapter 4).[26]

This respect for bread is reflected in the careful ways in which Egyptians handle bread within their homes.[27] Although those who buy bread tend to do so on a regular basis, they do not necessarily go to the bakery every day. Since most Egyptian breads do not have preservatives in them, they require particular care to maintain their quality over time.[28] When people buy bread for several days, those who have fridge-top freezers often freeze some loaves. Before eating, some wrap the bread in cloth and place it on the counter to defrost; others heat it. In addition, just as in Palestine, it is considered morally wrong to throw away bread. Within a home, for instance, women typically collect uneaten quarters or half loaves at the end of a meal, dust them off, and place them back in the bag to be served again. They even save small scraps to feed to household livestock, in rural areas, or in urban areas, to sell to the informal traders who buy stale bread for animal feed. In public spaces, too, it is common to see discarded bread on walls or ledges—a plastic bag with a couple of loaves in it, for example, or a half-eaten loaf laid bare. This is partly an offering to needy urban residents who might wish to consume this bread, and partly a result of the fact that it is considered unethical to throw a respected item of food on the ground.

These three characteristics of staples—foods that are defining features of meals, that accompany other foods, and that hold symbolic resonance—are not necessarily present in all cases. In the United States, for instance, although there is no clearly identifiable staple, there are still some foods that hold staple-like qualities.[29] Take, for example, milk and bread. The rush on these items in grocery stores when storms are approaching is indicative of how many people perceive them as basic items that they should have in their homes (even as a growing number of Americans choose not to eat them) (Du Puis 2002, Bobrow-Strain 2012). So while these foods may not hold the same kind of symbolism as the breads discussed in this book, they are foods that, like a staple, many American households are used to having on hand.

Staples are not fixed in time, as Mintz (1985) showed in his study of how sugar shifted from being a luxury for the elites to a staple among the working classes in England. Yet staples are associated with stability, with the consistent rhythm of the everyday, the meeting of basic needs. Any interruption in that stability, therefore—when people do not have enough of a staple to stave off their hunger, or cannot access a staple that tastes pleasing—carries a sense of threat. This is how a staple becomes a matter of security.

Security

For much of the latter part of the twentieth century, security was the domain of scholars working in the field of security studies. Emerging out of political science and international relations, this body of work focused primarily on organized violence and the strategies deployed to protect against military threats. Since the 1990s, however, security has been taken up in anthropology, geography, and related disciplines in response to changes in the political, economic, and geopolitical order after the Cold War. With the attacks of 9/11 and the launching of the war on terror, security has become a central motif of political rule. A number of anthropologists have looked at processes of militarization, surveillance practices, counterterrorism operations, and cultures of militarism that have emerged in the name of security (Lutz 2002, Maguire, Frois, and Zurawski 2014, Masco 2014, Samimian-Darash and Stalcup 2017, Gusterson and Besteman 2019, Rubaii 2021). They have also examined the mounting fear of racial, ethnic, and foreign others as security has come to the fore of the public imagination, as well as associated practices of policing (Fassin 2013, Diphoorn 2016), migration control (Feldman 2011, Besteman 2020), and residential segregation (Low 2003).[30]

Yet despite the scholarly interest in the current "security moment" (Goldstein 2010: 487), security is not a new concern. It can take on many forms, extending far beyond the military domain. Goldstein argues, for instance, that security is a characteristic of neoliberalism—a tool of state formation and governance that capitalizes on the fractures of inequality produced through free-market policies.[31] Such a multifaceted understanding of security is evident in Gusterson and Besteman's (2009) analysis of insecurity in the United States, which highlights the multiple unsettling forces that shape American lives, including anxieties about jobs, health insurance, and debt. These concerns about economic security are not discrete from their military counterparts but, rather, closely intertwined: the desire to secure supplies of economic resources has often been at the root of military interventions, just as military contexts have often shaped economic priorities.

When it comes to the Middle East, however, these broader conceptualizations of security are frequently obscured by an overdetermined global discourse on terrorism. Such is the weight of Cold War legacies and Anglo-American policy interests that security in the Middle East tends to center on what Abboud and his colleagues describe as "well-rehearsed framings of sectarianisms, conflict, underdevelopment and terrorism" (2018: 274).[32] But security does not only mean countering extremism, preventing terror attacks, or reinforcing borders in times of hostility. Moreover, such a vision of security says little about how security and insecurity are being experienced in the region by both state and nonstate actors. Speaking to Abboud et al.'s call to move beyond these prevalent framings, I adopt security as a framework in this book not because of my own preexisting interest in the concept, as someone who has lived in the United States through the contemporary "security moment." Rather, I draw on the notion of security because this is the lens through which, either explicitly or implicitly, the Egyptians with whom I conducted my research see bread and wheat.

Glück and Low define security as "a modality of constructing danger, enemies, fear, and anxiety, and the measures taken to guard against such constructed threats" (2017: 282). This definition points to two dimensions of security: an affective domain and a concrete one (Low and Maguire 2019). On the one hand, there is the imaginary of a threat, which evokes an emotional response. On the other hand, there are the infrastructural measures that are taken to counter that threat, which have a material form. The significance of the former—the framing as a threat—is that it justifies the latter, a particular form of action. At the same time, actions can either enhance or diminish the sense of threat, underscoring the deep interconnections between security's affect and practice.

Security is associated with threats of a certain magnitude. What generates this sense of danger, fear, and anxiety is not just any kind of threat, but an existential threat, something that is understood as threatening the very existence of a state or society. It is also a constructed threat. As Masco writes, "What a national community fears and how it responds to those fears are cultural forms as well as technologically mediated processes, the basis for a domestic politics as well as a geopolitics" (2014: 3). In the United States, for instance, given the high rate of car ownership and limited public transportation options, many people see gasoline as a staple. As a consequence, many Americans worry about gas prices going up and the national reliance on foreign oil (Huber 2009). In Egypt, there are similar concerns about wheat and bread.[33] Many Egyptians worry about bread prices going up and the national reliance on foreign wheat. The fact that it is possible to live without bread is immaterial; security is not about the assessment of "real" dangers, it is about the construction of a "collective understanding of something as a particular kind of danger, an existential threat to state, society, 'our way of life'" (Goldstein 2010: 492). Such national-level concerns generate what Masco (2014) terms "national security affect"—an atmosphere of anxiety stemming from the perception that a country is under threat, which in turn legitimizes a particular course of state-level action.

But the affective domain of security is not only linked to the possibility of a national crisis. Personal livelihood concerns also produce "ordinary affects" (Stewart 2007), which emerge in intimate spaces or mundane moments. Woven into day-to-day interactions, these security affects are tied to those things that an individual or household experience as directly threatening, such as a fear of crime that makes its way into dinner party conversations (Lemanski 2012) or the sense of hopelessness that emerges in the face of multiple precarities (Allison 2013). Affect encompasses multiple scaled domains, from the collective consciousness of the national body to an individual's mind, body, and emotion (Skoggard and Waterston 2015).

Within the literature on security, fear is a common trope. This is not, however, security's sole affective register. As scholars who have added a parenthetical prefix to the term—(in)security—have sought to demonstrate, insecurity and security are closely interlinked states. The duality of security and insecurity creates openings not only for negative affects like anxiety but also for positive affects like comfort (El Dardiry and Hermez 2020). Within an overarching context of fear, there may be times and places where people experience safety, albeit fleetingly. In the midst of an ongoing conflict, the domestic space and kinship network of an extended family may provide reassurance (Fluri 2011). In a context where buses are associated with the risk of a terror attack, a journey in a car may provide a sense of protection (Ochs 2013).

Security, therefore, is a *state of being*. It is a lived experience of fear and risk, punctuated by moments of refuge, which shapes everyday lives in contrasting ways across lines of social difference. It is a state that is both produced by and productive of varied affective registers.

But security is also a *form of action*; it is the measures taken to guard against perceived threats. The practices through which a range of actors seek to be secure run across scales, from the body to the city to the nation and beyond. They are deployed not just by states but by communities and individuals as they interact with one another and with various branches of the state. Security is not only something practiced at a military checkpoint, in an airport screening, through an encounter with a police officer, or by a border patrol. It is something that becomes normalized in quotidian acts, whether choosing to wear a particular type of clothing (Fluri 2011), turning on a burglar alarm before going to sleep (Low 2003), or navigating a daily commute (Ochs 2013). In some instances, the act may be a conscious form of threat mitigation; other times, it is a ritualized behavior that becomes instinctual. In all cases, security is not a matter of navigating between a binary of being either secure or not secure but, rather, a process of moving along a gradient of possibilities between context-specific understandings of being more or less secure.

My interest in this book is primarily in exploring security as practice. I am attentive to security's affective dimension—the pervasive sense of anxiety about the supply and quality of wheat and bread in Egypt, as well as the moments of reassurance that come from the presence of abundant wheat and good bread. But my data relate mainly to the realm of action—not surprisingly, perhaps, given the difficulty of capturing ethnographically that which is felt or sensed.[34] I examine the ongoing efforts by various individuals and institutions to counter the threat of insufficient or poor-quality wheat and bread. These are not novel threats, defined by a post–Cold War, post-9/11, or post-neoliberal era. Indeed, as Goldstein (2010) points outs, security, broadly conceived, has been a fundamental concern for nations and states since these concepts first came into being. So, too, vagaries in agricultural production have always been something that farmers have had to deal with, and the production and distribution of basic foods has been a matter of concern for states as long as people have been living in cities and not growing their own.

For many scholars and practitioners working on food and agriculture, engagement with questions of security is channeled through the concept of *food security*. In coupling security with food, however, it becomes harnessed to a concept with a particular history, rooted in international conferences, negotiated definitions, and policy approaches. The conceptual dyad of "food security" emerged in the 1970s, when increasing grain prices and limited grain supplies directed policy communities' attention toward how the world's food supply was being distributed and whose needs were being met.[35] Early definitions of food security framed the concept in terms of agricultural production and food availability at a national level, with a central focus on staple grains. Over time, scholars and policy analysts working in this field, inspired by the work of Sen (1983) and others, shifted the concept to a focus, instead, on access to food. They also expanded its scalar dimension, noting the importance of thinking about food security on scales beyond the nation, from the individual and household through to the global (Jarosz 2011). With increasing focus on nutritional deprivation, practitioners further widened the frame from cereal staples to consider the full spectrum of nutritional needs. In addition, they recognized that food security is not only a matter of having enough food but having enough food that people like to eat (Appendini and Quijada 2016). Today, academics and development practitioners working on food security commonly turn to a definition from the 1996 World Food Summit, which described food security as a state in which "all people, at all times, have physical and economic access to sufficient, safe and nutritious food to meet their dietary needs and food preferences for an active and healthy life."[36]

This conceptualization of food security has been taken up by a number of scholars working in the Middle East. Public policy analyses have surveyed how food security strategies have evolved in different countries of the region (Woertz 2013, Babar and Mirgani 2014, Harrigan 2014). Economists have debated the efficacy of particular food security policies, such as the investment in grain storage (Wright and Cafiero 2011, Larson et al. 2013). Several scholars have looked beyond the regional and national scale to probe household food security dynamics (Gertel and Kuppinger 1994, Khouri-Dagher 1996). International agencies have also produced a number of reports on the status of food security in Egypt and the Middle East (Breisinger et al. 2012, Maystadt, Trinh Tah, and Breisinger 2012, WFP 2013).

Yet despite the prevalence of food security within the scholarly literature and as a foundation for development planning, I argue that the concept has two key limitations. First, even with the inclusion of the word *security* in the term, explorations of security itself are remarkably absent from work on food security. Scholars of food security seldom discuss the links between this form of security and other securities, for example. There is little recognition of the fact that limiting food access through siege or sanctions can be a way of achieving military security objectives (see, for example, Winter 2016). Nor is there much discussion of the popular unrest that can result from food shortages or inadequacies, or how concerns about such instability may underpin political leaders' interests in food security. In focusing on a state of being in which all people have access to all the food that they need, food security sheds scant light on what might happen in its absence. A bland definition about people being able to access food stands in stark contrast to a square in downtown Cairo thronging with protestors.

Moreover, while food security scholars certainly recognize that access to food is mediated by physical, economic, and social variables, and consider the vulnerabilities associated with rising prices or reliance on imports, they pay less attention to the deep anxieties that accompany these vulnerabilities and efforts to obtain particular foods. In other words, the affective domain of the security imaginary—the way in which a particular threat is conceived and how that shapes everyday life, as well as the sense of comfort that comes when that threat is removed, even if only momentarily—is largely missing. The concept of food security offers little insight, therefore, into why Egyptian newspapers would report each cargo ship that arrives at a port loaded with wheat, politicians would deploy military metaphors of strategic storage and grain procurement campaigns, or fathers would fret over their children not having bread, even when there is plenty of other food for them to eat.

Second, food security is not very helpful for thinking about staples specifically, even though cereal grains were the focus of much of the early work in this field (Shaw 2007). An increasing awareness of the importance of a variety of food types has shifted the focus of food security to "nutritious" foods that meet "dietary needs." It is impossible to be food secure only by eating bread. This was brought home to me during my fieldwork for this book, when I found that none of my interviewees working on bread were talking about food security (al-amn al-ghidha'i) and none of my interviewees working on food security were talking about bread. For those concerned about food security, the taste of security is a combination of vegetables, fruits, grains, and meat, not a piece of flavorful bread. Similarly, few of the works on food security in the Middle East and Egypt include more than passing references to bread. Indeed, some would say that from a food security perspective, Egyptians eat too much bread (Ecker et al. 2016).

Thus, the concept of food security fails to capture how staple foods can become items of particular security concern, both to households and to the nation. Nothing about the notion of all people at all times having access to safe and nutritious food would explain why my entry into a bakery, for example, would be perceived as a security threat. Yet this is what I found the one time I tried to enter one. Accompanied by Hisham, a taxi driver I have known for a long time, I visited a bakery in his Cairo neighborhood. The workers were chatty and showed us around, but when the supervisor saw us she was very suspicious, insisting on taking Hisham's name and number, even calling while we stood there to check that the number was correct. She clearly felt threatened by my presence—without an official chaperone or formal paperwork documenting the purpose of my visit—as a non-Egyptian in a site of production for a subsidized staple. At the household level, too, people talk about their need for sufficient good bread in a manner different from that in which they talk about their ability to access other foods. There is a disconnect, therefore, between how people experience security related to particular foods and how policy scholars define food security.

The concept of food security has also come under critique by scholars working on food sovereignty. Emerging from peasant movements in Latin America, food sovereignty highlights questions of power, control, and rights in the production and consumption of food (see, for example, Patel 2009, Wittman 2011). Yet in spite of its peasant roots, food sovereignty has been taken up in Egypt as a largely elite urban project.[37] Egypt's small-scale farmers are not talking about food sovereignty (siyada ghidha'iya). The educated, wealthy Cairo residents advancing the concept are focused primarily on local seeds and the importance of challenging the hegemony of multinational seed corporations. For wheat, though, this is not a dominant concern, given that the wheat seeds being planted in Egypt are not imported from private companies but bred locally by the public sector (albeit from germplasm that is far from local, as I discuss in chapter 1). Food sovereignty activists are also concerned about the preservation of local foods—in the case of bread, Egypt's regional bread varieties (see chapter 5). However, in focusing their attention on these rare bread forms, they sideline the baladi bread that is consumed by the majority of Egyptians. Food sovereignty, conceptualized in this way, is removed from the day-to-day concerns of feeding a household. While work on food sovereignty has valuably critiqued food security for its failure to acknowledge the importance of justice and control over food supplies, security still matters as an important affective, bureaucratic, and political practice.

I use the term *staple security* to move beyond work on food security and its conceptual associations to probe the nexus of *food and security*. This concept focuses the attention on staple foods, since these foods have an affective valence that other foods do not. The existential importance of staples to people's daily lives and to the legitimacy of the state is why their absence or substandard quality poses such a threat. Staple security speaks to the special kind of security that staple foods both require and produce.

The first component of staple security is its affective dimension: the feelings that surround the potential absence of a quality staple. In the case of Vietnam, for example, Gorman (2019) describes the high degree of anxiety that permeates Vietnamese society around the rice supply and possibility of shortages. There are similar fears in Egypt over whether the nation could run out of wheat and bread.

From the perspective of the state, anxieties over staple foods are tied to the possibility of protest. The figure of the food riot—of people taking to the streets to protest hunger—brings into dramatic relief the link between food and security. Described by Patel and McMichael (2009: 9) as "one of the oldest forms of collective action," food riots have occurred throughout history. In diverse political and economic contexts, rising prices and poor-quality food have been a focus of popular unrest (Tilly 1971, McFarland 1985, Engel 1997, Orlove 1997, Francks 2003, Hossain and Scott-Villiers 2017). The food riot, in its varied manifestations, underscores how state legitimacy may be tied to the accessibility and quality of basic foods. It demonstrates the threat that food insufficiency or inadequacy can pose to national security, challenging the stability of a ruling regime.

In Egypt, the bread riot occupies a central place in the political imagination. Whether in politicians' speeches, conversations with people engaged in food policy, or newspaper articles, references to past bread riots in Egypt are common. People recall these riots—just as I did in the opening of this book—as a way of signaling the significance of this staple food. They use them to explain why, as Egyptian politicians are fond of saying, the provision of cheap bread is a "red line" that cannot be crossed.[38] For on the other side of that line is the specter of the riot.

Yet as a number of scholars have shown, food riots are seldom about food alone. Rather, they are typically the outcome of complex and historically rooted political-economic relations (Bohstedt 2008, Wolford and Nehring 2013). As Thompson (1971) argued in his seminal study, instead of being "rebellions of the belly," the food riot is more an expression of people's sense that the "moral economy" has been breached—that ruling parties have failed to fulfill their social obligation to meet certain basic needs of the poor. Hence while many commentators branded the protests that broke out around the world in 2007 and 2008 during the global food crisis as food riots, they were not so much about the high price of food as about people's perceptions that their entitlements were not being met and their frustration at the lack of political recourse (Patel and McMichael 2009). Similarly, Sadiki (2000) argues that, over the latter decades of the twentieth century, the uprisings across the Arab World that were labeled bread riots were in fact motivated by the rising cost of a number of commodities, as well as dissatisfaction with structural inequality and incompetent and illegitimate political rule.

In the case of Egypt, the bread riots most commonly recalled are those that occurred in January 1977. According to the common narrative, these protests—which are referred to as the intifadat al-khubz—broke out around the country in response to rising bread prices.[39] They were an expression of resistance to the Sadat government's proposal to cut back the bread subsidy as part of a package of reforms introduced to meet conditions attached to a loan from the International Monetary Fund. But the reforms also involved the reduction of other subsidies, including those on cooking oil and rice, and the freezing of state employee benefits and pay increases. In addition, the only bread price the government sought to raise was that of a white roll (fino), which was subsidized at the time; it made no change in the price of the widely eaten baladi bread. The protests, therefore, were not just about bread.

This book *is*, however, just about bread. Using the bread riot as a lens through which to approach questions of food and security hence provides only partial insight. The possibility of popular protest might loom large for government officials managing a subsidized bread program, but this is not the only level of security concern associated with the absence of quality bread. A political leader's fear of the bread riot is distinct from the unsettled feeling a parent has when there is no bread left in a home, a mother's frustration at her inability to bake the homemade bread her family prefers because she cannot afford the flour, or a family's vulnerability when they are unable to access subsidized bread and so have to rely on other people's donated bread. Such affective registers of staple security are linked not to abstract national threats but to very immediate individual livelihood concerns. They resonate with the stress that Garth (2020) describes in her account of Cubans' daily efforts to acquire food for a "decent meal," of which starchy staples comprise a key part. Garth describes how the dwindling of rice rations toward the end of the month impacts people's affective state, even when they still have pasta or other carbohydrates on hand. Recounting the experience of one middle-class resident of Santiago, Garth writes, "It may be somewhat acceptable to have one meal without rice, but when she has to go multiple meals or even days without rice she begins to panic" (2020: 48).

There is a class dimension to this anxiety. The presence of bread, a cheap and filling food, matters in the daily lives of Egypt's poor and middle-class majority in a way that it does not matter to Egyptian elites. There is also a taste dimension to this anxiety. The quality of bread, and the sensorial engagement of handling and eating it, is part of how people understand themselves to be more or less secure. Bread does not equal calories, just like being secure is not the same as being alive. Hence fear is not the only affect at work here. There is also the pleasure of eating a meal with freshly baked bread, the yearning, among some, for breads that taste of rural childhoods, or the satisfaction of bringing home good bread for a family. Staple security is as much about the desire for palatable bread as it is about the fear of no bread.

The second dimension of staple security is the concrete actions that are taken to ensure that people have a good staple to eat. Garth (2020) describes, for instance, the daily struggles of low-income residents of Santiago to acquire the rice, beans, and tubers that form the center of a decent meal, involving time-consuming journeys around the city to seek good prices, borrowing from neighbors and relatives, and tapping into the black market. Gorman (2019) recounts the lines forming outside of supermarkets in Ho Chi Minh City as rice prices rose in 2008, people stocking up on rice in fear of scarcity. These practices are not separate from the affective dimension of security but, rather, interwoven with it. This is evident in Ries's (2009) discussion of the common practice in Russia of storing enough potatoes to last through the winter, even among families that buy rather than grow them. One urban dweller explains how both the act of growing potatoes on a small household plot and storing them in large quantities helps her feel more secure: "You can trust that if everything *really* falls apart, you have the skills and habits to survive. And, you can look at your potatoes in the apartment hallway in dark November, and *see* your food for the winter" (Ries 2009: 200).[40]

Throughout this book, I describe similar efforts by Egyptians to ensure that they have access to sufficient decent bread. For some, this means growing and storing their own wheat and turning it into bread. For others, it means standing in lines at bureaucratic offices to get a working ration card and making daily trips to the bakery to get bread, relying on others to grow, trade, and store wheat, mill it into flour, and transform it into bread. Once bread is in the home, further everyday labors prevent wastage and preserve quality. The nature of these practices is closely tied to the materiality of the staples in question—grain has to be stored in a particular way because of its tendency to rot otherwise; loaves of hot bread must be handled with care or they will crumple, tear, or become soggy. These are some of the individual practices of staple security.

Staple security is also the purview of states, which have long mobilized to ensure that cities and armies have staples to eat. As Erkal writes, "An essential measure of government legitimacy and good governance in preindustrial societies, whether city-states or empires, was public food provisioning—most crucially, the supply of grain" (2020: 17). Thus, actions to maintain the supply of wheat and bread in Egypt have deep historical roots. In pharaonic times, for example, the state stored grain in large granaries to provide a buffer against variations in cereal productivity, in an effort to guarantee the consistent availability of bread (Murray 2000). The Ottoman administration of Egypt established and maintained a network of storage facilities, labor, and shipping routes, specifically designed to move grain within the country to supply the cities, and out of the country to supply the empire (Mikhail 2011).

In the contemporary era, many governments have taken actions to ensure that their populations have staples to eat. Some have promoted national self-sufficiency in staple crops as a way to mitigate vulnerability to volatile international market prices that could endanger the country's staple supply (Francks 2003, Clapp 2017, Zhang 2017, Gorman 2019). This goal of self-sufficiency is supply-focused; it is about ensuring that there is enough of a given grain within the country. It is a popular theme that has been taken up by successive Egyptian regimes. In 2009, the Ministry of Agriculture launched a strategy to raise wheat self-sufficiency from its current level of around 55 percent to 80 percent by the year 2030 (see chapter 1). After the 2011 revolution, President Morsi talked of Egypt becoming self-sufficient in wheat in just four years.[41] His successor, President al-Sisi, has stepped back from this ambitious goal but maintained a commitment to raising the self-sufficiency level. Whether or not wheat self-sufficiency is feasible, adopting a self-sufficiency target marks a government's dedication to securing the nation's wheat supply.

The other policy approach focuses on access, subsidizing staple foods as a way of ensuring that all members of the population are able to get them at an affordable price (Alderman, Gentilini, and Yemstov 2018). In India, the Public Distribution System provides subsidized wheat and rice to 800 million people (Bhattacharya, Falco, and Puri 2018); in Indonesia, the Rastra program provides subsidized rice to 62 million people (Timmer, Hastuti, and Sumarto 2018); in Jordan, until 2018, the government provided highly subsidized bread (Martínez 2017, 2018a). Even in the midst of conflict, during the Syrian Civil

War, the Assad regime, the Free Syrian Army, and armed Islamist groups have sought to provide subsidized bread in the areas they control, seeing the provision of bread as a way to prove their state-worthiness and bolster their authority among local populations (Martínez and Eng 2017, Martínez 2020). In Egypt, the government's commitment to providing cheap bread through its subsidy program has transcended major shifts in governance throughout the postindependence period, from President Nasser (1956–70), to Sadat (1970–81), Mubarak (1981–2011), Morsi (2012–13), and now Sisi (2014–).[42] Although Sisi's government has been cutting back a number of subsidies in recent years under the terms of a 2016 IMF loan, it has not made equivalent cuts to the bread subsidy.[43] This shows the lengths to which governments as well as individuals are willing to go to guarantee widespread access to a quality staple.

These practices, taken by governments and individuals, lead to momentary states of security, in which feelings of anxiety, fear, or yearning give way to those of reassurance, comfort, and stability. This sense of stability may come from there being more loaves on a table than family members can eat, a spreadsheet with figures showing the national silos full of grain, possession of a ration card that guarantees access to cheap bread, sacks of grain stored within a household, or a field of bountiful wheat. But even at such moments, the threat has not evaporated. The temporal horizons of security range from a day to a few months, but a horizon is ever present. The loaves will be eaten, the silo stores will be depleted, a ration card might stop working, the grain will be turned into flour, and the harvest could be disrupted by poor weather. The intensity of the labor may wax and wane, but the need to work for a good staple is a constant.

Staple security therefore describes a set of practices through which states, households, and individuals seek to secure the continuous supply of a palatable staple so as to address anxieties about staple absence and meet desires for staple quality. I use this concept to draw attention to a common dynamic that spans the varied domains I discuss in this book, but the staple security that features in these domains is not the same. The devices of staple security range from high-yielding seeds to procurement prices, bread specifications, grain quality standards, electronic ration cards, and shared baking labor. The metrics of success include yields per hectare, the amount of wheat harvested, silo capacities, contaminant percentages, bread prices, and preservation of traditional forms of bread production. The meanings attached to staple security are shaped by the social and political fields in which those acts are practiced. A woman who takes wheat harvested by her family to mill and bake into bread sees the grain differently from the breeder who develops new varieties, the government official who procures wheat, the silo operator who stores grain, and the trader who buys and sells it. The grain they work with is variously a source of a family's food, an object of scientific study, a matter of national security, and a way of accruing profits. A father buying subsidized bread for his household thinks about this bread in a different way from the owner of the private bakery that produces it, who in turn sees it differently from the official charged with setting its specifications. The loaf of subsidized bread they interact with is variously a source of cheap calories, a way to make a living, and a mechanism for preventing popular unrest. Staple security is a singular concept, but its manifestations are multiple.

The value of staple security lies in how it captures multiscaled practices and their affective resonances. Global supply chains are part of the narrative, given that they deliver half the wheat that goes into Egypt's bread. The security of the supply chain—the smooth functioning of a transnational set of infrastructures, labor practices, and regulatory procedures—is critical to the arrival of this wheat at Egyptian ports (Cowen 2014). But staple security goes beyond the singular scalar vision and logic of supply chain security, linking a large complex system of grain transport around the world and a vast food subsidy program with small individual acts, like a woman drying homemade loaves so that they last longer. This is not just a matter of bringing together a cluster of disparate things. Rather, my analysis moves from fields to ports to silos to bakeries to spaces within a home because it is through the everyday practices taking place at these sites—practices that are in some ways similar but also quite different— that the feeling of security reaches the bellies of the Egyptian people.

While my analysis is specific to Egypt, this story is not unique. There are many countries where staple foods hold a comparable degree of significance and many staples that have generated comparable levels of concern. The concept of staple security can, therefore, inform understandings of countries beyond Egypt and staples beyond bread. In addition, staple security has broader resonance for thinking about other environmental resources that are commonly framed in terms of security, like energy security and water security, and that are essential to life. It raises questions of what it might mean to approach these resource securities, too, less as states of being and more as modes of practice that are underpinned by historically rooted anxieties, deeply embedded in politics, and contingent on quotidian labor. Furthermore, in disaggregating the category of food to focus on staples specifically, staple security invites reflection on what insights might be gained from dismantling other resources that come to be matters of security concern. I return to develop these points in the conclusion.

Methods

I am walking through a Cairo neighborhood. It is December 2016 and I am looking closely for bread. In my head, I am making a mental list of observations, which I will later turn into written fieldnotes. What bread are people carrying? Where is bread being sold? How is bread being eaten? In my arms, I am holding a squirmy child, my eleven-month-old son Oscar. Newly walking, he strains against my arms, wanting to run. He cannot understand why I am not putting him down. He does not see the broken sidewalk, impassable with trees, parked cars, and cracked pavement. He does not appreciate how close the cars, motorbikes, and minibus taxis are skimming by the pedestrians as they walk down the road. He does not recognize that he and his mother lack the skill of longtime residents in easily navigating Cairo streets. I find a small patch where he can run—the forecourt to a metro station. I put him down just as a crowd of people is coming off a train. He runs up to a man, a stranger, and raises his arms in the air, his intent clear. The man picks him up with a smile. "Habibi [my darling]," he says. Oscar beams. The man brings a smiling child back to me and I feel a flash of happiness at the joys of sharing a moment in my fieldsite with my son.

I have worked in Egypt since 2007. My first book, *Cultivating the Nile: The Everyday Politics of Water in Egypt,* drew on the year of ethnographic fieldwork that I conducted in Egypt in 2007–8 as a doctoral student, as well as on follow-up trips in 2009 and 2011. This work was based in the village that I call Warda, in the western part of Fayoum Governorate, about three hours southwest of Cairo, where I lived in 2007–8.[44] Fayoum lies just west of the Nile Valley, its agricultural land irrigated by Nile waters through a network of canals (see map I.1). The village of Warda has around three thousand residents, many of whom are engaged in farming. It is also a village where a number of Cairo intellectuals, artists, and expatriates have weekend homes, which is the reason why I was able to live there without arousing the attention of the security authorities, who are wary of foreigners spending extended periods in rural areas outside the tourist zones. This makes the village in some ways anomalous. Many households have at least one member working in the construction of new villas, as house guards or gardeners, or catering to a growing number of mostly Egyptian day-trippers. But farmers having diverse income sources is not in itself uncommon, and most of these households also grow wheat and bake bread. My fieldnotes from this earlier fieldwork, therefore, constitute one of my sources of data for this book; my long-term experience working in Egypt comprises its ethnographic foundation.

By the time I began this project in 2015, however, I had two children, aged five and two, and was pregnant with my third. Although many ethnographers have reflected on how various aspects of their positionality and identity have shaped their data gathering, relatively few have written about how being a parent has affected their work. There remains a stigma attached to acknowledging that your personal life might influence your research. It is part of the "shadow side of fieldwork" (McLean and Leibing 2007) that is seldom discussed. By not talking about this issue, though, I think we miss opportunities to think through creative methodological approaches for balancing fieldwork with looking after children, caring for aging parents, or myriad personal responsibilities that might tie us to places distant from our fieldsites. I outline here, therefore, how I sought to combine my goals of writing a second book and raising, with my husband, three young children. In laying out my strategy, I hope to invite more conversation about methodological approaches that are both productive and accommodating of diverse personal circumstances.[45]

I conducted research for this book in Egypt between 2015 and 2019.[46] On my December 2016 trip, I took my youngest son with me. As other scholars have discussed, taking a child to the field is not only a good way to combine parenting and researching but can add to the research, creating space for different kinds of interactions (Cassell 1987, Flinn and Marshall 1998, Cornet and Blumenfield 2016). It was a wonderful experience bringing Oscar with me to Warda and introducing him to people with whom I have built friendships over the years. In a context where there is a strong identification of women with motherhood, it changed my relationships with people in the village for them to see me in a maternal role. But it was also mentally and physically exhausting. Typing up fieldnotes after getting my son into bed was even more tiring than typing up notes after a day of fieldwork on my own. Traveling across Cairo was challenging when I had to consider my willingness to take a child in a taxi without a car seat. Having a conversation in a rural home was tricky when also chasing after my toddler, who was heading for the gas burner on the floor where our tea water was being boiled. Assessing my comfort level with the security situation after a bomb in Cairo killed twenty-nine people was more complicated when I had to consider the safety of my son as well as myself. So in the absence of a broader support network of family or childcare in Egypt, and given that there are less mobile parts of my family, I decided to adopt a different approach in researching this book.[47]

Between 2015 and 2019, I made six research trips to Egypt. These were short (ranging from ten days to three weeks), but they allowed me to conduct interviews in Cairo with a number of people working on wheat policy, involved with the subsidized bread program, and working within various food and agricultural organizations. Some of those I interviewed I knew from my first period of fieldwork, so we were able to step into a rapport from the outset. Others were new contacts, but in a few cases I met with them multiple times over successive visits, gradually generating a greater ease of interaction. During each of these trips, I also returned to Warda, where I built on the strong relationships with several farming households that I have established since 2007 to talk more about their wheat cultivation, home baking, and bread consumption practices. In the context of my longer engagement in Egypt, time spent in the country, and knowledge of the language, this approach provided valuable data, even if the time frame limited the scope for the kinds of chance encounters that can be ethnographically revealing. To gain some insight into the world of grain trading, I also attended the 2017 Global Grain Middle East meeting in Dubai, where I conducted participant observation and informal interviews with Egyptian and non-Egyptian grain traders.

Throughout my fieldwork in Egypt, there were some sites that remained inaccessible to me. My experience attempting to enter a baladi bread bakery with Hisham, referenced above, left me wary of trying again, for fear of endangering my contacts or getting in trouble with the authorities, particularly at a time of heightened political tensions.[48] My attempts to visit an agricultural research station where scientists are working on breeding new wheat varieties were also in vain. I corresponded with an Egyptian breeder, who invited me to visit his station when I was in Egypt in August 2015. Three days before my visit, though, he emailed to say that his director had told him that I had first to get permission from a senior official in the Agricultural Research Institute. I duly made an appointment with this official, but when I arrived for it, he was not there. Instead, I was met by three other senior officials, who were cautious and cool toward me. After brief introductions, they ended our conversation saying that they could not talk with me unless I had a letter from the Department of Foreign Relations within the ministry. I went to that office, but the person in charge refused to speak to me. When I was instructed that I would have to send a request on headed paper listing all the people I wanted to meet and the data I wanted to gather, along with a copy of my passport, I decided that not only was this line of research unlikely to be feasible, it was unwise to pursue it further. Bakeries, agricultural research stations, flour mills, cargo ships, or grain silos might not be places that readers immediately associate with security, but in Egypt these are politically sensitive sites—sites in which the presence of a foreign researcher would raise questions that could put those who facilitated her presence in a dangerous situation. The gaps in my data, therefore, are in themselves revealing of the ways in which bread and wheat are tied to security, both in the affective sense of them being things that provoke danger or fear, and in the practical sense of them being things around which various groups actively take measures to guard against threats.

Since I was interested in the history of wheat breeding in Egypt and the subsidized bread program, there was an archival component to my work. I traveled to New York to conduct research at the archives of the Rockefeller Foundation, which has played a major role in funding research and training in wheat breeding around the world. I spent a week in Rome, in the archives of the Food and Agricultural Organization of the United Nations, which has funded several regional wheat breeding initiatives. I conducted research at the US National Archives, in College Park, Maryland, which has a valuable set of records from the US Department of Agriculture's Foreign Agricultural Service officers based in the American Embassy in Cairo.

While this research approach provided rich data, I understood from the beginning that it would not allow me to fully explore patterns of bread production and consumption in urban Egypt. I have spent considerable time in Cairo, meeting with government officials, policy experts, and international development practitioners, but I do not have a strong network in any residential neighborhood. Without such a base of established relations, I knew that it would be impossible to gain meaningful information about how urban peoples interact with bread in the context of short-term research trips. I decided, therefore, to work with a Cairo-based research assistant—a practice that has long been a feature of ethnographic fieldwork but one often obscured due to academic norms that privilege single authorship and sustain the myth of the proficient ethnographer as one who works alone (Middleton and Cons 2014). Collaboration, in its varied forms, has always been central to the production of ethnographic knowledge and a topic of much discussion in the literature, from early work in dialogical anthropology (for example, Rabinow [1977] 2007, Crapanzano 1980, Dwyer 1982) to more recent feminist and decolonial texts, which have underscored the critical insights that come from the integration of multiple voices (for example, Harrison 1991, Nagar 2014, Berry et al. 2017). My point here is to acknowledge how collaboration can also be a way to address the structural constraints that researchers may face at particular life stages, limiting access to their field sites.

Mariam Taher, the research assistant I found through a mutual acquaintance, is an Egyptian American who grew up in Cairo. She is from a relatively privileged background and studied overseas, obtaining bachelor's and master's degrees from universities in the United Kingdom and the Netherlands. When we met, she was managing a local foods delicatessen in the upscale neighborhood of Maʿadi. Between August 2015 and June 2017, Mariam conducted participant observation at two baladi bread bakeries in a working-class neighborhood adjacent to Maʿadi.[49] Three to four times a week, she went to these bakeries to buy bread (paying the nonsubsidized price, as she does not have a ration card). Since Mariam also felt the political sensitivity of the baladi bread bakeries, as sites so deeply linked to the governing regime through the subsidy program, she focused on observing other people buying bread and conversations between customers and bakery staff. She did not attempt any more explicit questioning, so as not to draw attention to herself and to maintain her personal safety, a priority we agreed was paramount. Mariam complemented her long-term observations at these two bakeries with occasional visits to bakeries in other parts of Cairo.

The research evolved collaboratively. Each week when Mariam sent me her notes, I wrote back with detailed questions about what she was observing, comments on what she had been doing, and suggestions for what she might look for, to which she then responded. The conversations that emerged in these correspondences became an important part of the data archive. The combined outcome was over one thousand pages of single-spaced typed fieldnotes. During my fieldwork in Egypt, I also visited these bakeries, which provided a helpful visual framework for engaging with this data.

In addition, Mariam kept a journal of bread-related observations. The journal included informal interviews that she conducted with key informants from the working-class neighborhood, as well as interactions concerning bread with members of her own more affluent community of family and friends. Mariam further assisted in a keyword search of seven Arabic-language newspapers, which we chose to gain a diversity in political perspectives.[50] Focusing on the period 2015–18, we used a series of keywords to search through online databases for relevant articles about wheat and bread.[51]

This approach of working with a research assistant proved highly productive for three reasons. The first was Mariam's skills as a researcher. Although she had only limited prior experience conducting fieldwork, Mariam proved an adept ethnographer. The detail of her observations and her ability to communicate what she saw to me through extensive fieldnotes were key to this becoming a valuable source of data. Second, my own experience living and working in Egypt and my command of the language were central to me being able to engage with, understand, and interpret Mariam's data. The final factor was our frequent communication throughout the research process. These conversations not only shaped the way the data collection unfolded, but also informed my analysis of the data. We coauthored a paper drawing on this research (Barnes and Taher 2019) as well as chapter 4 of this book, which draws largely on data that Mariam collected. The collaboration was mutually productive. Mariam gained from the experience participating in an ethnographic research project—she is now working on her own research as a PhD student in anthropology at Northwestern University—and from the remuneration she received. I gained from the data Mariam gathered, and from the process of talking through our different perspectives on things that we both observed and read.

Together, these varied sources of data offer insights into the perspectives and practices of the multiple parties engaged in producing, trading, and consuming wheat and bread in Egypt. They reveal the complex, and sometimes contradictory, interests that underpin these everyday acts. In illuminating how this staple food features as a quotidian concern, to a nation and to a family, they paint a portrait of staple security.

1. STAPLE BECOMINGS

In a 3,300-year-old tomb painting from the Ancient Egyptian village of Deir el-Medina in Luxor, two people stoop forward, moving through a field of ripened grain (figure 1.1). The man, wearing a white cloth wrapped around his waist, leads the way. He holds a scythe, cutting tall stalks of grain. The woman follows behind, wearing a robe of the same cloth, gathering the fallen stalks. The ocher background and stylized heads of grain give a sense of bounty. A similar abundance is evident in a photograph taken in the Egyptian governorate of Qalubiya in 2014 (figure 1.2). In this photograph, a man walks through a sea of wheat, the ears of grain bending in the wind. The man, dressed in the clothes commonly

THE GRAIN, THE SEED. *Photograph by Mariam Taher.*

FIGURE 1.1. Painting from the tomb of the artisan Sennedjen, Deir el-Medina, Luxor. Charles K. Wilkinson, Wikimedia Commons, https://commons.wikimedia .org/wiki/File:Sennedjem_and_Iineferti_in_the_Fields_of_Iaru_MET_DT257167.jpg.

FIGURE 1.2. Harvesting wheat, Qalubiya. Photograph by Hassan Ammar. Used with permission.

worn by farmers working in their fields, is carrying a scythe in his hand, ready-ing to harvest the grain. Across the gulf of time, the similarity in the imple-ments being used to harvest the wheat is remarkable.[1] Yet there is a notable difference. In the pharaonic painting, the wheat reaches over the heads of the people harvesting it. In the contemporary photograph, the wheat barely passes the farmer's waist. Even given the different postures—stooped versus upright—and potential differences in size of the individuals pictured, the contrast in the height of the crop is striking. The nature of Egypt's wheat has changed.[2]

In the second pair of images, wheat appears in its ready-to-eat form as bread. The first is a depiction of a painting from the tomb of Ramesses III in the Valley of the Kings (figure 1.3). The drawing represents scenes within the court bakery of the pharaoh, who reigned from 1186 to 1155 BC. The image is a hive of activ-ity. People are grinding flour, kneading dough, fashioning loaves, stoking fires, and baking bread. In the bottom left corner of the image, a man is carrying a tray full of loaves, balanced on his head. The similarity with the contemporary photograph, this one of a woman walking through the streets of Cairo in 2016, is once again striking (figure 1.4). She, too, is carrying a tray of bread balanced on the head, one arm out to steady it. Her loaves are also round, but rather than being the bread of the elite, they are loaves of government-subsidized baladi bread. The continuity in food type and mode of carrying are notewor-thy. The differences are less visible: the quality of bread made with emmer and barley versus bread wheat; the texture of a loaf made from flour ground by hand versus machine; the taste of bread baked in a wood- versus gas-fired oven. The nature of Egypt's bread has changed.

I start with these comparisons not because I have an orientalist fascination with Ancient Egypt but because such comparisons are commonly evoked in con-versations about wheat and bread in Egypt. During an interview with an Egyptian nutritionist, for example, she transitioned from talking about wheat imports to noting, "In Ancient Egypt they grew wheat for bread." In a conversation with a Cairo resident about baladi and shami breads she said, "These breads have been around since the days of the pharaohs." Talking with an agricultural policy expert about wheat in Egypt, he commented, "We are the only country that calls bread ʿaish, which means livelihoods, since pharaonic times." The longevity of this crop and food's production and consumption is central to their staple identity.

Indeed, these same two images from Ancient Egyptian tombs featured on the opening slide of a PowerPoint presentation given by an Egyptian grain spe-cialist at the Global Grain conference in Geneva in 2013.[3] "The early Egyp-tians depended on wheat and barley to provide the carbohydrates they needed for a healthy, energetic lifestyle," noted the slide accompanying the harvest

FIGURE 1.3. Illustration of a painting from the tomb of Ramesses III, Valley of the Kings, Luxor. Wikimedia Commons, https://commons.wikimedia.org/wiki/File:Ramses_III_bakery.jpg.

FIGURE 1.4. Carrying bread, Cairo. Photograph by Simon Matzinger. Wikimedia Commons, https://commons.wikimedia.org/wiki/File:The_Urge_(179657967).jpeg.

scene. "Bread was the most important part of the Ancient Egyptian diet," explained the text next to the bakery scene. It was as though the presenter was seeking to make a point for why the audience should continue listening to his presentation about the logistics of importing grain to Egypt. Stop. Listen. I am talking about something important. About a crop that has been central to Egyptian livelihoods for millennia. Yet despite how this continuity figures in Egyptians' relationship with wheat and bread, framing Egypt's main crop and food in terms of such continuities glosses over the intervening millennia and obscures the significant ways in which these staples have changed.

This chapter tells the story of how the wheat and bread that we see in Egypt today have come into being. While this story is one that began thousands of years ago, I focus on changes over the twentieth century and to the present. In their book *Ingrained*, Head, Atchison, and Gates (2012) challenge the idea that wheat's character and identity are fixed, arguing that wheat is "in a constant process of becoming." The word *becoming* points to how people have shaped the nature of this staple crop over time, and the fact that this process is ongoing.[4] In tracing how Egypt's wheat and bread have come to be what they are today, I seek not only to demonstrate the mutability of these staples but to highlight the rationale driving this process of change. I argue that the becoming of wheat and bread is one realm in which practices of staple security are manifest. The ways in which a range of actors have sought to shape Egypt's wheat and bread over the years have been oriented toward the specific goal of ensuring that Egypt does not run out of a quality staple crop and food.

The first part of the chapter traces the making of Egypt's wheat. This has been a process of countering two risks—the possibilities that Egypt might be unable to grow sufficient wheat for its growing population and that a disease epidemic might wipe out the crop. I look at the breeding of new varieties that are both productive and resistant and at how this has been tied to the circulation of germplasm and expertise between Egypt and other parts of the world. This has been a public endeavor; the scientists breeding new varieties are mostly based in government research stations, and the production and distribution of seeds is done by government agencies, with minimal private sector involvement. While these scientists may not make an explicit link between their work and bread, this is what drives the government's investment in this research—it is about maximizing the yield and resilience of domestic wheat cultivation to secure the steady supply of flour for Egypt's staple. I then examine the movement of these new varieties from experimental research plots into the fields. The points of tension in this process reveal how staple security does not necessarily mean the same thing to a farmer as it does to a national policy maker.

In the second part of the chapter, I turn to bread. While multiple breads circulate within Egypt, I focus on the government-subsidized baladi bread, since this is Egypt's most widely eaten bread and the bread that has come to be seen as a central part of the state's social contract. I look at how successive governments have altered three core elements of this bread—its price and size, composition, and style. I show how shifts in these elements have been linked to anxieties about ensuring a consistent supply of the bread and producing a bread that the general public deem satisfactory. New varieties of wheat have been integral to increasing domestic wheat production, but the supply of flour to the baladi bread program rests also on the government's ability to procure that wheat and import the remaining required grain. Moreover, the taste of the bread depends not so much on the variety of wheat but on the way in which it is processed into flour and whether it is mixed with other grains. Behind these policy decisions on bread specifications is the fear of public unrest should the bread run out or popular perceptions of its quality decline.

My analysis draws on the archives of the Food and Agricultural Organization of the United Nations (FAO) and of the Rockefeller Foundation, both of which have been involved in wheat breeding efforts in the Middle East. It also utilizes material from the Foreign Agricultural Service, an agency within the US Department of Agriculture (USDA) that is responsible for promoting US agricultural exports, and which has a close interest in Egypt due to the country's position as a market for US wheat exports. Although the regular reports on wheat and bread in Egypt produced by this agency present an account that is filtered through the eyes of their authors—American and Egyptian agricultural specialists based in the US Embassy in Cairo—they offer a detailed record of key developments since the mid-twentieth century.[5] Together, these sources tell us only limited amounts about the practices and perspectives of farmers and bread consumers, but they provide valuable historical contextualization for my ethnographic examination of cultivating wheat and buying and consuming baladi bread later in the book (in chapters 2 and 4).[6] They also illustrate how staple security is not something new. A concern with ensuring that there is enough bread for the Egyptian people has long underpinned wheat cultivation and bread policy in Egypt.

Pairing these two narratives reveals a disparity between how these stories of becoming are commonly told. When agricultural scientists narrate the history of wheat varietal development in Egypt, they do so in terms of advances in the breeding program across the decades. In such a narration, the course of scientific progress appears detached from major political events within and outside of Egypt. The scientific account of developments during the 1940s, for instance, contains little mention of the world war that occupied the first half of the decade; breeding histories of the 1950s pay scarce attention to how this was also the decade in which Egypt transitioned into being a republic (El-Togby and Talaat 1971, Ghanem 1994). Yet this political context did, of course, shape how the nature of Egypt's wheat changed over time. The transfer of seeds around the world, for example, was mediated by geopolitical relations; international donors supported agricultural development initiatives in the Global South in part to strengthen alliances and counter the communist threat.[7] While the framing of breeding in terms of scientific objectives alone obscures underlying political rationales, politics is impossible to ignore when this story is brought together with that of the subsidized bread into which much of this wheat goes. Subsidized bread is at its heart political, a project of garnering popular support by guaranteeing a low-priced staple. It is a bread that originated during the conflict of the Second World War, and whose evolution has been closely mediated by the governments of Presidents Nasser, Sadat, Mubarak, Morsi, and Sisi. It is a bread, too, that has been shaped by Egypt's shifting alliances with other countries and with international financial institutions. Staple security underscores the necessity of reading these stories together.

Becoming Egypt's Wheat

The scene is bucolic. President al-Sisi stands on a flower-adorned dais, in front of a large photographic collage of golden wheat and an assortment of smiling faces, flanked by a row of Egyptian flags on one side and a field on the other. It is May 2016 and Sisi is giving a press conference to mark the launch of the wheat harvest in Farafra, an oasis in the Western Desert where the government has recently sponsored the reclamation of thousands of feddans of desert. His speech documents what he refers to as unprecedented achievements over the previous years, from the expansion of the Suez Canal to road building, housing development, and new water treatment stations.[8] While the speech ranges widely, moving beyond agriculture, Sisi's choice of the wheat harvest as the venue in which to deliver it is notable, testament to the crop's national significance and to the Egyptian people's positive associations with wheat grown on domestic soil. This same harvest season is celebrated in a video posted on the website of the *Al-Wafd* newspaper. In the five-minute clip, combine harvesters cut straight lines across vast fields to a soundtrack of nationalist-themed pop songs. In large farms like these, machines are commonly used to harvest rather than the scythes still utilized by many small-scale farmers in the Nile Valley

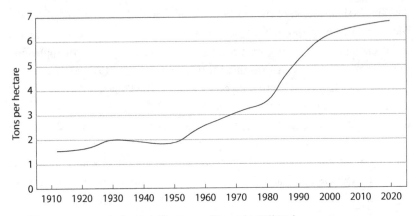

FIGURE 1.5. Average wheat yields, Egypt. Figure by Bill Nelson.

Note: Early data taken from Ghanem (1994: 12); data since 1961 taken from the FAOSTAT database, http://faostat.fao.org/faostat.

and Delta. With their khaki green color, Egyptian flags flying on top, and unloader tubes jutting out, the combine harvesters bear an uncanny resemblance to tanks.[9] Nation and crop blend seamlessly into one another.

Wheat is Egypt's staple and it is a crop that Egyptian farmers grow well. Egyptian agricultural experts often comment on the quality and productivity of Egypt's wheat. "For some reason, *our* strain coupled with *our* conditions gives really good yields," one scientist said to me. This is not happenstance, though, but rather an outcome of deliberate efforts over the years to alter Egypt's wheat in particular ways. A Sudanese wheat breeder, who works for an international agricultural organization based in Cairo, explained to me that "Egypt is one of the countries that has progressively made great improvements in the quantity of wheat produced." He described how wheat yields on an average Egyptian farm are more than 6.8 tons/ha.[10] To contextualize this figure, he gave some international comparisons. "When I was working in Mexico in CIMMYT [the International Center for Wheat and Maize Improvement], we got 3.5–4 tons/ha," he said. "In Africa, the average is 2 tons/ha. Even in the most favorable environment, like in the Ethiopian Highlands, it's maybe 2.5–3 tons/ha. Egypt doubled that! Chile, on the Mediterranean climate side, South Africa, and Egypt are top in terms of yields."[11]

The agricultural success story this breeder narrated is represented in the graph shown in figure 1.5. The line's upward trajectory, steady then more dramatic, reveals a marked increase in wheat yields over the course of the twentieth century. The graph symbolizes a transformation that has enabled the production of increasing quantities of bread. A hectare of Egyptian land now produces more than four times as much wheat as it did a century ago. The Sudanese breeder explained this transformation in terms of "varietal development and good management." It is an outcome of both breeding new varieties and then getting those varieties out into the fields and cultivating them in a particular way. It is a story not just of high-yielding seeds but also high applications of fertilizer. Indeed, alongside Egypt's superlative status in wheat productivity, a number of people told me that Egyptian farmers have one of the highest rates of fertilizer usage in the world.[12]

Military metaphors abound in this story of becoming. It is a revolution, labeled *green* by international experts. A battle, waged against diseases and pests. A resistance, captured in seeds' genetic material. The leaders of the revolution are the Egyptian and non-Egyptian experts trained in plant breeding and plant pathology. Yet their work would be incomplete without the farmers who plant the resultant varieties. These various actors all play a role in the project of staple security, but their interests do not always align.

Breeding

A longer history of the becoming of Egypt's wheat since ancient times would center on the labor of farmers, year in and year out, to identify the best plants from each crop and select seeds to plant the following year, gradually modifying the crop over time. Within the limited timeframe of the last hundred years or so, however, the dramatic changes shown in figure 1.5 rest on the work of what Kloppenburg (2005) terms "scientific breeding." This mode of seed development takes place in the laboratory and on experimental plots and lies primarily in the hands of scientists trained in plant breeding. In the case of Egypt, this work, led by scientists in the Ministry of Agriculture, has been channeled toward two goals: fighting rust and raising yields. Both of these goals are ultimately about trying to ensure that nothing threatens the supply of bread for Egypt.[13]

FIGHTING RUST Egypt's formal breeding program dates back to 1914.[14] The goal of the program was to develop wheat varieties that were high yielding and had good agronomic characteristics, but, above all, that were resistant to disease.[15] Rust was the main disease of concern, a fungal disease that has been present in wheat-growing regions since ancient times.[16] Caused by the *Puccinia* pathogen and coming in three forms—stem rust, leaf rust, and yellow (also known as stripe) rust—this disease can result in yield losses of up to

50 percent (Draz et al. 2015). Breeders were deeply aware of the import of their research. One breeder described his work as a "continuous battle" with rust, motivated by the threat of a "catastrophic situation" should a virulent race of rust appear in an epidemic form and "wipe out . . . whole areas of wheat."[17] Another justified his efforts to reduce disease losses by noting how wheat is "so badly needed in the world today and the future to feed the burgeoning human population."[18] These breeders may not have written about bread, but they were clearly thinking about the staple food their research subject would become and about people's reliance on it.

The early years of Egypt's wheat breeding program were illustrative of how this battle with rust advanced. In the 1920s, Egyptian breeders incorporated seeds from India into their breeding program, mixing them with local varieties to develop varieties whose names—Hindi D and Hindi 62 (*hindi* means *Indian* in Arabic)—bore testament to their origins. But while these seeds had some promising characteristics, they were attacked by stem and yellow rust. In response, breeders looked for new "parent" seeds with rust-resistant traits that they could bring into their breeding program. They found such resistance in seeds being grown in Kenya. A crossing of Kenyan and Egyptian varieties led to the development of a successful variety known as Giza 139 (named after the research station in Giza where it was developed) (El-Togby and Talaat 1971). A prominent Egyptian wheat breeder of that time described this variety as "the milestone in combating these diseases." When, however, this variety was widely released in the 1940s, although it proved resistant to stem rust, it was subject to "serious attacks" of leaf rust.[19]

Efforts to try and understand more about rust, the threat it posed, and the best way to counter it therefore continued apace. In the late 1940s, the government established a Rust Laboratory at the Giza research station, and plant pathologists began to explore the races of rust found in Egypt and the epidemiology of this disease. They worked, also, to screen varieties to identify which ones were resistant to rust. This knowledge was complemented by data collected through international nurseries coordinated by several institutions, including the Food and Agricultural Organization of the United Nations (FAO). These nurseries were packages of seed sourced from around the world, which were distributed to participating breeders to grow on their experimental plots, so as to generate data on different varieties' growth under contrasting conditions and a closer understanding of their relative merits. The seeds were exchanged free of charge, although the archival records reveal traces of other things that impeded their flow across borders, from insufficient envelopes to missing phytosanitary certificates and mislabeled seeds. One of these nursery initiatives was specifically focused on identifying varieties' resistance to rust.[20] Through the testing of varieties, not only did Egyptian scientists contribute to a broader body of understanding about rust resistance, but they identified varieties that they could then incorporate in their breeding programs. As an FAO report from 1968 explained, "Increasing wheat production means fighting with rust. Therefore, the UAR's [Egypt's] plant breeders have for many years relied on FAO's nurseries and also other agencies."[21]

These efforts led to a marked success. In the 1960s, Egyptian breeders released a variety named Giza 155 (a cross between local, American, and Indian lines) that was resistant to all three prevailing forms of rust in Egypt and that produced a quality grain. When an officer from the FAO visited Egypt in 1969 he noted, "because of great importance given to breeding resistant varieties, the losses due to the three rusts are on average about 2 to 5 percent, and only in some years do they reach 10 percent."[22] By 1970–71, Giza 155 was being grown on about 90 percent of the total area under wheat cultivation (El-Togby and Talaat 1971).

Through a battle waged in laboratories and experimental fields, not just in Egypt but around the world, in tables of data logging different races of wheat, inoculations applied to artificially infect crops so as to test their susceptibility, and packets of seed sent across oceans, these early decades of the breeding program saw the becoming of a rust-resistant crop in Egypt. But this was not a process that had an endpoint. Since rusts are always evolving, wheat varieties, too, have to evolve if they are to be resistant to emergent races. Moreover, there were further risks that the breeding program strove to address.

PRODUCING MORE The 1960s and 1970s saw a shift in emphasis within Egypt's wheat breeding program toward a primary focus on yields, although disease resistance continued to be an important consideration. Such an interest in yields was not new. Earlier breeders had certainly sought to produce productive varieties, and yields had increased by 67 percent over the fifty-year period from 1912 to 1962 (Ghanem 1994: 12). What was new, however, was the horizon of possibility of what constituted a high-yielding variety and the unprecedented scope for how much wheat Egypt could grow—and, consequently, how much bread it could produce.

The goal to make Egypt's wheat more productive was underpinned by a Malthusian logic. In 1966 John Gibler, an official from the Ford Foundation, reported on his recent trip to the Middle East. "Egypt is sitting on top of a volcano and doesn't know it," he wrote. The looming disaster, as he saw it, was the product of millions of people crammed into a narrow strip of land along the Nile Valley, a rapidly increasing population, and limited land on which to grow food.[23] While Gibler suggested that Egyptian officials were unaware of this threat, concerns about the so-called food gap—between the consumption needs of a rapidly growing population (largely defined in terms of bread) and production potential of a restricted natural resource base (largely defined in terms of wheat)—were a prevalent theme among Egyptian officials at this time. As Mitchell (2002) has argued, this framing of the problem as one of geography versus demography erased important questions of power and inequality but helped legitimize a technical solution to overcome these "natural" limits. In terms of increasing food production, the technical possibilities were twofold: Egypt could increase the amount of agricultural land by expanding into the desert (so-called horizontal expansion) or increase the amount of food grown on existing agricultural land (so-called vertical expansion).

Since the formation of the Egyptian republic, successive governments have taken up horizontal expansion through desert reclamation as a central policy objective (Springborg 1979, Voll 1980, Meyer 1998, Sowers 2011, Barnes 2012). The 1.5 Million Feddans Project to reclaim land in Egypt's Western Desert, the site of Sisi's speech to launch the wheat harvest in 2016, is the latest iteration of this kind of initiative. The government has framed this project explicitly in terms of the imperative to produce bread for the people. Reflecting this official narrative, one newspaper article from 2016 on the project began with a reference back to the revolution: "About five years ago, the square of Tahrir was aloud with calls of protesters for bread, freedom, social justice. Now, with the beginning of a new year and the fifth anniversary of the January 25 revolution, the state is still fighting to keep bread on the table of Egyptians. It has specified that about half the land of the 1.5 Million Feddans Project will be used for wheat production."[24] Yet commentators remain skeptical about whether this project will achieve its ambitious targets.[25] Past attempts at large-scale reclamation have raised questions about the feasibility and sustainability of turning Egypt's desert into cultivated land. Of the land that has been successfully reclaimed, much has been used for high-value fruit and vegetable crops rather than cereals. So although the rhetoric of expansion continues, the role that growing wheat in the desert has played in securing Egypt's staple has been limited.

Meanwhile, the work of vertical expansion has continued with less fanfare. Over the last fifty years or so, Egyptian scientists within the government's agricultural bureaucracy have been working in collaboration with international networks to produce more from the given area of land. The seeds that, back in the 1960s, unlocked the potential for a jump in productivity came from the Mexican Wheat Program, a Rockefeller Foundation–funded initiative under the leadership of Norman Borlaug, an American agronomist with a PhD in plant pathology from the University of Minnesota (often credited as being the "father of the Green Revolution"—work for which he went on to receive a Nobel Peace Prize). Borlaug and his colleagues, drawing on genetic material from diverse geographic roots, developed shorter-stature varieties of wheat, which could support larger heads of grain without lodging (falling over) and thus could be fertilized more.[26] Judging these varieties to be the way forward, they included these so-called Mexican dwarfs in the packages of seed they sent around the world, sometimes in one-to-one exchanges with breeders, other times in larger nursery collections.

It was through such channels that these varieties made their way to Egypt. But for those varieties to shape the becoming of Egypt's wheat, there had to be a spark of interest among Egyptian breeders to incorporate them into their breeding program. This spark came, in part, from the Egyptian scientists who went to Mexico for training. Between 1966 and 1986, the FAO and the Rockefeller Foundation sponsored eighteen Egyptian scientists to attend training courses in Mexico (CIMMYT 1988: 130). Through this training, these scientists had a chance to see dwarf varieties being cultivated and to learn about their advantages.

In addition, a number of foreign experts made trips to Egypt during the 1960s, some sponsored by the Rockefeller Foundation, others facilitated by the FAO and a regional program to support crop breeding, the Near East Wheat and Barley Improvement Project.[27] During these trips, they interacted with Egyptian breeders and shared their conviction that short-stature Mexican varieties were what Egypt needed. One wheat breeder from the Mexican program, Charles Krull, who visited Egypt in 1966, was struck by the problems of lodging that he saw in the wheat fields. He explained, "None of the present varieties . . . have adequate straw strength for even the presently used fertilizer levels, and the situation will rapidly deteriorate as fertilizer applications are increased." Underscoring the sense of threat, he noted, "It is essential that this be done, or wheat will not be able to retain its present place in UAR [Egyptian] agriculture." He concluded, "The Mexican dwarfs are in general well adapted in the UAR. Their straw strength is definitely what is needed in the breeding program now."[28]

It is notable that Krull framed his statement about the necessity of new varieties in terms of a future of increased fertilizer applications. Indeed the two—new seeds and fertilizer—went hand in hand. International experts spent considerable time debating what levels of fertilizer use would be "adequate," "economic," or "advisable." But what they all agreed on was that levels should be increased. Borlaug noted how, with the old varieties in Egypt, farmers were unable to apply more than 50 pounds of nitrogen, "because above 50 pounds of nitrogen [per acre], all their own breeding material is flat on its back on the ground, lodged, and no matter how much more fertilizer, no matter *what* you do to the crop from there on out, you get no additional yield." He then contrasted this with the Mexican varieties. "These small wheats—short ones—could be fertilized 100 pounds, 120 pounds, 130 pounds and still pay big dividends with the yield going up progressively as a result of this."[29] In his mind, there was no contest. Borlaug talked about this rapid increase in fertilizer use as a central part of his strategy for working in the Middle East, a center of origin for wheat, where you have to be a "better showman," dealing, as a breeder, with "attitudes like—well, we've survived on it like it is for all these thousands of years, let's not rock the boat too much." It was for this reason, he said, that he was "not willing to go through applying 20 pounds of nitrogen and 40 pounds and 60 pounds and 80 pounds and fighting all the bureaucrats and government politicians along the way." Instead, he explained, "I want the difference in yield to be so big, that everything they've believed in—that has been basic to their very survival—comes down in a shambles all around them."[30]

But some of Egypt's senior plant breeders were not immediately receptive to the showman's message. They knew that farmers valued the stem of the wheat plant as well as the grain, cutting and drying it to use as straw for animals. Not only was straw an important part of provisioning for household livestock, but it was also valuable (at times, wheat straw has been worth more than the grain in Egypt). Foreign breeders maintained that these dwarf varieties could actually produce as much straw as tall varieties because of their increased tillering—the way in which they generated more lateral shoots per plant—and their ability to be highly fertilized. But the perception that smaller varieties would produce less straw was persistent.[31]

One of the most vocal initial critics of the dwarf varieties was Said Dessouki, who was head of Egypt's wheat breeding program at that time. Dessouki, like Borlaug, had a PhD from the University of Minnesota and considerable experience in wheat breeding, having played a key role in the development of important varieties like Giza 155. In the notes from his 1966 trip, Charles Krull wrote, "Dessouki seems to be the primary road block to the use of dwarf wheats. He claims to be interested but finds lots of reasons why they might not work and makes sure that the staff at Sakha [one of the government research stations] where the little work being done . . . is kept at a minimum."[32]

While Dessouki's intransigence lay in part in concerns about the grain-to-straw ratio, there may also have been an underlying sense of professional threat. Krull reflected that the "real reason" for Dessouki's resistance "is that he feels that a significant impact by such varieties might reflect on the breeding he has been doing the last twenty years."[33] As another officer working for the Rockefeller Foundation noted after his visit to Egypt, "Egyptian workers are extremely proud of their varieties, ones which they have bred for high yield and for resistance to rust diseases." He called this the "cult of the variety."[34] Egyptian breeders were not the only ones to develop a relationship with their varieties—Borlaug talked about this relationship in terms of "love"—but the foreign commentator's dismissal of this attachment in cultish terms was revealing.[35] It implied that Egyptian scientists' attachment to their seed was excessive rather than legitimate, nostalgic rather than the forward-facing.

Dessouki was eventually won over, however, after the Rockefeller Foundation funded a two-month trip for him and the head of Egypt's plant pathology department to visit wheat research stations in Mexico, the United States, Canada, and Sweden in 1967. At the end of their trip, Dessouki and his colleague expressed excitement about what they had seen and their keenness to "get into the streams of international flow of improved materials."[36] The following year, in 1968, an initiative began to facilitate the "extensive exchange of wheat material" between Egypt and the Mexican program, now established as an international organization called CIMMYT, the International Center for Wheat and Maize Improvement (El-Togby and Talaat 1971: 27). At a 1969 conference, Dessouki heralded a "new era in wheat breeding" referring to a "number of promising dwarf lines."[37]

When scientists were called upon to rationalize their work, they did so in terms of meeting Egypt's food needs. The becoming of a productive wheat was tied to the perceived need to secure Egypt's bread supply by producing more. A 1969 report noted that "the successful introduction of high yielding Mexican varieties . . . has partly removed the great anxiety which was caused by food deficit in the Near East countries."[38] With their high yields, these new varieties were to wipe out the threat of grain scarcity.

Yet it was not these Mexican varieties alone that led to the transformation of Egyptian wheat. Local breeders had to do considerable work to adapt these varieties to local conditions and to respond to locally valued quality characteristics. Farmers did not like the dark-colored grain of the initial dwarf varieties, for instance, because it impacted the quality of the bread that they made at home. (Notably, there is no record in the archives of similar dissatisfaction with the grain among bakers who made subsidized bread, perhaps because grain color was less evident when this grain was mixed with other local and imported varieties during the process of being milled into flour for the subsidy program.) In response to the farmers' complaints, Egyptian breeders adjusted the coloring in their subsequent releases.[39] It was also important for Egyptian breeders to adapt these varieties to ensure their resistance, for not only were many of the Mexican varieties susceptible to rust but the conditions of their production exacerbated the disease risk. The director of the FAO's Near East breeding project warned that the "spread of varieties more or less of similar genetic constitution on large contiguous areas using high doses of fertilizer could create serious outbreaks of diseases and pests." He described the "virtual merry-go-round of breeding and releasing new varieties as fast as new races of pathogens appear on the scene."[40] The fact that such serious outbreaks were not manifest is indicative of the success of Egyptian breeders' efforts to meld productivity and resistance traits. While scholars often talk about the Green Revolution in terms of the combination of seeds and fertilizer that produced such plenty, it was also a triumph of resistance.

Since the 1960s, Egyptian breeders have continued to incorporate dwarf lines into their crossing program, while breeding in resistance, and have released a series of high-yielding dwarf varieties (table 1.1).[41] The logic underpinning their actions has been that the more wheat Egypt can produce, the better. To plant breeders, staple security means increasing the productivity and resilience of the seed. The metric they use to assess success is yields per hectare. The domain in which they engage the staple crop is science. However, for this process of seed development to translate into the pattern of national average yields shown on figure 1.5, the seeds have to move from the hands of scientists

TABLE 1.1
The Becoming of Productive, Disease-Resistant Wheat

	Primary seed sources	Key bread wheat varieties
1910s	Egypt	Baladi 116
1920s	Egypt and India	Hindi D, Hindi 62
1940s	Egypt and Kenya	Giza 139
1950s–1960s	Egypt, United States, Canada, Europe	Giza 144, Giza 145, Giza 146, Giza 147, Giza 148, Giza 150, Giza 155
1970s–1980s	Egypt, United States, Canada, Europe, Central and South America	Super X, Mexipak, Chenab 70, Sakha 8, Giza 157, Giza 158, Sakha 61, Sakha 69, Giza 160, Sakha 92, Giza 162, Giza 163, Giza 164
1990s–2010s	Egypt, United States, Canada, Europe, Central and South America	Gemiza 1, Gemiza 6, Gemiza 7, Gemiza 8, Gemiza 9, Gemiza 11, Sakha 93, Giza 168, Shandaweel 1, Misr 1, Misr 2, Giza 171, Sids 1, Sids 12, Sids 13, Sids 14

to the hands of farmers. This has not always gone smoothly, for farmers have their own interests and practices of staple security, which do not always match those of the breeders and government bureaucrats seeking to secure the nation's wheat supply.[42]

Into the Fields

In 1953, Egypt's Minister of Agriculture noted that "the good seed will have no effect on the raising of the general production of the country unless the use of selected plant and animal seeds is broadly spread to every farmer."[43] Thus at the same time that the ministry invested in plant breeding, it also worked to develop an infrastructure for producing and distributing the new varieties. Producing seed for a cereal crop, in which the grain is the seed, means growing a promising variety and gathering its harvest not to consume but to replant. This is the responsibility of the ministry's seed department, which contracts with private farms to grow the crop for seed. Government officials supervise to ensure that the seed meets its standards for varietal purity and the absence of insects, pests, and diseases. The seed is processed in processing plants, which clean the seed, treat it with insecticide, bag, seal, and label it. The government then distributes the seed at controlled prices via the agricultural cooperatives.

Between 1952 and 1961, the ministry increased the amount of "high-quality seeds" that it was producing and distributing to farmers for planting each year from 10,000 tons to 43,000 tons.[44] This had the desired effect, for an expert review panel from the FAO reported in 1960 that "definite progress is being made in replacing native and the older improved varieties with more productive ones."[45] In 1964, the new varieties were being grown on more than 70 percent of the area under wheat.[46] By 1978, the ministry announced that it had produced sufficient seeds of two of its high-yielding varieties—Giza 155 and Chenab—to cover "the entire area." It also announced that it had produced enough seeds of several new Mexican varieties—Giza 157, Giza 158, and Sakha 8—to cover 100,000 feddans.[47]

It was with these Mexican varieties, however, that the government encountered some resistance. To encourage farmers to plant the dwarf varieties, the government (as the sole purchaser of domestic wheat) offered to buy the grain from these varieties at a higher price—73.3EGP/ton in 1978 compared to 66.7EGP/ton for older varieties. In 1980, the government increased the price to 86.7EGP for Mexican varieties and 80EGP for older varieties.[48] But the good prices did not counteract the farmers' aversion to these varieties' squat architecture.[49] Just as some of Egypt's leading wheat breeders had recognized, farmers valued the straw of the wheat (which they could sell or use as fodder) as well as the grain, which they could sell or use for baking. Furthermore, although the procurement price for the grain of Mexican varieties was higher, it was still not all that inviting; at this time the government was essentially taxing producers to support consumers through the baladi bread program (see chapter 2).[50] As a result, farmers could actually earn more from the straw of their wheat than from any grain that they wished to sell. Not only were fodder prices high at this time (the straw-to-grain price ratio rose from 0.2 in 1970 to 0.9 in 1979), but in traditional varieties the yield of straw outweighed that of grain by about 50 percent. Farmers, therefore, had no economic incentive to switch to the dwarf varieties (Byerlee and Moya 1993: 28). If their current wheat seeds were producing enough for household bread needs and they were also benefitting from selling straw, the new varieties held little appeal. The farmers' security criteria did not align with those of the government.

Farmers were also resistant to the way in which these varieties had to be cultivated. In particular, not all farmers wanted to use the amount of fertilizer that breeders thought they should. This was not due to the limited availability of fertilizer or its cost, for at this stage the government kept fertilizer prices stable.[51] Rather, it was a reflection of how farmers perceived wheat in relation to other crops (chapter 2). An official working for the Rockefeller Foundation noted that Egyptian farmers often "plant the wheat and sell the fertilizer to their neighbors for putting on more profitable crops." He concluded, "This sure isn't conducive to increasing wheat production."[52] He placed the burden for Egypt's insufficient wheat production on farmers' inappropriate "cultural practices"—on them not doing what they should with their fertilizer. But whereas the government has an interest in maximizing wheat production to supply the subsidized bread program, from the farmer's perspective, so long as they have enough wheat for household use, it may make more sense for them to use their fertilizer to enhance the production of another crop.

Furthermore, farmers were concerned not only about straw quantity in the dwarf varieties but also about quality. Many continued to think that the straw of these new varieties was too rough to work well as fodder. They also complained about the darker grain and flour that these varieties produced, which did not make the kind of bread they were used to.[53] The farmers' resistance was reflected in the government's statistics. By the end of the 1970s, less than 10 percent of the wheat area was planted with high-yielding dwarf varieties, despite the fact that those varieties yielded 14 percent more than older varieties and the fact that the government paid higher prices for their grain.[54]

These same indicators show that something changed over the following years. By the mid-1990s, officials reported that roughly half the wheat being planted was high-yielding dwarf varieties.[55] Part of the reason for this change lay in the government's reversal of its pricing policies during the 1980s in favor of grain over straw. This made the new, grain-heavy but straw-limited varieties economically attractive to farmers (Byerlee and Moya 1993: 28). Breeders also addressed some of farmers' other concerns in their development of the next wave of varieties, lightening the color of the grain and making the straw less rough.[56] In 1998, officials reported that more than 70 percent of the wheat area was planted with dwarf varieties, a substantial increase from just three years prior.[57] By 2003, the Ministry of Agriculture claimed that the entire wheat area was being cultivated with these varieties.

Thus, over the latter half of the twentieth century, the ministry bred, produced, and distributed new varieties of wheat throughout Egypt—shorter in stature, higher in yield—displacing both the modern varieties that preceded them and the landraces that had developed over generations.[58] But while the ministry's seed production and distribution program has introduced new wheat varieties to all parts of the country, it does not generate enough seed for each farmer's annual needs. The key distinction in terms of what Egyptian farmers are planting today, therefore, is not between modern and traditional varieties but between certified and uncertified seeds.

Certified seeds are produced by the ministry and quality-checked by officials. Uncertified seeds are saved by farmers, sourced either from previous harvests or from neighbors or friends. Embedded in these two seed types are different degrees of government control. To crop scientists, uncertified seeds carry the risk of a disease outbreak, since they have not been checked for contamination (the assumption being that any checks conducted by farmers are insufficient). Uncertified seeds also tend to have lower yields over time, because they produce crops that are not consistent in height or form. As one Egyptian scientist explained to me, "Each generation, the phenotype suffers. The crop may start to lie down [i.e., lodge]. After three generations, you can't plant it anymore."[59] From the government's perspective, therefore, certified seed is a way to ensure that Egyptian farmers produce the maximum amount of wheat possible.

Each year, the ministry produces a number of certified seeds for distribution to farmers. In 2015, for example, it produced eighteen wheat varieties that it recommended for use.[60] But many of the agricultural specialists I interviewed maintained that there is not enough seed to go around. Often they recited figures of the proportion of the cultivated area being grown with certified seed, ranging from 40 to 50 percent. This issue was highlighted in an article in the opposition newspaper, *Al-Badil*, which noted that although the Ministry of Agriculture claims that it provides 70 percent of wheat seeds, "experts" assert that it only provides enough for 40 percent of the area grown with wheat. According to the article, uncertified seeds produce yields that are only 70 percent of those of the varieties distributed by the ministry and are one reason for the "inability of the state to reduce the food gap."[61] From the national vantage point, uncertified seeds are undermining the security of Egypt's wheat supply.

From the local vantage point, on the other hand, uncertified seeds mean something different. Indeed, the term itself—*uncertified*—is not one that farmers typically use, since governmental certification is not the yardstick by which they evaluate their seeds. For farmers, seeds saved from a previous harvest bring the security of knowing that they will be able to plant their fields without having to buy seed alongside all the other costly inputs. From one year to the next, farmers may not be so concerned about attaining the highest possible yields, so long as they can grow enough to meet their household bread needs (chapter 2). Over the long term, though, the reduced yields of saved seeds could compromise a farmer's staple security objectives. Hence certified seeds have their advantages. This raises the question of which farmers are able to access these seeds, given that there are not enough to go around. Inequalities in access are not as pronounced as they are in places where seeds are controlled by corporations that ramp up prices. Still, it is not surprising that farmers in positions of influence are those more likely to be able to access them. As one agricultural expert said to me when talking about access to certified seeds, "Farmers have to use power or pay to get those seeds."

Hence, to return to the image in figure 1.2, the short stature of the wheat, reaching just to the farmer's waist, is a reflection of how a new kind of wheat has come to dominate Egypt's agricultural landscape. This high-yielding wheat is a champion for meeting the nation's bread needs. It also provides farming households with grain that they can consume or sell. In contrast with the fixed portrayal of the crop in the photograph, however, this wheat is not in stasis.

Still Becoming

Egypt's wheat is still becoming. Breeders continue to work on the crop. Farmers continue to select seeds from their best plants. Researchers continue to exchange germplasm across borders. Egyptian scientists continue to attend CIMMYT training courses. The resistance and yield of wheat remain driving imperatives.

The specter of the nation's crop being wiped out by a disease is an ongoing concern, although the enemy to which the wheat must be resistant is constantly changing. One agricultural expert told me that the most pressing current threat, for instance, is Ug99, a race of stem rust that was first discovered in Uganda in 1998. An international institute founded by Borlaug to continue his work against rust describes on its website how this virulent rust "threatened to invade the wheat fields of the world's bread baskets of the Middle East." It warns of the "disastrous impact on world food security if Ug99 and/or other rusts were to spread unchecked" and advocates for a "global campaign to counter wheat rust epidemics and mitigate the potential impact on food security." Such a campaign must be led by the "world's wheat warriors." The account concludes with a quote from Borlaug: "Rust never sleeps."[62] Thus the threat continues and plant breeders and pathologists must remain ever vigilant.

Over the past decade, Egyptian breeders have sought to integrate Ug99 resistance into new varieties such as Misr 1 and Misr 2, which they released in 2011.[63] Plant pathologists screen the various varieties being grown in Egypt for their resistance to rust and make recommendations regarding resistant varieties that farmers should plant and breeders should incorporate in their breeding programs. As scientists based in the Ministry of Agriculture's research center noted, there is a need to "continuously monitor [the] rust situation and evolve resistant varieties to ensure [the] food security of Egypt" (Draz et al. 2015: 37).

There are also non-disease threats to which Egyptian breeders are seeking breed resistance, namely, the threat of higher temperatures and possibly more stressed water supplies due to climate change. Given projections that climate change will have a negative impact on Egypt's wheat production (Asseng et al. 2018), breeders are aiming to develop varieties that are resistant to heat and low in water use.[64] These varieties will be key to Egypt's continued ability to secure its food supply in a warmer world.

At the same time, the impetus to increase yields persists, haunted by the lingering ghost of Malthus. In many of my interviews, people recounted markedly similar narratives to those circulating in the 1950s and 1960s about Egypt's limited agricultural land, growing population, and need for greater wheat production. The Ministry of Agriculture's goal is to increase national average yields to 11.5–12.5 tons/ha.[65] Such goal setting is part of the government's staple security practice; it is an effort to maximize domestic production so as to reduce reliance on imports and attendant risks to Egypt's wheat supply (see chapter 3). The further expansion in yields is to be achieved not only through new seeds but also through new cultivation techniques. One of these is known as raised-bed cultivation.

I first heard about raised beds during a 2015 interview with Walid, an agricultural engineer who works as a water management specialist for an international agricultural organization. (This technique was not in use during my earlier fieldwork in 2007–8.) With raised beds, rather than broadcasting seed across a flat field, the farmer plants wheat in rows along parallel raised beds, which are interspersed with furrows. Sitting with Walid in his Cairo office, he talked me through a PowerPoint presentation that outlined the promising results of his organization's work to demonstrate the efficacy of raised beds in a pilot area of the delta.[66] By the time I had an opportunity to accompany Walid to the field to see this technique in practice, four years later, there were 900,000 feddans of wheat being cultivated in raised beds, almost a third of the wheat-cultivated area, and the approach had been adopted as a central part of the Ministry of Agriculture's program to increase wheat production.

We headed out of Cairo toward the eastern part of Fayoum Governorate, which is one of the sites where Walid is now leading an initiative to demonstrate use of this technology so as to extend its adoption beyond the delta. During the journey, Walid took out his phone and showed me photos of a gleaming yellow and red machine. This is the machine that has made the expansion in raised-bed cultivation possible. It is a raised-bed seeder, which Walid adapted to meet the needs of Egyptian smallholders. It is a durable, low-cost machine, pulled behind a tractor, which makes the beds and sows the seeds in a single pass through the field. Whereas manually preparing and seeding a feddan of wheat in raised beds takes ten laborers a whole day—which, based on a daily rate of 100EGP per laborer, amounts to 1,000EGP—a farmer can rent the machine to do this in half an hour at a cost of 150EGP.

We arrived in Fayoum and stopped to look at a field. The field was small, only two qirats in size (less than a tenth of a feddan). Recently planted, the order was noticeable: neat raised beds, running parallel down the field, and straight lines of wheat plants, running parallel down each bed (figure 1.6). Walid was happy with what he saw. As so much technology is made for use on larger farms, he is pleased to have helped develop a technology from which small farmers can benefit. In the neatly ordered beds, he saw the security of Egypt's domestic wheat supply. What struck me, though, were the gaps between the beds. I wondered what farmers thought about leaving this land uncultivated. Most farmers have such small pieces of land, they tend to make use of every part. Walid responded that this had indeed been an issue at first. "They see this and they say, 'You are crazy! We're losing a third of the land!'" But, in his recounting, they were won over when they saw the results at harvest time.

FIGURE 1.6. Cultivating wheat in raised beds. Photograph by the author.

As we moved from field to field, it was these results that Walid told me about, over and over again. Initially, the rationale behind promoting raised beds was to save water—flooding furrows requires less water than flooding a field. But the field trials showed a number of other benefits. Walid listed them for me several times, a mantra of this technology's wonder, as I nodded and scribbled them down in my notebook. Water savings of 25 percent. Increased yields of 25–30 percent, up to almost 9 tons/ha. Lower fertilizer usage by 30 percent. Fifty percent fewer seeds required. Even reduced social conflict. Not all these benefits come directly from raised beds, for the project is introducing the beds in combination with a package of interventions, including certified seeds of high-yielding varieties, laser land leveling, changes in the irrigation infrastructure, and agronomic advice. Still, raised beds lie at the heart of the transformation.

Walid's narrative of success was seductive, the prospect of what might happen if this technology were extended to all of Egypt's wheat fields exciting. But I wondered to myself whether there was another side to the story. Walid did not share any problems, but I got a couple of glimpses over the course of the day. In among the perfectly ordered fields, we saw a few fields of disorder where, in place of the neat beds, the green had crept across the field and the crop was uneven. These were fields where farmers had made raised beds but then broadcast seed in the ditches between them to maximize their use of the space—an act that ironically, according to Walid, results in lower yields. There is also the question of cost. When raised beds are combined with all the other inputs, the package costs significantly more than just the cost of bed preparation: around 5,000EGP/feddan, in contrast to the 1,200EGP/feddan it typically costs farmers to prepare a field for wheat cultivation and sow the seed through broadcasting. In this pilot area, the project has covered the cost, but as the initiative rolls out, the question remains of who will pay and, if that responsibility falls on farmers, which farmers will be able to pay. Indeed, none of the wheat farmers in Warda, the area of western Fayoum where I have been doing fieldwork since 2007, are planting wheat in raised beds (see chapter 2). They have not benefited from a development project targeting their area, and even if this package were to be available for purchase, it is doubtful that many could afford it. Nonetheless, despite the possibility of not all farmers being entirely convinced, and despite the associated costs, the government is committed to expanding use of this technique. The ministry has set a goal for 1.9 million feddans of wheat to be planted using raised beds by 2023, which would be roughly 60 percent of the total wheat-cultivated area (Alwang et al. 2018).

Hence the becoming of wheat is not just about what wheat is but how it is planted in the soil. Over the twentieth century, Egypt's wheat has evolved from a tall crop, like those depicted in ancient tomb paintings, yielding 1.5 tons per hectare, to a shorter crop, resistant to disease—at least temporarily, until the next disease emerges—which produces over 6.5 tons per hectare. Farming practices have shifted along the way, from changes in the seeds farmers use to how they prepare their fields and the amount of inputs that they apply to the soil. Farmers' varying degrees of openness to these new seeds and practices have been shaped by their individual interests. From the government's perspective, though, such transformations have been key to increasing the production of domestic wheat and its resilience, so as to secure the supply of wheat for Egypt's bread.

I turn now to this bread, the ultimate reason why the staple crop is of such significance. While Egyptian farming households transform some of their own wheat into homemade bread (see chapter 5), the second part of this chapter focuses on the widely eaten subsidized bread, which is made from both domestic and imported wheat. Over the years, government officials have changed the nature of this bread with the specific goal of maintaining a consistent supply and quality that the general public deems acceptable.

Becoming Baladi Bread

Egypt's subsidized baladi bread is a round loaf, roughly seven inches in diameter, dark in color, with a loose layer of bran coating each side. It is mild in taste, not that salty, rough in texture, and chewy. These loaves of bread, which cost five piasters each (0.05EGP), are eaten by most Egyptians three times a day (figure 1.7). They are omnipresent, especially in urban areas where home baking is rare, found within homes, wrapped in cloths on kitchen counters, and outdoors, on the laps of people breakfasting by the side of the road, in plastic bags dangling from hands, or balanced on racks, like the one the woman carries home from the bakery in Cairo (figure 1.4).

This bread is different from the loaves being prepared for Pharaoh Ramesses III in the tomb painting (figure 1.3). It is also different from the subsidized bread that was first introduced during the Second World War as the "national loaf" (raghif watani) (Schewe 2017). Over the last eighty years, the authorities have changed the nature of this bread, and, as with efforts to change the nature of Egypt's wheat, these changes have been driven by the need to ensure the constant availability of a decent staple. Yet unlike with the crop, where the threat is a more abstract fear about the national food supply, with bread, as the staple that Egyptians eat daily, the threat is more immediate. It is the threat of what people might do if they do not have good bread to eat; it is the fear of the bread riot.[67] Egyptians care about whether there is bread in the bakeries that they can afford to buy, and they care about what that bread tastes like. Hence in determining the price, size, composition, and style of Egypt's subsidized staple, successive governments have sought to counter disquiet and the threat of protest.[68]

Price and Size

For millions of Egyptians, their ability to get bread at a low price is central to their families not going hungry. In setting the price of a loaf, therefore, government officials are determining whether or not this bread will be affordable to Egypt's poor majority. But they are also determining the magnitude of the government's expenditures, given that it is the government that makes up the difference between the cost of producing the bread and what the consumer pays. While the government can pass some of this burden onto wheat producers by

FIGURE 1.7. Recently baked baladi bread. Photograph by Mariam Taher.

buying the grain from farmers at below market prices, as it did in the 1970s and 1980s (see chapter 2), the government continues to shoulder the significant cost of any imported wheat that goes into baladi bread. For every loaf of bread sold for five piasters today, the government reimburses sixty piasters to the bakery.[69] The total cost of the program is substantial; in the 2019–20 fiscal year, the government allocated 52 billion EGP ($3.32 billion, 3.3 percent of its total expenditures) to the bread subsidy.[70]

Thus, in deciding how much to charge for baladi bread, government officials have to weigh the acceptability of a price against the impact on its budget. Alternatively, the government can tweak the size of the loaves as a potentially less controversial mechanism for reducing costs. At its inception during the Second World War, the government set the price of the national loaf at half a piaster. Indicative of how a particular price can come to take on a significance that perhaps goes beyond what initial price setters had in mind, Schewe (2017: 54) writes that in the aftermath of the war it became enshrined "practically as a civil right of all urban and rural Egyptian subjects to purchase [bread] for five millemes (0.5 piaster)."

At this time, there was some variation in the size of the bread, but the average size was around 225 g. The loaves shrank in the postwar years; in 1952, the Ministry of Supply, which manages the baladi bread program, issued an order setting a minimum weight of 156 g.[71] An agricultural attaché based in the American Embassy in Cairo noted in a 1953 report, "While the price of the popular bread has not been changed, the public complains that it now costs them almost twice as much for the bread, normally consumed in one meal, as it did several years ago." The attaché went on to give an example. "Before 1947," she wrote, "the average worker took one loaf of bread, and some fruit or vegetables as a lunch—he now claims he has to eat almost two loaves to get the same satisfaction. In any case, one loaf now does not suffice and what is left over of the second loaf is generally wasted, so his cost of bread has doubled."[72] From the patchy archival records, it is impossible to know if this public disgruntlement had any effect, for they contain no documentation of official changes to loaf size in the 1950s through 1970s. At some point prior to 1980, however, the size of a loaf of baladi bread stabilized at a lower weight of 135 g.[73]

Cost was not a particular concern to the government in these years. The food subsidy program remained small, so its cost was not too much of a burden (Ali and Adams 1996). In the 1970s, however, President Sadat's government expanded the food subsidy system to cover eighteen different food items. The cost of the bread subsidy also grew due to rising expenditures on wheat. Despite

the efforts breeders were putting into increasing wheat yields, domestic production was still far from able to cover the needs of the subsidized bread
program, once farmers' own uses were deducted. After the United States suspended flows of subsidized wheat to Egypt in 1966, Egypt was left vulnerable
to fluctuations in world wheat prices. When those prices peaked in the early
1970s, increasing from $60/ton in 1972 to $250/ton in 1973, it hit Egypt hard
(Trego 2011). In 1974, the bread subsidy program constituted 15 percent of total
government expenditures (Dethier 1991: 58). Facing mounting debt, the government was forced to enter into loan agreements with the International Monetary Fund, which made support contingent on the government reducing its
public expenditures. In 1977, the government tried to make cuts to a number
of subsidies, including to one kind of bread (discussed more below). This led to
two days of riots around the country in which protestors attacked shops, government buildings, and police stations. The government responded with force,
bringing in the army; at least 77 people were killed and 214 wounded (Mitchell
2002: 249). The government rescinded the subsidy cuts and, in the aftermath,
adopted a more gradual approach to reform.

But the international pressure on the government to cut costs continued.
This was compounded by domestic pressure to address shortages of baladi
bread, which had become a growing problem in the late 1970s. Reports at-
tributed these shortages to the bread's low price, which resulted not only in
high consumption in urban areas but also among rural villagers, who formerly
used to bake their bread. There were further accounts of people feeding baladi
bread, which was cheaper than fodder, to their animals.[74] It was in this context,
therefore, that the prime minister convened a committee of high-level officials
to look into the cost and size of baladi bread. The committee produced a report
in 1979 that laid out seven policy options comprising different combinations of
baladi bread size (ranging from 135 g to 160 g) and cost (either a half-piaster or
one piaster). The committee calculated the savings associated with each option
(up to 163.6 million EGP), underscoring how the government's desire to cut
costs was what was ultimately motivating these reforms.[75] The following year,
the Ministry of Supply took action, doubling the price of a loaf (to one piaster)
and increasing its size by 25 percent (to 169 g).[76]

Yet the impetus for further subsidy reform persisted after Mubarak became
president in 1981 and continued his predecessor's neoliberal policy agenda. In
1984, a report noted that, although the government was managing to maintain
the bread supply by importing lots of wheat, "below the surface, the government is considering an unappealing choice between the continuation of the

current policy and the burdensome subsidies this entails and, as some inside and many outside the country are urging, raising bread prices, hoping that the domestic political consequences would be manageable." The report also noted that the government had at that point "shelved plans to raise bread prices following the results of this action in Tunisia."[77] That the government was looking to other countries in the region and observing the violent demonstrations that broke out when the Tunisian government increased bread prices as part of an IMF-imposed austerity program, was notable. Clearly, though, government officials decided that the benefits of change were worth the risk, for later that year, they doubled the price of a loaf again (to two piasters) and reduced its size to 160 g.[78] In 1989, the ministry further increased the price of a loaf to five piasters (Abdalla and Al-Shawarby 2017). Thus, over the course of ten years, the price of subsidized bread increased tenfold, with just a slight increase in loaf size. The fact that there were not widespread protests in response to these changes suggests that this gradual approach to reform was successful, from the government's perspective, in achieving its objective—cutting costs while maintaining stability.[79]

Nevertheless, the government's fear of what might happen if it raises the price of bread remains, and it has not deployed this cost-cutting mechanism since then. The price of a loaf of baladi bread has stayed the same since 1989. Five piasters has become a symbolic marker, an emblem of the government's beneficence and concern for the poor. Most people, or 70–80 percent of the population—not just the very poor but also the lower middle classes—can get bread for less than half a US cent a day, paying 0.05EGP for a loaf of bread rather than the 1EGP that most nonsubsidized breads cost.[80] This five-piaster price generates a sense of reassurance—the knowledge that whatever else happens, however much a family's income might fluctuate or market prices might go up, they will still be able to afford bread. Politicians are well aware of this price's affective significance. In a 2017 speech, President al-Sisi reassured the public that "the price of the loaf of bread will not be touched." Emphasizing what this means for the government, he went on to note that this was in spite of the cost of bread production almost doubling since the economic restructuring of 2016. He made a distinction between bread and other basic food commodities, like oil and sugar, for which prices have increased, and between bread and other subsidies, like fuel, which the government has cut under conditions of the IMF loan. The message he was keen to make was that bread was different and that the public should rest assured that the loaf's price would stay at five piasters.[81]

Yet the stability in this price gives an impression of continuity that obscures significant changes in the size of the bread. In 1991, the ministry reduced the size of the baladi bread loaf from 160 g to 135 g as part of its efforts to cut expenditures under ongoing neoliberal reforms. In 1998, it reduced it again to 130 g, and in 2014 to 110 g (Abdalla and Al-Shawarby 2017). When the ministry announced a further reduction in 2020 to 90 g, officials went to lengths to highlight that they were not interfering with the price, apparently assuming that the public would not make a connection between the price they were paying and the amount of bread they were receiving. "A set of constant factors will be preserved in the bread subsidy system," the ministry stated, "the most important of which is the price of a loaf . . . (5 piasters)."[82] While there were hints that a change might be coming when Sisi made a comment in 2021 that the price of bread should be increased—noting that "it's incredible to sell 20 loaves for the price of a cigarette"—the government has yet to take action and is clearly wary of raising the price.[83] Hence, at the time of writing the price remains the same, but five piasters buys just a little more than half as much bread as it did three decades ago.

A reduction in loaf size may be a less politically controversial mechanism of cost saving. However, it does not go unnoticed by those who eat this bread on a daily basis. When baladi bread comes up in conversation, people often mention how its size has decreased. They do not talk in terms of grams, but in comparisons, recollecting the bread of the past as being bigger, or commenting on the bread of today as being small. During one of my earliest conversations with my research assistant, Mariam, who is in her late twenties, she talked about the changes that she had noticed since her childhood. "I don't know if it is just a romanticization," she said, "but I remember the baladi bread as being better. The loaves were bigger." Several months later, she recorded a conversation that she had about baladi bread with her father. Her father commented, "I remember how big the subsidized loaf used to be," gesturing with his hands to indicate the loaf size that he remembered. The circle enclosed within his hands was at least double the size of what a loaf of baladi bread is today. Mariam responded, "So I'm not crazy for remembering that, it really was a lot bigger?" That Mariam has any doubt in her recollection speaks to the different ways in which people might perceive changes in loaf size versus price increases; a memory of a size change is likely to blur in a way that a doubling of price is unlikely to. Her father nodded, moving his hands closer together to indicate the size that a loaf is today. "Wow, yes," commented Mariam, "it really is such a difference!" After the most recent size reduction in 2020, an elderly woman whom Mariam has known for a long time reported the change to her over the phone. "They made it smaller. Now it is *light*," she said, elongating the word for emphasis (khafiiiif), "like paper." Another man expressed his frustration at the government's failure to meet people's basic sustenance needs, saying of the newly sized bread, "It's so tiny you eat it in two bites."

Loaf size is also an arena that is more easily open to manipulation by bakers than price. Mariam's father spoke to this during their conversation as he moved his hands still closer together, outlining the circumference of an even smaller circle. "Sometimes," he said to her, "if you are unlucky, the loaves are this small." While the government sets the specifications for what baladi bread should be, whether or not the bread conforms to those regulations is up to the private bakeries that produce this bread. (Bread quality also depends on how people handle the bread as they convey it home, as I discuss in chapter 4.) One man wrote into the newspaper *Al-Youm Al-Sabi'* with a complaint that the loaves in his Cairo neighborhood were not meeting the ministry's size requirements, referring to the specified size—17 cm diameter—rather than weight. He submitted a series of photos as evidence: a loaf with a measuring tape laid across it, the loaf extending just beyond the 13 cm mark; another looking small in an adult's outstretched palm, not touching the ends of the fingers; and one propped up beside a 1.5-liter water bottle, not reaching as high as the label.[84] Over the course of her twenty-two months of fieldwork, Mariam occasionally weighed the loaves of baladi bread that she purchased. The range in weights she recorded was notable (between 75 g and 90 g), as was the fact that every loaf she weighed was less than the 110 g mandated at that time.

That bakery owners might seek to cut costs by producing smaller loaves, or by substituting ingredients, is not altogether surprising.[85] The government reimburses them according to the number of loaves of baladi bread they sell, so the cheaper they can produce those loaves, the more profit they will make. Just as this is a matter of complaint today, the archival records contain numerous references to bakers' violations. When bakeries used to receive flour at a subsidized price (rather than being reimbursed after they sell the bread, as they are today), it was not uncommon for bakery owners to divert that low-cost flour to the production of goods that they could sell at a higher price. A report from 1978, for instance, noted how some bakers were "cheating on the weight of the loaf of baladi bread" and using some of the subsidized flour, instead, "to produce more profitable pastries."[86]

Such acts by private bakers can, however, compromise the government's interests. If baladi bread is too small or tastes unpleasant, people are just as likely to blame the government as they are to blame the particular bakery that produced the bread. The Ministry of Supply has inspectors whose role is to visit bakeries and ensure that bakeries are producing the right size loaves (in addition to meeting some of the other quality parameters discussed below) and to fine those who are found to be infringing. The ministry is keen to show that it is serious about this. In 2015, for instance, one newspaper ran a story about the Minister of Supply himself going to a bakery in the city of Qena to check the weight of baladi bread. A photograph accompanying the article shows the minister in a tan suit carrying out his inspection within a bakery. A man in a galabiya, presumably a bakery worker or owner, has placed five loaves of baladi bread on the scales. The minister leans forward, intent in concentration, checking the weight of the loaves on an old-fashioned display. The message: high-level officials care about bread weight.[87]

Yet the fact that Mariam found the loaves to vary so much in size between bakeries is indicative of the limitations of this regulatory process. Government inspectors see what they want to see; bakery owners make changes that it is in their interests to make. There is a range of actors who do not necessarily share the central government's concerns with the threat to national stability posed by shrunken loaves. These actors do not have the same stake in staple security on a national level. They are looking out for their own livelihoods, doing what they need to do to secure their own households' needs. In the process, their practices may undermine the government's goal of ensuring the quality of baladi bread.

Composition

The second key dimension of baladi bread that successive governments have altered over the years is its composition. This too, is linked to security considerations, given that the ingredients that go into the bread shape its taste and that bad-tasting bread poses the risk of protest.[88] Such a concern was evident during the Second World War, when, as Schewe (2017: 57) writes, "Even tampering slightly with the flavor and color of the nation's bread . . . was cause for anxiety among supply bureaucrats." Bread specifications also determine what ingredients the government has to procure and, as a result, can have security ramifications depending on the availability of those inputs.

The ingredients that comprise bread are simple: flour, yeast, water, and salt. In the case of Egypt's bread, it is the first of these—flour—that is the key determinant of taste.[89] Despite the multiplicity of wheat varieties discussed in the first part of this chapter, the breeding of these varieties has been more about yield and resistance than flavor. In all my discussions about bread and wheat in Egypt, I have not heard anyone talk about different wheat varieties as producing different tasting bread.[90] So unlike staples like rice, where the variety is key to the taste of the food that the grain becomes (see Avieli 2012), bread in Egypt owes its taste more to how that grain is processed into food. The taste of baladi bread stems primarily from the degree of refinement of the wheat flour and from whether any other grains are added.

MIXING GRAINS In the early twentieth century, bread made from corn was common in rural Egypt. From the outset, though, the government-subsidized bread followed the model of the wheat-based bread that was more common among urban residents. In times of scarcity, however, the Ministry of Supply, which is responsible for supplying the baladi bread bakeries with flour, has supplemented this wheat with the flour from other grains like maize, rice, and barley. This was done during the Second World War, for instance, when the government's wheat flour reserves fell short. Yet even as government officials ordered bakeries to mix in rice or maize flour with their dough, they were concerned about how this might affect the taste of the bread. Such concern was evident in a meeting that took place between the prime minister and several high-level officials in 1942, in which they spent an hour discussing the relative taste merits of bread made with one-third yellow maize versus one-third white maize (Schewe 2017). That such a subject should have been a topic of discussion among these high-level politicians is in itself notable. They were concerned about the taste of bread because they understood that taste was a matter of security; they saw the potential for popular unrest if the bread was not acceptable to the masses.

In the postwar era, there was some intermittent mixing of other flours into wheat in response to wheat shortages. In 1950, for example, the government required millers to mix 15 percent rice or corn flour into the wheat flour being used for baladi bread so as to make the wheat stocks go further.[91] But by and large, wheat flour remained the central constituent of government-subsidized bread. Schewe sees this as "a political and cultural shift" from wheat bread being a "prestige food for urban areas" to being "the new national right for all Egyptians" (2017: 50).

In the 1990s, though, the continued imperative to reduce expenditures, as well as mounting concerns about reliance on imported wheat, led the Ministry of Supply to reconsider the use of corn. In 1995, the ministry began conducting experiments making baladi bread with a composite of 80 percent wheat flour and 20 percent flour from domestically produced white corn. This was not only a mechanism to increase the country's self-sufficiency but also to cut costs, given that the local white corn flour was at this time cheaper than imported wheat.[92] But the initial results were not promising. Corn flour does not contain gluten—the protein in wheat flour that helps dough rise and hold its shape—so its inclusion affected the taste and texture of the baladi bread. One person who works for an international development agency told me that 20 percent corn was too much; she and her colleagues had calculated the "optimum mix" to be only 5 percent corn flour to 95 percent wheat. There were also concerns about the initiative's technical and economic feasibility.[93] Not as many mills ended up participating in the project as the government had hoped.[94] Nevertheless, in 1998 the Ministry of Supply issued a ministerial decree stating that wheat and corn flour should be used in the production of baladi bread at a ratio of 80 to 20. Evidently, the benefits of reducing reliance on wheat outweighed quality concerns.

Fifteen years later, in 2013, the ministry reversed this policy. Reports that covered this policy change explained it in terms of quality, the implication being that bread made entirely from wheat was inherently better than bread with corn mixed into it.[95] Yet when I talked about the mixed-flour bread as being lower in quality with someone who previously held a leadership role in the ministry, he disputed this. "Where did you read this?" he asked me, slightly confrontationally. "This bread is good, I ate it." He told me he grew up in a village where they ate bread that was 80 percent corn flour. "And the look of it! It was golden, shiny, crunchy," he smiled at the memory. "It wasn't a problem of taste." According to him, the mixing of corn into the wheat flour had largely come to a stop by the early 2010s anyway. When he took on his position in the ministry, shortly after the revolution, he had been excited about pursuing corn as a component of baladi bread. But when he tried to promote this, he found that the ministry no longer had the infrastructure needed to incorporate corn flour in the production system. "This is the problem," he said sadly, "you lose things." Baladi bread today, therefore, is all wheat. But a singular grain can produce different tasting bread, depending on how it is milled into flour.

EXTRACTION RATES When talking with practitioners engaged with Egypt's bread subsidy program or reading policy reports, the nature of flour is typically captured in a percentage. This percentage is the flour's extraction rate—the amount of flour that is extracted from a given quantity of grain. It is an indicator of how much of the grain's bran (the multilayered skin of the kernel) and germ (the embryo) are removed during the milling process. Whole wheat flour, for instance, has an extraction rate of 100 percent because it contains all parts of the edible grain—the bran, germ, and endosperm (the starchy portion). If, on the other hand, a mill removes some of the grain's bran and germ so as to produce, for example, only 80 kg of flour from 100 kg of grain, the flour's extraction rate would be 80 percent. A highly refined white flour, from which all the bran and germ has been removed, would have an extraction rate of around 70 percent.

Baladi bread is a dark bread, made with a relatively high extraction rate flour. It has a high concentration of the nutrient-rich bran—something that those who eat this bread sometimes comment on. During a conversation with one Cairo resident, for instance, he referred to baladi bread as "father of the bran" (abu rada), a colloquial expression used to describe the main characteristic of something, going on to point out how this attribute makes baladi bread healthier than other breads.[96] While people who engage with baladi bread as an object of consumption rather than an object of policy making do not typically talk about extraction rates, they can clearly see and taste a bread that is made from a darker flour and contains more bran. If the extraction rate of the flour being used to make the bread changes, shifting the loaves' coloring slightly darker or slightly lighter, consumers notice the difference. So the extraction rate is significant because it affects the quality and acceptability of the bread. It also determines how much flour can be derived from a particular quantity of grain. The more refined the flour, the less flour can be produced from that grain. Over the course of the baladi bread program, officials have deployed the extraction rate as a way of balancing the taste of the bread with economic concerns about grain procurement.

In the immediate postwar period, the subsidized bread was being made with 86.6 percent extraction flour. In 1952, however, the Ministry of Supply issued an order to increase the extraction rate to 93.3 percent, resulting in a darker flour containing even more bran and germ. The minister justified this change (along with the accompanying slight decrease in the size of the loaf) in terms of the cost savings that they would bring. A memo written by the US agricultural attaché noted that "the new loaf will be about the same size, but a little lighter weight, darker in color, and having a slightly different taste." The memo continued, "The Minister stresses the added nutritional value of the new loaf, and expects the population to cheerfully accept the new bread in the interests of the national economy."[97] The notion of "cheerful acceptance," whether or not people found the darker bread palatable, is striking. Anyone who did not like this bread, the report added, could always buy whiter bread on the market, if they could afford it. It was the poor, therefore, who were being asked to make sacrifices for the sake of the nation. As the minister called for cheerful acceptance, no doubt he was able to afford whiter bread if he preferred it.

The official flour extraction rate for baladi bread remained at 93.3 percent for some time. Occasional references in archival material suggest, however, that this might not have been entirely consistent. In 1967, for instance, after the US government suspended flows of subsidized wheat to Egypt through the PL480 program, a telegram from the American Embassy in Cairo to Washington, DC, noted that the "'baladi' type bread of kind eaten by general populace [is] becoming darker in color indicating increase in percentage extraction of wheat."[98] The subtext of the telegram was that the Egyptian government must be trying to stretch its wheat stocks further through increasing the extraction rate, in light of the interruption in its supply of cheap wheat from the United States. The high extraction rate, in other words, was an indicator that Egypt's wheat stocks might be in danger.

It was not until the late 1970s, though, under pressure to cut public expenditures, that the government returned to consider officially changing the extraction rate specifications. In 1980, the ministry issued a decree to change the extraction rate from 93.3 percent to 82 percent.[99] According to a report written by the US agricultural attaché, the objective of this move, first and foremost, was to "improve the quality of baladi bread." While bran and germ are full of nutrients, the assumption was that slightly reducing their content would make the taste of the bread more pleasing. This change was also designed to reduce the cost of the subsidy program. Although grain milled to 82 percent extraction yields less flour than grain milled to 93.3 percent extraction, at this time the government did not subsidize the former to the same degree, charging bakeries 50EGP/ton for 82 percent flour but only 25EGP/ton for the 93.3 percent flour. Thus, by changing the bread specifications to a more refined, less subsidized flour, the government was able to reduce its costs to ensure the ongoing consistent supply of bread. The government was, in essence, shifting some of the cost of the subsidy onto bakeries, which saw their flour expenses double but were unable to recoup that money by raising the bread price. The archival records contain no reference to bakery owners' complaints, but such policies provide important context for understanding why bakers might seek to cut other costs and not precisely follow the government's specifications when producing baladi bread.

The required extraction rate for the flour used in the production of baladi bread has not changed since 1980. Yet as with the government's size regulations, this does not necessarily reflect the actual flour being used by baladi bread bakers on a daily basis. I learned about this in a 2015 conversation that

I had with Ahmed, an Egyptian in his fifties with a background in business administration, who worked for over two decades for a major wheat exporting country's market development organization before becoming a freelance grain expert. This work led him to interact closely with grain traders, millers, and representatives of the baking industry, and he has a wealth of knowledge about how wheat moves into and through the country. Sitting in the cool lobby of a five-star hotel on the outskirts of Cairo, drinking Italian coffee, it did not take much prompting from me for him to launch into a long account of the wheat commodity chain. I asked him about the flour that is used to make baladi bread. "They say it's 82-percent [flour]," he told me, "but it is actually 85-percent." A few years later, during another conversation with Ahmed, he narrated the same story, just with slightly different figures. "In the baladi bread business," he said, "they don't do 82-, they do more 87-percent. It's very dark." The reason he gave for this was the need to compensate for "leakage" (see chapter 4). He gave me an example: "Say you are a mill licensed by the government to produce 82-percent flour. You get 10,000 tons of wheat; you're meant to produce 8,200 flour. But you only received 9,500. Or you did receive 10,000 and leaked off 500 to markets. So you make up for this [by milling at higher extraction rate]." To him this was no secret. "The government knows that everyone is fixing," he said.

Hence the extraction rate is a way for the government to secure its position, ensuring that its subsidized bread is just white enough to be acceptable, but not too white as to be overly costly in its grain requirements. But it is also a point where this security can be jeopardized, where the leakage of a valuable resource can be covered up through the production of a bread that people might not find to be to their taste. The owners of the baladi bread bakeries operate at this critical juncture. Through their everyday acts of baking baladi bread, they help the government meet its social contract with the people. Yet the kind of bread they produce is driven more by their own livelihood interests than by the imperative to maintain the legitimacy of the state.

Baladi bread is not a singular thing, therefore, but a food whose nature has changed over time and space (figure 1.8). The government has deployed extraction rates, mixing ratios, weights, and prices as devices of staple security— tools to manipulate subsidized bread, with the central goal of ensuring that the supply does not run out and that the general public is satisfied with its quality. But some elements within the process of transforming wheat into subsidized bread elude government control, contributing to a sense of continual precariousness.

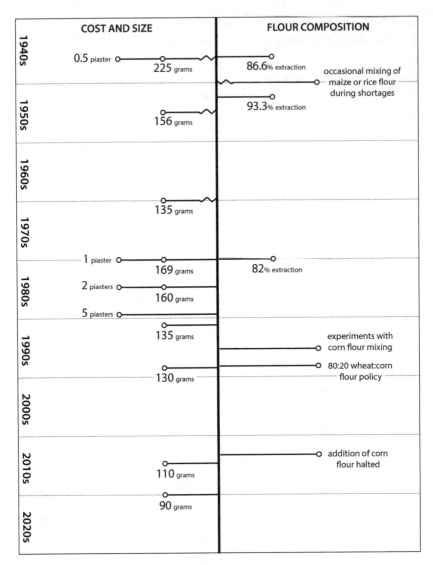

	COST AND SIZE	FLOUR COMPOSITION

1940s — 0.5 piaster o———o **225** grams ⌇ 86.6% extraction — occasional mixing of maize or rice flour during shortages

1950s — **156** grams 93.3% extraction

1960s

1970s — **135** grams

1980s — 1 piaster o———o **169** grams — 82% extraction
2 piasters o———o **160** grams
5 piasters o———

1990s — **135** grams — experiments with corn flour mixing
130 grams — 80:20 wheat:corn flour policy

2000s

2010s — **110** grams — addition of corn flour halted

2020s — **90** grams

FIGURE 1.8. The becoming of baladi bread. Figure by Bill Nelson.

Style

As the bread that the Egyptian government has subsidized from the 1940s to today, baladi bread is the most staple of staples, a bread so essential to the general public that successive governments have gone to great lengths to ensure its continuous availability at a low price. Yet up until the 1990s, the government also subsidized two other kinds of bread, known as fino and shami. These are both whiter breads, made from more refined flour. The first, fino, is a baguette-

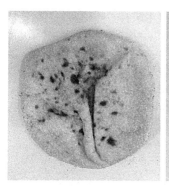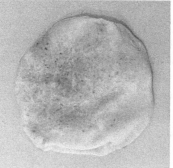

FIGURE 1.9. Defining a staple: baladi (*left*), shami (*middle*), and fino (*right*). Photographs by Mariam Taher.

style roll, soft and fluffy in texture, not very filling, and slightly sweet in taste. Unlike other breads in Egypt, fino is not typically eaten as an accompaniment to a meal (to dip or scoop up a sauce) but for sandwiches.[100] It is particularly popular among children and is often used as a snack to be taken to school. Shami bread is a round, flat bread, similar in shape to baladi bread but often larger and always whiter, softer, less chewy, and finer in texture. The government's changing policies on these breads show how the line between staple and luxury, between something the government should subsidize to maintain national stability and something people should pay for themselves, is far from fixed (figure 1.9).

In the 1950s–70s, the government subsidized fino and shami breads, setting their price at one piaster, which was more expensive than the baladi bread but cheaper than their cost of production. In 1977, however, when the government was under pressure to reduce its expenditures, it singled out the fino bread price as the one to increase. Archival records do not document the rationale that government officials gave for this, but maybe they assumed that increasing the price of this sweet, white roll would be less controversial, given that baladi bread would still be available at the same price. The violent outbursts that broke out in response suggest that the public did not see it in this way. (Alternatively, the fact that people protested even when the government had made no change in the price of the baladi bread that most of them ate may say more about the inaccuracy of describing these as "bread riots.")

Whether or not the change in fino price was a key factor driving the public unrest, the government backtracked and reinstated the lower price. For a number of years, fino and shami bread continued to be available at a subsidized price of one piaster for a small loaf or two piasters for a large loaf (Abdallah and Al-Shawarby 2017: 134). In 1989, however, when the ministry increased the price of baladi bread to five piasters, it did the same for these breads. Then in 1991, the government stopped subsidizing fino bread. Shami bread was the next candidate for a potential cut. Some officials were concerned, though, that this might signal bias toward certain populations. Shami bread was more popular in the northern part of the country, in the city of Alexandria and throughout the Nile Delta, in contrast to Cairo and southern Egypt, where the consumption of baladi bread predominated.[101] Nonetheless, several years later, the ministry phased out the shami bread subsidy, presumably because the cost savings outweighed concerns about how this would be received by the public. With the exception of a short-lived experiment to reintroduce a subsidized fino loaf for schools (2003–8), for the last twenty-five years or so, the subsidized bread program has coalesced around the baladi loaf.

Fino and shami are now breads that non-elite Egyptians buy on special occasions or for particular needs but not, typically, for daily consumption within the home. In 2015, a loaf of fino bread cost twenty-five piasters, a loaf of shami cost fifty piasters—considerably more than the five-piaster loaf of baladi bread. This difference became even more marked after the currency devaluation and the phasing out of fuel subsidies in 2016, when the costs of all nonsubsidized breads skyrocketed. In 2019, a loaf of fino cost sixty piasters, twelve times that of a loaf of baladi bread, and a loaf of shami cost 1 EGP. The importance of baladi bread, as a reliably cheap staple, has thus become even more pronounced for the majority of Egyptians, who are either poor or susceptible to falling into poverty (chapter 4). It is this bread, therefore, whose supply and quality the government must secure for the sake of national stability.

Conclusion

To return to the images with which I began this chapter, while Ancient Egypt is often evoked in conversations about wheat and bread in Egypt, change is as much the story of this staple crop and food as continuity. The past century has seen pronounced transformations in the nature of wheat being grown and subsidized bread being eaten in Egypt. These stories of becoming bring together contrasting sets of actors, from farmers to plant pathologists, bakers to bread consumers, breeders to bureaucrats in the ministries of agriculture and supply. But they are underpinned by a shared sense of threat—the threat that Egyptians will not have decent bread to eat. In the case of baladi bread, this threat, encapsulated in the figure of the bread riot, is vivid. In the case of wheat, it is less tangible but still present, captured in the ongoing anxieties about whether the government will be able to access sufficient wheat for its subsidized bread program. The becoming of wheat and bread—the breeding of seeds to be productive and disease-resistant, and the altering of specifications for the size and composition of baladi bread—are, in themselves, practices of staple security. They are all about ensuring that Egyptians have sufficient and good-quality wheat and bread.

These practices of shaping the nature of Egypt's wheat and bread in specific ways continue today. Yet this process of becoming is only one of a number of everyday practices that seek to secure consistent access to a quality staple food for the Egyptian population. The next chapter takes the seed from its point of implantation and traces its growth in Egyptian fields. The story of baladi bread is continued in chapter 4, which probes the work of private bakeries in translating the government's specifications into loaves and the labor of those who buy, take home, and consume this bread.

2. GOLD OF THE LAND

The soil is bare; dark, turned, fertilized, ready for planting. A farmer walks through the field one December day, his sandals picking up small clods of earth. He takes handfuls of grain from a sack and broadcasts the seed across the carefully prepared soil. Over the following days, shoots break through the surface, fingers of green emerging from the brown. Soon the fields become full of what look like tufts of grasses as the individual wheat plants tiller, producing clusters of side shoots. Within several weeks, the landscape in this part of Fayoum Governorate, where most farmers grow a winter crop of wheat, is a mosaic of grassy shoots of various heights depending on when

BUNDLES OF GOODNESS. *Photograph by the author.*

FIGURE 2.1. Wheat field in mid-December (with fields of clover, maize, and onions in the background, as well as olive trees and date palms). Photograph by the author.

the farmer planted, interspersed with fields of other crops like onions and clover (figure 2.1).

Through the following months, the wheat continues growing, the stems elongating, developing joints, and beginning to produce heads. The farmer keeps an eye on the field, checking the crop for rust but, in the absence of any evidence of it, does not spray fungicide. Every three weeks, he opens a gap to the irrigation ditch, flooding the field then leaving the water to infiltrate. At two points over the growth cycle, first at tillering and then at flowering, he sprinkles the fertilizer granules that are needed to coax the high-yield potential from the seed over the soil. Otherwise, the field is largely quiet as the plants develop.

By early April, the wheat is tall and its head fully formed. Over the coming weeks, the crop matures and the grain ripens, changing from a deep green to a warm yellow. This color change sweeps across the landscape, blanketing the land in a rich golden glow. Late in the month, the farmer comes to the field, carrying a scythe in his hand. Through the cooler hours of the evening, as the nighttime dew coats the grain, protecting it from damage, he moves through the field, cutting each stalk at its base. The next day, he bundles the cut stems into sheaves, stands them on their end, and leaves them to dry. A week later he rents a thresher from a man in the village. He feeds in the wheat and the machine separates the heads from the stalks. The straw puffs out of an elevated shoot at the front and falls to the ground, forming a pile. The grain pours out of an outlet tube on one side, into a sack which the farmer's wife holds open beneath. From a bare piece of soil to the source of a staple food.

Egyptians sometimes refer to wheat as the "gold of the land" (dhahab al-ard), a moniker that reflects not only the crop's golden color as it approaches maturity but the value attached to it. Whereas the previous chapter looked at wheat breeding as a realm of staple security, examining efforts to develop seeds that are more productive and resistant, this chapter looks at what staple security means to rural households that cultivate wheat, following the seed from its moment of implantation in the soil. At the center of this story is the relationship between those who farm wheat and those who claim a national stake in this homegrown staple. At times this relationship between farmers and the state is mutually beneficial. At other times it is conflictual, just like the state's relationship with the owners of the bakeries that produce subsidized baladi bread (chapter 1). On the one hand, Egyptian farmers growing wheat is a way for their families to ensure that they have enough wheat to produce the homemade bread that many prefer to eat (chapter 5). Without this wheat, unless households can afford to buy grain or flour, there would be no bread baked within the home. On the other hand, Egyptian farmers growing wheat is a way for the government to ensure that it has enough wheat to produce the baladi bread upon which most of the population relies (chapter 4). Without this wheat, along with the wheat imported by the government (chapter 3), there would be no subsidized bread. Hence, the government's securing of wheat for the bread subsidy program depends not only on farmers growing wheat but also on the government being able to buy that wheat. Procuring domestic wheat is the mechanism through which the government moves wheat out of the domain of household bread production and into the domain of national bread production.

The significance of domestic wheat procurement came to the fore in 2020, when the spread of the coronavirus around the world disrupted wheat supply chains, causing some major wheat exporters to curb exports. In late April, just as Egyptian farmers started heading into the fields to harvest their crops, President al-Sisi gave a televised address to the nation. He began by announcing, "We have organized ourselves well and have good reserves," seeking to allay any fears of an imminent shortage and to reassure the population about the nation's grain stores. He went on to note, however, "Because of the uncertainty until this coming December, I say to farmers it would be better if you don't keep more than necessary and sell it to the government." His plea was explicit. For the sake of the nation, he wanted farmers not to hold onto their harvested grain. Any wheat that farmers sold, he said, "the government will keep and it will benefit many"—a quote that captures the tension between wheat that farmers save to eat themselves and wheat that they sell for others to eat.[1]

In the first part of this chapter, I contrast the national and household visions of wheat by examining the seasonal cycle of cultivation through the lens of Egyptian newspapers and the lens of a farming family. The detailed media coverage of cultivated areas and harvest totals demonstrates the national significance of homegrown wheat. Given the vulnerabilities associated with relying on imported wheat (which I examine in the next chapter), domestic production is a way of countering the threat that Egypt might run out of its staple by ensuring that at least some of the nation's wheat needs are not dependent on global supply chains. After harvest, coverage of the reception season—the period during which the government buys domestic wheat—marks the key moment when this wheat transitions from farmers' property to part of the national food supply. The government's metric of success is tons of domestic wheat purchased. Notably, quality does not enter the discussion much, for there is a widespread presumption that Egyptian-grown wheat is good. The figures that accompany the news stories, of hundreds of thousands of tons of grain harvested and procured, may not be all that accurate, but they conjure a picture of security—a sense that the domestic wheat supply is bountiful and sufficient to meet part of the nation's demand.

Looking at the everyday practices of farming wheat through the lens of the home, on the other hand, shows domestic cultivation as a process of providing for a family rather than meeting a national need. This is a process playing out on millions of smallholdings, for wheat is grown on over 90 percent of Egypt's farms, many of them smaller than a feddan (roughly equivalent to an acre) in size.[2] My site for exploring these practices of growing wheat is on the margins—a village in Fayoum, one of the poorest governorates in the country.[3] Although wheat yields for the governorate as a whole are close to the national average of 6.8 tons/ha (McGill et al. 2015: 15), the village of Warda lies in the remoter, western part of the province, where irrigation water is scarce and resources for agricultural inputs and mechanization limited. Farmers in Warda plant high-yielding varieties, but often use grain from the previous year as seed rather than buying certified seeds from the government. Their yields are around 5 tons/ha—far from the yields of almost 9 tons/ha that can be achieved with raised beds and the associated package of interventions discussed in chapter 1. Following the cycle of wheat cultivation through a family in the village highlights the role wheat plays as something that small-scale farmers both eat and sell.

In the second part of the chapter, I turn to procurement as a practice that transfers domestic wheat from something a farming household eats as homemade bread to something the nation eats as subsidized bread. I look at the procurement price as a device that the government employs to incentivize farmers to grow wheat and sell their harvest, so as to secure the domestic wheat that it needs for the subsidized bread program. I show how this effort has been successful at times but has at other times backfired. I then contrast the attention given to the wheat procurement price in policy making circles with the lack of attention given to it in farming households. While price certainly matters to small-scale farmers who sell wheat, they grow this crop primarily for household bread production rather than profit. I illustrate this through a comparison between wheat and onions. The multiple approaches to wheat cultivation and sale between policy makers and farmers underscore how staple security means contrasting things to differently positioned actors.

The Fields

From Cairo

My research assistant, Mariam, and I began our analysis of Egyptian newspapers with a simple keyword search for wheat. Among the prolific results returned by the newspapers' online search engines, we found a clear pattern of reportage on domestic wheat. The detailed coverage of each stage of wheat cultivation in newspapers across the political spectrum, evident not only in the number of articles but their repetitive nature, was striking. This is a kind of attention that is not given to other major crops like cotton, fruits, vegetables, or other cereals. While analysis of this coverage alone cannot shed light on how this information is received (although circulation figures do suggest a relatively small readership), given that these articles are based on statements and data released by government ministries, it provides insights into what the state is hoping to convey.[4] The articles have a distinct temporality over the course of the year. Together, they offer an alternative way of reading the seasonal cycle of wheat cultivation to the changes written in the landscape with which I opened the chapter.

Starting in mid-October, the articles on planting begin. Take, for instance, this string of headlines from the popular independent newspaper *Al-Youm al-Sabi*: "Sharqiya Agricultural Department: 433,000 Feddans Planted with Wheat with an Increase of 10,000 over Last Year"; "Planting of 150,000 Feddans of Wheat this Year in Gharbiya"; "Planting of 143,000 Feddans of

Wheat in Beni Sueif."[5] The headlines signal the place of origin and, with their large-sounding numbers, the promise of plenty. The figures imply a clarity of knowledge that belies the roughness of the estimates on which they are based. Since farmers choose what they plant, the government lacks the data it used to have when it set cropping patterns; officials therefore have to employ various approximation techniques to gauge the area planted in wheat. Logged in a headline, though, the round figures with the series of zeros do something; they articulate a sense of security that comes from a staple-in-progress. Just as a farmer walking through a field of newly planted wheat feels some peace of mind in the knowledge that wheat is on its way, these figures seek to generate a similar affect among those who are removed from transitions across Egypt's countryside but who might read a headline in a newspaper, hear a story on the radio, or watch a report on the television.[6]

After the articles that mark the start of wheat cultivation, a period of sparser reporting follows; wheat growing gradually in the fields is not as newsworthy. In late April, though, as the harvest approaches, coverage in the news reflects the growing air of anticipation. "Qena Sings to the Harvest: Wheat, Your Hair Is Beautiful and Your Goodness Will Fill My Purse," notes one headline.[7] In another article, the Minister of Agriculture introduces his optimistic forecast for the upcoming harvest with the statement that "wheat is considered one of the most important strategic crops in the world and in Egypt." He goes on to emphasize the centrality of this crop for the nation and to explain why the wheat harvest is a matter of national interest: "It is the main source for the loaf of bread for most inhabitants of Egypt. The case of wheat is a case of national security of the highest priority."[8]

In the weeks that follow, newspapers are full of articles about harvesting. "Asyut Agricultural Department Announces the Harvesting of 850 Feddans of Wheat"; "Harvest of 60,700 Feddans of Wheat in Munufiya"; "Sohag Agricultural Department: Harvesting 191,000 Feddans of Wheat."[9] Documenting the harvest in different parts of the country, these articles tell the story of a nation coming together in the common project of wheat production, each governorate doing its part. They also draw comparisons, ranking the governorates against one another and lauding those most successful. One headline notes, for instance, "Al-Qalyubiya Produces 305,000 Tons of Wheat and Holds the First Place in Egypt for the Year," celebrating the governorate's contribution to the national objective of securing Egypt's wheat.[10] Once again, the clarity of the figures masks a process of approximation. As Ahmed, an Egyptian who has long worked in the wheat trade explained to me, "In terms of production, there are no accurate statistics, even though they [government officials] say there are." Officials estimate production based on assessments of the area planted with different varieties of wheat and average yields those varieties attain, as opposed to actually summing harvest totals. "They say that people go out into the fields [to collect data]," he told me, "but that's not true."

These governorate-specific figures sum up to Egypt's total harvest—in the year of those headlines, 2015, about 8.3 million tons—an indicator of national agricultural progress. Yet this figure is of less relevance to the broader population than the amount of domestic wheat that moves into government hands for production of the bread that most Egyptians eat. The process of the government "receiving" (istislam) wheat is the focus of the next wave of newspaper articles, which coincide with and extend beyond the harvest period. The government is the sole official purchaser of domestic wheat and thus receives any grain that farmers want to sell, either directly or via traders (although in practice there are some illicit sales to the private sector). Despite the apparent passivity of the verb *receiving*, the government is actively engaged in ensuring that it has the roughly 9 million tons of wheat that the subsidized bread program needs to function. Each year the Ministry of Supply, in coordination with the Ministry of Agriculture, sets a goal for how much of this wheat it will procure domestically. Over the course of the reception season—the government-designated period during which it buys domestic wheat—news reports tally the government's progress toward its procurement goal, the total edging higher as the season unfolds. A promising opening to the 2015 reception season on May 1, for instance, "Minister of Subsidies: Receiving 750,000 Tons of Local Wheat from Farmers since Mid-April"; steady progress on May 20, "Ministry of Agriculture: Receiving 3.7 Million Tons of Wheat in the New Season"; and a triumphant conclusion on June 20, "Minister of Supply: We Achieved a Leap by Receiving 5.3 Million Tons of Wheat Last Harvest Season."[11]

Given the role this staple crop plays in Egyptians' daily needs, these figures hold considerable political weight. The higher the figures, the more positive the outlook. But figures that are too high can raise questions. When in 2015, for example, the ministry claimed that it had purchased 5.3 million tons of Egyptian wheat, a much larger figure than ever before, it prompted an inquiry. The inquiry revealed a significant amount of foreign wheat being sold to the government by traders under the pretense that it was locally grown. So too, when reported totals do not reach the government's stated goal, it opens officials up to critique. Shortly after the 2017 reception season closed, I spoke with a reporter based in Cairo who covers wheat for an international news agency. The previous day, the government had reported a procurement total of 3.4 million tons. Just before our conversation, however, the reporter had received a phone call from a man in the Ministry of Supply. The official was calling to tell him that the total was actually 3.75 million tons. The reporter was skeptical. "They are trying to inflate the figures," he said. "I think this is because we published a story suggesting they didn't hit their target. Their target was 3.5." He concluded, "It's unclear how much they bought." Hence there is a lot of uncertainty around these figures, magnified by the fact that those who supply the data have an interest in showing a successful domestic procurement season.

Any uncertainties are hidden, though, in the news reports through which the stages of Egyptian wheat cultivation—from a bare piece of soil to the source of a staple food—ripple through the national sphere. As the numbers cited by government officials get picked up in newspapers and reports, they stabilize and tell a complex story. They coalesce to form a picture of security: Egyptian farmers are growing large areas of wheat; the harvest is abundant; the government is buying lots of domestic wheat; Egypt will not have to rely too much on other countries' wheat; there will be plenty of flour for making subsidized bread; there will not be shortages; fear not.

Yet such articles and figures offer little insight into the day-to-day lives of the four million smallholder farmers on whose labor this domestic wheat depends, nor into what happens to the millions of tons of wheat that are not sold to the government. I turn now, therefore, to a contrasting picture of domestic cultivation—through the lens of a farming household. Whereas to government officials staple security means monitoring wheat-cultivated areas around the country and directing as much of the harvest as possible into the subsidized bread program, to those cultivating this crop, it means sustaining a household.

From a Village Home

I first met Marwa in the summer of 2007, when I arrived in the village of Warda to begin my doctoral fieldwork. We were introduced by her older brother, Khaled, who was one of the first people I got to know in the village. A kind, distinguished man with sparkly eyes, Khaled was one of ten children, many of whom still live in the village with their families. At the time I met him, Khaled was in his fifties, living with his wife Habiba, a strong woman with a warm smile, and their four children. As a younger man, Khaled had traveled to Saudi Arabia, Libya, and Syria to work as an agricultural laborer, gradually saving money that he invested in parcels of land back home. Over the years he amassed twelve feddans, making him a relatively large and wealthy landowner for this area. He still lived in one of the older houses in the village—a basic, single-story structure incorporating space for livestock—but had built an apartment for his first married son and was hoping to build a new house for his family soon. His younger sister Marwa was in her late thirties, a big personality with a wonderful sense of humor. Like many in the village, her husband was then working in Saudi Arabia as a building caretaker, leaving Marwa at home with five children (one of whom was married). Marwa is not as rich in land as Khaled—she and her husband own a couple of feddans—but her relative wealth from her husband's remittances is revealed in small details of her domestic space: a house with a tile rather than dirt floor, painted walls, upholstered furnishings in the room for receiving guests, and a clearly separated area for livestock.

The year I lived in the village, in 2007–8, Marwa decided to cultivate a half-feddan of land with wheat. Such a small scale of production is not atypical. Most Egyptian farmers only own small pieces of land (63 percent of Egypt's farms are smaller than a feddan, 95 percent are smaller than five feddans), which they divide between multiple crops (McGill et al. 2015: 12). Still, Marwa's decision to grow wheat was not taken lightly. With her husband in Saudi Arabia and two sons in school, along with the various health problems she faces, her household lacked labor for working the fields. She considered selling or renting out her land, but was unable to find a buyer or sharecropper. In these circumstances, wheat was a good choice; it is not too labor-intensive and she knew it would be of value to her household.

One day in October 2007, I arrived at Marwa's house at 7 a.m. as her family was about to have breakfast. She sent her sons to buy bread as they were out of homemade bread.[12] When the boys returned, they breakfasted on bread, cheese, eggs, and olives as I sat with them, drinking sweet black tea. Afterward, we went to visit Marwa's land. We walked through the village and into the fields that border it on each side. We weaved through fields with long stalks of corn, the cobs almost ripe; fodder maize with thick leaves; recently planted clover, still close to the ground; and deep green leaves of infant onion seedlings. Dotted between the fields were clusters of olive trees and date-laden palm trees. We stepped over the irrigation ditches that run alongside each field, some with water in them, others without. Among the patchwork of small fields in cultivation lay dark brown fields, soon to be planted with wheat, clover, transplanted onions, barley, or beans. In some of the plowed fields, water buffalo, cows, and donkeys grazed the grasses that littered the turned soil (figure 2.2).

We came across two farmers whose land abuts Marwa's and sat down together in the shade of a tree. They chatted among themselves about the crops they were growing, a broken canal bank, and their desire for covered drainage. After a while, their conversation turned to manure, which farmers apply to their fields before planting to boost the soil's fertility, if they can afford it. The three of them talked about what they were doing to get the manure they

FIGURE 2.2. A patchwork landscape. Photograph by the author.

needed to prepare their fields for sowing wheat in December. The wheat was not yet in the fields, but it was on people's minds and work was underway in anticipation of its cultivation. Deciding what seed to plant was part of these preparations, farmers either selecting grain from the previous harvest, exchanging with others, or purchasing certified seed from the government. But this did not feature in Marwa and her neighbors' conversation; indeed, in contrast with government scientists' close focus on breeding new varieties of wheat (chapter 1), seed choice was not something that I heard farmers in Warda discuss. On the one occasion I specifically asked Marwa's brother Khaled how he chose which wheat seeds to plant, he talked about how he sometimes changed seeds to find the variety best adjusted to his soil but made no mention of the fact that some varieties might bring higher yields.

Over the next seven months I followed Marwa's small parcel of wheat, not through my regular presence in her fields but my regular presence in her home. This was in part an outcome of methodological constraints that I faced as a woman, being unable to spend extended periods of time in the fields, which in this region are a primarily male domain. But it was also a reflection of the dominant space that Marwa occupied. Although she was responsible for managing her land, like many women in the village whose husbands work overseas or have died, she left much of the in-field work to others due to her poor health and limited mobility—a choice she was able to make because she had the financial means to employ laborers. Situating myself in the household—a domestic space in which I would have been unable to spend extended periods of time had I not been a woman—gave me different insights from those I would have gained situated in the fields. It taught me not so much about the day-to-day work of cultivating wheat but about how this cultivation is integrated into household priorities.

The annual cycle of wheat can be narrated also, therefore, through the conversations I had with Marwa inside her home. These conversations did not take place every time I talked with Marwa. Unlike livestock, which must be fed every day—clover brought to water buffalo, food scraps cut up for poultry—wheat does not require constant work, and thus is not something that people in the village discuss on a daily basis.[13] Rather, these were intermittent references that materialized when something of note happened, or when my arrival in Marwa's home happened to coincide with her thinking about the wheat she was cultivating. Together, these moments reveal how this crop is embedded in broader calculations about household staple security.

It is early January and I am drinking tea with Marwa. She tells me that they have been working on their wheat fields. Her two sons went with a laborer the night before to fertilize and irrigate. Nighttime is a good time to irrigate because fewer people irrigate then, so the water supply is more plentiful.[14] In a place where there is scarcely any rain, ensuring that water from the irrigation system reaches the field is fundamental to ensuring that the crop continues to grow.

When I drop by Marwa's house a couple of months later, I find her baking bread with her teenage daughter. They are sitting in the hallway, taking a break as the dough rises, and talking about a recent scandal in the village. A distant relative of Marwa's called Sharif got embroiled in a dispute with a man from a neighboring village over a contested piece of land. The dispute escalated, they were both carrying guns, and ultimately Sharif killed the other man. A substantial compensation payment will have to be paid by members of Sharif's extended family to the family of the deceased. Marwa says they have all been sad and worried, crying and unable to eat.

Later in our conversation, Marwa comments that flour has been getting increasingly expensive. She has been buying flour because she has no grain saved from the previous year. A 50 kg sack of flour, which is sufficient for her to bake three times for her family, each time producing enough loaves to last a few weeks, now costs 140EGP; it used to cost only 40EGP. This is something Marwa has told me several times over previous weeks. Reiterated in the context of her worries about the Sharif saga, the rising prices underscore her sense of vulnerability. Marwa's phone rings. It is her husband, calling from Saudi Arabia. I hear her recite these same figures regarding the cost of flour to him. The increasing flour prices threaten her ability to make the homemade bread that her family prefers to eat. Marwa does not spell out the direct connection between flour prices and her decision to grow wheat, but herein lies one of the key values of that crop to her. When she harvests her wheat, she will no longer have to buy expensive sacks of flour because she will be able to mill her own.[15]

It is not surprising, then, that Marwa is anxious for her crop to be successful. She had been to check on her wheat that morning and was concerned by what she saw. "It's growing too high," she tells me. Dwarf wheat varieties may be shorter in stature than their taller ancestors (see chapter 1), but height still carries the risk of lodging. She is worried that the crop might be ruined by the strong winds that day. These are the kinds of worries that farmers have to deal with— the vagaries of the weather, the uncertainties of disease blights, the possibilities of irrigation disruptions—any of which may affect the progress from seed to crop. They are worries that are magnified when flour prices are high, raising the stakes attached to homegrown wheat. Luckily, in this instance, the crop survives.

As the harvest season approaches toward the end of April, wheat becomes a more common topic of conversation as people discuss when they will harvest their wheat and comment on other people's harvests. When visiting homes, I see the sleepy eyes of older children who have been out harvesting the night before, or the glint of adventure among those due to head into the fields after dinner in the dark.[16] One day I arrive at Marwa's house to find her looking tired. The electricity has been out for a couple of days and, without fans running, the mosquitoes have been keeping her family awake. The scandal over Sharif continues. Marwa's brother Khaled has a 1.7-feddan piece of land near the village from which the murdered man came. He needs to harvest the wheat planted on this land but, due to the ongoing conflict, is unable to go. He sent four laborers to harvest, but someone alerted the people of the village, and they came out to prevent the laborers from working. Fortunately, Marwa's land is closer to Warda. She rouses her teenage boys from the floor, directing them to go and tie up the wheat that they cut recently. "Tie it well, in small bundles!" she instructs. When her sons begin to protest she explains, "I want to leave them for ten days so they dry well" (figure 2.3). For the grain to last in storage and cover her food needs for the year, it must be fully dry; otherwise it will rot.[17]

FIGURE 2.3. Sheaves of wheat. Photograph by the author.

By the end of May, the Sharif scandal has finally been resolved. Marwa's extended family will be paying 300,000EGP to the family of the deceased, each household's contribution calculated according to their means and number of grown sons. Marwa will not have to pay, as her husband is from another family, but she is worried about her siblings. Due to his relative wealth, Khaled must pay 20,000EGP. He will have to put off construction of his new house in order to cover the payment. Two of Marwa's sisters are in more tenuous economic situations. They must pay 5,000EGP each but have few resources: their houses are not fully equipped with electricity and they have many children yet to marry. I meet one of these sisters one day at Khaled's house. She farms 2.75 feddans while her husband works in Saudi Arabia, but he only earns 600 riyal a month (compared to Marwa's husband, who earns 1,000 riyal, or 1,460EGP). The worry is etched in her face. "Where will I get that 5,000 from?" she asks. "I don't have any money." She bursts into tears. Unexpected circumstances like this reveal the importance of savings and the vulnerability that comes with not having any cash on hand.

Marwa, though, shielded by her marital status from the need to come up with a compensatory payment, is upbeat about her own situation after the harvest. She is pleased with the 6 ardab (0.9 tons) of wheat that she harvested from her half-feddan. This grain is now piled in sacks in the storage room at the back of her house. The yield may be lower than the national average, but that figure is not the barometer by which she assesses her yields.[18] She has already taken some of the grain to the village mill to be ground into flour and has baked from it. The 6 ardab will be enough for their household needs for the year, with a bit left over. She will sell anything they will not eat, and she also got some money from selling the straw.

Marwa's experience growing wheat encapsulates a contrasting view of the crop—from a bare piece of soil to the source of a staple food—from the perspective of the home. Just as in the patterning of the newspaper coverage of wheat, there is a temporality to wheat in farmers' day-to-day lives. The crop is prominent at particular moments—planting, irrigating, harvesting—and recedes at others. But while farmers may not talk about wheat all the time, it is just as vital a concern to them as it is to the government officials who oversee national wheat production. In the quotidian scene of Marwa's family eating bread for breakfast, the complaints about the price of flour needed to produce homemade bread, or the contentment upon baking with recently harvested grain, the importance of the crop—and the staple food it becomes—is an unstated constant. This is not the only constant. The Sharif scandal was an exceptional occurrence, but it was a reminder of the unusual events that may arise and the need for cash to cover such costs on top of everyday expenses. If people sell their grain or other parts of the crop, like the straw, wheat can be a source of cash. But for Marwa, and for many farmers like her, wheat's cash value is not a driving motivation. As I discuss further below, farmers typically turn to other crops for income generation.

A view from within the household, therefore, reveals a different way of thinking about wheat. In scaling down from the nation to the home, the overt language of security evaporates but the affective orientation remains. For Marwa, growing wheat is a way of securing her family's staple for the coming year. After Marwa harvests her grain, however expensive flour becomes, she will be able to make her family's preferred bread because she has grain stored in the home. This practice of household staple security has implications, though, for the national project of securing wheat for subsidized bread. I explore this relationship in the following section as I consider a key device that the government has employed to bring domestic wheat into its orbit: the procurement price.[19]

The Price

The fact that many farmers, like Marwa, keep a substantial portion of their wheat for household use is reflected in national statistics, which show that in recent years, the government has procured less than half the total harvest (figure 2.4).[20]

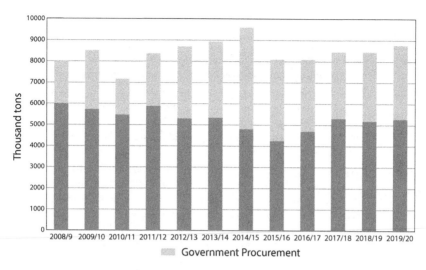

FIGURE 2.4. Domestic wheat production and procurement. Figure by Bill Nelson.

Note: Data from 2008–14 taken from McGill et al. (2015: 36); data from 2014–20 taken from the USDA Foreign Agricultural Service's *Egypt Grain and Feed Annual* reports, https://gain .fas.usda.gov. These data represent approximations, and for some years there is considerable variability between sources. In 2015 and 2016, for example, a number of agricultural experts challenged the government's figures, alleging corruption, and estimated much lower totals for the procurement of domestic wheat.

Maintaining or even increasing the amount of domestic wheat that enters circulation is critical to the stability of the subsidized bread program given the vulnerabilities associated with imported wheat (see chapter 3). The national government has a close interest, therefore, in farming households' decision-making process over whether they grow wheat and—as was evident in Sisi's address to the nation in the midst of the coronavirus crisis—what they do with the harvest.

Past governments sought to control this process directly through a centrally planned agricultural system (table 2.1). From the 1940s through the 1980s the Ministry of Agriculture set cropping patterns, which specified what proportion of each farmer's land should be allocated to wheat. The decision of how much wheat to plant was out of farmers' hands, in theory at least (in practice these crop rotations were not always enforced). At the time, due to the national prioritization of other crops, this policy operated as a restrictive one—it kept the wheat-cultivated area low, at only 33 percent of all agricultural holdings in 1955, later reduced to 27.5 percent in 1970. In addition, through much of this period the government set delivery quotas, which determined what proportion of each farmer's harvest—typically 1–3 ardab/feddan—had to be sold to the government

TABLE 2.1

Wheat Policy in Egypt

1940s	Fifty percent of all agricultural land holdings is allocated to wheat production. State control over the production and trading of wheat is gradually increased.
1950s	Increasing state control over agriculture. In 1955, allocation of wheat area is reduced to 33 percent of all agricultural land holdings. Delivery of wheat quota is made compulsory (1–3 ardab/feddan) at fixed prices lower than the world market price. From 1955, Egypt starts to receive subsidized wheat from the United States through the PL480 program.
1960s	The government introduces strong centralized control over the agricultural sector, determining which crops should be planted where and requiring farmers to deliver their crops to the government. Agricultural cooperatives are created in each village to control the production and marketing of major crops, including wheat. Transport of wheat without permission from the Ministry of Supply is prohibited. In 1966, the United States suspends its shipments of subsidized wheat to Egypt.
1970s	In 1970, the government reduces the wheat area to 27.5 percent of all agricultural land holdings. The government begins controlling marketing, distribution, and imports. In 1975, the US government reinstates flows of subsidized wheat to Egypt through the PL480 program. In 1976, the government rescinds its compulsory wheat delivery and replaces it with an optional delivery program.
1980s	In 1985, the government reinstates compulsory wheat delivery. This is only temporary, however, and the following year the government abolishes mandatory area allocations and delivery quotas, introducing an optional delivery program at a guaranteed procurement price.
1990s	Under agricultural liberalization, the government continues to open up the wheat sector. In 1992, the private sector is allowed to import, produce, and trade refined (72 percent extraction) flour. In 1993, the government eliminates all restrictions on marketing refined flour, but mills are still permitted to produce only one type of flour. In 1996, the government introduces a requirement that private and public millers producing refined flour use imported wheat. The government begins offering Egyptian farmers a procurement price that is higher than the world market price.
2000s	The government continues to use the procurement price as a way to incentivize wheat cultivation, in most years setting a price that is higher than the world market price.
2010s	In 2017, the government ends its policy of announcing a high procurement price prior to planting and starts paying the world market price for domestic wheat.

Sources: Kherallah et al. 2000, Abdalla and Al-Shawarby 2017, and the USDA Foreign Agricultural Service's *Egypt Grain and Feed Annual* reports.

at a fixed price (Kherallah et al. 2000: 4). The decision about how much wheat to sell, therefore, was also out of farmers' hands. The fixed price for these delivery quotas was lower than world market prices, allowing the government to keep down the costs of the bread subsidy. The government was, essentially, taxing farmers, transferring some of the burden of providing huge amounts of low-cost bread for the urban population onto the shoulders of rural producers.

In the late 1980s, however, these centralized controls on the agricultural sector became a target of critique from international and bilateral donors like the World Bank and USAID, which argued that they produced inefficient distortions. In terms of wheat, international experts were concerned that the government's system of delivery quotas, area allocations, and low purchasing prices was suppressing wheat production, causing the government to rely more on imports and escalating the costs of the subsidized bread program. So in 1987, as part of a broader package of reforms to liberalize the agricultural sector, the government abolished the area restrictions and delivery quotas, facilitating an expansion in the wheat-cultivated area.[21] At the same time, despite the pressure to open up agricultural markets, the government maintained its price controls for wheat and a small number of strategic crops. As a way of encouraging farmers to plant wheat, the government introduced a new policy to announce an attractive procurement price before the beginning of the planting season (Kherallah et al. 2000).

Since then, the procurement price has become the government's primary technology for incentivizing farmers to cultivate and sell wheat.[22] It is a mechanism for maximizing domestic production so as to counter the threat that the wheat supply will run out.[23] But just as the government has to weigh between a low price for bread and a subsidy program it can afford to fund (as discussed in chapter 1), it must also weigh between a high price for wheat and a procurement plan it can afford to fund. Furthermore, not all farmers necessarily think about the procurement price in the same way that government officials do.

From Cairo

What makes an attractive price? The point of comparison through which government officials and grain trade professionals assess the procurement price is the world price. By this, they mean the price at which Egypt buys foreign wheat.[24] While I have never heard farmers in Warda compare what they get for their wheat to world prices, this is the metric that nonfarmers use to evaluate how likely farmers are to plant and sell this crop.

After the neoliberal reforms of the late 1980s, the government began paying farmers around the same or slightly more than the world price for their wheat.[25] From the mid-1990s, the government started paying substantially more than the world price, as a way to incentivize wheat production. The high procurement price, relative to the global indicator, became a pillar of the government's efforts to secure the wheat supply. Such was its role as a symbol of government support to those who farm this crucial national crop that, even when world market prices fell, it was politically difficult for the government to reduce it. The government made no adjustment to the procurement price, for instance, when world prices declined from a high of $262/ton in 1996 to only $126/ton in 1998 (Kherallah et al. 2000: 10). This policy of supporting wheat farmers by paying them an inflated price continued through the 2000s and into the 2010s. In almost every year during this period, the government purchased domestic wheat at a price that exceeded the world price.[26]

I talked about this approach with Gamal, an economist who for a short while held a senior office in the government that was formed after the 2011 revolution. As we sat in the office of his slightly rundown Cairo penthouse apartment in August 2015, he told me, "Bread is very dear to my heart, as a person and as an economist." His conversation was peppered with the phrase "as an economist," a conscious reflection on how his academic training has shaped his vision of the relationship between the state and those who produce and consume the nation's food. "It is fine to aim for social justice," he said, "fine to be subsidizing consumers—but not if that is at the expense of producers." He told me that, when he held office, he "struggled to offer local producers of wheat a price that was higher than world prices, higher by 10 to 15 percent." His use of the term *struggle* suggested the work it took to convince other parts of the government to raise the price and his pride at having succeeded.

However, while this policy was designed to encourage farmers to grow wheat, it had consequences that ultimately threatened the security of the nation's wheat supply. The first problem was budgetary. In committing to the price at which it would buy wheat prior to the planting of the crop, the government opened itself up to the possibility, if world prices fell, of having to procure local wheat that was much more expensive than wheat it could have procured elsewhere.[27] This is precisely what happened the year I met with Gamal. "This year the wheat world price decreased," he explained to me. "The price offered to farmers back in October was much higher. The difference was huge, 30 percent or even more! This had very serious consequences." The government was locked into a commitment of having to buy millions of tons of local wheat at an inflated price, increasing the already substantial costs of the subsidized bread program.

This situation had another effect. As Gamal continued to explain, "Clever merchants bought foreign wheat and sold it on to the government and pocketed the difference." Hence while the high procurement price was meant to help the government secure the wheat needed for subsidized bread, it actually jeopardized that supply. It increased the cost of the government's wheat procurement, raising the possibility that financial constraints could limit the government's ability to meet the wheat needs of the bread subsidy program. In addition, it prompted the illicit substitution of foreign for domestic wheat, which also—given the widespread perception of foreign wheat as being inferior to domestic (discussed in chapter 3)—raised questions about the quality of the resultant bread.

After the problems with the 2015 procurement season, the Ministry of Supply and Ministry of Agriculture proposed a change in policy. Instead of setting an artificially inflated procurement price, they suggested that the government should buy domestic wheat at the market price. The proposal included a stipulation that the government continue to support wheat farmers through a direct payment (1,300 EGP/feddan, up to an area of 25 feddans), but it still met with outrage from the three main agricultural unions, which argued that the new pricing would make it unprofitable to grow wheat. Such a policy, they claimed, would be unconstitutional, since under Article 29 of the constitution the state commits to "buying staple agricultural crops (al-mahasil al-zira'iya al-asasiya) at appropriate prices to achieve a profit margin (hamish ribh) for farmers" (Government of Egypt 2014). A group of farmers with backing from several parliamentarians took these concerns to the prime minister, ultimately leading him to reverse the government's decision.[28]

Following similar problems with the 2016 procurement season, though, and a corruption scandal that culminated in the resignation of the Minister of Supply in August 2016 (see chapter 3), the government took action. In January 2017, as wheat was growing in the fields, the Ministry of Supply announced that it was switching to buying wheat at the world price. This meant that it would no longer declare the procurement price prior to planting, but would calculate it at harvest time based on the average price of imported wheat in the two months prior. The new procedure is designed to prevent the government from paying above-market prices for domestic wheat. It is also meant to reduce the possibility of traders—who play a key role in staple security through their movement of grain across borders—from passing off imported wheat as domestic.

This time the policy measure did not prompt such a backlash from farmer groups, perhaps in part because it took place after a major change in the economic context—the November 2016 currency devaluation. The new exchange rate after the devaluation had a profound impact on what it meant to translate a world price, calculated in US dollars, into Egyptian pounds. After equalizing the procurement price with the world price, the amount paid to farmers for their wheat increased by 29 percent (from 2,800EGP/ton in 2016 to 3,600EGP/ton in 2017), even though the dollar price decreased by 37 percent.[29] Things went smoothly with that year's procurement season. The government bought 3.4 million tons of domestic wheat, which was generally considered satisfactory even if some government officials, as I discussed earlier in the chapter, were interested in inflating the figure.

The following year, however, problems arose. The Minister of Supply forecast a procurement of over 4 million tons of domestic wheat, but the government only managed to buy 3.15 million, one of the lowest totals in recent years. This may have been due in part to bad weather, which affected the harvest, but grain traders maintained that prices were at the root of the problem.[30] Although the new procurement policy was meant to prevent fraudulent substitutions of imported wheat for domestic wheat by equalizing their cost, because the procurement price is fixed whereas world prices are variable, there remains the possibility that opportunities for arbitrage can open up. When farmers came to sell their wheat in 2018, due to an upward trend in global wheat markets, the government price ended up being lower than the price of imported wheat (3,600EGP/ton compared to 4,150EGP/ton). As a result, many private-sector mills that produce highly refined flour for specialty breads, cakes, and pasta—which by law are only permitted to buy foreign wheat (so that they do not compete with the government as buyers of domestic wheat)—chose instead to purchase local wheat illegally, offering farmers a more attractive price of 3,950EGP/ton. Consequently, less wheat was channeled into the subsidized bread program.[31]

Some farmer advocates continue to call for higher procurement prices, arguing that, with the increased cost of production, current prices do not make farming wheat profitable.[32] A former official from the Ministry of Agriculture, who spoke out against the new procurement policy, argued, "Wheat is a strategic crop, which means that farmers should receive financial support to grow it and thus reduce imports." He went on to note, "Increasing wheat cultivation would help to save foreign currency as well as achieve food sufficiency in one of the most important staples for Egyptians."[33] To him, a guaranteed high procurement price is important for the security of this staple. Yet despite these voices of critique, the new procurement policy remains in place at the time of writing in 2021.

The procurement price is therefore a political object, much discussed among policy makers and in the media, circulating widely as a figure of Egyptian pounds per ton. Underpinning this discussion is an assumption that there is a clear link between the price offered for wheat and how much of the crop farmers choose to plant and sell. Illustrative of this premise, a report written by an agricultural expert within the American Embassy notes, "The key driver for wheat production is the government's procurement price policy. High government procurement prices encourage farmers to make early cropping decisions, discouraging them from switching to other crops such as clover or sugar beet."[34] By encouraging Egyptian farmers to grow this staple crop and sell their harvest to the state, the procurement price plays a role in ensuring that there is sufficient flour for the subsidized bread program. Just as the state seeks to shape the nature of the wheat being planted around Egypt through scientific breeding and the distribution of certified seeds (chapter 1), it seeks to shape the choices farmers make through its pricing policy.

The link between price and behavior seems commonsensical. Of course farmers will plant more wheat if the procurement price is high. Yet a view from within a farming household offers a different perspective.[35] While the procurement price is a frequent topic of discussion among policy makers and in media accounts, as well as a matter on which agricultural unions and influential farmer groups have lobbied, it did not feature at all in my discussions with Marwa. Over the course of her wheat cultivation cycle, she barely mentioned how much she would get from selling her wheat. This speaks to a disjuncture between how policy makers and small-scale farmers understand wheat. Staple security is as much a part of small-scale farmers' everyday lives as it is for government officials charged with securing the nation's wheat, but it operates on a different scale and is underpinned by a contrasting imperative—not to sustain a politically significant bread subsidy but to support a family.

From a Village Home

Before Marwa planted her wheat in 2007, the government had already announced the price at which it would be purchasing the crop the following spring, but she never mentioned this to me as a factor in her decision to grow wheat. Nor did she, when she harvested her 6 ardab (just under a ton) of grain in 2008, mention price as being a factor in her decision to sell some of that wheat. She simply told me the amount of wheat her family would need for the year's bread production—5 ardab—and said she would sell the remainder. Although prices and costs were something she frequently talked about, she did not say how much she got from selling this wheat. As for Marwa's brother Khaled, his harvest that year was 8 ardab of wheat, less than anticipated (as he was unable to harvest some of his land due to the Sharif conflict). The 8 ardab came from land he had sharecropped out to a relative, so his share of the harvest was 5 ardab. Of this 5 ardab, he gave 1 ardab to the poor for zakat (the acts of charity required of Muslims), and kept the remaining 4 to cover part of his household needs, not selling any.

Marwa's and Khaled's labors in their wheat fields from the fall of 2007 through spring of 2008 were primarily, therefore, about feeding their families; only 1 ardab of the grain they harvested was channeled to mills to become flour for subsidized bread. Like most farmers in Egypt, they grow wheat for themselves first and to sell only secondarily. When a farmer sells only a small part of their harvest, this raises the question of the role price plays in shaping their decision making. From what I observed in Warda, the amount of wheat that farmers choose to sell and to save varies from year to year, but these variations are driven more by changes in total harvest and household needs than by price. Typically, farmers with sufficient land and production keep about 1 ardab (150 kg) of grain for each household member's bread needs during the year.

When I returned to Warda seven years later, during the 2015 harvest, Marwa told me that she had harvested 10 ardab of wheat. That year, with only two children left at home to feed, she kept 3 for the household and sold 7. I also talked with Habiba, Khaled's wife, asking how much wheat they planted and whether they sold it. Her immediate response was: "No, we don't sell it." It was only on further questioning that she added, "Well maybe we'll keep 10 ardab for the family and the rest we take to the weighing site [for sale]." That year, Khaled had harvested 30 ardab of wheat, meaning that they actually sold two-thirds of their crop. Yet for Habiba, this sale was an afterthought. She was certainly aware that they would earn some money from selling this wheat, but her primary concern was the grain they saved for use within the home. Neither Habiba nor Marwa mentioned the connection between the wheat they had sold and the national subsidized bread program it would support (despite the fact that they, too, sometimes eat this bread [chapter 5]). For farmers like these, sale—and thus the price at which wheat is purchased—is secondary to the primary purpose of providing for the home. In contrast with the depiction of wheat cultivation in the national newspapers, they think about the supply of bread on a household rather than a national scale.

This association of wheat more with domestic consumption than with the market that transfers wheat into an object of national consumption was evident in the way people talked about the crop. Early on in my time in Warda, I was chatting with one farmer when, without my prompting, he gave his judgment on the relative value of different crops. "Onions are best [mufadal]," he stated. "What about wheat?" I asked. He responded, "Wheat is also useful [mufid]." I was struck by his evocation of use value in relation to wheat. He continued, "You can use it to make bread for the house, and when you have lots of children, they eat a lot." This usefulness comes into relief when the price of flour or nonsubsidized bread (for those who do not have access to baladi bread) increases, rendering homemade bread from homegrown wheat particularly desirable. When I was talking with one group of women in December 2007, for example, their conversation turned to how expensive wheat flour had become—something about which they, like Marwa, were concerned. They wished their household had planted more wheat, they said. The order in which Marwa reported her use of the 2008 harvest to me, therefore, was not coincidental. She told me first about the bread she had just made from her newly harvested wheat, then about how she planned to keep most of the 6 ardab she harvested for her baking throughout the year, and only at the end about how she would sell the rest. Finally, she mentioned the money she gained from selling the straw—an added bonus that seemed peripheral to the primary purpose of growing wheat (unlike in the past when, as I discuss in chapter 1, farmers at times valued straw over grain).

Marwa's and Khaled's approaches to wheat are not representative of all wheat farmers. While they are well off in relation to many other households in Warda, their wealth is small compared to that seen in some other farming regions. Khaled's land may place him in the top 1 percent of Egyptian farmers, whose landholdings exceed 10 feddans, but his 12 feddans are a fraction of the size of the large commercial farms found in other parts of Egypt. For large-scale farmers, who in Egypt are referred to as "agricultural investors" (mustathmirin) rather than farmers (falahin), price means something different. If the only purpose of growing a crop is to sell it, the price that crop will fetch is obviously a central factor in their decision making. I talked with one man, for instance, who runs the exports for an agricultural company that owns thousands of feddans. He told me that his company grows large areas of wheat on reclaimed land in the Western Desert. I expressed my surprise, since most of the investors I had met previously were growing high-value fruits and vegetables. "Are large-scale commercial farmers interested in wheat?" I asked. "Yes, definitely," he responded, "for the last ten years, since the government has been putting a premium on the international prices." The government's high procurement price—which he referred to as "tempting"—thus had the desired effect of inducing this investor and his colleagues to grow wheat. This is a particularly positive outcome from the government's point of view, since the grain from such large-scale production moves directly into government channels without consumption losses.

For investors, the government's procurement of wheat is attractive not only for its inflated prices but for its reliability as a confirmed market. One small investor, for instance, told me about how he decided to grow wheat after a failed venture with onions (a crop whose potential for high profits but also high losses I discuss further below). He planted wheat on 25 feddans of land that he had rented as a way to recoup some of the 250,000EGP he had lost on onions. The procurement price was high that year—he described it as "good money," although, he added, "it didn't make up for the onions." But he benefited, too, from the cash bonuses that the government gave that year to farmers who grew wheat. His goal with growing wheat, in other words, was not to make huge profits, but to capitalize on the government's economic supports and on the knowledge of how much revenue he would make.

To those who grow wheat as a commercial venture, the procurement price is key. It is not surprising that such farmers—affluent, well-connected, and powerful—would express resistance to any changes in the government procurement price policy. Yet these investors' interest in procurement prices was not matched in my conversations with farmers in Warda. To understand more about why small-scale farmers do not place so great an emphasis on the procurement price requires a look at some of the other crops that compete with wheat for space in the winter fields. Egypt's main winter crops by area after wheat are clover, barley, onions, and fava beans.[36] Clover is an important source of fodder for household livestock and a crop to which most farming households devote at least a small piece of their land.[37] But over the decade that I have been working in western Fayoum, onions have been wheat's main competitor.[38]

Onions are not worth as much as wheat per unit weight (in 2016 the prices were around 3,760EGP/ton for wheat and 1,300EGP/ton for onions), but their yields per unit area are higher. Farmers in Warda say that they can get 10 tons/feddan with onions—or, on the best land, up to 25 tons/feddan—whereas wheat yields in this area are typically only around 2–2.5 tons/feddan. Onions also operate in a different kind of market from wheat—one with multiple buyers and that is open to exports. Without government intervention to control the crop's price, onions bring the possibility of huge profits if market conditions are good. They also bring the possibility of ruin.

Obviously, potential profits are not farmers' sole concern in choosing what to plant. In Warda, for instance, many farmers have parcels of land that has been cultivated for centuries and has clay-rich soils, as well as parcels of so-called new land, which is more recently reclaimed and has sandier soils. Farmers say that clay soils are better for wheat, sandy soils for onions. Cropping decisions are also affected by labor needs and labor availability. Onions, for example, are labor-intensive during the planting stage (at the harvesting and processing stages, the costs are not so different from wheat). Farmers plant onions first as seeds in a nursery, weed them carefully by hand, and then transplant the seedlings one by one into the field (figure 2.5). This high labor requirement was the reason Marwa did not plant onions in 2007. Yet over the course of my

FIGURE 2.5. Transplanting onions. Photograph by the author.

fieldwork in Warda, the most striking distinction between onions and wheat has been the preponderance of onion price talk over wheat price talk.

The export potential of onions, which is the key determinant of price, circulates in an almost mythical way. One of my first conversations in Warda in the summer of 2007 was with the owner of a small guesthouse who has some agricultural land. Sitting in the fields together, he told me that Egypt had recently started exporting onions to Russia.[39] To make vodka, he added with a conspiratorial grin, seemingly designed to demonstrate his positioning apart from other villagers as someone comfortable discussing alcohol and his closeness to me as a foreigner. This, he said, had had an amazing impact on prices, which rocketed up from 600–700EGP/ton the previous year to around 1,300EGP/ton that year. While he was the only one to mention vodka, many people spoke to me that summer about the price of onions—many more than spoke to me about the price of wheat. As a result of this optimism about the potential returns, many farmers in the village decided to grow onions that year in place of wheat.

The price of onions remained a common topic of discussion as the onion market started to fall. One day in late November 2007, Khaled and I took a pickup taxi back from a morning in the 3 feddans he was planting with onions. The driver asked Khaled if he had been transplanting onions. The fields were abuzz at this time of year with laborers bent double, carefully placing the transplanted seedlings in raised beds.[40] When Khaled replied that he had been, the driver responded, "Onions are going down in price. It's better to grow something that you need, like wheat." The driver cemented his judgment with a personal reflection, telling us, "We still have wheat from last year that we are using in the house for bread." Later that day, I accompanied Marwa to collect clover for her young water buffalo. We bumped into a relative of hers who was on her way to transplant her onion seedlings with her married daughter. "They say the price of onions is not going to be good," the daughter commented. "They say that," echoed the woman. "You shouldn't grow a lot of onions," the daughter told her mother. "You should grow wheat instead." By this time, though, there was no going back for this woman, Khaled, or for others in the village, as they had already made the decision to invest in onions.

The sense of doom mounted as the months passed, the May harvest came and went, and the already disappointing prices declined even further. Sacks of onions piled up in the corners of fields. There was no point in farmers taking them back to their homes, for unlike wheat, this was not a crop that farming households could eat in large quantities. Their only option was to sell, so farmers held off, hoping that the prices might rebound. Passing by one of these piles of unsold onions in June 2008, the two men accompanying me began talking about how the price of onions had fallen to only 350 EGP/ton. "And the price will continue to go down, ruining us," said one.[41] "To think that people in the beginning sold for 800, but some waited," commented the other. They pondered what might have caused the low price. There were stories going around that the government was restricting exports to depress the price, "because the government wants people to grow wheat next year," one of the men commented. I found no documentation to suggest that this was in fact the case, but the man's explanation was a notable indication of how the government's efforts to encourage wheat cultivation at the national level might not necessarily be perceived in a positive light at the local level.

One evening I went to chat with Khaled and Habiba, who were drinking tea at home, having just woken from siestas. They were in low moods. "The government has destroyed the farmers," Khaled said. "The price of crops is so low and even the price of livestock is low. The government should support us, but instead they destroy us." It soon became clear that their main concern was onions. They narrated the sad tale of the declining prices, which started off at 800, then went down to 500, now to 350, rendering all those farmers who waited to sell their onions in a desperate situation. Although wheat procurement prices were also low this year compared to world prices (which increased during the global food crisis), this was not a prime concern for people in Warda. Later in the conversation Khaled did refer to wheat, but his disappointment with regards to that harvest was not so much about the insufficiency of the price at which he could sell it as about the insufficiency of the harvest to cover their household needs. The 4 ardab of grain that they kept from that year's small harvest (after 1 ardab went to zakat and 3 went to the sharecropper) would not be nearly enough for the family's year-round bread consumption.

The following week I went for a walk in the fields with Khaled, just before sunset. As we walked through his grove of olive trees I asked him if things were better now that farmers have the freedom to choose what to plant. The wording of my question betrayed my preconception that having an ability to choose what you grow would be preferable to having that decision imposed on you through a designated cropping pattern. To my surprise he responded, "No! It used to be better. Then you wouldn't have the onions destroying the farmers." He recounted the same story: how so many farmers had chosen to plant onions because they had sold for 1,100 EGP/ton the previous year but that this year the price had fallen. "The government should support us," he concluded, "otherwise the farmer will die." The fact that the government was supporting him and other farmers through buying wheat at inflated prices was clearly of little relevance; price supports for a crop he grows primarily to eat do less for his sense of security than they would for a crop that he grows primarily to sell.

Such patterns, which I first noticed during the year I lived in Egypt, were further reflected in my visits to Warda over subsequent years. After the low price of onions in 2008, fewer farmers planted onions that fall. In April 2009 when I returned to the village, Habiba explained that her family had decided to grow more wheat for household use rather than onions because of the previous year's onion price decline. As she told me this, she recited the figures—how they sold their harvest for 500 or 400, rather than the 700 they had been anticipating. This kind of figure recitation is a way of communicating a trend of worrisome nature—either down, as in the case of the onions, or up, as in the case of other costs, like those associated with marriage. But while wheat often features in a similar way, through recitations of the cost of a sack of flour, procurement prices for wheat do not, even though they too change from year to year.

Two years later, in 2011, the position of onions had further declined, rendering wheat, by comparison, once again more attractive. During fieldwork in Warda in November 2011, I asked Khaled and Habiba how their crops had been that year. Habiba replied, "Good, we had lots of wheat. We made flour and stored wheat to make bread in the house." It was interesting that she referred first to the household use. Later that day, I returned to their house and talked with them some more. This time when Khaled referred to the wheat being good, he mentioned how they use it both in the house and sell it. "The price of wheat was good," he said. This was the year of the revolution; it was the same year that Gamal, the economist and former politician who I interviewed, had been in the administration and had campaigned hard to ensure that the price of wheat was higher than the world price in time for the 2011 harvest. Yet the world price was not Khaled's point of reference. Rather, his comparison was with onions. He continued, "The price for onions was not so good, so people are not focusing so much on it this year."

During my fieldwork in 2015, high wheat procurement prices were under debate in the media and were mentioned in many of the interviews that I conducted in Cairo with people working in policy. But these high prices did not seem to register prominently with the farmers I talked to in Warda like they had back in 2011. In a discussion with Marwa about how farmers decide what to plant, she explained, "Well if they have lots of land maybe they will choose onions, if they fetched a good price last year. So if they have 50, 60 feddans perhaps they will grow 30 feddans of onion and 30 feddans of wheat. But if you have just a little land, like us, maybe you will grow some wheat, some moonflowers, some clover." In other words, onions are a crop for investment, but for smallholders a diverse set of crops, including wheat, is a way of mitigating risk. I followed up, asking her, "But the price of wheat was good this year, wasn't it?" "Yes," she responded, "an ardab was for 460 [Egyptian pounds]." Price, though, is not her chief concern for wheat, unlike for onions. She added that wheat is good for the family, in case of a crisis.

Khaled told a similar story. When we chatted in September of that year he commented that the price of onions was so low. With the high cost of the inputs required for growing onions, such as chemicals and labor for transplanting seedlings and the harvest, farmers are stuck if they "don't find a market"—or, in other words, if they cannot sell their crop at a sufficiently high price to recoup their costs. After his experience planting 6 feddans of onions in 2014, he said he was not planning to cultivate so much the following year; maybe they would grow 2 feddans. He did not mention wheat, of which they had grown 2 feddans that year, until I questioned him about it. "How was the price of wheat this year?" I asked. "Not bad [mish batal]," he responded. This price, which was at that time under intense debate in policy circles for being artificially inflated, clearly did not register with him as being all that remarkable.

Through these early years of my fieldwork, therefore, for Khaled and Marwa the cultivation of wheat was a way to secure their households—a central part of their livelihoods and yet one so mundane it often went uncommented upon. They grew wheat, stored it, and turned it into bread. If there was any extra left over, they sold it to the government. But their primary focus, so far as wheat was concerned, was on producing a homemade staple that their families preferred and that was not subject to the vagaries of flour or bread prices. The degree to which they planted enough wheat to sell the excess, and the degree to which they contributed to the national project of staple security, depended less on the price of wheat, as compared to the world price, and more on the price of onions. Thus, whereas the government has the appearance of control over wheat markets through setting the procurement price, farmers' household livelihood strategies confound this control, revealing the limits to the state's attempts to move domestically grown wheat into the national domain.

Yet a household's mode of securing its staple can change over time as family circumstances shift. This was evident following major changes that took place in Khaled's and Marwa's households in 2018. The first of these was the tragic death of Khaled following head injuries sustained from a road accident. The loss of this wonderful man left a big gap in the family. The eldest son, Mohamed, who is in his thirties and has five children of his own, took over responsibility for work in the fields, helped by his second brother (the third brother is intellectually disabled and so stays closer to home). But 12 feddans was a lot for them to manage. When I visited in 2018, they were growing onions, banking on the prices being good, along with 3.5 feddans of wheat and some smaller areas of chamomile and clover. The burden of financing the necessary inputs, however, was weighing heavily on them, the costs of chemicals, manure, fuel, and labor all having increased markedly since the currency devaluation. When I returned the following year, they told me that the price of onions had been strong and their production profitable. That year, though, they had decided to rent out half their land and put all of the remainder into onions, saving just a small piece of land near the home to grow clover for fodder. This was the first time since I met the family in 2007 that they had not grown wheat. When I asked Habiba what they would do about getting grain to make bread, she responded, "We can fill our room for 4,000 EGP." It made more sense, in other words, for them to buy grain for their year-round bread needs—enough to fill the room where they would store it until they needed to mill it into flour—than to grow it themselves. For this household at this point in time, growing wheat was no longer the best way of securing the family's bread. Planting crops that had the potential to bring large profits and buying grain had become their practice of staple security.

Marwa's household also saw a change in household composition around this time, with the return of her husband from Saudi Arabia and the departure of her two sons, one to do his military service and the other to study in Cairo. Growing wheat was hard on her husband, Marwa told me. He finds working in the fields increasingly difficult as he gets older, especially with no sons to help him. In 2018 they decided that, instead of planting wheat, they would just tend their olive trees. She still had some wheat stored in the house from the previous year, which she used to bake for special occasions, but refilling this stock was less of a concern. Like a number of households in the village, she had started getting subsidized bread (chapter 5). Buying subsidized bread had become her way of ensuring that her family had bread to eat each day.

The view from within Marwa's and Khaled's households hence reveals the disjuncture between different types of staple security. To both the government and farming families, staple security means minimizing risks and securing the supply of wheat and bread. But the ways in which they go about doing this are divergent. To policy makers, the procurement price is a device of staple security, a mechanism for encouraging farmers to plant wheat and sell their crop to the government. Agricultural investors who grow wheat commercially may share this vision, recognizing the value of a strong procurement price for making wheat a profitable crop to grow. But this group comprises only a small minority of the farmers who cultivate wheat (even if their contribution to total production is disproportionate, given the yields they are able to generate with high levels of investment). Among the small-scale farmers who produce the majority of the nation's wheat, the procurement price occupies a less central place; they think about wheat primarily as a crop they will consume rather than sell. Still, there are multiple ways for a rural household to ensure that its members have good bread to eat, the appropriateness of each strategy depending on a number of factors. Growing wheat to produce grain to bake homemade bread may be a way of securing the household staple, but so may growing other more profitable crops and using the proceeds to buy grain, or to buy subsidized bread.

Conclusion

To return to the figures reported in Egypt's newspapers: to get to the point that those newspapers document—millions of feddans of land planted with wheat—farmers have to decide to grow wheat over other crops. To get to the figure of millions of tons of wheat supplied to the government, farmers have to decide to sell rather than keep their wheat. These decisions are mediated by a number of factors, including not just the price of wheat but the price of other crops, labor availability, and household priorities. They are decisions that are key to securing domestic wheat for the subsidized bread program, shielding the country from some of the vulnerabilities of imports that I discuss in the next chapter. Yet while they are decisions with national ramifications, they are also decisions that are part of household strategies for meeting staple needs and building livelihoods.

Staple security, therefore, is different things to different people. National and household priorities, the interests of the state and those of the farmers, and the need for flour to make subsidized bread and flour to make homemade bread are sometimes aligned and other times in conflict. This confluence of factors may produce an experience of security at a particular point in time—when, for instance, a farmer harvests a good crop of wheat and brings the grain back to her home, or when a government official sees high figures for an area planted with wheat. Such moments carry a sense of reassurance that future needs will be met: a family's need for homemade bread over the coming year or nation's need for subsidized bread over the coming months. But these are transient and not stable states of being—the sacks of grain in the home are eaten, poor weather may impact a harvest, and the threat returns. Thus staple security is not something that a country or individual attains. Rather, it is these varied actors' ongoing efforts, day in and day out, to access the wheat required for baking bread, whether that may be cheap bread for the nation's poor or homemade bread for a family.

3. GRAIN ON THE MOVE

The Craigslist site for Egypt hosts a range of advertisements for housing, jobs, services, and things for sale. It is a site people might associate more with finding an apartment or selling used furniture than with buying grain. But it was here, in May 2015, that I came across an advertisement for 25,200 tons of "Russian Milling Wheat in Bulk" for sale in Cairo. Below a dusky photograph of a pile of grain inside a silo, the advertisement explained that this lot of wheat from Russia had been "rejected due to fungus contamination (*Tilletia spp.*)." It went on to explain that the wheat is being "offered for sale on behalf of owners in order to minimize losses." The posting directed interested parties to a page on

---

FRENCH WHEAT DESTINED FOR EGYPT. *Photograph by Pascal Rossignol. Used with permission.*

the Salvex website, an online marketplace for salvage goods, where they could view additional photographs of the mound of grain from different angles—the darker kernels characteristic of grain damaged by *Tilletia* just visible—and place a bid.

When I mentioned the advertisement several years later during interviews in Cairo with a number of grain trade experts, they too expressed surprise.[1] Most said they had not heard of Craigslist and were unaware of online trading platforms for rejected wheat. Some wondered at who had managed to bring such a large quantity of contaminated wheat to Cairo. Others were skeptical that the port inspection process would not have weeded out such wheat. Sensing a degree of discomfort among my interviewees, I did not ask many follow-up questions. I was aware that I was treading on politically sensitive terrain. The prospect of a mound of the country's staple grain, contaminated with a fungus that would cause yield and quality losses were it to get into Egyptian fields, sitting in a warehouse in the capital city, ready to enter into circulation when someone clicks on a website link and types their credit card information, was troubling. How had this wheat made its way from Russia to Cairo? What were the chances of this fungus infecting Egyptian wheat and reducing domestic production? Where was this grain being held? Such questions of grain procurement, quality, and storage are unsettling because they underscore the threat posed by both the presence of bad wheat and the absence of good wheat.

In this chapter, I approach these domains of procuring foreign wheat, assessing wheat quality, and storing wheat as practices of staple security.[2] They are efforts to ensure the continuous supply of decent bread for the Egyptian people by moving grain that has the desired attributes across space and, at particular moments, holding it in place. I start with procurement. Whereas the last chapter looked at how the government procures domestic wheat, I focus here on how it procures foreign wheat. Roughly half of Egypt's imported wheat is purchased by the government for use in its subsidized bread program. This is the foreign wheat that is most closely tied to staple security (the remainder is imported by the private sector to be milled into refined flour and used in the production of luxury foods such as specialty breads, cakes, cookies, and pasta). Without the government-imported wheat, a crucial supplement to the domestically grown wheat, there would not be sufficient flour for the production of baladi bread. The government agency responsible for importing this wheat is the General Authority for Supply Commodities (GASC), which is part of the Ministry of Supply. I look at the factors that shape the ability of this agency to secure the wheat required for subsidized bread from global markets. I also trace the popular and political anxieties that surround this procurement process and the question of whether Egypt will be able to access enough wheat for its population's bread needs.

Second, I look at the quality of imported wheat. The government sets a number of quality requirements that impact the types of wheat that enter Egypt and the country's ability to secure the wheat that it needs. Sometimes the government chooses one shipment over another because of particular quality specifications; at other times it tweaks its quality requirements in favor of a cheaper shipment. The possibility of contaminated wheat entering the country is a matter of considerable concern, both within the general public and among government officials. This is partly because Egyptians eat a lot of bread; if contaminated wheat were to be used to make that bread, it could pose a major public health threat. It is also because Egyptians grow a lot of wheat; if the grain brought into the country carries disease, it could undermine domestic production. Indeed, the fungus for which the Russian wheat on Craigslist was rejected is, in theory, banned from entering the country because it causes a range of diseases, known as bunt, that result in lower yields and poorer-quality grain. I explore these questions of quality, trust, and security through the case of a recent controversy over ergot, another fungus found in imported wheat.

Third, I look at storage. Given the temporal and spatial mismatch between when and where wheat is harvested and imported and the daily bread consumption needs around the country, storage is key to ensuring a consistent supply of the staple grain. This plays out on multiple scales, from national concerns about the amount of wheat in the country's silos to the security that sacks of wheat stored within the home provide to farming households. A mass of grain in storage embodies the affective state, albeit transient, of staple security—the knowledge that, at least for the near future, there will be enough grain to make bread. In contrast, the absence of storage with sufficient capacity and adequate protection to prevent deterioration in grain quality jeopardizes the reliable supply of this grain. The government cannot procure either domestic or foreign grain if it does not have somewhere safe to put it. At the same time, the 22,500 tons of contaminated wheat advertised on Craigslist indicates how certain kinds of storage run counter to security imperatives. Storage is not only a place where good wheat can be held in reserve but one in which bad wheat can be hidden and good wheat siphoned off.

Through exploring the procuring, assessing, and storing of wheat, this chapter shows how movements of grain are underpinned by a deeply perceived need to secure a steady supply of Egypt's staple food. Foreign grain traders, port inspectors, mice, fungi, silo bins, sacks, and exchange rates might not be commonly associated with a loaf of bread, but the following analysis demonstrates just how closely interrelated they are. The various people involved in moving and holding grain may not necessarily see their work as securing a staple; they may be more interested in making money. But all play a role in shaping the availability and taste of the dark baladi bread that is eaten in most Egyptian households multiple times a day, alongside eggs for breakfast, stuffed with beans for lunch, or dipped in a tomato and spinach stew for dinner.

Procurement

In our analysis of Egyptian newspapers, my research assistant Mariam and I found not only extensive media coverage of domestic wheat production and procurement (see chapter 2), but also prolific coverage of wheat imports. Headline after headline documented the government's successful completion of wheat purchases and the arrival of wheat shipments at Egypt's ports. The articles were formulaic, each headline containing two crucial details—the tonnage of wheat purchased and its source—taken from press releases from the Ministry of Supply. After Mariam spent some time compiling numerous pages of near-identical headlines, we began to wonder about the utility of this exercise. Yet as I read through these records, I realized that what to us was repetitive almost to the point of disinterest was also revealing. Read together, the articles offer a window into a message the government is trying to communicate to the public.[3]

In announcing every act of international wheat procurement, the Ministry of Supply is seeking to reassure the Egyptian people (and perhaps other parts of the government and political leadership, too) that the nation's wheat needs are covered. Such figures detailing concluded wheat purchases are one of the ministry's success metrics. The newspaper articles that document these purchases often note that this wheat is destined for use in the production of subsidized bread. This draws a link between the far-from-food-like wheat in question—grain held in a warehouse or in the hold of a cargo ship—and the food it will one day become. It reminds readers that they, the citizens, are the ultimate beneficiaries of this government expenditure.

The government's subsidized bread program requires 800,000 tons of 82 percent extraction flour per month.[4] This program is contingent, therefore, on procurement driving that quantity of grain from field to silo to mill to bakery. The role of the government is to supply the privately owned bakeries that produce baladi bread with the flour that they need.[5] In the two or three months following the Egyptian harvest, most of the grain sent to the mills producing 82 percent extraction flour comes from wheat procured domestically. For the remainder of the year, the production of baladi bread depends on imported foreign wheat, at an annual budgetary cost of around $1.5 billion.[6]

To understand the nature of international procurement as a practice requires a look at the dynamics of the global grain trade.

In May 2017 I attended the Global Grain Middle East conference, an annual meeting that brings together grain traders, buyers, and brokers who have an interest in the Middle East region. Held in a five-star hotel on the outskirts of Dubai, the conference comprised a series of workshops, presentations, and panel discussions, interspersed with coffee breaks for networking over platters of dainty sandwiches and miniature pastries. As I sat listening for three days in various meeting rooms, sponsor-embossed notepads in front of me, I gained a crash course in grain as a global object. The acronyms flowed around me—CIF, FOB, SRW, HRW—so much a part of the everyday worlds of the conference participants that they required no explanation.[7] Bears and bulls, calls and puts, long and short came up in each conversation, the lexicon of the grain trade. Business cards exchanged hands, my university affiliation eliciting slightly baffled looks. In spaces like these conference rooms, wheat is abstracted from its earthly origins, captured in figures of thousands of tons, its movement across borders and between different storage sites mediated by the vagaries of another set of figures—those of currencies and exchange rates.

In one presentation by a vice president from a Fortune 500 financial services company, the speaker used Egypt as an example to illustrate a core concept—the distinction between the physical market and the futures market. The graph on his PowerPoint slide showed the difference between the price at which the Egyptian government procures foreign wheat and the price on the MATIF futures exchange, based in France (figure 3.1). "In July," the Irish analyst explained, gesturing to the beginning of the lines, "this is when Egyptians buy the cheapest wheat." At this point, Egyptians pay a price close to or even slightly under the MATIF price. Following the upward trending lines, he continued, "Then, very consistently, after harvest you have a window of pressure. Suddenly sellers keep stepping back and they [Egyptians] have to pay a bit more." Like many of those I observed talking through graphs of price data, his speaking took on a patter style that reminded me of how weather forecasters talk. "That usually persists until November or December. [*The day will start sunny . . .*] Then things can evolve a few different ways. [*But as the day moves on . . .*] Typically, after a while the producer countries start freaking out. [*We'll have some patches of cloud . . .*] They still have lots in their stores, so start selling more. [*Then some late afternoon storms . . .*]" He pointed toward the midpoint of the graph, where—with the exception of the one for the current year—the lines mostly started to fall. Gesturing toward this plateauing line, the presenter explained, "As for Europe, we don't have a buffer stock like last year, a big carryover. We're

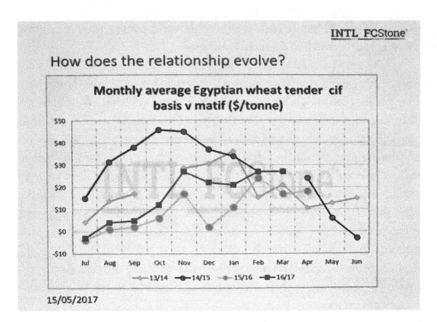

How does the relationship evolve?

Monthly average Egyptian wheat tender cif basis v matif ($/tonne)

15/05/2017

FIGURE 3.1. Egyptian wheat purchases in a regional grain trading meeting presentation. Photograph by the author.

not getting so involved in the game, because we don't have much wheat. That's why it's still quite expensive for Egyptians to get wheat."

The presenter's words captured the variability in the price that Egypt pays for wheat over the course of the year and how that is tied to the temporality of harvests in far-removed countries and the quantities of grain in those countries' silos. Egypt's buying price is determined through a tendering process, which GASC holds roughly every ten to twelve days between July and February—the period during which it is not focused on procuring domestic wheat. First, GASC issues a tender document, which lays out the quantity and quality of wheat that it wants to purchase for delivery during a particular period, generally around six weeks later. Then, global trading houses with operations in Egypt and regional commodity trading firms respond with offers. Based on these offers, which must include both an FOB price—meaning "free on board," or the cost of the wheat not including the delivery—and a separate cost for freight, GASC officials select the winning bid. These deliberations take place behind the closed doors of the ministry offices in Cairo, an imposing edifice on one of the main streets leading to Tahrir Square, to which traders must deliver their bids in sealed envelopes. The news filters out through the financial media, however, as officials from GASC pass information to

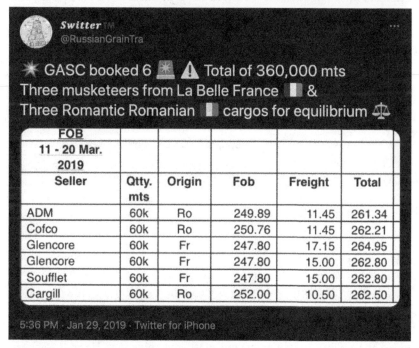

FIGURE 3.2. Egyptian wheat purchases on Twitter.

journalists from business news agencies and as traders post their own up-
dates on social media.

Take, for example, a series of tweets from the director of an international
commodities trading firm based in Switzerland. This man tweets about a number of countries' grain tenders; GASC, as the world's largest single purchaser
of wheat, is a regular feature in his Twitter feed. One set of tweets begins on
January 28, 2019, with an explosion emoji (figure 3.2): "GASC in [*sic*] back in the
market for wheat tomorrow March 11–20th delivery," he writes. Early the next
morning, his narration of the process begins with another explosion emoji and

two tables of data showing the "GASC LINE UP"—the thirteen offers that have been submitted on paper to the GASC offices in Cairo that morning. One table contains the quantity (55,000–60,000 tons), country of origin (United States, France, Romania, and Russia), port of origin, and FOB price. The other table shows the associated shipping costs. This is the starting point of the contest.

An hour later, he tweets the next development. This one is titled, "GASC 'landed' LINE UP." The attached table gives the total price of each wheat shipment including shipping costs. The list of potential offers has by this point been whittled down to seven, the higher freight costs from certain ports making some shipments uncompetitive. The tweeter notes his opinion: "It'll be Romania for sure. Probably 2 cargoes . . . Maybe 1 or 2 from France?" Each country's name is accompanied by the corresponding flag emoji. He concludes: "RUSSIA NO LONGER COMPETITIVE," followed by a surprised and then a sad emoji face. Given that he specializes in trading Russian grain, his disappointment at the Russian wheat losing out is not surprising.

A few hours later, he gives an update: "GASC to buy 5 vessels? 3 x Romania, 2 x France. Haggling is ongoing . . . Results soon!" I am on the edge of my seat. Luckily, I do not have to wait long. Seventeen minutes later, he gives an update: "GASC BOOKS FIVE," he writes, "3 Romania, 2 France. The Famous Five adventures . . ." He then lists the five trading firms that will be supplying the grain.

It seems like the end of the road, but no. Thirty minutes later another tweet arrives: "BREAKING NEWS," with a triangular warning sign emoji. "GASC update," he tweets, with three explosion emojis. "It's not over. It might be 5 . . . or it might be 6!" He then lists the prices for all the shipments except one, noting, "Cargill still negotiating Romanian flag price it seems."

The finale comes an hour later: "GASC booked 6" (figure 3.2). This is followed by a police car light emoji and another warning sign. He adds some poetry to his final summary, "Three musketeers from La Belle France & Three Romantic Romanian cargos for equilibrium," and finishes with a balanced scales emoji. Below that, he copies a table giving the final prices paid and the trading companies that will be delivering each cargo at some point between March 11 and March 20. The tweeter does not add up the total cost of the day's transaction, for it is of little concern to him, but it comes to $94.6 million for 360,000 tons of wheat. He also does not convert that wheat into loaves of bread—enough for roughly two weeks of baladi bread production—for that, too, is of little concern to him. Grain traders may be critical to staple security, but the staple food is not their focus of interest.

In this tweeted account of Egypt's wheat tendering process, price features prominently. This is due in part to the audience to whom this trader is speaking. Such are the size of GASC's imports that they have a strong influence on price formation in the regions from which Egypt sources most of its wheat. The price GASC pays for its wheat is thus of interest to the broader grain-trading community. The tender process acts like a "public noticeboard," providing insight into what constitutes a competitively priced offer from traders selling wheat from one of the world's major exporting regions—the Black Sea (Heigermoser, Götz, and Svanidze 2018). Egypt is in the powerful position of being able to shape global markets. "The whole world waits for Egypt's request, and it determines the price," one Egyptian who works in development said to me—the notion of the "whole world" waiting on you having a satisfying ring to it. Yet at the same time, the size of Egypt's wheat imports and its degree of reliance on imported wheat is widely understood as being a source of vulnerability.

Vulnerabilities

One day in May 2015, I sat in Leila's living room, chatting over a cup of tea. Leila is in her late twenties and is married to the youngest son of the extended family that I used to live next to in Warda. We were talking about baking bread and farming wheat. Our conversation centered on elements of Leila's day-to-day experience, such as whether she finds making bread for her family to be hard work and the price at which farmers in the village sold their wheat that year, rather than on national-level issues. So I was slightly surprised when Leila paused and then commented, "You know, Egypt has to import wheat." It was clear from her tone that she did not see this as being a good thing. She went on to suggest that Egypt should reclaim more desert land and use it for growing wheat. "Then," she said, "we would produce enough wheat for ourselves." That Leila would mention this to me is revealing. Leila is smart, curious about life beyond her village, and often talks about things going on in the news; unlike the other women in the household, she has the benefit of literacy and having been able to complete her schooling. But her world is far removed from that of grain policy making in Cairo, a city she has never visited. Nonetheless, she has an opinion on this policy. It matters to her that Egypt is not self-reliant; to her, it is a marker of national weakness. Leila's position reflects the pervasiveness of the anxiety about the foreign source of much of Egypt's grain.[8]

This perceived vulnerability is evident in the media, where concerns over Egypt's reliance on imported wheat are a common topic of discussion. "He who does not own his food does not own his freedom," noted one commentator in the opposition newspaper, *Al-Wafd*.[9] Another journalist expressed dismay at how Egypt has to go "begging for a loaf of bread from Russia a bit, and from America a bit." In translating wheat imports into loaves of bread, the writer sought to bring this issue home to readers.[10] To this journalist, such reliance means that Egyptians have to "live in fear and oppression, subject to the whims of these powers, either of which could decide not to cooperate on wheat deals." There is also the uncertainty over quality. "Often we have received bad wheat," the journalist added.[11]

This sense of vulnerability is underpinned by a concern over what would happen if Egypt did not have sufficient foreign exchange to import wheat. Such a crisis point could be produced by a shortage in the government's foreign currency reserves, since the government needs dollars to buy foreign wheat. This has been a problem in the past, for instance in the 1980s, when the drop in oil prices led to declining oil revenues and remittances from migrants working in oil-rich Gulf countries.[12] In 1988, the FAO representative in Egypt noted, "Egypt is facing a critical situation in that its consumption of major food commodities such as wheat . . . significantly exceeds the domestic supply. . . . With a shortfall of hard currency earnings, the importation of these food commodity items is putting a heavy burden on the budget and the balance of payments and is causing a great deal of concern to the Government."[13] This is also an issue in the present. Indeed, several times during 2018, the government had to delay its payments for wheat shipments due to a lack of dollars.[14]

The other dynamic that could produce such a crisis point would be a dramatic increase in prices, like that seen during the global food crisis in 2007 and 2008, when international wheat prices doubled (Headey 2010).[15] During this period, the government had to increase its budget for the baladi bread program significantly (from 3.8 billion EGP in 2006–7 to 9 billion EGP in 2007–8) to cover the cost of the more expensive imported wheat.[16] In one conversation I had back in 2008, a woman who worked for an international development agency talked about how there was a "very big concern at the policy level with the issue of the food price crisis." Newspapers at that time carried stories about the price increases and their impacts on the government's import bill and on food costs for the poor.[17] When wheat prices rose again in 2010, these concerns resurfaced. Economists warned that the high bill for imported wheat would impact the national economy. Officials issued assurances that the government had raised the necessary funds to cover these costs and to ensure that there would not be any shortages.[18]

A decade on, conducting interviews at a time when international wheat prices and GASC tender prices had returned to lower levels, I found this sense of vulnerability still to be a prevalent theme. "Egypt is the largest importer of wheat, which makes it vulnerable to the shocks of the market," commented one man who works for a foreign embassy and is involved in several agricultural projects. Similar statements, regarding Egypt's superlative status as the world's largest wheat importer and the related risks, recurred in many of my conversations. Through this lens, a dominant position in a global market is associated not so much with power as with weakness.

Some interviewees couched the threat in relation to historical moments when Egypt's reliance on imported wheat proved a point of vulnerability. A few people referred back to the year 1966, for instance, when the United States suspended flows of PL480 subsidized wheat to Egypt due to political differences between Lyndon Johnson and Gamal Abdel Nasser (Burns 1985, Mitchell 2002). The sense of threat and Egypt's desire to move beyond a position of such vulnerability are evident in the archival records from this period. In a speech that President Nasser gave in 1966, for instance, he described America's actions as a "war of starvation," pledging to expend greater effort and savings so that the country could "stand on its own two feet and not fear sanctions from the United States or anyone else."[19] The following year, after some uncertainty over whether the PL480 deliveries would resume, Nasser withdrew Egypt's request for this wheat, explaining, "We are a people having dignity . . . so we preferred to rely on ourselves." He added, "We therefore need to save 60 million pounds in hard currency to buy wheat and get rid of all traces of economic pressure"— an addendum that illustrated the costs associated with securing the nation's supply.[20] Despite the bravado of Nasser's words, another report issued that same year noted that, due to the elimination of PL480 sales, high demand for wheat, and limited domestic production, grain stocks were almost absent and Egypt was living "from hand to mouth."[21]

Thus the fluctuating price of foreign wheat, availability of funds to pay for it, and possibility of political influences on trade flows combine to produce a threat to the continuity of Egypt's wheat supply. The Russian invasion of Ukraine in February 2022 brought Egypt's vulnerability into stark relief. The prime minister called a special cabinet meeting to plan for how this conflict between Egypt's two largest suppliers might impact grain imports or increase prices. Policy makers issued words of reassurance, but many Egyptians were still worried about whether a disruption to Egypt's wheat supply or rising grain prices could drive up the price of the bread on which they depend.[22]

There are also internal factors relating to how Egypt manages the importation process that threaten the continuity of Egypt's wheat supply. Since there is only one conduit for sourcing foreign wheat for the baladi bread program—the government's tendering process—the smooth operation of that process determines the reliability of the wheat supply. Any problems in the process, or risks that traders perceive may affect the delivery of their shipments, are factored into the cost of the wheat and, therefore, its affordability to GASC.

I talked about this one day with Ahmed, an Egyptian grain trade professional (introduced in chapter 1), when we met in a restaurant on the banks of the Nile. Over a lunch of grilled chicken, rice, and salad, served with white pita bread, Ahmed explained to me the complexity of Egypt's tender process and how it affects the price Egypt pays for wheat. He drew a comparison with Saudi Arabia, which is another major wheat purchaser. Whereas Saudi Arabia's tender document is two pages long, Egypt's document is twenty, containing multiple requirements and lengthy annexes. Traders factor each of these requirements into the price. Ahmed pointed at my glass of freshly squeezed orange juice as an example. "So you want orange juice," he said. "This is one price. You want it cold, it's a bit more. You want a straw, it's a bit more." The result is that Egypt pays much more for its wheat than many other countries.

Ahmed's words imply a level of inefficiency underlying the tendering process and the fact that it produces costlier wheat. Yet he understands that one of the reasons why GASC sets so many conditions is because of its concerns about quality (discussed in the next section). Referring, for instance, to the Egyptian government's strict quarantine regulations—one of the complications within the tender documents—Ahmed noted, "Saudi has no agriculture, so they're not afraid of diseases. But here we are relying a lot on agriculture." He recognizes, therefore, the potential security ramifications of contaminated wheat entering the country and wreaking havoc on domestic wheat cultivation. The problem is that, in seeking to secure safe foreign wheat, the government may undermine its ability to secure affordable foreign wheat.

Traders also play a role, mediating both how much and what kind of wheat flows into Egypt. While GASC could in theory purchase its wheat directly from foreign sellers, the size of its purchases and the associated logistics render this, in practice, unfeasible. The agency is hence reliant on the Egyptian and foreign traders who work for the global trading houses and regional commodity trading firms that operate in Egypt. Traders are more interested in making money than making sure there is no disruption in the supply of quality wheat to the baladi bread bakeries. The trader's attempt to resell a contaminated shipment of wheat on Craigslist in order to recoup losses, with which I began this chapter, is a case in point. Gamal, who formerly held a leadership position in the Ministry of Supply, told me about a trip he made to Kazakhstan, where he met with the chairman of a grain company that deals with Egyptian traders. He recounted how the Kazakh chairman said he would sometimes make agreements with Egyptian traders to sell, say, a ton of wheat for $300 but to record the price as $350/ton. The traders could then submit that paper to GASC and charge a higher price for the shipment. Often, the chairman added, this would be low-quality wheat. This story was Gamal's way of setting himself and his government apart from the traders. In Gamal's narrative, he and his colleagues are the upstanding ones, seeking high-quality wheat for the people's bread, whereas it is the traders who put Egypt's wheat supply at risk. Although the corruption case I discuss below raises questions about this portrayal of officials as moral guardians, it is a politically convenient framing of the beneficent state.

Ultimately, however, traders are in a powerful position. If they are unsatisfied with the government's terms, they can boycott GASC's tender process. Low trader participation in a tender means less competition and higher prices; no participation means a rupture in the country's wheat supply. Traders have used this influence at a number of times in the past to push for policy changes, such as a cap on port charges or lowered quality specifications, as I discuss later in this chapter.

While the government has little choice but to work through traders, it has various tactics for managing the vulnerability posed by its high reliance on imports. For instance, GASC keeps its expenditures as low as possible by typically selecting the cheapest tender offers. Freight costs play a big part here, often rendering wheat from the United States (which costs $28–30/ton to transport) uncompetitive compared to wheat from the closer Black Sea countries (from which transport costs only $10–12/ton). This is the reason why the US wheat fell out of the running in the tender narrated in the trader's Twitter feed, despite the fact that it had the lowest FOB price. It is also the reason why the United States has largely lost its share of the Egyptian market after having been the primary supplier for many years.[23]

But the government does not always buy the cheapest wheat. Any time it makes an alternative choice provides telling insight into government officials' strategic thinking. In November 2018, for instance, Egypt bought two shipments of American wheat—something it has rarely done in recent years. When I talked about this with Ahmed, he did not find this strange. "It was political," he said. On this occasion he told me that GASC "bought the first on the list [i.e., the cheapest offer], which was maybe Ukrainian, Russian, or Romanian—and the second, and then the fourth which was the US offer." I asked him why GASC would choose this more expensive American wheat. "For political reasons," he responded. He explained that GASC is keen to demonstrate to Russia and the other Black Sea countries that they should not take their position of dominance in the market for granted or assume that Egypt will always buy from them. Having multiple potential sources of imports is important so as to be resilient to shocks. In a telling juxtaposition, a leading government official stated in a newspaper interview, "Diversifying our sources of [wheat] imports is important, the same as it is with weapons."[24] It was just such diversification, for example, that allowed GASC to maintain its supply in 2010 when the government of Russia, one of Egypt's major suppliers, placed a ban on wheat exports due to a severe drought. Turning to France and the United States, GASC was able to source sufficient wheat to make up for the canceled Russian contracts, allowing it to continue to supply flour to the bakeries without disruption. It was also this diversification that a government spokesman drew on after the Russian invasion of Ukraine, reassuring the public that Egypt has 12 other countries from which it purchases wheat."[25]

The procurement of foreign wheat is therefore a key component of staple security at the national level; it is what enables the baladi bread program to continue. This practice is not only, however, about securing access to wheat but securing access to quality wheat.

Quality

In May 2015, I had coffee in Cairo with two young professionals involved in Egypt's nascent local foods movement. "Did you hear about the scandal surrounding the poor-quality wheat from Russia?" they asked me. I had not. Just that morning I had actually been reading some articles about the superior quality of Russian wheat and how its high gluten levels make it ideal for bread making. These two people were not, however, thinking about quality in terms of protein content. They were thinking about quality in terms of potential foes like funguses, insects, and carcinogens that could be harmful to people's health. They were scanty on the details as they talked about a recent case and about another a few years prior, but they were clear on their association of Russian wheat with scandal. It was evident that, to them, there is something risky about Russian wheat.

Popular anxieties about bad wheat underscore the deep threat posed by bread that might make you sick.[26] Given that bread is a food that most Egyptians eat three times a day, every day of the year, this concern is not surprising. Egyptian newspapers across the political spectrum fuel this sense of threat with regular articles reporting the seizure of "bad wheat" (qamh fasid) from various places around the country, a few thousand tons here, several tens of thousands there. This is wheat not fit for human consumption, full of worms, infected by funguses, mixed with dust and gravel, or littered with dead insects. The heroes of these stories are the investigative authorities who find such wheat, foil egregious attempts to sell it, and prosecute guilty parties (the possibility of bad wheat slipping through unnoticed—as with the bunt-infected grain on Craigslist—is not mentioned). Yet while the tenor of these articles is in part celebratory—a testament to the rigor of the government's investigative procedures—they are also an unsettling reminder of the mixed quality of wheat circulating through Egypt.

Some of the bad wheat in question is domestic in origin, linked in part to quality problems that emerge in storage, as I discuss in greater detail below. But there is particularly heightened anxiety around imported wheat. One newspaper article referred to shipments arriving at Egyptian ports as carrying "what are really the worst kinds of wheat in the world, only fit for animals"—a charge designed to generate outrage since those consuming this wheat will not be animals but the Egyptian people.[27] This sense of imported wheat as bad permeates a number of domains. Many Egyptian doctors, for example, see imported wheat as a "toxic vector" (Hamdy 2012: 182). To these medical professionals, the problem comes not from the quality of the foreign wheat per se, but from the aflatoxins and ochratoxins (linked to liver and renal carcinomas) that can grow in the wheat as it sits in ports in hot and humid weather. Although such toxins could also develop in storage facilities holding domestically produced wheat, in many doctors' minds, this is a problem associated with foreign wheat alone.

Concerns about imported wheat are underpinned by the prevalent sense that locally produced agricultural products are superior. When the government procures locally grown wheat, inspectors grade each delivery according to the Egyptian measure of purity, the qirat. This measure is based on a scale with a maximum grade of 24, and the government only accepts wheat if its purity is 22.5 qirat (94 percent) or higher.[28] They also check that the wheat is free from insect infestation, sand, and stones. Yet beyond those directly involved in the procurement process, few people know about these quality controls. The common valuation of domestic over foreign wheat hence lies less in this bureaucratic procedure and more in a sense of value ascribed to its origins, coming from Egypt's land and cultivated by Egyptian farmers.[29] One journalist contrasted, for instance, "imported wheat of the worst kinds" with "Egyptian wheat grown on good soil."[30]

Despite popular concerns, imported wheat is subject to strict regulations, and the government only buys from countries that it believes meet its quality expectations. These quality standards cover a range of parameters (table 3.1). When grain traders talk about grain quality, they typically talk in terms of protein levels: the higher the protein, the higher the quality, based on an assumption that wheat will be used for bread and thus that a strong network of proteins is needed to help the bread rise and maintain its shape.[31] For other people, different quality parameters on the list might seem more pressing. Some of these quality criteria, such as the limit on pesticide residues and the absence of rodents, are established with human health concerns in mind. Others, such as those related to various fungal contaminants, are intended to protect Egyptian agriculture (and in some cases, human health as well).

TABLE 3.1
GASC Tender Specifications

Moisture level of 13 percent or less
Falling number (a measure of sprout damage) of 200
Limit on impurities of 0.5 percent
Minimum protein content of 10–12 percent
Specific weight of less than 76 kg per hectoliter
Safe for human consumption and free of unpleasant odors and tastes
Meets international limits on pesticide residues, ergot, mycotoxins, and heavy metals
Defects amount to <5 percent of the weight, with the following specific limits: grain admixture <1.5 percent of weight; dead insects <1 percent of weight; damaged grains <4 percent of weight
Free of live insects and dead rodents; if two insects found within 1 kg sample, fumigation required
Other organic materials less than 5 percent of the weight

Source: McGill et al. 2015: 79

Nonetheless, there is a politics to the enforcement of these regulations—as can be discerned in the circumstances of the Craigslist posting—and to their setting in the first place. These quality standards are not just about the needs of the subsidized bread program or the safety of the wheat that Egyptians eat. They are also economic decisions about what wheat the government is willing to buy. Quality characteristics factor into price, and sometimes economic imperatives eclipse quality concerns. In February 2018, for instance, GASC reduced its protein requirements to allow lower-cost wheat to be imported.[32] Thus, as GASC assesses grain shipments, it works to balance concerns about the quality of the wheat with its need to provide the quantities demanded by the government.

Hence the many actors who play a role in delivering a continuous supply of bread to the Egyptian people are driven by a range of motivations. Grain inspectors think about wheat in a different way from those charged with ensuring that the baladi bread bakeries always have sufficient flour, whose priorities in turn differ from those of the traders who coordinate shipments of foreign wheat to Egypt's ports. The tensions that can arise as a result are illustrated by a recent controversy over ergot, a fungus found in imported wheat.

Ergot

In December 2015, Egyptian inspectors turned away a 63,000-ton shipment of French wheat from the port of Damietta. The wheat had been purchased by GASC from Bunge, one of the world's largest grain trading companies. The reason for the rejection was the wheat's contamination with the ergot fungus.

Although ergot is quite common throughout the world, it is highly toxic to both humans and animals and can cause severe health problems, even death. The shipment had already been checked and approved, though, by Egyptian inspectors at the French port before it set sail. Moreover, according to the trader, it met international safety guidelines, containing only a relatively small amount of ergot. Nonetheless, Egypt maintained that it would not accept wheat with any ergot in it at all. The ship turned around, eventually delivering its cargo to a client in Spain for use as livestock feed.

The case sent shockwaves through the global wheat industry. Egypt was demanding a quality of wheat that few of the world's major wheat exporters would be able to meet, a position that had major ramifications given Egypt's prominence as a buyer on international wheat markets. Indeed, two years later, when I attended the Middle East Grain conference in Dubai, Egypt's quality regulations were a topic of discussion. The opening presentation began with the conference chairman encouraging people to their seats by projecting a picture of Kate Moss—scantily clad in a short denim skirt and sleeveless top, draped over silver convertible—and saying with a smirk: "Why is everyone still drinking coffee? Will this get them to come in?" The audience, almost entirely male, chuckled quietly as the presenter continued to his overview of the previous year and outlook for the next. One of the five key trends he identified going forward concerned Egypt, his slide noting that "Egypt could come up with specific quality requirements which will bring the desired Volatility in the Wheat complex." Quite apart from his assumption, as someone who makes money off global trade flows, that volatility is a good thing, the presenter's focus reflected how Egypt's quality standards resonate across these disparate spaces of the global wheat industry. As he talked through the slide, he explained, "Egypt has been fluttering around and trying to work out what to do about quality." His use of the word *fluttering* implied that the attention to quality among Egyptian officials was somehow trivial—a suggestion I return to later. He concluded with a statement of uncertainty: "We'll have to see how they start to think of quality parameters." He did not talk specifically about ergot, but it was the elephant in the room.

Ergot is caused by the fungus *Claviceps purpurea*, which can affect a number of grains, including wheat.[33] The fungus is found in many countries around the world and thrives in wet, cool climates. When the fungal mycelia harden on a plant they form what are known as sclerotia. Ergot sclerotia contain significant quantities of toxic compounds called alkaloids. Long-term or high-level exposure to these toxins results in a potentially fatal condition, ergotism, which causes either gangrene or convulsions. In the past, the impacts of ergot poisoning were horrific. Today, severe outbreaks of ergotism are much less common, not due to a decline in the prevalence of the fungus but to an increase in practices designed to identify and remove ergot sclerotia at various points in the production process.

One of the striking things in the ergot controversy was the contrasting viewpoints on quality and safety that it elicited.[34] There were notable distinctions, for example, in how Egypt's rejection of the French wheat, and the subsequent ergot crisis, were framed within the widespread media coverage. In English-language international news sources, like Reuters or Bloomberg, the term *ergot* typically appeared followed by the subclause, "a common fungus found in grains." In this phrasing, the elaboration after the comma emphasizes the pervasiveness of the fungus, the frequency of its occurrence, and the fact that it affects multiple kinds of grain. Climatic differences that influence how common that fungus is—the fact that it is more likely to infect wheat grown in France, the United States, or Romania, for example, than wheat grown in Egypt—are erased in a simple characterization of commonality. Although these news stories often went on to mention the potential health impacts of ergot poisoning, introducing ergot in this way acted to normalize, or undermine the sensationalism and sense of threat. Through such a lens, Egyptian inspectors were being unnecessarily anxious—a judgment resonating with a longstanding North-South dynamic in which the Global South is rendered irrational in contrast to the dispassionate expertise of the North (Escobar 1994, Bergeron 2005).

In the Arabic-language media coverage, by contrast, the emphasis tended to be on the severity of the potential health impacts. In one headline in the independent newspaper *Al-Badil*, for example, the clarifying subclause attached to the ergot fungus was: "which causes cancer and miscarriage."[35] The reference to miscarriage points to the uterine contractions that can result from ingestion of ergot toxins. The reference to cancer is not a link I have read about in English-language texts, but is not surprising given the symbolic valence of cancer in Egypt. In everyday conversation, cancer often appears as a catchall for something that is impure or bad for the health. Polluted water, bad seeds, or poor-quality wheat, for instance, may all be talked about as cancer-causing. Similarly, in the Egyptian press ergot is often accompanied by the adjective *cancerous* (al-argot al-musartan). In such wording, what comes to the fore is the danger.

For the inspectors who work to mediate what wheat enters Egypt through its ports, the line between danger and safety crystallizes in a percentage figure. What proportion of grain contamination with the ergot fungus is safe? Under the Codex Alimentarius, a set of internationally adopted food safety standards, 0.05 percent is the key threshold—the maximum level of ergot contamination that is deemed not to pose a health risk.[36] I asked Ahmed, an Egyptian who works in the grain trade, to explain this threshold to me during one of our con-

versations. I was wondering whether it related to the ease of removing a relatively small amount of sclerotia, or to the fact that at a low concentration the
toxins they contain are considered unproblematic. It was clear from his response
that he did not really know. His faith in the threshold came from his faith in
the process rather than his understanding of how it mitigated the danger posed
by sclerotia. "It's an international standard," he said, "scientists have studied it!"
He went on to explain the origins of this figure. "To come up with tolerances,
they [unspecified experts] study it and do a risk assessment. It's a long process. If
somebody did the research you don't have to reinvent the wheel. It's the Codex
Alimentarius!" To him the procedures of international risk assessment, the science, and the unnamed experts render no further questions necessary.

Back in 2015, however, the quarantine inspectors working at the port of
Damietta took a different stance. They turned away the shipment of French
wheat, despite the trader's insistence that it met the standards of the Codex
Alimentarius. Whether or not this was in fact the case (GASC officials maintained that the contamination level exceeded 0.05 percent) was immaterial,
for the inspectors took this opportunity to call for a more stringent, zero-
tolerance position. They were, in other words, not only rejecting the grain but
rejecting an international guideline. Reversing the common dynamic of the
Global South as dumping ground for the North's detritus, Egyptian inspectors
were seeking to forestall contamination from the North. They were deploying
the tolerance level as a security device.

The rationale that the inspectors gave for their actions was nationalistic in
tone. This was an effort to protect Egypt's crops and people. Egyptian farmers
do not, at present, have a problem with ergot. Agricultural officials are worried
that imported grain carrying ergot could inadvertently contaminate Egyptian
fields—were, for instance, any ergot-infected grain to fall from the trucks that
carry it around the country and to implant in the soil. As the head of the Quarantine Authority said in a newspaper interview, "I am obliged to do this [to call
for zero tolerance] as it would be very harmful if any level of contamination
reached plants in Egypt."[37] There are also concerns about potential impacts on
human health. As one member of parliament stated, "Wheat contamination is a
national security issue, because it affects the health of large numbers of citizens
and can lead to permanent disability or death."[38] The severity of the threat is tied
to bread's staple identity and its high levels of consumption. In one article, for
instance, a professor of agriculture at Cairo University made his case for zero
tolerance on ergot by drawing a comparison between "the Egyptian citizen,"
who eats 182 kg of bread a year, and "the European citizen," who consumes
only 60 kg, concluding that "the rate of damage that the Egyptian citizen is

liable to is very dangerous and not comparable to the levels consumed by other populations."[39]

This sense of a national threat circulated widely. As one journalist commented to me, "You'll see in *Al-Ahram*, the state newspaper, there's lots of stories about the need to protect the population from toxic stuff." He added, "This is how ergot was talked about in talk shows also," referencing the medium that reaches a broader audience than newspapers. Such was the political sensitivity of this matter that the Ministry of Agriculture issued a statement confirming that "not a single wheat grain infected with ergot has entered Egypt so far"—a statement that would be difficult to verify but which was obviously designed to alleviate concerns and assert the government's control over the matter.[40]

However, the grain traders—some of whom are Egyptian, others foreign—pushed back, stating that the government's strict quarantine regulations were unfeasible. "No country anywhere in the world can provide wheat with zero ergot in bulk volume," commented one European trader.[41] To the traders, the government's quality expectations were unrealistically high. To move toward a resolution, the government launched an investigation into the risks that ergot posed to wheat cultivation in Egypt. (There was no similar investigation of the risks ergot posed to bread eaters in Egypt, which is notable given that several political leaders drew on these concerns in their public statements.) To conduct the study, the agricultural ministry commissioned an international expert—referred to only as "al-khabira," the (female) expert—from the Food and Agricultural Organization of the United Nations (FAO). The study, written in English, was never made public, but the ministry released a single-page summary, translated into Arabic, to the media. The summary presented the report's conclusion—that ergot poses no threat to Egyptian agriculture—but gave few details as to how that conclusion had been reached. This was a politically convenient result, for while government officials might have expressed public concern about ergot, they still had to find wheat somewhere. They were well aware that the stricter their regulations, the more limited their potential sources, and they were wary of compromising their supply. When the results of the FAO study were published, in July 2016, the Quarantine Authority backtracked and said that, in light of the report's findings, it would accept wheat with up to 0.05 percent ergot.

Meanwhile, though, experts within the ministry's Agricultural Research Center were conducting their own study. This report, too, was kept from public release. A copy was posted, though, on a Facebook site called al-Mawaqif al-Masri (The Egyptian Position), an anonymous site that seeks to "help in shaping opinion change with the assistance of experts."[42] The eight-page report in Arabic was authored by ten specialists in the research institute. It was a critique not only of the science in the FAO report but of their perceived marginalization in the process of its preparation. They began by criticizing the FAO report for not being a "real, proven, scientific" (haqiqa ʿilmiya thabita) study, and described their dissatisfaction with having met with the FAO expert but then receiving no further communications or access to the full report. They questioned the central foundation of the FAO report's argument, presumably based on the parts of it that they were given access to. The expert's judgment that ergot poses no threat was predicated on an assumption that Egypt's climate is too warm, since the fungus needs a twenty-five-day cooling period, with temperatures between zero and ten degrees Celsius, to germinate. The specialists from the research institute challenged this assumption, citing five studies which found that ergot can still germinate without a cooling period. They concluded that Egypt's temperatures "are suitable for germination and completion of the life cycle of the fungus" and reasserted that Egypt should not "permit any percentage of this dangerous disease to enter Egypt with imported wheat."

When this study was published, in August 2016, the Quarantine Authority reinstated its total ban on ergot, and GASC changed its tender documents to specify the zero-tolerance level. As a result, two further shipments—from Romania and Russia—were rejected for ergot contamination. The response from the grain traders was swift. They boycotted the government's tenders, refusing to sell wheat to Egypt under these terms. Ultimately, it was this threat to Egypt's wheat supply that led the government to reverse its stance, reinstating once again the 0.05 percent tolerance level for ergot. As Ahmed explained to me, the government decided to conform with the international standard in the end "because anything different from this will make problems with the supply." In his view, the government's attempt at a more rigid stance on ergot came at a price: "It cost the country money and reputation. It made Egypt seem risky." The government's decision to return to the international standard for ergot was a clear indication of how quality standards are shaped both by the assessment of risks and by the imperative to secure the continual supply of a good.

This case drew attention to the role of the inspectors who are charged with determining whether or not a shipment of grain meets the government's standards.[43] These inspectors carry the responsibility for the health of the Egyptian people and fields on their shoulders, but they are also individuals trying to build lives for their families on low government salaries. In the case of the initial rejected French shipment, one of the things that made the trader, Bunge, so outraged was the fact that Egyptian inspectors had already approved the grain at a port in France, before the ship set sail. The government's standard practice at this time was to send a team of inspectors to test the wheat at the port of origin before the cargo departed for Egypt. Yet the inspection trips also created opportunities for kickbacks. One journalist I interviewed explained, "That's how they [the inspectors] would make money. They'd force the trading company to wine and dine them, maybe take a bribe if there was any issue [with the cargo]. In some countries, they'll even get prostitutes." According to news reports, each inspector would typically get $3,500 in "pocket money" from the trading firms.[44] Wheat, for these inspectors, was not flour for subsidized bread but a source of upward mobility.

In the aftermath of the ergot crisis, the government stopped sending inspectors overseas to examine shipments at their ports of origin, relying instead on international inspection companies. When it reinstated its policy of Egyptian inspectors carrying out preshipment inspections in 2019, the regulations it set in place were noteworthy. The ministerial decree stated that for an inspector to participate in an inspection trip, "There must be no evidence that the candidate has previously misused the authority of Plant Quarantine through abuse of power for personal gain." It added that "any offence against honor and integrity" is reason for disqualification.[45]

While the specific standards for imported wheat have receded as a matter of controversy, political tensions over the inspection process remain. During a meeting between government representatives and private traders facilitated by the FAO in 2018, the chairman of the Egyptian Grain Traders Association explained that, from the point of view of the traders, the problem is not so much the quality requirements but the sampling process. "We can all agree about the specification and the limits," he said, "but the name of the game is the sample that goes to the lab. The sampling process is extremely, extremely important." He continued, "The transparency, of course, in all those things, starting at the sampling through to the analysis—the transparency has to be there."[46]

This was also an issue when ergot returned to the news in 2018. In May 2018, quarantine officials found a 63,000-ton shipment of Russian wheat to contain 0.06 percent ergot, just exceeding the 0.05 percent limit, and announced that the shipment would be rejected.[47] Russia responded with a swift denial and sent a delegation from its agricultural safety administration to Egypt. Following further testing of samples in Cairo, quarantine officials revised their claims, announcing that the levels were within acceptable limits, and the wheat was released into the country.[48] This struck me as curious. Was the change in decision actually related to new testing results? Or pressure exerted by the Russian delegation? Or GASC's imperative to source grain, especially given that three of its other shipments were at that time held up due to a dispute with a trader?

I questioned Ahmed about this when I talked to him later that year. "Why did the government change its mind?" I asked. He smiled, correcting me. "They didn't change their mind, they re-tested it!" He spoke with conviction. Yet his subsequent statement undermined the apparent neutrality of the testing process. "The problem is that some inspectors are stricter." Assuming the position of a trader, he continued, "You know that if you are sending a shipment to Safaga you may have problems [because the inspectors there are more rigorous], but not so much to Damietta or Alexandria." There is, therefore, a political layer to the mediating of grain quality at the ports.

The following year, in 2019, the same thing happened. Inspectors rejected a French shipment of wheat, which they had found to contain 0.1 percent ergot. The trader requested a retest; this time, the results indicated a level of 0.01 percent and the shipment was accepted.[49] Testing is hence a key gatekeeping process that determines what wheat enters Egypt. Inspectors and traders are important intermediaries in the circulation of wheat, playing a role not only in the assessment of quality but the production of quality.[50]

All the same, quality concerns do not come to an end once the wheat arrives in the country. The quality of wheat may change during the process of conveyance, just as the quality of bread does (chapter 4). This is one reason why storage—a moment of pause during the act of conveyance—becomes an important consideration for staple security. I turn now to consider these practices of storing both domestic and foreign wheat.

Storage

It is the end of May in a village. A threshing machine hums in a field as a laborer feeds in sheaves of wheat. The farmer holds open a sack to catch the grain that comes out of the outlet tube. When the sack is full, he secures it tightly shut with a tie. This is the beginning of the grain's life detached from the plant. When all the sheaves are threshed, there are thirty 50-kg sacks lined up in the field. The farmer loads the sacks of grain into a rented pickup. Back at home, he unloads the truck and piles the sacks in his hallway. He opens eighteen of the sacks and adds a chemical treatment, which he refers to as a "pill" (birsham). These sacks hold sufficient grain for the year-round bread needs of his family of six. He reseals the sacks and leaves them in a closed, darkened room for several days. He says that the fumigation treatment should ward off insects, mice, and other critters, allowing the grain to last for a year or so. He then piles the sacks in an alcove under the stairway. Here the grain stays, protected under the roof of the house and by the treatment, until the farmer's wife opens a sack and scoops some grain to take to the village mill to be ground into flour for homemade bread (chapter 5). This is the first place where Egyptian-grown grain comes to rest, at this point still closely linked to the fields in which it was grown and the hands that harvested it.

A short drive away, grain is also sitting in sacks. These sacks are not within the domestic space of a home, though, but in a large open area, stacked on a dirt floor. This is a storage site known as a shona. The sacks are piled on top of one another, some piles over fifteen feet high. This is the site to which the trader, who bought and collected the twelve remaining sacks from the farmer, delivers the grain. As the shona operator piles these twelve sacks on top of similar-looking unlabeled sacks purchased from other farmers, the link between grain and field is severed, the farmer's grain becoming part of a larger entity. The shonas are managed by the Principal Bank of Development and Agricultural Credit, which is one of the government agencies that procures domestic wheat. The piles of grain peak at this time of year. Over the coming months, gaps will be etched in the profile of the grain mountain as the sacks are gradually transported to silos for further storage or to mills for transformation into flour. Six months from now, the space will be empty.

Two hundred miles to the north, at the port of Damietta, a gleaming silver silo stands close to the berths where the bulk carriers dock. When the ships begin to arrive in a month or so, it will be filled with the GASC's wheat imports. Here the grain is stored in bulk rather than in individual sacks, accumulating in a tall vertical structure made of steel. Operated by two government agencies—the General Company for Silos and Storage and the Egyptian Holding Company for Silos and Storage—these are public silos.[51] The silos located at ports act as "buffer bins"; they are places where traders can swiftly unload their imported grain and thus minimize costly demurrage charges. The grain does not stay long. Soon, it will be transported on to one of the inland silos for storage, carried by truck or possibly by train or barge. At the inland silos, the imported grain is mixed with domestic grain, which by this point has been extracted from the sacks in which it was transported. Accumulated in the silo, the wheat is divorced from the Egyptian and foreign fields in which it was planted; the labor, varietal choice, and selected inputs that went into its production are erased in a mass of grain.[52] Here the grain is stored until it is taken to a mill to be processed into baladi (82 percent extraction) flour.

These three sites—farmer's house, shona, and silo—are key points in the grain's passage through Egypt. They are nodes where the grain comes to a temporary halt. Unevenly distributed throughout the country, these storage sites are concentrated in the most densely settled and cultivated lands of the Nile

Valley and Delta, but also scattered through the Western Desert in places of groundwater-based agriculture, and linked by a web of roads, as well as by some rail and river connections (map 3.1).[53] Trucks, railway cars, and barges play a vital role in moving wheat, but since transportation was not a prominent issue in my interviews with policy makers and grain experts, and I was unable to access these sites for direct observation, I focus here on the storage structures in which the grain comes to rest.

Farmers' homes do not feature on the government's map of storage infrastructure. Yet for farming households that grow wheat and bake bread, the grain they store plays an important role in securing their staple food, insulating them from fluctuations in the market price of flour. One day in March 2008, for example, while I was living in Warda, I was invited to lunch with a family in a nearby village. In front of their home, they had five large, mud-domed structures for storing wheat, each with a small hole at the base.[54] Ten months after harvesting their fields, three of the domes were empty, but two were still closed and full of grain. At a time when flour prices were increasing rapidly, these domes and their contents afforded this family the ability to produce their preferred homemade bread. It was a striking contrast to the many other families I talked with at this time who were struggling to afford the flour they needed to bake bread (see chapter 5).

Stored grain acts as a form of savings, bolstering a household's security in multiple ways. Take, for instance, the case of Salma, wife of the second son in my former neighboring household. Salma and her husband live with five of their seven children, one having left to work in Libya and another to get married. They are relatively poor, their only source of income coming from a small piece of land that Salma's husband farms. During my December 2016 visit, Salma showed me two sacks of wheat in the corner of her bedroom, the grain left over from their harvest seven months prior. In contrast with the domes of wheat storage that I had seen in the other farming household, Salma's two sacks did not seem very much. Clearly, she was unable to keep the three sacks (one ardab) of grain per person for year-round bread needs that other farmers in Warda typically store.[55] But when I asked her if it was enough (kifaya), she said yes. She then added, "If we need more, we can get subsidized flour from the bakery and mix it in and the bread comes out nicely." Whereas I had been thinking of "enough" as meaning an amount of wheat that would cover the year-round bread consumption of her household of seven, to Salma "enough" meant having some wheat in the house, so that it is not always necessary to buy flour to bake the kind of homemade bread that your household prefers. In addition, grain in storage is something of value that can be exchanged. Sometimes

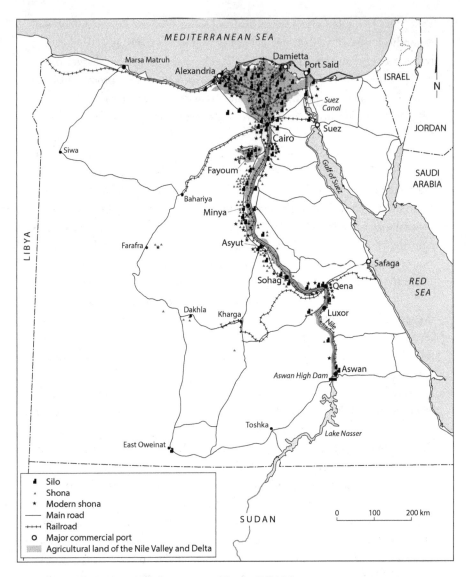

MAP 3.1. Grain storage infrastructure. Map by Bill Nelson.

FIGURE 3.3. Wheat in the home. Photograph by the author.

Salma swaps grain with her sisters-in-law in return for something else of use to her. Other times, Salma's husband will sell some grain if he needs cash during the year. Wheat may not generate big profits, but it has a consistent value and can help cover small expenses.

Sacks of grain in the living room bring peace of mind—the knowledge that a family will have good bread to eat in coming months (figure 3.3). People in rural households do not talk about this in terms of security, but this is the affective state produced by growing, harvesting, and saving grain—a temporary state achieved until a family eats through those stores and must plant the next crop. Grain stored in huge silos produces a similar affect, a sense of reassurance in the knowledge that immediate needs are covered, even if the threat of scarcity is still present. In the domain of national grain storage, however, the language of security is explicit.[56] Just as the government sees wheat as a strategic crop, it also talks about *strategic storage*, a term that indexes security as the framework for understanding the allocation of and interests in grain as a resource. Storage is a key part of the day-to-day functioning of the wheat supply chain, a vital precondition to the procurement of both domestic and foreign wheat: the government cannot buy wheat if it has nowhere to put it. Storage also breaks the link between demand and supply, buffering the country against fluctuations in international prices and problems in major wheat-producing countries like poor harvests or export bans. With an ability to store grain, the government has more freedom to buy when prices are good, rather than being forced to respond to immediate needs. There is a close link, therefore, between procurement and storage.

The policy of the Ministry of Supply is that it should have a five-month supply of wheat in storage at all times—that is, sufficient wheat to cover five months of baladi bread production. This includes wheat in the pipeline, which means foreign wheat that has been purchased through a GASC tender but has not yet been delivered. So at any given time, the government typically has around three months of wheat in the country's silos and shonas and another one to three months' supply on its way. Maintaining this reserve is a longstanding policy, although the exact number of months' supply that the government has deemed to constitute a strategic stock has changed over time.[57] When, for instance, the coronavirus pandemic hit in 2020, President al-Sisi instructed the government to bolster strategic reserves and maintain six months of wheat in storage, in case the pandemic led to disruptions in grain supply chains.[58]

To some non-Egyptian experts, the Egyptian government's policy to hold months of wheat in reserve makes little sense.[59] During a senior traders panel at the 2017 Global Grain Middle East conference, for instance, the moderator asked the panelists what they thought about strategic reserves. One panelist, head of trading for a large company, dismissed this method of "hoarding grain in large infrastructure" as "old-school." In his opinion, "The conversation has morphed into understanding the supply chain and what are the risks." Another panelist, a manager for a major grain trading house, said, "A strategic reserve doesn't have to be the amount of tons in silo. It can also be a matter of supply, how quickly it can come." In his view, it is all about trade—an unsurprising perspective from someone who makes his money on international flows of grain. "It's all fundamentally about connection to the world," he said. Over one of the coffee breaks, I followed up with him, asking his thoughts on Egypt's policy to keep grain in storage. "The government doesn't need strategic grain reserves," he responded, "Why have all that wheat in a silo?" To him, the strategy is illogical.

These traders' comments reflect their belief in the notion of supply chain security, a framework that has become predominant in managing global circulations of goods (Cowen 2014). Security, through this lens, is about protecting global supply chains, understanding linkages, anticipating potential disruptions, and taking measures to mitigate those threats. But although a global supply chain is responsible for bringing enough grain into Egypt to cover half the nation's consumption needs, staple security is about more than just protecting this supply chain. Egypt's ability to access wheat through global markets is not enough to reassure the Egyptian people; it does not address the affective domain of staple security. Full silos speak to the deep anxieties that many Egyptian officials and members of the public have about Egypt's wheat running out, in a way that measures for managing risk in global wheat markets do not.

During one conversation with an American development practitioner who has long worked in Egypt, we talked about the Egyptian newspapers' coverage of each act of wheat procurement by the government. "Have you noticed," he asked me, "how these reports are always accompanied by a statement 'and so our stocks are good for three months, or through month so and so?'" This recurrent framing is indeed notable. These headlines from the government-affiliated newspaper, *Al-Ahram*, are illustrative: "Supplied 4 Million Tons of Local Wheat, and the Reserve to Last until October" (May 23, 2015); "Purchasing 175,000 Tons of Russian Wheat, the Reserve to Last until Mid-February" (July 23, 2015); "Importing 240,000 Tons of Wheat and the Reserve to Last until April" (October 17, 2015).[60] After a while, the numbers and dates blur into each other, but the pattern is clear. The Ministry of Supply is communicating to the population that its stores of wheat are abundant and sufficient for the bread needs of the near future. As stated explicitly by the Minister of Supply in words captured in another headline from that year, "The strategic wheat reserves exceed the bounds of security."[61] Similarly, when in 2020 the coronavirus shook global wheat markets, Sisi gave a speech on television, reassuring the public that Egypt had "no issue" with its strategic reserves of wheat.[62]

Any indication that these stocks might be depleted is a source of popular disquiet. In response to reports early in 2015 that the stocks were running low,[63] for example, the left-leaning newspaper *Al-Badil* published an article with an attention-grabbing headline: "Strategic Store of Wheat Is Nearly Empty." The author critiqued the government for failing to ensure that it had stocks that could last at least three months. The article quoted a former advisor from the ministry as saying, "This is a catastrophe, because there has always been enough for at least 70 days, even during the 1973 war and other difficult times." The journalist concluded, "This means we have arrived at a point of imminent danger."[64]

The journalist's reference to former times of war is telling. The sense of a need for wheat in storage is embedded in these histories (just as the sense of risk surrounding reliance on imports, discussed above, is embedded in memories of past interruptions to those imports). In a conversation with one agricultural specialist who works for the FAO about the government's wheat policy, he reflected back to what had happened during the Gulf War. "At that time, there was only a twelve-day supply of wheat, and they [the Egyptians] needed to import." It was this imperative, he thinks, that drove the government's subsequent actions. "When Saddam invaded Kuwait, Egypt had to make a decision about what to do. A key factor was the twelve-day [wheat] supply. They needed a shipment from outside." In his account, this absence of wheat in storage was the reason Egypt aligned with the international community against Saddam Hussein.

Hence the threat surrounding the possibility of Egypt running out of wheat is existential; it challenges the very existence of the nation. Storing grain is one way of countering this threat. But this practice of staple security is contingent on Egypt's storage infrastructure being sufficient in capacity and quality.

Capacities and Qualities

In December 2019 I met with an Egyptian engineer who is an agricultural expert for a foreign-funded project working on grain storage in Egypt. We sat in the small conference room of the donor's office suite, the air thick with cigarette smoke. He began by asking if I knew about the storage system in Egypt. I responded that I knew a little bit, prompting him to launch into a lengthy discussion of the relative merits of shonas and silos. After a while, he opened a report that he had brought with him to the meeting and said, "So you probably want to know about the storage capacities?" I did not, really. I had read about the capacity of Egypt's silos and shonas in a number of policy reports and newspaper articles, talked about this in several previous interviews, and had always found these figures of hundreds of thousands of tons difficult to appreciate. To me, they did not mean much. But to him, they lay at the heart of the issue. I smiled, poised my pen, and said, of course.

The engineer flicked through the pages of the report, which was in Arabic and bore the logo of the Ministry of the Supply, until he came to a table that he had highlighted with a scratch of bright ink. He started to read it aloud to me. "So you have 430 shonas, run by the Agricultural Bank, Egyptian Holding Company, and General Silos Company, with a capacity of 2.44 million tons. Of those, 122 are asphalt[-] or cement[-floored]. The rest are dust[-floored]. Then you have 46 silos, which are metallic and concrete." He paused, his finger on the page to keep his place, and looked up. "That's now changed I think," he said, explaining that a number of silos were being constructed through a UAE-funded project. His spoken caveat captured one of the problematic things about such figures. They are typically presented as static, but the country's storage capacity is not a constant. Sure enough, after noting that the figures in the table might not be up-to-date, he continued with a definitive conclusion. "This makes a total capacity of 4.6 million tons."

To many of the Egyptians who work in agriculture and trade, the country's storage capacity is insufficient—a marked departure from the non-Egyptian experts who see the storing of large amounts of grain as nonsensical. There is insufficient space in the shonas, for example, to store the amount of domestic harvest that the government might like to procure. Homegrown wheat is purchased entirely during the three-month reception season (unlike wheat imports, which are spread over the remainder of the year), presenting a huge amount of grain to be stored at once. As one Egyptian agricultural specialist explained to me, "Say farmers said they wanted to sell all their wheat to the government [rather than consuming about half of it, as they currently do]: there would be nowhere to store it!" This limits the amount of domestic wheat that the government can buy with local currency, adding to the country's reliance on imported wheat. Even at the current rate of procurement, there are sometimes problems with full shonas turning away farmers. A news report from May 2016 showed images of trucks piled high with sacks of grain waiting in a street under the headline, "Oh Wheat, Who Will Buy You?" The report explained how farmers in one part of the country were finding shonas closed because they were full, leading to delays in their deliveries (and, as a result, increased transportation costs, since farmers typically rent trucks to deliver their wheat). It quoted one farmer who described the situation as a "slow death."[65]

There are also concerns about the quality of storage. Storage is only of value if it can hold grain without deterioration. Many grain experts say that Egypt's storage infrastructure is inadequate. As Ahmed told me, "Storage is a mess." Concerns center primarily on the shonas and their open storage. Shona managers fumigate the sacks of grain and cover them in a layer of burlap cloth or plastic sheeting, but this thin covering offers little protection. Exposed to the air, sun, and precipitation, there is no way to manage the temperature or humidity within the sacks; sometimes the grain molds. The bags tear and birds and rodents eat the grain; the grain gets contaminated with dirt and stones. Silos, on the other hand, offer more protection—separating the grain from ground and sky and allowing greater control of atmospheric conditions—but many of them are in a dilapidated state.

These problems are manifest in what experts refer to as grain "losses." These losses may be physical (grain carried away by mice, wind, or rain) or they may be quality-related—as in the case of grain becoming contaminated by insects, mold, dirt, or stones and deemed unfit for human consumption. (There are also grain losses that are related not to the quality of the storage infrastructure but to the efforts of some to intervene in the use of these infrastructures for their own wealth generation, as I discuss in the next section.) Thus while grain quality might be evaluated by government agents at particular points in time—when a truck arrives at a shona, or when a bulk carrier arrives at a port—quality is not fixed; it may decline as the grain is conveyed through time and space. Estimates suggest that between 10 and 30 percent of the wheat in storage is lost—a cost that must be borne by the government.[66] Media coverage presents this issue as one of national disgrace; one newspaper account was titled, "Wheat for Mice."[67]

There is a link, therefore, between storage and the supply of baladi bread. Without sufficient high-quality grain storage, the daily production of bread for 70 million people may be at risk. Recognizing this fact, the government has embarked upon a massive investment program to develop its storage infrastructure.[68] This program has been funded by a number of international donors.[69] A short video posted on the Ministry of Supply's Facebook page showcases this program. Set to dramatic music and with fast-paced editing, the video is almost like a trailer for a thriller movie. It starts with imagery of old, open-air shonas—desolate plots of land with sacks of grain piled up and exposed to the elements—along with shots of aged, concrete silos. From that bleak beginning, the video charts a smooth narrative of progress that culminates, at the end of the short clip, with shiny new steel silos, sophisticated electronic monitoring systems, and bold statements about the millions of tons of storage capacity added.[70]

I learned more about this program in December 2018 during an interview with Sami, an Egyptian engineer who managed a UAE-funded project that constructed twenty-three new silos around the country. Sami works for a Danish company that specializes in grain storage.[71] We met in his office in Heliopolis, a sprawling neighborhood toward the outskirts of Cairo, where new roads—studded with cookie-cutter villas housing families and small businesses—spread like tentacles into the desert. He was excited to tell me about the contract that his company had finished the year before. It had been the biggest contract for grain storage ever completed worldwide, unlikely, in his opinion, ever to be surpassed. At 60,000 tons each, these twenty-three silos increased Egypt's storage capacity by 1.38 million tons. Sami described the logistical feat of designing and manufacturing the silo bins in Denmark, shipping them to Egypt in pieces, and assembling them using local contractors under the watchful eyes of forty-five Danish supervisors flown in for the job—all in under two years.

He handed me a folder full of information that he had prepared in advance of our meeting. The folder contained a map showing the locations of the silos the company has built in Egypt over recent years, including those built under the UAE grant as well as those financed by Saudi Arabia, Denmark, Finland,

and OPEC. The folder also included the company's glossy annual report from a few years earlier, which featured a photograph of one such new silo on the front cover. This silo is located at El-Marashdah in Qena Governorate, in the Nile Valley. It is a striking image. Taken from a height and up close, the silo bins appear gigantic, dwarfing the truck parked in front of them and a tree off to one side. They are silver, shiny, perfectly symmetrical, emblazoned with the logo of the Danish company, arranged in groups of two, linked by the elevated piping of the grain conveyor. A ribbon of blue lies behind them—the waters of the Nile, on which some of the silo's grain deliveries arrive by barge. Behind that, the green of the floodplain—the wheat-growing land—punctuated by villages, and in the distance, the sandy cliffs that border the edge of the Nile Valley, their pale color almost blending with the clouds that dot the sky. This is the silo that Sisi inaugurated in May 2017, accompanied by the prime minister, three other ministers, and four hundred people described in the press release as "VIPs."

Sami invited me to look at some photographs of the inauguration day on his computer. In two of the photographs, the president, dressed in a dark suit and dark glasses, walks among the silos with his entourage. The dark of the suits contrasts with the silver of the silos, which shine with modernity. I commented on how small the men look next to the silos. "Yes, the silo bins are twenty-five meters tall," Sami responded. In another photograph, the president is in the control room listening to an explanation, from a worker dressed in a jumpsuit, about how the electrical system works. The final photograph was one I had seen before; it was printed in a number of the newspaper articles about this storage project. In this picture, Sisi stands within an air-conditioned tent set up in the silo's forecourt, inspecting a model of the silo complex while the major general in charge gestures with a long pointer, his mouth open in explanation (figure 3.4). The series of photos, juxtaposing Sisi and the silos, gives a powerful impression of the political significance of grain storage and its links with the security apparatus.

As we looked through the images and the other materials he had prepared for me, Sami provided more details. He described these silos as "state-of-the-art technology." He explained, "They have a modern TMS, temperature measurement system. If the temperature arrives above a certain level, then an aeration system blows air through from the bottom to the top. Above a certain temperature could allow for infection. And there is also an IMS, an inventory measurement system." He was keen to explain why such features are significant: "It's very important when you are storing grain," he noted, "preserving the condition of the grain. *Safe* [he emphasized the word] storage. Almost zero percent losses. And to protect the grain, we use fumigation." He documented several

FIGURE 3.4. President al-Sisi inspects a model of a silo complex. Photograph by CIMBRIA. Used with permission.

other features. The plant is equipped with precleaners, including a magnet separator that takes out any metal and a dust remover, which he described as "modern machinery for removing waste." All these descriptors were designed to communicate to me the quality of this storage infrastructure and how well it works. These silos are key to the work of staple security, sustaining the supply and quality of the wheat that goes into the subsidized bread.

Gesturing to the different parts of the silo complex in one of the images, Sami explained how the grain moves into and through the system. The grain enters the silo through the weighbridge—this is where staff take samples and measure quality. Trucks then proceed to the road intake, where the grain is transferred from the truck into the conveying system. The system operates at 200 tons/hour. He explained how the fast processing capacity poses a problem when the grain arrives at the silo in sacks, as much of the domestic harvest does. His words conjured in my mind the image of workers in a frenzy, desperately slitting open bags and trying to get the grain onto a conveyor belt before it progresses onward. The grain moves through the elevator—he pointed at the system for lifting up the grain—then enters into the chain conveyor. This is the elevated bridge that transports grain around and empties it into the grain bins, which open at the top through a computer system. When it is time to empty a bin, the grain discharges through gravity, through a door in the bottom.

These large silos have added valuable capacity to the government's storage infrastructure, but ambitions to further build this capacity remain. When I communicated with Sami in 2021, he told me about his company's involvement in a subsequent phase of the silo project, initiated in 2019 and funded by Saudi Arabia. Clearly proud of his work, he suggested that I might like to write about how his company had contributed, in total, 2.5 million tons of modern storage silos to Egypt's infrastructure. These silos are known as "central silos" and are the main nodal points where large quantities of grain, both domestic and imported, gathers. But they do not address the issue of where wheat should go most directly when it is harvested from the fields. As Sami noted, it is difficult for these large silos to receive grain directly in sacks from small-scale farmers, although they can do so in limited quantities. In addition, the problem of the particularly high losses from shonas remains. Addressing the shonas has, therefore, been another governmental priority over recent years.

In 2015, the Ministry of Supply embarked on a program to upgrade the shonas, lining the floors with concrete, adding roofs and monitoring systems. The government's goal was to turn what it referred to as "dirt shonas" (shona turabiya) into "modern and technological shonas" (shona haditha wa tiknologiya). From many foreign commentators' perspectives, this was unwise. A number told me that they thought the government should have adopted a less costly system of adding concrete floors to existing shonas and erecting basic tent structures over them to protect the grain. It is not surprising, though, that government adopted a more visibly high-tech option. Partnering with an American company called Blumberg Grain, the ministry built a hundred modern shonas. However, the technology proved problematic. The grading system, for example, required the grain to be emptied from its sacks, so that it could go through the grading machine, only to be bagged again. Some of the new shonas were not supplied with electricity, rendering the equipment useless. The project also proved extremely costly. Ultimately the government said that it could not afford to sign for the second phase of the project.

Since then, the ministry has shifted its emphasis, turning its focus away from shonas and toward smaller silos, which it believes are easier to keep aerated. The government now has a plan to build a number of silos that are each around 5,000 tons in capacity. With funding from the Italian Debt Swap program, the ministry is currently working on building ten of these. These small silos will act as what the government terms "collecting centers." Located in agricultural areas, they are designed primarily to replace shonas and store domestic wheat. Given that these silos have a lower conveying capacity, it is easier for staff to manually empty the sacks of grain into the system than it is with the larger silos, so they can act as intermediate points where the grain is shifted from bags to bulk. Since domestic wheat is only stored for a relatively short time—in theory, three months or less—the government intends also to use these smaller silos to store the wheat that it imports during the remaining nine months of the year.

This expansion in the quality and capacity of its Egypt's grain storage infrastructure contributes to securing the continuous supply of baladi bread. It is a key part of staple security for government officials charged with getting the necessary flour to the bakeries that produce baladi bread on a month-to-month basis to cover all their production needs. However, at the same time, this infrastructure holds the potential to undermine that security. Storage is not only a place where good wheat can be held but a place where good wheat can become bad. It is also a place where bad wheat can be concealed or good wheat diverted to other purposes.

Imaginary Wheat

In 2016, Egypt's storage infrastructures became the focus of a high-profile corruption scandal. The government announced in June of that year that it had procured 5 million tons of domestic wheat. This was meant to be an achievement, a marker of the bumper harvest that Egyptian farmers had produced and of the efficacy of the government's procurement process. Yet the figure—significantly higher than the 3–3.5 million tons of domestic wheat procured by the government in previous years—struck a number of leading grain industry officials, traders, and politicians as suspicious. Were there really two million tons of additional wheat in the government's stores? A number of allegations of fraud began to emerge. Such allegations of fraud in the wheat sector were not new, but, having pledged to weed out corruption, Sisi's government took the decisive step of appointing a parliamentary fact-finding commission to look into the issue.

The commission visited silos and shonas around the country. It found substantial discrepancies between the quantities of grain listed in registers and the actual quantities in the silos and shonas. About 40 percent of the domestic wheat procured by the government that year seemed to be missing.[72] In some cases, the storage structures were not as full as the records suggested they should be; in other cases, the storage sites could not actually hold the amount of grain that was recorded as being there. There was ample evidence of what the press termed "imaginary wheat" (qamh wahmi). The commission also found widespread evidence of silos that were meant to be filled with locally grown wheat actually being filled with (cheaper) imported wheat.

When these charges became public, a blame game ensued. The ministry issued press releases on its website stating that it was waging a "war against corruption."[73] Head officials blamed the owners of the privately operated silos and shonas whom the ministry had contracted to manage some of their storage that year in the absence of sufficient public storage capacity. Placing the blame here also added justification for the government's investment in storage. But other commentators pointed to the fact that many government officials must have been involved. "Ironically it is the Storage Silos Company [one of the major government buyers and storers of domestic wheat] that has the most corruption," one journalist told me. "The ones who do the wheat tallying and reporting." The commission's conclusion was that the responsibility was shared, the corruption stemming from collusion between a number of government officials, farmers, domestic traders, and private silo operators—a group the press referred to as the "wheat mafia" (mafia al-qamh). Prosecutions were launched against a number of individuals and the minister resigned.

The word *corruption* (fasad) comes from the same Arabic root as the adjective used to describe bad wheat (fasid); it signals something that is rotten, decayed, bad, or spoiled. This corruption was a source of widespread public outrage. The reason for the outrage, first, was the financial loss incurred by the government. Many of the news stories referencing the amount of "imaginary wheat" presented figures detailing what this nonexistent wheat had cost the government: by some estimates, as much as 2 billion EGP.[74] But more deeply, the outrage centered on the fact that these corrupt individuals, in pursuing their own wealth, were jeopardizing production of the nation's staple. Just as reports rhetorically tied this imaginary wheat to money, they also tied it to the hundreds of millions of loaves of bread lost as a result. A parliamentarian gave a statement saying, "The government should not have given a chance to thieves and deceivers to tamper with the livelihoods [luqmat al-ʿaish] of poor people," his expression for *livelihood* literally meaning "a morsel of bread."[75] In another commentary, a journalist wrote, "Sadly the worms [sus] came and ate the harvest, and the worms this time are the human thieves . . . who are tasked with the wheat transport and supervision. . . . The thieves permitted themselves to steal the food of the poor and the work and toil of the peasants and to steal public money with all tyranny and confidence."[76]

Attention to corruption in the wheat sector has led to calls for heightened surveillance of the storage infrastructure. Part of the design of the new shonas and silos has been tailored toward increasing the authorities' ability to "see" the grain that lies within them. This was explicit in the goals of the Blumberg shona modernization project. A spokesman for the company stated, "One of the key benefits of the Blumberg Grain system is that it will combat corruption, through the use of electronic scales that ensure fair and accurate weights, barcodes that digitize the inventory, continuous digital audits of the system that call out discrepancies, and a security system that can investigate and identify the perpetrators."[77] The spokesman's reference to fairness, accuracy, discrepancies, and perpetrators underscores some of the perceived threats to national wheat storage. The modernized shonas were also tied to a new command and control center, which was designed to collate data on temperature and humidity levels, as well as on grain contamination, in each shona. In one interview, the CEO of the American company was pictured in front of a bank of screens displaying footage from cameras trained on mounds of grain within different storage structures. His suited body, flanked by these surveillance images, projected an aura of authority, signaling the government's newfound ability to keep track of grain.[78] What has become of this surveillance apparatus since the Blumberg project was terminated, though, is unclear.

Similar efforts to increase surveillance have been evident in the projects to build silos. When Sami described the new central silos to me, he explained how, as part of the inventory measurement system, "each cell has a laser camera giving the volume and amount of grain." Enhanced monitoring is also a component of the government's ongoing program to build smaller silos. Ten percent of the funding from the Italian Debt Swap program is going toward developing an information, communication, and technology system for the whole country. When I asked people working for that program why this was important, they emphasized the strategic nature of wheat as a crop. When grain is a matter of security, those in power want to know how much they have in stock.

The degree to which these efforts to develop an all-seeing state of grain succeed remains to be seen. Not only will it cost a lot of money to maintain and continue to develop these computerized systems, but it may not be in all government officials' interests to do so. The involvement of bureaucrats at different levels of the government administration in the 2016 corruption scandal highlights how not everyone within the government is committed to the project of staple security. The efforts of some to pursue their own profits run counter to the efforts of others to secure a consistent supply of baladi bread for the people. Whereas, for the latter group, knowledge of what wheat is where at all times is key, for the former, such knowledge may not be desirable. A surveillance camera might take footage, but that footage has to be seen and acted upon to have an effect. Data in a database might log what wheat is where, but that data can be adjusted. Storing wheat may be a way of securing the nation's staple, but not everyone is equally invested in that practice.

Conclusion

Procuring, assessing, and storing wheat are part of a complex network of interactions that results in the Egyptian people having bread to eat each day. But while these practices have a shared outcome, their underlying logics are multiple. For national officials, these practices are designed to ensure that the government has enough quality wheat for use in the government-subsidized bread program (see chapter 4). For farming households, they are practices designed to ensure that a family has enough quality wheat for use in the production of homemade bread (see chapter 5). Within and between these levels, at each point in the grain's movement through the country, there are a number of competing interests at play—between traders for whom rising international wheat prices are a source of profit and government officials for whom they pose a threat; between those primarily concerned about the quality of imported wheat and those who see cost as a more pressing consideration; and between those for whom grain in a silo is a strategic reserve and those for whom it is a mechanism of personal gain.

Different forms of knowledge underpin these contrasting positions. From the posting on a classified ad website to a trader's Twitter feed, headlines in an Egyptian newspaper to laser cameras within a silo, there are many ways of knowing how much and what kinds of wheat are moving into and through the country. These knowledges can do multiple things—allow traders to make money, facilitate surveillance, or make people feel safe. They are both contingent and incomplete. The government is investing in computer systems to monitor grain in storage, but there are some stores, like those within farmers' homes, about which it knows little. Inspectors employ laboratory tests to know the quality of wheat, but assessment is dependent on the sample of grain tested and the standards adopted. The press reports the government's procurement of foreign wheat, but much of the process goes on behind closed doors. Thus both knowledge—and its corollary, ignorance—shape staple security.

4. SUBSIDIZED BREAD

with Mariam Taher

The bakery sits back from the booth where the bread is sold, behind a small courtyard. Located in a working-class neighborhood of Cairo, along a busy street, it is identifiable less by its appearance, marked only by a small sign, and more by the stream of people heading away from it carrying bread. I visit one morning in August 2015, accompanied by Hisham, who is from this neighborhood and whom I met in 2007 when he was working as a driver for the development project with which I was affiliated during my doctoral fieldwork. When we arrive, the dough—a simple mix of flour, water, salt, and yeast—has already been kneaded in a giant mixer, which now stands silent. A man sits on

BALADI BREAD IN HAND. *Photograph by Ahmed Elabd. Used with permission.*

a stool next to a trough of dough, a sack of flour open between his knees. On his other side is a pile of large wooden trays, which a boy is coating with a thin layer of bran. The man covers his hands with the flour, takes a scoop of dough out of the vat, and pats it between his hands a couple of times, shaping it into a round, then places it carefully on the tray of bran. He is deliberate in his scooping motion and the rounds are remarkably similar in size. The boy carries the trays over to the other side of the room where another man receives them, pressing each ball of dough to flatten it slightly and sprinkling it with flour. There the dough sits until it is ready to be carried into the neighboring room.

The next-door room is occupied by a large oven the size of a caravan. The space is hot but surprisingly calm despite the constant motion. Two walls are lined with green sacks of flour. At one end of the oven, a man perches on a high stool. He places the dough circles, each around seven inches in diameter, onto a conveyor belt, which moves into the oven. Over the course of a ten-minute journey, the conveyor belt passes the dough through the top part of the oven, down, around, and back along the bottom, before it comes out just below where the man on the stool is sitting. The loaves of bread emerge, now puffed and browned. This is Egypt's subsidized bread.

Small-scale, privately owned bakeries like this one produce most of the baladi bread that is eaten around Egypt each day.[1] This subsidized bread is not the only bread Egyptians eat. Some people bake their own bread (see chapter 5). Others buy different kinds of bread, like fino rolls to make sandwiches for their children to take to school, or whiter and softer shami and siyahi loaves if they prefer their taste and can afford them. These alternatives are sold from small bakeries, similar to those that sell baladi bread, scattered around urban areas; they are also widely available from numerous informal bread stands set up along the street.[2] Yet among these multiple kinds of bread, baladi bread is distinct. It is distinct in its darker color and bran-rich taste, and it is distinct in its price, which is a twentieth of the price of any other kind of bread.[3]

For the roughly one third of the Egyptian population that lives in poverty, on incomes that provide less than 24EGP a day to cover all expenses, the difference in cost for five loaves of bread—between 0.25EGP and 5EGP—is significant.[4] Even for those earning 1,000EGP or 1,500EGP a month, this difference in price is not trifling when buying twenty or thirty loaves a day for your household. Baladi bread hence meets a central need. For the poorest segments of the population, it is the only bread they can afford. For those with slightly more means—the 60–65 percent of the population not below the poverty line but far from affluent—baladi bread is a daily expenditure that is reliably inexpensive, whatever the fluctuations in other market prices, and a food that can be turned to when times are tough.[5]

The position of baladi bread in relation to other breads is evident in how people talk about their bread-buying patterns. One woman who works as a caregiver in a children's nursery in Cairo, for instance, explained, "I get baladi bread, that is the basis. I also get fino, but just for the school, for the kids, for their sandwiches. Outside of school, it's baladi." A man who works as a driver described his bread-eating practices this way: "Baladi bread is the standard bread I eat. Sometimes I also eat shami bread, like on vacation or a day off. But all week I have baladi bread, it's what I'm used to. I get it all the time." Even in rural households in which homemade bread is the primary bread consumed, baladi bread acts as a valuable supplement or staple to fall back on. On one of my visits to Warda, for instance, Khaled, a farmer in the village who grows wheat, told me that he had been buying baladi bread recently. His wife was sick and his daughter-in-law heavily pregnant, so there was nobody in the house who could bake their harvested grain into homemade bread.

Thus although Egyptians eat multiple kinds of bread, baladi bread is foundational, a linchpin of many people's daily sustenance. This centrality resonates across multiple domains, from everyday conversation to references in popular culture. On one episode of the widely watched talk show *Al-Qahira al-Youm*, the host, Amr Adib, sits with a pile of baladi bread in front of him. "That," he says, holding a loaf in his hand, "is the most important thing (da al-awal)." He stares intensely at the camera. "More important than electricity," he points with his finger for emphasis, "more important than water," another jab of the finger, "and more important than security."[6] The significance of baladi bread thus outweighs that of even the most basic of needs, water, as well as other things—electricity and security—whose importance is a given. This is why the possibility of there not being enough baladi bread, or of baladi bread not being good enough, poses such an existential threat.

This chapter is about the everyday practices of countering this threat by securing the supply and quality of baladi bread. Whereas chapter 1 looked at this historically, tracing the development of the bread subsidy over the past seventy years and the actions taken by successive governments to tweak the price, size, and composition of baladi bread in order to ensure the steady supply of acceptable bread at a national level, this chapter focuses on the contemporary period. Building on my analysis of how the government accesses the wheat that it needs for the subsidized bread program from Egyptian farmers (chapter 2) and from overseas (chapter 3), this chapter looks at the next stage of transforming that wheat into baladi bread and bringing it into the home. The national supply of baladi bread is dependent on the government ensuring that flour is available and covering the cost of selling the bread at a reduced price. It is also dependent on the work of the privately owned bakeries that produce most of the country's baladi bread.[7] At the same time, the securing of sufficient, quality baladi bread for a home rests on the quotidian acts of individuals going to bakeries and bringing home good bread for their families to eat.

This analysis is based on ethnographic work conducted in collaboration with my research assistant, Mariam Taher, who is the coauthor of the chapter. The focus is primarily urban, reflecting the predominance of baladi bread consumption in areas where home baking is rare, and drawing on Mariam's twenty-two months of participant observation at baladi bread bakeries in a working-class neighborhood of Cairo. Since, however, baladi bread is eaten in rural areas as well, the chapter also includes data from my fieldwork in Fayoum.

The first part of the chapter considers practices of securing *sufficient* baladi bread. It looks at bread lines, which are emblematic of scarcity, and the efforts of the Ministry of Supply, which manages Egypt's food subsidy program, to reform production and purchasing practices at bakeries so as to address shortages. While these reforms, implemented in 2014, have ensured that there is typically enough bread available at the bakeries, access to this bread is now mediated by an electronic ration card. The analysis therefore turns to the everyday labors of getting a so-called smart card and keeping it working, which determine whether or not people are able to buy baladi bread at the subsidized price. Looking at these contrasting domains of action—government officials making policy reforms and individuals trying to get a smart card—as different types of staple security highlights a contradiction. Whereas the government puts a lot of money and consideration into ensuring that there is enough cheap bread for poor Egyptians to eat, its bureaucratic procedures are such that a number of Egypt's poor are unable to access this bread.

The second part of the chapter looks at practices of securing *quality* baladi bread. The 2014 government reforms also addressed quality concerns. They did so not through introducing new regulations but through the market device of competition. By changing the way the subsidy is channeled through bakeries and having them vie for business, the government has sought to incentivize bakers to produce good-quality bread. These actions only shape quality through to the moment of sale, though. Between that moment and the bread's arrival at home, the quality of the bread can change. Hence the final part of the chapter examines people's everyday practices of handling bread at the bakery and on the street, which shape the taste and texture of the loaves that they end up eating.

Through this analysis, the chapter shows how securing the continuous supply of a quality staple is about national-level policy decisions regarding the logistics of a vast subsidy program, but it is also about people standing in lines at bureaucratic offices and filling out paperwork to get a smart card. It is about the Ministry of Supply thinking of ways to get privately owned bakeries to produce good bread, but it is also about how an individual arranges her loaves and puts them in a plastic bag. Staple security offers a conceptual lens through which to view these disparate realms of action together. It underscores how it is not sufficient simply to look at how a policy translates into loaves of cheap bread in a bakery, nor to focus on food production and distribution practices within a home. Rather, the momentous must be considered alongside the mundane, the public alongside the private, the visible alongside the less visible. For only if all these domains are considered can insight be gained into how different people within Egypt access their staple food and what that food ends up tasting like.

Baladi Bread Supply

I am traveling through the Fayoum countryside with an official from the Ministry of Irrigation and a driver. It is April 2008 and the yellow of the wheat, glowing in the late afternoon sun, stands out from the patchwork greens of the other maturing winter crops. I comment on the color of the wheat, and they tell me that the wheat is nearing harvest in fifteen days or so. "All that," says the irrigation official, gesturing toward the fields around us, "and people are still hungry!" The driver, a friendly man, always ready with a smile, uses this as an opportunity to segue into a joke. "A man wants to marry a woman," he begins, a fitting opening in a place where marriage constitutes a major life event as well as a substantial economic burden for both the bride and groom's families. "So he goes to the woman's family, who ask him, 'Have you got an apartment? Have you got gold?' 'Yes, yes,' says the man." The driver pauses before the punchline. "'And have you got bread?' they ask. 'No,' he replies." We chuckle at the comedic tragedy of a figure who has all the expensive trappings of marriage—the jewelry he will give his wife and the apartment for the bride's family to furnish—but not the most basic of needs, bread.

The joke was a telling reflection of people's concerns, at this time, about the limited availability of baladi bread. During 2007–8, when I was conducting fieldwork for my first book, lines at bakeries were prevalent. Passing through small towns as I traveled around Fayoum with staff from the irrigation ministry, I would often see throngs of people in front of bakeries, pushing and shoving, every so often racks of bread emerging through a window and being passed over the heads of the crowd to be whisked home by the lucky one. "Bread is a problem," an irrigation engineer commented to me one day, pointing at a cluster of people screaming at a bakery outlet. "People are worried that there won't be enough left for them."

The bread shortages were a frequent topic of conversation and theme on the news. The crowds of angry people outside bakeries, arms raised as they thrust their money toward the sales windows in the hope of a bakery worker taking it in exchange for bread, made for dramatic images to accompany the headlines of crisis. The stories of people waiting two or three hours for their bread, sometimes getting to the end of the line only to find that the bread was finished, were striking. Over dinner one night in Warda, the conversation turned to the bread crisis. One woman, an Egyptian academic who has a house in the village, joked, "It is like Ethiopia, six months feast then six months famine." While her tone was light, in evoking Ethiopia, the poster child of food scarcity, her joke underscored the seriousness with which she perceived the situation. On another occasion, I was sitting with a small group when someone told the story of what had happened the previous week to an Egyptian artist who lived in the village. The artist had taken a couple of friends on a trip into the desert nearby, where his car had been stopped in an attempted carjacking. When the narrator got to the part about "they wanted to steal . . ." another man interrupted saying "Bread! They wanted bread!" Once again, everyone laughed. Yet beneath the laughter was a deeper current of anxiety.

While the people with whom I interacted in Fayoum did not make a connection between the shortages they were experiencing and global patterns of food production and distribution, this was a time of global food crisis.[8] During 2007 and 2008, food prices on international markets peaked, leading to higher prices for many goods in Egyptian markets, including other kinds of bread. Baladi bread was something people could turn to in these times. It was an affordable option that people could draw on to help sustain their families when other items were becoming too expensive. In doing so, though, they created additional demand pressure that the production system was unable to keep up with, contributing to the scarcity (Trego 2011).

President Mubarak responded to the crisis by calling on the National Service Projects Organization, the part of Egypt's military that manufactures a number of military and civilian products including bread (Abul-Magd 2017: 147). The production capacity of the large-scale industrial bakeries operated by the military is limited relative to the demand, but military trucks arriving in areas of shortage to distribute loaves of bread created a politically powerful image of the government taking decisive action to provide for the people.[9] The Ministry of Supply also introduced several policies to ease the crowding, including a requirement that bakeries sell their bread from booths, separated from the site of production, and a trial bread delivery program (Trego 2011). These policy changes did not, however, fully address the underlying issues. As a result, even when food prices declined in the aftermath of the global food crisis, the baladi bread shortages continued.

When protestors took to the streets in the Egyptian Revolution of January 2011, the availability of bread was a central theme in their list of grievances as they called for "bread, freedom, and social justice." Some protestors brandished loaves of bread above their heads. One of the protestors' slogans featured the absence of bread as a key rationale for their uprising: "Mish hanuskut, mish hankhaf / ahna mish la'yin al-'aish al-haf! [We won't be quiet, we won't be intimidated, we can't even find plain bread to eat!]" (Srage 2014). In the months after the revolution, once again the Ministry of Supply called on the military to assist in bread production and distribution (Kamal 2015). When President Morsi came to power, bread was one of five central items that he pledged to address in his first hundred days in office. Under his administration, bureaucrats began to talk through options for more significant subsidy reform (Frerichs 2016). These were not new ideas. A number of Egyptian and non-Egyptian policy experts had been advocating reforms to the bread subsidy program for years (Alderman and von Braun 1986, Gutner 1999, Ahmed et al. 2001, Al-Shawarby and El-Laithy 2010). But the postrevolution political context created a renewed impetus and space for policy change. The following year, the Ministry of Supply began a pilot study for what was to become in 2014—under President al-Sisi's administration and the leadership of a Minister of Supply who was committed to subsidy reform—a major overhaul to the subsidized bread program.

The Line

The reforms introduced by the Ministry of Supply in 2014 fundamentally altered the way in which Egypt's bread subsidy program operates. They were a national-level response to the threat of baladi bread running out, as well as an effort to curb costs. They were one of a multifaceted set of practices that the government has adopted in its attempt to secure the continuous supply of the nation's staple and ensure that Egyptians can get their daily bread.

The reforms sought to address issues on both the demand and the supply sides that the government understood to have been causing baladi bread shortages and adding to the burden on its budget. In terms of demand, the 2007–8 food crisis had underscored the way that popular demand for baladi bread fluctuates with broader economic circumstances. Humans were not the only consumers of concern, though. The bread was so cheap, many claimed, that people were feeding it to animals, such as the poultry that some urban dwellers raise on their roofs and which are commonly kept in rural households. This point was often mentioned when I asked people to reflect back on past scarcity, both during interviews and in casual conversation. I talked a lot about bread, for example, with Hisham, with whom I visited the bakery in Cairo. In his narratives about the bread lines of the past, greedy animal owners often featured as the culprits. "Farmers used to come in from the countryside and buy 3, 4, 5EGP of bread," he told me on one occasion, his tone revealing his outrage at this practice. He implied that this was common behavior, describing people from rural areas taking the train into Cairo to stock up on a hundred or so loaves of cheap bread before returning to feed it to their poultry. Not only were people buying bread for their own animals but to sell on to others; the economics made this a profitable enterprise. As Gamal, an economist and former government official explained to me, "For a kilogram weight of baladi bread, that's about seven loaves, you could sell it as food for humans for 35 piasters or as animal feed for 2 to 3 or 4EGP."[10]

A central part of the reforms, therefore, was the introduction of a limit on the number of loaves of baladi bread that people could get each day.[11] The ministry set a daily limit of five loaves per person—more than enough for most Egyptians (government studies suggest an average consumption of three loaves a day) but not enough for hungry chickens.[12] At the same time, it introduced an incentive for individuals to consume less bread, by allowing them to exchange any unused bread points for other subsidized goods at the end of the month. For each loaf uneaten, an individual gets 10 piasters to use at the special Ministry of Supply stores. (I refer to these stores as "tamwin stores," since *tamwin*, which means supply, is a common colloquial way of referring to the ministry.) Uneaten bread can therefore become free oil for cooking, sugar for tea, rice, or one of fifty or so other subsidized goods.

This new substitutability has changed the way people think about subsidized bread. Now baladi bread is not just a matter of loaves that can be eaten but what can be obtained for loaves-not-eaten. This is evident in how Hisham, for example, talks about baladi bread. Hisham earns a modest income as a taxi driver in Cairo. Now in his late fifties, his two children are in college and his wife has retired from her low-level government position due to poor health. He seldom gets his family's full allocation of baladi bread. "If I only take fifty loaves a month," he explains, "I can use the remainder for other things." Fifty loaves are not sufficient for his household of four over the course of the month, but he often buys other kinds of bread. He prefers the taste of the whiter shami and siyahi loaves, likes the convenience of being able to pick them up on his way home without having to make a special trip to a baladi bread bakery, and has the means to pay more. In addition, the 550 loaves of baladi bread that he does not buy over the course of the month translate into 55EGP that he can spend at the tamwin store, where he likes to get oil, sugar, soap, and pasta.

The other part of the reforms sought to address problems on the supply side. Since the early 2000s, policy experts had been pointing out the opportunities for what they term *leakage* within the subsidy program (Ahmed et al. 2001, Croppenstedt, Saade, and Siam 2006, Al-Shawarby and El-Laithy 2010, Coelli 2010). Bakeries would not use all the subsidized flour that they received from the government to bake baladi bread but instead would either sell it on the black market for a higher price or use it to make more profitable kinds of bread.[13] Ragib, an agricultural expert who works for a foreign embassy in Cairo, explained the problem to me. "If he [the baker] got five bags of flour a week, each bag fifty kilos, maybe he would bake two [bags] and sell three on the black market." As a result, the bakeries were just not producing that much bread. "They would only open 8 to 10 in the morning then close," Ragib said. The long lines of the past were in part an outcome of this limited amount of bread being baked and such short opening hours.

The reforms addressed this problem by changing the way the subsidy was conveyed through the bakeries. Instead of enabling bakeries to sell very cheap bread by providing them with a very cheap primary input—flour—bakeries now have to buy flour at the market price. For every five-piaster loaf of bread they sell, the bakery owner can claim reimbursement from the ministry to cover the full cost of production as well as a small profit. To keep track of the number of loaves people are purchasing, and the number of loaves bakeries are selling, the ministry introduced an electronic ration card, known as a smart card. Bakers have raised some objections to the new system, arguing that the reimbursement is not sufficient to make profits and that delays in the reimbursement process are problematic, but most commentators consider the reforms to have been a success.[14]

The success of these reforms is encapsulated in the absence of lines at bakeries. Although a line does not in itself necessarily mean that there is not any bread—it may just mean a glitch in the production process such that there is no bread available when customers arrive, or a large number of customers arriving at once and so not being able to be served immediately—it is a symbol of scarcity.[15] People still remember the lines of the past that ended in disappointment. One woman who lives in a poor neighborhood of Cairo recalled, for instance, "We used not to have enough. I used not to be able to get bread from the bakery. It would be crowded, and then when it was finally your turn and you would get there, you would find it empty. He [the baker] would tell you there is no more bread." This experience is the frame through which she interprets the impact of the reforms. "Now there are fewer lines," she says, "because everyone is entitled to a certain amount of bread." Her account of what was the problem previously matches that of the policy analysts. "Before," she explains, "they [bakery owners] used to sell the flour on the black market, in the street. Now it is better. You have your assigned quantity."

Those who work in policy and see the baladi bread program through that lens, rather than through the lens of eating this bread every day, are similarly pleased with the transition. Ragib, who writes regular reports on Egypt's wheat policy and food subsidies, talked about the reforms as "stopping the stealing." His use of the verb *steal* reflects the government's perspective that when bakery owners directed subsidized flour to non-baladi bread use, they were, in a sense, stealing it from the state and from the nation of hungry citizens. "This has led to an abundance of bread," he said. "There are no lines, bread is available all day." Another elderly Egyptian economist who I interviewed described this change as being monumental, unprecedented not only in his lifetime but in that of his father's, who was born in 1899. "Wherever you go," he said, "people now for the first time are saying there is enough bread." "Try!" he challenged me. "Go to any Egyptian village and ask, '*Fen al-ʿaish al-baladi?* [Where is the baladi bread?]' and everyone will say there is lots. This is the first time no one is complaining about bread. This is the achievement! Bread is now available and there are no lines like there were in the past. Never in the history of Egyptian politics has there been this bread availability!"[16]

This is not to say that there are no longer any lines at all in front of baladi bread bakeries. It is not uncommon to see small groups—maybe of ten or so people—waiting to buy bread, typically clustered into two lines segregated by gender.[17] But these lines do not seem to count as lines anymore, perhaps because of their shortness (relative to the lines of the past) or because the presence of bread at the end of the wait is more certain. Seldom do these lines lead to violent fights as they did in the past.[18] During Mariam's twenty-two months of participant observation, she rarely had to stand in line for more than five to ten minutes at a baladi bread bakery. On one of the few occasions when she did have to wait longer, the conversation around her was telling.

It was Ramadan 2016, the month when Muslims fast during daylight hours, and Mariam was buying bread from a bakery located in a narrow alleyway off a market street. In the small space in front of the bakery outlet, bordered by dilapidated apartment buildings on each side, a number of people were waiting for their bread. Most were buying thirty or forty loaves, some purchasing not only for themselves but for other people whose cards they had brought with them, a practice which is fairly common. As Mariam stood in the line for about twenty-five minutes, the women around her chatted. Much of their conversation centered on the line as they clarified their positions, who was behind them, who was in front, and who had been there the longest. An old woman was standing behind Mariam. "Hopefully there will be enough bread for everyone," she commented, the worry etched on her face. To Mariam there seemed little reason to assume that there would not be enough, but she does not have memories of standing in long lines to no avail. Nor did the bread Mariam was planning to buy feature in what she was planning to eat in the coming days in the same way as it likely did for this woman. But for the old woman, anxiety was an easy position to slip into. She clarified, "We do not mind waiting, just as long as we know there will be enough." Every now and then, a fear about there not being enough for everyone spread through the crowd. Whispered rumors about the bread running out trickled through the huddle and people started looking anxious. Then voices of calm countered those rumors, reassuring that there would be plenty of bread. The momentary sense of staple security returned and bodies relaxed back into their waiting stance.[19]

The presence of a line still brings the fear of an absence of bread. Illustrative of this concern is a video titled *Baladi Bread*, posted by a comedy group of young Egyptian men on their YouTube channel in 2015.[20] The video begins with a young man leaving his house. Another man, playing his mother and dressed in a black galabiya and pink headscarf, asks him, "What should I tell your siblings if you do not return?" To a dramatic soundtrack, similar to that heard on Egyptian soap operas, the first man turns and says, "Tell them I died a martyr, going to get bread ['aish]." His use of the word 'aish here reflects the word's dual meanings, as the Egyptian colloquial term for bread and as the word for livelihoods. At this point in the film, the viewer does not know if this man is going to a bakery, facing the risk of a long and potentially violent line, or, like many Egyptian young men, migrating for work and facing the associated risks of travel. The music changes to "Soul Bossa Nova" as the camera shifts to a new scene, titled "At the bakery," and the man approaches the bakery with another young man. Despite the jaunty tune, there is an ominously large crowd gathered in front of the bakery. The screen then goes black; white writing announces, "After three weeks at the bakery," the wait in line extended for comic value. The music changes to a nationalist-themed pop song by an

Egyptian singer and the camera shows another Cairo street. The two men come running around the corner triumphantly waving loaves of baladi bread in the air. They kiss them. They cry fake tears. They strike silly poses with their loaves. They snap selfies taking bites. In the end, they pray, bowing down onto the dirty asphalt, the loaves clasped in their hands. The video is playful, but speaks to something less playful—the continuing resonance of having to wait at a bakery and the fears about whether or not you will be able to get bread to take home to your family at the end of that wait.

The fact that bread lines continue to circulate as a source of concern is an indicator of the sense of underlying threat regarding the bread supply. Yet the key determinant of an individual's access to baladi bread today is not so much whether bakeries are producing enough and how long they might have to wait for those loaves, but whether they have a working smart card to allow them to get that bread at the subsidized price. The smart card has become the new security device. It is the means of accessing cheap bread, but it is also the means by which that access can be terminated. At a simple modification of a database entry, a bureaucrat can delete someone from the list of eligible recipients, stop their card from working, and prevent them from getting this bread.

The Card

A customer approaches the booth of a baladi bread bakery (figure 4.1). Within the darkened space, a woman sits behind a counter. The customer holds a handful of coins in one hand and a plastic card in the other. He places several coins on the counter, hands over the card, and asks for 2EGP of bread. He has no need to translate the monetary figure into a loaf equivalent, for both he and the server are well versed in thinking about bread in five-piaster units. Two pounds, forty loaves. The server places the card in a small handheld reader and types the amount of bread requested. She then reaches for loaves from the shelves that line the booth and places the bread on the counter. As the customer gathers his bread, she takes the money and hands back his card, along with a receipt indicating how much bread he has purchased and how much he has left for the month.

In this quotidian transaction at the baladi bread bakery, the smart card is pivotal. While not necessarily visible to a casual observer, the presence of a card reader at the counter, or of cards at-the-ready in customers' hands, is one way of distinguishing a bakery that sells baladi bread from one that sells the similarly shaped and colored siyahi bread (figure 4.2). The smart card—typically referred to just as "the card" (al-bitaqa) or sometimes as the "subsidy

FIGURE 4.1. Booth of a baladi bread bakery. Photograph by Ellen Geerlings. Used with permission.

FIGURE 4.2. Baladi bread and smart card reader. Photograph by Asmaa Waguih. Used with permission.

card" (bitaqat al-tamwin)—is a rectangular plastic card, divided with a curvy diagonal into blocks of bright green and yellow, with the national coat of arms at the top. Faded into the background of the so-called family card is a generic image of a family, striking in its departure from the reality of most families that hold these cards—two parents, two children, the father in a shirt, tie, and waistcoat, the mother without her head covered, long hair loose over her shoulders. There is a gold chip on one side of the card. In the other corner, the name of the card holder is followed by two rows of numbers—the first the ID number of the individual, the second, the number of the card. Management of the card system involves the Ministry of Supply, which assesses eligibility, checks documents, and interfaces with citizens; the Ministry of Military Production, which reviews applications, manages the information database, and orders the cards; and several private companies, which print the cards and deal with technical issues regarding the smart card readers.

These cards turn a surveilling eye on those buying baladi bread, keeping track of how many loaves each individual buys to ensure they stay within the five-loaf limit and facilitating the transformation of uneaten bread into other subsidized commodities. As Hisham says one day while we are chatting as we drive through Cairo, "The card has organized everything." Not only is the card a way of allowing access, but it is also a way of precluding access. During a conversation at a coffee shop with Ragib, the agricultural expert who works for a foreign embassy, he explained to me, "There didn't used to be any database or targeting. Now through the new smart card, we can see who needs or who deserves [the subsidy] and filter out those who have died."[21]

The cards also provide a way of surveilling those baking baladi bread, keeping electronic track of bakeries' production practices. At each transaction, the smart card reader logs how many loaves of baladi bread a bakery has sold and to whom. These are the metrics by which the ministry assesses the reach of its subsidy program. For every loaf sold at the subsidized price, the government transfers money for reimbursement into the bakery owner's bank account.

The cards, therefore, are a key part of the new subsidy program. But they do not work on their own. The system requires not only cards but card readers that are operational, paper to go into the card readers to print receipts that customers can check, and network connections to link the handheld devices to the national database. The system rests, also, on people acting in a particular way: bakery staff typing in the correct numbers, people bringing their cards with them to the bakery and keeping track of their receipts, and technicians readily on hand to fix faulty machines or repair broken network connections.[22]

Each of these points presents a juncture where the supply and receipt of baladi bread can be interrupted. If the network is down or the card machines are out of operation, for instance, this can mean that people are unable to access bread. The interruption may also be deliberate, as various actors seek to tweak the system for their own interests. One woman who lives in Cairo talked about her experience with this. "When I get bread from the bakery," she said, "for example ten loaves, I sometimes find that they have written on the paper [i.e., entered into the system to appear on the receipt] fifteen. Once I took nothing, and he [the bakery owner] said I did." She says that she reported this to her husband, but there was little he could do. Rumors about how people cheat the system abound. The woman talked about how there are things that "they [bakery staff] fake on the machine." "There is still cheating," she explained. "Some have not taken [bread] and are told they have taken. They know how to play inside the machine. They will take several thousand [EGP] and split it between themselves." Another man talked about how bakery owners sometimes make illicit arrangements with customers. The customers will give the owner their cards, so that he can claim reimbursement from the government for loaves not sold, in exchange for small monetary payments. "Say you give the baker your card, and he holds onto it," he explains. "Maybe you have 500 loaves a month, but you took only 250 and left the rest. The bakery guy will give you money for them." Often, people point the finger at the technicians who manage particular pieces of the system. "Some technicians have struck deals with the bakers," one man told me, "so they log larger numbers of baladi bread sales in the database." These kinds of tweaks can have profound impacts on individual card owners. "Sometimes you might order bread for only 1EGP and they will charge for 3[EGP]," one woman explained. "You might not realize it until at the end of the month, then you see that everything is gone, all your money that you thought you had saved up."

Despite the ways in which the smart card system can be made to work for particular interests, it remains the mediator of daily access to cheap bread. For an Egyptian to get subsidized bread, they need a smart card. Obtaining a smart card requires a particular kind of laboring with the bureaucracy. It requires standing in lines not at the bakery but in various offices; filling out paperwork; photocopying; and paying fees, some official, others not. While the plethora of bureaucratic paperwork and documents required to access government assistance is not necessarily surprising, it is notable when positioned next to politicians' statements about cheap bread being a right for *all* Egyptians.[23] Once someone has a smart card, their continued supply of subsidized bread depends on them ensuring that the smart card keeps working. These practices of card accessing and maintenance are everyday practices of staple security at the individual level. They, too, are ways people make sure they have cheap bread to eat.

GETTING A CARD According to the Ministry of Supply, obtaining a smart card is a simple process, laid out step by step on the ministry's website. One must just submit the necessary paperwork, pay a fee of 10EGP, and collect the card when it is ready. The required paperwork includes an identification card, birth certificates for children and marriage certificates if applicable, proof of address, and documentation proving eligibility. Yet in practice, the process is often not this smooth.

The eligibility criteria, for one, are not entirely clear. Income level is obviously part of what determines access to baladi bread.[24] But the fact that an estimated 70–80 percent of Egyptians eat baladi bread and only 30 percent of the population is classified as poor shows that subsidized bread is not only intended for those below the poverty line. Nonetheless the ministry has, in recent years, been seeking to tighten its criteria and remove those it deems not needy from the system so as to reduce the cost of the subsidy. As an Egyptian economist at Cairo University who has worked on the subsidy program explained to me, "They want to eliminate some people, but don't want to direct it only to the very poor." She estimated that the government's goal was to reach, "maybe 50–60 percent [of the population]"—in other words, to include some of the middle class because, she noted, "for those middle classes, it [cheap bread] helps them not fall into poverty." In 2019, the government introduced additional criteria to determine noneligibility, including ownership of assets or high monthly payments for other services.[25] Although the way in which the ministry assesses these criteria and their efficacy at determining need are matters of dispute, as I discuss further below, they remain a mediator of access to baladi bread.

In addition to the complexity and opacity of the eligibility criteria, some people do not have easy access to the required documents or are unsure where they should go to submit all the forms. In one Warda household that I have known since 2007, for example, many of the family's documents are not in order. They have not registered all the children's births and some of the young men have not done the mandated military service. Each year when I returned to Warda after the smart card system was implemented in Fayoum, I would ask the female members of this extended family if they had obtained a card. In response, they would talk about not having the right papers, or their husbands not having made the trip to the relevant bureaucratic offices, located in a small town about fifteen minutes' drive away. Not until 2018 did they manage to compile the necessary paperwork to receive their cards. While in the case of this household the delay was not a huge issue, since the women of the family are accustomed to baking and family members prefer the taste of homemade bread (chapter 5), for those not in the position to bake their own bread, such paperwork-related delays can pose a huge challenge. Indicative of these problems, on the Facebook page of the Ministry of Supply, below its listing of the card application information, there is an extensive list of complaints in the comments section.[26] One after another, the commenters detail problems such as difficulties in adding newborns, delays in receiving cards, and their suffering as a result. Without a smart card, they have to buy baladi bread at the nonsubsidized price of fifty piasters, purchase another kind of bread for one pound per loaf, or go without this basic component of their diet.[27]

At the same time, there are informal means through which people without smart cards manage to access cheap baladi bread. It is common, for instance, to see people waiting by bakeries to ask other customers if they will buy bread for them on their cards. One day as Mariam approached a bakery, a man asked, "Do you have a card? Are you getting bread with a card?" Before she could reply, he continued, "You are a lucky one [ya bakhtik]. I am waiting around, just waiting for someone with a card to get me bread." While on this particular instance the man voiced his request, such is the commonality of this kind of exchange that it often proceeds with few words spoken. The person will stand by the bakery, ask an approaching customer for a certain monetary amount of bread, based on a five-piaster price per loaf, and hand over some coins. If the customer is willing to give some of her loaf allocation to this individual, she will take the money, buy the corresponding amount of bread, then pass back the loaves.

Hence the smart card is the mechanism through which Egyptians obtain the cheap bread that comprises a major part of their daily caloric intake. But even for people who have cards, obtaining a card does not necessarily secure a consistent supply of bread. There is also work that needs to be done to ensure that the smart card keeps working. These are practices of card maintenance.[28]

CARD MAINTENANCE As with any small plastic card carried around on a daily basis, the smart card requires basic kinds of care. Sometimes you will see cards tenuously held together by bits of tape. Other times people buy protective plastic covers for their cards to ensure that they are not damaged. Occasionally, misplaced cards can be seen lying on the ground near a bakery. Some people are particularly concerned about the chip in the card and believe that placing the card in proximity to certain other things can cause the information to be wiped. One woman commented that the card and coins must be kept in two separate hands, "because if the card comes into contact with the coins, it will be ruined. The silver money deletes its contents."

The central practice of card maintenance, however, is not so much about maintaining the material nature of the card, itself, as maintaining the connection between that piece of plastic and the broader network system. This depends on regular use of the card to get bread. According to the ministry's regulations, a card must be used at least three times a month or else it will be terminated. Although the frequent use of a card that gives access to a daily staple might appear to be a nonissue, there are a number of circumstances in which people might not want to buy baladi bread every day but still want an active card. Some people in rural areas, for instance, bake their own bread but are keen to have operational cards, so that they can get baladi bread if they ever need to. Others choose to buy other kinds of bread, because of health restrictions or taste preferences, but still want to have baladi bread to fall back on if they, or others to whom they are close, are in times of need. The access to other subsidized goods in return for bread-not-eaten is another reason why people have an interest in keeping their card active, regardless of their desire for baladi bread each day.

As a result, people work specifically to ensure their card stays active. Some will use their card to get bread even if they do not need it, and then donate the bread to beggars on the street, or to poor families who do not have enough.[29] One time when she was at a bakery, Mariam observed a woman hand over her card and ask for 75 piasters of bread. The server put the card into the reader. When, however, he started placing loaves on the counter, she responded that she did not want the bread, only the card. She may not have wanted baladi bread on this occasion, but she clearly wanted to keep open the possibility of getting bread (or other subsidized goods) in the future. It might seem strange for someone to pay for something and then not take it home, especially if their means are limited. But leaving the fifteen loaves at the bakery was evidently preferable to taking them and bearing the responsibility for not wasting them, either by freezing them for future use or by passing them on to someone else to consume. Indeed, the fact that the server did not ask any questions or seem surprised suggests that such a request is not unusual. Instead, he just removed the bread from the counter, placing it back on a rack to sell again, waited for the card reader to finish computing the transaction, and then returned the card to her with the receipt.

If a card stops working, this also necessitates certain kinds of work. The switch to nonoperational status is sometimes an outcome of the ministry cutting off someone whom it deems ineligible. After introducing its new eligibility criteria in 2019, for instance, the ministry cancelled 400,000 cards. The minister characterized these card owners as "board chairmen, board members, head judges and generals, people like that"—people, in other words, who are clearly not in need of cheap bread. Yet the number of people who gathered in the tent set up in Cairo for processing in-person petitions in response to this move suggests something different. One man who had been disqualified on account of a high monthly phone bill—which according to new regulations marked him as too wealthy to be eligible for baladi bread—insisted that the figures were wrong. With a pension of only 650EGP/month, it was ludicrous, he said, for the ministry to suggest he was spending over 800EGP a month on his phone. Another questioned his alleged electricity bill, given that there is no electricity meter for his home.[30] The petitioning that these individuals were doing, traveling from across the country to make their cases and claim their access to subsidized bread, is illustrative of a particular kind of labor. It is a labor that those faced with a nonworking card, who consider themselves entitled to one, have to go through to get it to work again, all the while not being able to access baladi bread. Such labor may not have a successful outcome—indeed, the following year the minister gave a jubilant television interview saying that the ministry had succeeded in removing 10 million citizens from the bread subsidy program, saving the state 5 billion EGP—but it is indicative of the efforts individuals put into trying to secure their staple.[31] The following case of Fayza and her card demonstrates the complexities and frustrations of the bureaucratic process, in contrast with the simple, transparent process set out on the ministry website. It shows the lengths to which people may have to go to ensure that they have a working smart card in order to get baladi bread.

FAYZA AND HER CARD Fayza is a widow in her sixties whom Mariam has known since her childhood. She lives with her three adult children, granddaughter, and sister in a small two-bedroom apartment in a working-class neighborhood of Cairo. She complements her deceased husband's meager pension (600EGP/month) with irregular short-term jobs; nobody in her household

holds permanent, full-time employment. Yet the household income is sufficient that she will sometimes purchase other kinds of bread, like fino rolls for
her granddaughter, or whiter shami bread for her sister, who has dental problems and so appreciates its softer texture. Only rarely does she get her full share
of bread for the household of six. But it is important to her that she maintains
this possibility, so she tries to remember to use her card regularly.

Early in 2016, however, Fayza becomes sick. Unable to leave her apartment,
she does not use her card, either to get bread or to buy other subsidized goods
from the tamwin store for several weeks. Preoccupied with her illness, she does
not think to send someone to get baladi bread with her card; her sister goes
out to buy some shami bread, so there is enough bread in the home to keep
the family going. By late February, she is beginning to feel better. One day, she
takes a minibus to the tamwin store to stock up on some products. She hands
her card to the man sitting at a desk near the front of the store with the card
reader in front of him. He tells her that her card is no longer working. The
problem, he says, is that it has been too long since she last used it.

The owner of the store is an acquaintance of Fayza's, for she has been buying from him for a long time. He expresses sympathy and tells her that she can
still have 16 kg of sugar and some oil. He also offers to take her card to the local
branch of the Ministry of Supply to see if he can activate it. (I refer to these
local branches of the ministry as "tamwin offices.") She is grateful and leaves
her card with him. Over the following weeks, she calls by the store and phones
him regularly. Each time, he reports that the card is still not working. She says
she trusts him, but given the stories that circulate about card fraud, Mariam
and I wonder why he is holding onto the card.

By early April, Fayza has decided that the man is unlikely to be able to solve
her problem. She starts the bureaucratic process of getting a new card. She is
optimistic because she has been told that in the meantime she will receive a piece
of paper which will allow her to obtain bread and other subsidized goods until
her card is ready. Several weeks later, though, she has made little progress. "They
keep sending me to different places, different offices, no one takes any responsibility," she complains to Mariam. She finds these offices challenging places to be.
"There were lots of people everywhere," she recounts, "people in difficult situations, people whose papers have been left for a long time. It is so difficult for
me to manage. Everyone is fighting, no one helps you, they all just want to get
ahead."

She considers going back to the owner of the tamwin store. "He is not a
stranger to the system," she says, "he must have a way to get things done." But
when she inquires, he says he will charge 200EGP for the service, and she is

unwilling to pay. She returns to the tamwin office, braving the crowds once again. When she finally gets to the front of the line, the clerk tells her she does not have the correct paperwork. She talks to other people in the line who have been waiting for months for their cards, unable to get bread. Every time they go to the office, they are told, "lissa [not yet]."

As the months go on, Fayza is absorbed in the bureaucratic saga. In each conversation with Mariam, she talks about how desperate she is to get the card and how annoyed she is at the difficulties she is facing. While the problem was precipitated by her not using the card, her sense of vulnerability without it is palpable. She might not need the card every month, but it makes a difference when she does not have it for months on end. Her income is unreliable and fluctuates. With a number of health problems, it is increasingly difficult for her to do the occasional work she used to do, cooking for families or helping with their children. Her sister does not have a job, and her children are unable to contribute much, all of them lacking full-time, stable positions. Some months, she has to cover the full household's needs on the 600EGP pension alone. Fayza's expenses also fluctuate. One month she might get nonperishables like sugar and rice in bulk and then will not have to restock for a while. But when they run out, she has to find the money to replace them. If her medical problems flare up, she has to buy expensive medicines; her current medicine regime costs 1,000EGP for a month's supply. This is all at the same time that prices in general are going up, rendering nonsubsidized goods increasingly expensive. So cheap bread and other subsidized goods provide an important safety net.

During a meal with Mariam early in 2017, Fayza comments, "Everything is becoming more expensive." She goes on to note, "Without the card, it is difficult. Even the bread now we cannot get from the [subsidized] bakery." Fayza's sister, who is eating with them, says that she tried to get baladi bread, but the bakery would not allow it, even when she said that she used to have a card. She castigates Fayza for not solving the problem. "I'm trying," Fayza responds, "but it is so hard." She is frustrated at the process. "Why do they make us go through all of this?" she says. "I am an old woman and it is tiring for me. Why do they make me run all around just to get bread? I do not know."

Finally, in May 2017, she is told that her application is complete and her card should be ready by the end of June. But it is not. And it is not ready in July. Or August. When she goes to inquire, the office tells her that the card has been issued and activated, but has not arrived. The woman who is next to her in the line suggests that she just go to the man who owns the tamwin store and ask him to get a card for her, but she is still unwilling. She says to Mariam, "You used to be able to give him [the tamwin store owner] 50 or 100EGP, and he would go and get the card for you, in an instant. Now the price has gone up to 300EGP, and this is too much." She concludes, "They can all eat together"—an expression that signals a sense of "them" (the subsidy managers) versus "us" (the subsidy recipients), the rich getting richer, splitting the money to profit out of poor people's suffering.

Shortly after this conversation, Mariam leaves Egypt to begin her doctoral studies. She talks with Fayza intermittently on the phone, who reports that she has still not received a card, despite submitting all her paperwork twice. In the meantime, she has had to buy bread at a much higher price—paying either the 0.50EGP/loaf that baladi bread bakeries charge to those without cards, or buying another kind of bread for 1EGP/loaf. Occasionally her friends will share some of their baladi bread with her, if they do not need it all. But her lack of a card remains a big concern.

When Mariam returns the following summer during her break, Fayza still does not have a functioning card. Mariam offers to accompany her to the tamwin office for her neighborhood. One morning, in early September 2018, they take a taxi to the office, which is in a building on a small side street. Visitors form lines outside to wait for a turn to speak with clerks through small barred windows (figure 4.3). When Mariam and Fayza arrive just after 9 AM, the office is not yet open, its service windows shuttered, but the forecourt is full. The women who are waiting have organized themselves in order, taking names in a numbered list for when the office opens. Fayza is number 41 on the list of the women's line. She and Mariam find some plastic chairs from a sandwich shop across the street to sit on.

Around 9:30 AM, the metal shutters are pulled upward and the windows appear. Immediately, the crowds swarm. Numbers 1 through 20 are already somewhat neatly aligned and excitedly awaiting their turns. But despite constant activity at the window—women waving papers, plastic folders, and cards, shouting and pushing—there is little movement in the line. An hour later, Number 20 has moved less than a few feet forward. Mariam and Fayza sit, watching, every so often walking over to ask which number is being served. One woman near them has a lot of paperwork spread out on the back of a car; she is here to add a new child to her card. Another group of women have come to fix a mistake; their paperwork says that their husbands are deceased, but they are not.

Suddenly, two new windows open. It is unclear what these windows are for or why the line has not shifted over to them. But keen to grab the opportunity to speak to someone, Mariam and Fayza make their way over through the crowds.

FIGURE 4.3. Waiting at the window, tamwin office. Photograph by Mariam Taher.

Fayza explains her situation to the clerk behind the window as other women thrust their hands over her and call out questions, hemming her in on all sides. The man tells her that everything she has done has gone from the system; she will have to do all the paperwork again. He starts listing the steps she will have to take. She needs to bring photocopies of her ID and those on the card with her; an electricity bill; a statement of her social support status; and a paper proving what pension she receives. Fayza asks him to write everything down. "These are all new instructions," she says, irritated. "They keep changing the requirements!"

Deflated at their lack of progress, Fayza and Mariam decide to try at least to get some of the necessary paperwork. They take a taxi to another office to get the documentation of Fayza's pension. This goes relatively smoothly. Just a short line, some information typed into an ancient computer, and Fayza is handed a piece of paper, which she gets stamped in another office. They then take another taxi to the office to get the statement of her social support status. The woman they speak to at this office tells Fayza that she does not in fact need this piece of paper. "The man who told you that you did is an idiot!" she says. "He does not know anything." She starts rattling off a detailed set of instructions, which are completely different to those that they were told before. Mariam takes notes, they thank her, and leave. It is now 1 PM. Four hours, three offices, three taxi rides, many lines later, and still no card.

The woman has told Fayza that she must phone a call center to find out the number of her now defunct card. Over the following days, Mariam tries repeatedly to call the five-digit number they were given. Each time, she receives a recorded message and is put on hold, never to get through. Fayza also tries calling, again and again, using up her valued phone minutes, to no avail. Later, it becomes clear that she has not realized that she has to press a digit to advance beyond the recording; she has been expressing her woes to a taped voice. When Mariam tries again, she finds that the phone number is no longer operative.

They decide to return to the tamwin office, this time trying a branch in another slightly more affluent neighborhood, closer to Fayza's apartment, where they think there may be fewer people. This office is smaller, with a bit of green space outside offering some shade to those waiting at the windows. They arrive before the office opens at 9 AM. It is less crowded than the other office was; there are around sixty people in front of the two windows. Fayza is number 11 in the informal ordering system. She takes a seat to one side while Mariam stands in line as the office opens, occasionally moving slowly forward, most of the time immobile. When she gets to the front, Fayza joins her, and they explain how Fayza wants to apply for a new card. The clerk behind the window tells her she has to get a form at the next window.

Fayza returns to her seat, a little fed up, while Mariam moves to the back of another line. It is now 9:55 AM and getting hot. Bodies are pressing in on all sides, pouncing at any opportunity to move forward. Around Mariam, everyone is asking questions, unsure of the process. Is this where I get the form? Does the clerk fill in the form for me? What form are you getting? Are you applying for a replacement card as well? Nuggets of information circulate through the crowd, collected eagerly by those who are waiting as they seek to piece together how the system works. The line inches forward. The sun is getting stronger and flies are increasing.

Eventually, Mariam and Fayza arrive at the window. The clerk starts going through Fayza's papers and filling out a form. There is a problem, she says. Fayza must have proof that she no longer has a card; she needs to file a report at the police station. At Mariam and Fayza's crestfallen faces, others in the line seek to reassure them, telling them not to worry, that there is a police station nearby, and it is easy to file a report. They leave the office and head to the police station. To their surprise, it takes only about fifteen minutes to get the police report. The officer fills out a form, Fayza signs the form and a handwritten ledger, she pays a 2EGP fee, and gets stamps on all the necessary papers. They return to the tamwin office, where they stand in line again.

When it is Fayza's turn she presents her papers. The woman goes through them, fills out a form, and staples everything together. She tells them they have to take these papers to another window. They join yet another line, which does not seem to be moving. It turns out the system is down. One clerk turns the computer screen toward the crowd to demonstrate. He clicks a button; the page does not load. They wait. People keep coming to ask about how they update their personal information so as to make a change to their smart card coverage. The clerks tell them, "On the net, Sir [min 'ala al-net yafandim]." Some people are not sure what this means. "Where do I get this net? [agib al-net da minin?]," they ask. A few people comment that they have tried the website multiple times but it is not working. The clerks admit that the system has been failing this week. There has been too much pressure with too many people accessing it. They are working on fixing it. It should be working by next week, inshallah.[32] One woman in the line is waiting for a new card. She is lucky, she confides to those around her. Her husband knows the owner of a baladi bread bakery and he lets him take ten loaves a day. If she had to wait for the card before she could get bread, she would not be able to manage.

The system begins working and the line starts edging forward. Eventually it is Fayza's turn and she hands over her paperwork. The clerk glances through her documents and tells her, with an apologetic tone, that she is at the wrong office. She has to go to the office she is zoned for. Fayza is unhappy and challenges him, asking why she cannot come to this office, since it is the one located closest to her apartment. The man is sympathetic but insists that she has to submit her paperwork elsewhere.

Tired but determined, Fayza and Mariam decide to go that day to finish the process. They return to the same office they visited on the previous occasion. The office is calmer on this day, with only twenty or so people lining up outside. They ask directions to the correct window, which they are happy to see has no line, and hand over the papers. The woman flicks through Fayza's documents and tells them that they are missing a photocopy of one document. They hear the words and feel their frustration bubbling up, almost ready to implode. Then, over their shoulders, less than two meters away, they see a

photocopier in the shade of a tree, a young man sitting beside it, ready to operate for a small fee. A piece of luck. They pay their 2EGP and return with the
copies to the window. After a bit more paper shuffling, the clerk takes Fayza's
phone number, stamps some papers, and says the process is complete. She will
receive a text message when her card is ready and then she must return to the
office and pick up her card. It could take only fifteen days, the woman tells her.
Or it could take one or two or three months.

The weeks and months pass. Every so often, Mariam checks in with Fayza.
She also calls Fayza's daughters and asks them to look at their mother's phone
and ensure that she did not miss a message. Finally, after nine months, Fayza
receives a card. But she never receives the PIN number that she needs to activate it. She goes to the tamwin office several times to ask. Each time, the
office staff tell her to wait. According to a ministerial directive issued in 2018,
designed to clarify what is evidently unclear to others as well as Fayza, the
PIN number is delivered to the card owner via their mobile phone, and if not
received, must be retrieved by sending text messages to a series of numbers.
The challenges of this final step can prove insurmountable for the elderly, like
Fayza, or illiterate, who struggle with managing mobile phones, as well as for
those who do not have SIM cards in their phones, or who have working phones
but do not have any credit on them. After multiple trips to offices to ask, Fayza
finds out that the problem seems to be that the phone number on record for
her is wrong; it is for a phone that she no longer has. She goes to a mobile
phone store and buys a SIM card for her old number, but is still not sure who
to call. The card remains safe in her apartment, unusable, while she continues
to buy ten loaves of bread for 5–10EGP instead of 0.5EGP, and to pay 100EGP
for a bottle of oil that she could receive for free from the tamwin store. "I don't
know what to do," she says to Mariam. "Should I go and sit on the steps of
the ministry?" She is disillusioned with Egypt's politicians. "They keep talking
about 'the Egyptian woman' and how they honor her, like a mother," she comments, and yet she feels far from honored.

When Mariam returns to Cairo for a visit in September 2019, she offers to
put money on Fayza's SIM card so that they can try sending a message to receive the PIN. Fayza has a scrap of paper on which someone has scrawled an
instruction—"send an empty message"—and the number to which that message must be sent. Fayza tries to show Mariam how to compose a message on
her phone, but keeps navigating to the calling section. It seems she has tried
to call the number many times. Mariam finds the messaging feature and types
in the number, but is unable to send an empty message. On Fayza's phone,

the icon for sending a message does not appear until you type something into the composition box. Eventually, frustrated, Mariam types, "Al-raqam al-siri feeeeen? [*Where* is the PIN number?]," and presses send. Several minutes later, to their surprise, the phone buzzes. The screen shows a reply with a four-digit code and the notification that Fayza's card will be operational by October 4, at the latest. In early October, Fayza's card starts working, and the nearly four-year saga comes to an end.

Fayza's experience is not unique. Newspapers carry stories of strikingly similar cases. One documented an individual whose card was damaged, submitted paperwork for a new one, received a card that did not work, and filed repeated complaints to no avail, leaving his family without bread for months. The journalist described this situation as "one of an untold number of cases that remain unresolved in Egypt, where some of the population's most economically vulnerable citizens are being denied access to a key social safety net, calling into question the credibility of the government slogan, 'providing support to those who deserve it.'"[33] Another article quoted a parliamentarian complaining about nonfunctioning smart cards, which "remain damaged for months at a time, which makes people's everyday lives more difficult," and lamenting the situation of those who are "unable to get hold of their cards for a period of six months to a year."[34]

Fayza also has stories. She talks about her friend, a widow with two disabled children, who has been waiting to receive a new card for a year and can barely manage buying everything for the full price. She describes another woman who has been waiting for two years for a card. This woman lives with her husband and four children in the small space under the stairs of the apartment building in which he is a doorman, earning 1,000EGP a month. Neither she nor her husband are literate; they feel helpless, unable to navigate the government bureaucracy. She talks about an old man she met one day at the tamwin office who was dizzy and tired. He had submitted all his paperwork and made several administrative payments, had been told numerous times that his card was on its way, but had been waiting for six months. He was pleading with the office, saying he was willing to go anywhere to get his card, but did not understand the mobile phone system; he cannot read the small writing of text messages. As Fayza recounts the many experiences she has seen and heard, she concludes, "There are a lot of really tough cases. Everyone has a story. A long sad story. It is all difficult. Difficult."

The line has shifted from the highly politicized and much-photographed space of the bakery to the less visible and more sparsely media-covered space of the bureaucratic office. In the process, opaque bureaucratic procedures have created a new set of barriers to access to bread that work to disadvantage those with low levels of literacy, who are unfamiliar with using online systems, or who do not have the time or physical strength to spend hours at busy government offices. While the bread line is a clear symbol of systemic failure and individual humiliation, in offices and mobile phone networks these conditions are less tangible but still present. For an elderly person like Fayza, or for the almost one third of the adult population that is illiterate, an inability to navigate the system and its challenges brings not only frustration but a sense of shame.[35]

What these cases illustrate is that not everyone's efforts to secure their daily supply of bread are equally successful. Even when a government subsidizes a staple such that its price is sufficiently low as to be affordable to all, other things may impede access. Getting bread for a family can, therefore, require many different forms of practice. Dealing with bureaucratic paperwork may be just as important as going to a bakery.

Furthermore, practices of staple security among baladi bread consumers are not just about what people do to get bread, but about what they do to get *good* bread. They are motivated not just by the fear of no bread but the desire for pleasurable bread.

Baladi Bread Quality

A group of friends is sitting together. Two men start talking about their military service—the obligatory period Egyptian men have to spend in the army.[36] They remember it as a time of humiliation, describing how their superiors sought to beat any sense of will, pride, or independence out of them. Food was central to this, always poor in quality, often infested with insects or going bad. They recall the bread in particular. Fresh baladi loaves, nice and soft, would be delivered to the army base. The officer on duty would receive this bread and then spread it out over the sand in an open space. It would be left there to dry out completely over two or three days. Only then would the loaves be collected and distributed to soldiers to eat. If you were caught taking even just a tiny piece from the fresh bread, you would receive severe punishment. In these men's telling, it is clear that their story is not about their bodies having suffered as a result of eating stale bread. Rather, it is about their sense of outrage that such a thing would be done to bread and the inhumanness of the people who would do it.

That bread would feature in these men's accounts of their time in the military service says something about the positioning of this food in people's daily lives. Their lingering anger over how the officers handled their bread speaks to the deep significance attached to bread quality. Eating bread is central to most Egyptians' diets, particularly among the poor for whom other staples, like rice, are unaffordable on a regular basis. But eating is not just about meeting caloric needs, even for people reliant on free or subsidized food. It is also about taste—hence the military conscripts risking punishment to tear off a piece of fresh bread—enjoyment, and the social bonds forged in and through food.[37] The quality of baladi bread shapes the experience of an everyday meal within the home, whether that might be a breakfast sandwich with falafel, greens, and pickles, or vegetable stew with bread on the side. As a food served with almost every meal, baladi bread also impacts the experience of feeding others, whether those others are children, a spouse, or guests.

The government is widely understood as being responsible for the quality of the baladi bread, even though this bread is mostly produced in privately owned bakeries. The quality of the bread is therefore one medium through which people assess the quality of the state.[38] Occasionally people complain about particular bakeries, but more commonly they direct any wrath about bad baladi bread at the government. Poor-quality bread thus poses a threat not only to the day-to-day existence of those who have little choice but to eat that bread but, more broadly, to national stability. Efforts to ensure the quality of baladi bread are, therefore, practices of staple security, operating both at the national level, through regulations and checks within the production chain for subsidized bread, and at the household level, through individual labors to provide good bread to go with a meal.

Around the same time that there were bread shortages, in the late 2000s, there were also complaints about the quality of baladi bread.[39] On one human rights website designed as a space for Egyptians to log their complaints (between 2008 and 2011), commentators described baladi bread as being "bad" (zay al-zift), "worse and worse," "so bad not even the livestock will eat it," and "not edible." Some critiqued the bread for being small. Others mentioned contaminants that they had found in the bread, like threads or pebbles.[40] Indeed when I found a hair in a loaf, one of the first times I bought baladi bread back in 2007, I remember that none of the people in the irrigation ministry, where I was then conducting fieldwork, were the least bit surprised. A 2011 article in the opposition newspaper Al-Wafd noted that baladi bread "is in a state that would not please your enemy or loved ones, as it suffers from deterioration in its appearance and size." The article went on to mention how the bread was full of insects and impurities and cited various citizens as describing baladi bread as bad (say'ia) and "the worst kind of bread."[41]

When President Morsi came to power, his manifesto pledged not only to deliver sufficient bread but to standardize the quality of the loaf (dabt gawdat al-raghif). In the postrevolution context, making the quality of baladi bread more consistent was part of the government's efforts to maintain stability. The government has long used regulations to shape the nature of the baladi bread that private bakeries produce, altering the composition and size of baladi bread in part with quality in mind (see chapter 1). Inspectors employed by the Ministry of Supply are a key part of this regulatory approach, charged with checking that bakeries comply with these regulations. Yet the frequency of the complaints about baladi bread suggests that this process has not been entirely effective. This is not all that surprising. The work of bakery inspection is tedious and low-paid, creating an incentive for inspectors to accept payments from bakers in return for not implementing fines and enforcing regulations (Kamal 2015).[42]

In the aftermath of the 2014 subsidy reforms, the government ramped up the inspection process. As one Egyptian economist I spoke with about the subsidy program explained to me, "At the beginning, with the new system, they [government officials] were keen to make it a success story, so they did lots of monitoring." More significantly, though, the reorganization of the reimbursement process has given bakers an incentive to produce good bread. Bakeries no longer receive flour at a below-market price; instead, the government reimburses them for each loaf that they sell at a below-market price. If they fail to sell their bread, they are unable to claim reimbursement to cover their production costs and so take a loss.

Many urban residents talk about baladi bread as being better now than it used to be and ascribe this change to competition. (In rural areas, in contrast, there is typically less choice. In Warda, for instance, there are only two baladi bread bakeries, and when people express taste preferences, as I discuss in the next chapter, it is generally for homemade bread over baladi bread as opposed to for baladi bread from a particular bakery.) This came up in a conversation with Ahmed, the Egyptian grain trade professional whom I introduced in chapter 1. "The quality has improved," he told me. "So in this neighborhood say you have three bakeries, they are competing on quality. If you don't like bread in one you will go to another." While Ahmed's income and social positioning is such that he does not eat baladi bread himself, as someone who engages professionally with people at each stage of the wheat supply chain, he has an opinion on this policy change. "This was a great move by the government to fix the problem," he said. Another man who drives buses for a travel company and regularly eats baladi bread described it as "wonderful." He went on to explain, "There are five bakeries in my area. If I do not like the bread in one, I can go to the other, I have all the choice, it is up to me. . . . With the new system, all the bakeries have to always improve their bread in order to sell more."

People talk about their preferences for bread from certain neighborhoods, describing their favored bakeries with terms like nidif, which means "clean" but can also be used to signify quality. "The bread of Fayda Kamil is always very nice [hilu awi]," Fayza says. "The bread in Maʿadi is dust[y] [turab]." Some alter their movements around the city so that they can buy from a bakery whose bread they like. Before her card stopped working, Fayza would often buy bread from Fayda Kamil, even though a detour to that neighborhood on public transport can take over an hour in heavy traffic. Her sister, on the other hand, would buy bread from their neighborhood but would walk to a bakery a little farther from their apartment rather than to the one closest, because she found its bread to be slightly softer.

This is not to say that there are no longer any complaints about the quality of the bread. There are occasional complaints about the bread being too small (chapter 1). The economist who reflected on the increased monitoring in the aftermath of the reforms also mentioned that the government had since relaxed its inspection process, and that some bakeries had been reducing the weight of their loaves in response to the rising costs of production. Sometimes people talk about finding dubious contaminants in the bread that suggest unsanitary production conditions. "I eat baladi bread . . . it's my favorite," said one woman, "but sometimes there are problems with it. You might find a cigarette butt or fingernail inside it." The media delight in the most alarming stories, like a gecko found in a loaf of bread, photographs showing its little body embedded in the top of the loaf, or a rat's tail.[43] But such occurrences are relatively uncommon given the vast quantities of baladi bread being produced and eaten on a daily basis.

Among those who eat baladi bread on a regular basis, there seems to be a general level of satisfaction with this bread.[44] A video produced by the Ministry of Supply in 2015 contains a number of clips from individuals talking about how the bread has improved since the reforms. Given the source of the video, it is not surprising that the featured quotes are positive; the ministry is, after all, keen to highlight its achievements. Still, it is notable that the success the ministry is showcasing relates to the improved *quality* of the bread. One woman interviewed on the street describes the bread as good, great (kwayis, zai al-ful), another describes it as a lot better than before (ahsan min al-awil bi-kitir), a third describes it as very good (kwayis gidan). The video then moves to a scene from the talk show *Al-Qahira Al-Youm* in which the talk show host is holding a loaf of bread. "They say," he says with a grin, "the Minister of Supply says, that *this* is for a shilling [5 piasters]!" It is evident, from the large size and the white color of the bread in the host's hand, that what he holds is not a loaf of baladi bread, but perhaps the show's production team assumes most viewers will not notice. The host tears off a piece of the bread and stuffs it in his mouth. As he chews he continues, "As enjoyable as can be. Very strange. It tastes nice [hilu]!" Pulling apart the loaf he adds, "and it opens!"—a valuable characteristic for bread if you want to make a sandwich out of it.[45]

The ministry's efforts to ensure that baladi bread meets some basic quality requirements appear, by most accounts, to have been largely successful. But the quality of baladi bread that Egyptians eat on a daily basis does not only depend on the ingredients and production conditions within bakeries. There is a final stage—the conveyance of the bread between the bakery and the home—which is critical for shaping the bread's taste, form, texture, and ultimately its quality as perceived by those who consume it. Conveyance is a liminal phase during which good care can lead to bad bread being rejected and bad care can lead to good bread becoming inedible (Barnes and Taher 2019). The next section turns to the quotidian practices of handling baladi bread through which people seek to ensure that their families have good bread to eat.[46]

Everyday Handling

AIRING One bright day in December 2018 I take the metro from the guesthouse where I am staying in downtown Cairo and walk the route that Mariam typically walked when going to buy baladi bread. I cross under the metro line, through the tunnel, down a street thick with fruit and vegetable stands and lined with small shops, around the corner, along another market street, over the bridge above the metro line, and back along the main road, passing four baladi bread bakeries along the way. I find a space by a wall close to one of the bakeries, pause, as though waiting for someone, and watch.

A stooped old lady in a long black galabiya is at the booth, where she has just bought around forty loaves of bread. The server passes her the bread on a rectangular lattice tray made out of palm fronds, known as a rack (qafas). A young woman helps her carry the rack of bread to one side. There is a set of metal shelves just in front of the bakery, next to the sidewalk. The old woman pushes her rack onto the shelves and starts moving around the loaves of bread. She takes a few from the front and places them at the back, a few from the left and places them on the right. She turns some of them over. After several minutes, she starts packing the loaves into a plastic bag she has bought with her, then pauses, realizing they are still too hot, and waits some more. A middle-aged woman with a similar number of loaves lays her rack beside the old woman's on the shelf. She puts her two palms on the loaves to feel their temperature, first in one place, then another. She packs a couple of loaves in her plastic bag, then waits. A middle-aged man brings his rack of approximately fifty loaves and slides it onto a higher shelf of the shelving unit. He uses the rack of the older lady, who has by now departed, to spread out his bread. He moves his bread between the two racks, laying out the loaves, rearranging them, turning them over. He pauses occasionally, standing and watching the traffic, then returns to arranging his bread.

These people are doing something mundane, a seemingly insignificant task, but one that is in fact critical to the quality of the bread that they will later eat. They are airing the bread, allowing it to cool before they pack it. Within baladi bread bakeries, as bread emerges from the oven over the course of the day, workers place the bread on racks to cool. Depending on fluctuations in demand and production, though, the bread may have little time to sit on a shelving unit before it is passed to a customer. While some might think of bread's warmth as a positive characteristic, to baladi bread customers, it is not. To them, temperature is not an indicator of freshness and good taste, but a quality they interpret in relation to the plastic bags they use to carry the bread home.[47] If a customer places hot bread directly in a plastic bag, the hot air condenses on the inside of the bag, rendering the bread soggy. Egyptians talk about this in terms of the bread sweating (al- 'aish biyi'raq). Sweaty bread is unpalatable. For baladi bread to be tasty, therefore, people have to closely manage its temperature after they buy it.

In the case of the bakery described above, the shelving unit on the side of the street provides a place where this airing can take place. More commonly, people temporarily commandeer a slice of public space to lay out their bread. If they have received the bread in loose piles, they may lay it on a cloth or bench. If they have purchased a whole rack of bread, they balance the rack on whatever they can find—a rock, table, crate, or car—allowing air to circulate around the bread to cool it before they pack their loaves and return the rack to the bakery (figure 4.4). Sometimes they actively manage the airing process, constantly rearranging their loaves so that they all have a chance to cool. Other times they

FIGURE 4.4. Airing bread on a rack. Photograph by Mariam Taher.

just stand beside their bread, speaking on the phone, smoking a cigarette, or chatting with a companion.

This labor is important for maintaining the texture of the bread. As Fayza once explained to Mariam, hot bread packed before it cools will "stick together" and "become doughy." By airing the bread, on the other hand, any moisture in the hot bread can evaporate into the atmosphere as the bread cools. Airing is critical, therefore, for preventing baladi bread from becoming wet. Other quality characteristics, such as the bread's shape and color, require different kinds of handling practices at the bakery.

REJECTING, STACKING, AND PACKING One day Mariam stands in line at the booth, observing a girl who is buying forty loaves of bread. The server has placed the bread on the counter in stacks of ten. This batch of bread has already cooled so does not require airing. The girl removes each loaf one by one and makes two new taller stacks of bread. As she does so, she sets aside four loaves. She does not say anything, but it is clear that she does not want to take these loaves. They are a bit burnt and slightly deflated. The server also does not say anything. Without a word, she sets the rejected loaves aside and replaces them with four new ones. When the girl finishes going through the rest of the bread, she takes her two stacks of loaves off to one side. She starts packing the bread into a large plastic bag that she brought with her, alternating between one pile and the other, building the loaves into a neat stack in her bag. Once the loaves are packed, she leaves.

Although customers at baladi bread bakeries are not able to pick bread off a shelf, many, like this girl, check their loaves as they receive them over the booth counter. They are looking for quality, which is not uniform across loaves due to the only partially mechanized nature of the production process in small-scale bakeries. They assess by eye and sometimes by touch, looking for defects in color or texture, feeling for temperature, and squeezing for freshness. They do not typically smell the bread, perhaps because it does not have a pronounced smell. Tasting is also not an option, rendering some dimensions of quality—like its occasionally sandy or metallic taste—indecipherable. But through sight and feel customers can detect the material characteristics that are commonly understood to distinguish a defective loaf from a good one—a burnt patch, flatness, hardness, discoloration, tear, crack on top, wetness, or absence of two distinct layers. This quality assessment process is not done in a very studied fashion but with a casual glance or feel as customers rifle through their piles of loaves.

If they do not like a loaf, they reject it. The girl's silence as she returns her loaves and the server's lack of verbal response as she replaces them indicates that rejection is not an unusual practice. No words are required to clarify the intention; the mere gesture of putting a loaf to one side suffices. Those working in the booths are typically baladi bread consumers themselves. They are not surprised that the customers are paying attention to the quality of the loaves they take home. They understand that customers have a right to choose and that some loaves, like darker loaves, are less appealing. The server-customer interaction over the returned bread therefore unfolds in a straightforward manner, without contestation.

Once the customer is satisfied with her loaves, she handles them in a particular way, carefully stacking them before placing them in her plastic bag. This is a small task, but a significant one. Thirty or forty loaves are not very heavy, but they are bulky. Unlike other food products where the packaging is incorporated in the process of production and sale, with baladi bread it is up to the customer to pack it. If the customer just shoved this bread in a plastic bag, it would crease or crack—characteristics that are widely understood as being undesirable. Through making little stacks of loaves in their hands or on the counter, though, and then transferring those stacks into their plastic bags, people make sure that the bread arrives home round and flat, not torn, its integrity intact.

The efficacy of these handling practices is evident in what goes unsaid. People do not complain about baladi bread being soggy or squashed, because they handle it to ensure that this is not the case. They do not complain about it being unevenly cooked, burnt, or poorly risen, because they select it to ensure that they do not bring home such loaves. While in these everyday encounters at the bakery the language of security is absent, these practices are just as integral to ensuring a supply of a quality staple as the practices of those who manage the subsidy program, who see their work explicitly in terms of the maintenance of national stability.

Conclusion

The production of baladi bread rests on the work of the farmers who grow wheat (chapter 2) and the officials who manage the importation of wheat (chapter 3), providing grain that is mixed together in mills to make the flour that constitutes this bread's chief ingredient. It is an outcome of the work of the staff of mostly small-scale, privately owned bakeries, who combine that flour with bran, water, salt, and yeast to turn it into bread. It is a reflection of the specifications that the government sets, which are supposed to determine the shape and composition of the loaves that those bakers produce (chapter 1).

Yet baladi bread is not only an object of policy making but a food that is woven into Egyptians' daily lives. This chapter has shown the contrasting perspectives of the government officials who run the baladi bread program and the individuals who consume the bread delivered by the program. Government officials employ policy reforms as a way to restructure the operation of the baladi bread program to influence the quantity and quality of bread that the private bakeries deliver to customers. But baladi bread consumers also play a role, going through various bureaucratic steps to ensure that they have a functioning smart card so that they can get this bread and, once at the bakery, handling their loaves in particular ways to maintain their quality.

This analysis highlights the multiplicity of what I mean by staple security and the different spaces in which these efforts to secure sufficient decent bread play out. Staple security is as much about individuals working within a bureaucracy as it is about governments making policy decisions, as much about those who buy baladi bread being careful with how they carry their bread home as it is about bakery owners improving their product to compete for business. Sometimes these practices unfold in contradictory ways. The smart card can facilitate access to baladi bread, but it can also preclude it. Thus as different actors seek to mitigate the threat of Egyptians not having good bread to eat, that threat and its associated ramifications both within households (on people's sense of wellbeing) and within the nation (for political stability) remains a constant presence.

5. HOMEMADE BREAD

The small hut has a rough dirt floor and plain brick walls, covered in dust and cobwebs. Slants of bright light shine in through gaps in the roof, which is patched together out of palm fronds, pieces of wood, and cardboard. In one corner, a mud brick oven is giving off heat. It is September 2015 and a group of women from a household in the village of Warda are baking bread. Khadiga has a pile of wood next to her. She is carefully monitoring the fire in the base of the oven, feeding in sticks to boost the flames when necessary. Her sister-in-law Salma and her thirteen-year-old daughter are sitting on the floor, preparing loaves. They take balls of dough, one by one, and place them on their

AT THE OVEN. *Photograph by Mariam Taher.*

FIGURE 5.1. Baking bread. Photograph by the author.

bran-covered matrahs, round wooden implements, about fifteen inches across, with handles. Tilting the matrah to one side and swinging it up and down, they gently toss the dough in the air to spread it out. The daughter works on each piece of dough first, beginning to expand it, before handing it to her aunt to complete the task, forming a perfect circle that reaches exactly to the edges of the matrah. Another of Khadiga's sisters-in-law, Magda, then takes the matrah and reaches into the mouth of the oven, flipping the thin round of dough with a practiced jerk onto the smooth surface. She uses a hooked metal pole to poke the top of the loaves a few times and move them around (figure 5.1). After about forty-five seconds, she pulls the bread—by now puffed and browned on top—to the front lip of the oven and flicks it onto a low, round table where a growing mound of bread is cooling.

This bread—made from wheat, molded into shape by women, baked in ovens within the home, and eaten in many rural households as well as in some urban households—is the focus of this chapter. For Egyptians like Khadiga and her family, a quality staple is a homemade staple. To them, therefore, staple security means securing a continuous supply of homemade bread. Such practices are not driven by the fear of absence; if homemade bread is not available, there are other affordable breads, like baladi bread, to which they can turn. Instead, these practices are driven by a desire for pleasure; people want to eat a bread that tastes good to them, which brings satisfaction when served alongside a once-a-week meal of meat or when eaten first thing in the morning for breakfast. This is not a matter of indulgence. The taste of a staple, eaten multiple times a day, shapes day-to-day sustenance, both the experience of eating and that of feeding others.[1] Moreover, taste is not only about the flavor sensation that comes from a particular kind of bread but the social relationships that surround the making of that bread.

In this chapter I look, first, at homemade bread in a rural context. Drawing on my work in Warda, I examine the value that residents attach to homemade bread. I then discuss the practices they employ to secure its constant presence in the home: sharing labor, accessing the necessary inputs, and handling the loaves in particular ways so as to preserve their quality. Second, I look at homemade bread in the city and at urban residents who also value homemade bread. While the consumption of homemade breads in Cairo is far outweighed by the consumption of baladi bread, the fact that some urban residents, even those of limited means, choose to buy more expensive homemade breads is revealing of the importance they attach to taste and of what taste means to them. I examine the tactics that these urban residents use to secure their supply of homemade bread in the city, including identifying street-side vendors through local knowledge networks, making informal arrangements with home bakers, and bringing bread from rural areas. Finally, I look at homemade bread as a matter of national concern. I follow narratives of Egypt's bread-baking heritage and explore stories about a national decline in baking knowledge and bread varieties. I examine the efforts of Cairo elites to sustain Egypt's homemade breads as objects of cultural value rather than consumption, logging them in museum exhibits, encyclopedias, and online databases.

The language of security is not explicitly present in the realms of everyday engagement discussed here, in contrast with the policy debates around wheat and baladi bread discussed in earlier chapters of this book. Yet to the people profiled in this chapter, the actions they pursue are just as significant for ensuring that they have their desired staple to eat. These practices may result in a momentary state of staple security—a pile of freshly baked loaves for a rural household offering the reassurance that a central part of each meal will be covered for the coming weeks; bread brought back from the village by an urban resident conjuring up a rural childhood and the taste of security; a written log of Egypt's diverse homemade breads setting a food activist's mind at rest that these breads will not be lost. But such moments pass, and the quotidian labors of sourcing a good staple continue.

In the Village

Early in the morning in Warda, the dirt roads that wind between the houses of the village are quiet. A few men walk their water buffalo toward the fields, and small groups of kids, hair neatly brushed, head toward school, but most front doors remain closed as families get ready for the day. From within come wafts of bread being heated for breakfast, the odd cry of an infant, and tinny recordings of Quranic recitations. On the asphalt road that borders the southern edge of the village, linking Warda with neighboring communities, the two baladi bread bakeries are hives of activity. Their service windows are open and small groups of mostly women wait outside. A steady stream of people head to and from the bakeries, in one direction carrying empty racks and plastic bowls, in the other direction, their receptacles loaded with loaves.[2] Just over a mile to the west, at the road's intersection with another main road, there is a small cluster of shops, a gas station, a coffee shop, and another bakery. This bakery, still shuttered, sells the slightly sweet white rolls known as fino. Later in the day, the small stores and fruit and vegetables stands scattered between the houses of the village will open, selling bags of shami and siyahi bread sourced from bakeries in larger villages nearby.

These are the places where bread can be bought in the village. The two baladi bread bakeries sell to the growing number of villagers who have smart cards; the other sites sell bread to anyone. Some residents buy bread regularly, others only occasionally. A farmer might get baladi bread to feed his laborers during a big work day, for instance; a mother might buy fino for her children's school sandwiches; or a family might buy a bag of bread if they have run out of homemade bread and have not had a chance to bake.

However, to many of those who live in Warda, homemade bread is preferable. The large, round, flat bread that women bake in this part of the country tastes different from the breads that can be purchased in the village (figure 5.2). It is less bland than the baladi bread, not as sweet as the fino, has a different texture than the siyahi, and more bran than the shami. When I asked people why they preferred this bread, though, they tended not to pinpoint specific taste characteristics. Instead, their answers referred to a general preference for foods made at home. "The bread from the bakery ['aish al-tabuna] is not good [mish hilu], I don't like it," one woman told me.[3] "The homemade bread is better." Another said, "Always people prefer the bread baked in the home—just like the food cooked in the home—because you know how you mixed and kneaded it and what you put in it." A third woman, commenting on her preference for homemade bread, explained, "Sometimes the other bread is good but

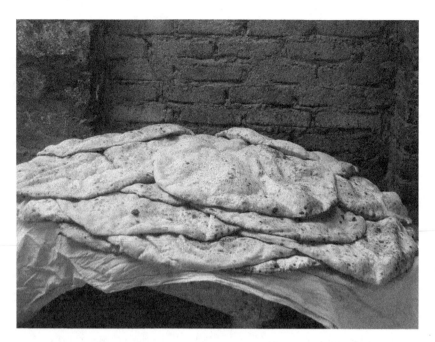

FIGURE 5.2. Homemade bread in Fayoum. Photograph by the author.

sometimes it isn't"—bringing up the question of reliability and consistency. She concluded, simply, "Ours is better." Embodied in a loaf of homemade bread is the knowledge of where the bread comes from—the ingredients that went into it and the labor that produced it; with a loaf of purchased bread, by contrast, its origins are hidden from the consumer's view.

Not surprisingly, therefore, homemade bread is the bread served on special occasions in Warda, for instance at weddings or during religious holidays to accompany specially prepared meat dishes. But it is also the bread that many in the village eat on a daily basis. When it is not available, this can be a source of complaint. Once when eating dinner with Khadiga's family, her husband expressed dismay at the baladi bread served with the meal. "Bake! You must bake!" he said to Khadiga. In ordering his wife to bake despite the plentiful bread in front of him, he demonstrated how staple security takes on a different register within rural households that produce their own staple. Unlike with the practices of obtaining and maintaining a smart card and taking it to a bakery to buy baladi bread discussed in the previous chapter, baking is not typically an act that determines whether or not a family will have any bread to eat. Even if Khadiga does not bake, she will still be able to feed her family because she can get subsidized bread. Khadiga's husband demanded she bake, though, because he prefers homemade bread and the social dynamics of the household are such that when he returns from a day's work he expects a good meal with good bread. To him, baladi bread is no substitute for homemade because not only does he find it less palatable but it also disrupts his expectations of gendered household roles.

The valuing of homemade over purchased bread is reflected in the preferential allocation of the former to certain people within the home. When families eat together, the women will pass around a piece or two of bread to each individual to use to eat from the shared dishes in the center of the table. If there is both homemade and purchased bread in the house, the homemade bread will always be given first to the higher-status members of the household, like the older men or, if I am eating with a family, to me as an outsider. Just as the norms of hospitality dictate that guests should have more bread (and other food) in front of them than they are able to eat, to ensure that they can eat until they are full, so those norms also dictate that the guest should be given the best bread. During my fieldwork in September 2015, I stayed in a small apartment above another family's house. When I talked with the father one day and asked him about his household's baking practices, he said that they had baked specially just before I arrived, "because we knew we had a guest coming."

Indicative of the value ascribed to homemade bread, it is sometimes given as a gift. Embedded in the gift is not just the bread's pleasing taste but the knowledge of the labor that went into its production. (Baladi bread, by contrast, while still something that one might give to a person in need, is not a food that people would give as a gift.) On baking days, women may send a few fresh loaves to close relatives living nearby, or to neighbors.[4] When I am in the village, the families that I know best will often give me some loaves when they bake. The bread is a symbol of their care for me, a way of showing their concern for my welfare—embodied in their knowledge that I have good bread to eat—and of cementing the relationship between us. But homemade bread is not something that people sell. Thus for those who consider a quality staple to be homemade, the practices required to secure its continuous supply relate not to daily trips to purchase it but daily acts to produce and maintain it.

Sharing Labor

Khadiga's house sits next to the house where I lived during the year I spent in Warda in 2007–8. It is a single-story home that has been added onto at various times as the family has grown, recently assembled walls of concrete blocks next to peeling paint, newly finished doors alongside ramshackle old ones. Khadiga lives here with her husband and six children, three of whom are now married and live in a newly built three-story building next door: one floor for each son along with his wife and children. Khadiga shares the household with her widowed father-in-law and his new wife, three brothers-in-law, their wives (Salma, Magda, and Leila), and fifteen yet-to-be-married children. The family owns land, which Khadiga's father-in-law farms with the assistance of his second son, Salma's husband. The others do not work in the fields. Khadiga's husband has built a successful business constructing villas in the village for wealthy Cairo residents, and the other two brothers work with him as laborers. Most household members, therefore, are not involved in growing wheat—unlike those in Marwa's and Habiba's households, featured in chapter 2. All of the women, however, bake bread. Each family has its own private space, a set of three or four interlinked rooms where they sleep, cook, and eat as a unit. In the middle of the home is a shared courtyard. This is where the oven is located.

On the particular morning described at the start of the chapter, Khadiga—the wife of the eldest son—was baking bread for her family and for her husband's second wife, who lives in a separate house close by but does not typically bake for herself due to health problems.[5] She was baking a dough made with 50 kg of flour, the amount necessary to feed nine people for a few weeks. She had been up since before dawn, preparing the dough by sieving flour, adding salt and yeast, then gradually mixing with water, before kneading by hand—a process women often do standing up, bent at the waist, so that they can put their whole body weight into pummeling and flipping the dough. By the time she had finished baking around a hundred large, round loaves of bread, and preparing it to be stored, it was early afternoon.

Shared labor was key to this bread production process. While women can bake on their own when making bread for a small family, it would be difficult for a woman to produce bread on this scale by herself. So, within the extended household, the women help one another. On this occasion, Salma and Magda were helping Khadiga, as were Khadiga's daughter and a couple of nieces. They help her, knowing that she will help them when it is time for them to bake for their families. It is a reciprocal relationship, tied to relations of kin within the extended family—relations that are in turn reinforced through such shared acts as baking together. Baking is a social activity, a time when the women get a chance to sit and talk together. They discuss goings-on in the village, who will marry whom, the price of things in the market, and recent events. Just like working with other women to prepare time-consuming meals like stuffed cabbage (Ghannam 1995), baking bread is a way of building community. Crafting a food is also a process of crafting social relations and one's sense of self, whether that food may be an artisanal cheese (Paxson 2013) or a loaf of bread.

This is not to imply that the household is tension-free or only a space of cooperation. Leila, for instance, the wife of the youngest brother, was not helping. As the only woman in the home who completed her schooling, and the only one who is literate, she sees herself as somewhat removed from the rest of the household and tends to keep to herself. She is able to do this in part because she only has a small family to provide for and so is less reliant on shared labor; with just a husband and three children, she can bake enough bread for them on her own.

In other cases, the relations of reciprocity stretch beyond the household. In homes where there are few women to help bake but lots of people to make bread for, women sometimes work together with neighbors (who may also be relatives) on baking days. Some women who have married and live with their husbands' families return home to their mothers to help them bake, maintaining bonds with their natal homes through the production of bread.

On special occasions when very large amounts of bread are being baked, these forms of mutual assistance are particularly important. For weddings, for instance, brides' families host meals for large numbers of guests. Relatives and neighbors will help the bride's family bake the necessary bread to accompany the wedding meal. When Salma's daughter got married, in addition to the bread baked by Salma and her sisters-in-law, the family distributed 100 kg of flour to neighboring households to bake on the day of the wedding, so that there would be fresh bread to go with the 125 kg of meat and vegetable dishes they served to guests. The women, in turn, do the same for others when they have weddings to cater. This is not only a matter of sharing labor but also of sharing some of the other costs that go along with baking, such as the cost of fuel. Taking advantage of this moment of shared burden, sometimes women will add in a bit of their own flour to that provided by the bride's family, so that they can take some of the loaves for their own families' use.

While baking homemade bread for a family is time-consuming, a morning spent baking can produce enough of the staple to feed a household for several weeks. When I asked women about their baking, many underplayed these labor requirements. "Does it take a lot of time?" I asked Leila. "Not really," she replied, even though producing bread for her family of five takes her a number of hours. Marwa responded to a similar question by saying, "wala waqt, wala haga [no time, no thing]"—in other words, it is not a big deal. Although women might not articulate baking as labor per se, the centrality of their manual work to the production of homemade bread is evident in what happens in its absence.

When there are not enough women in a household to mix and knead dough, shape loaves, and place them in the oven one by one, households are unable to produce and eat homemade bread. Such a labor constraint may come from women taking jobs outside of the home, leaving them less time for domestic tasks. Bread, in this way, can index broader societal changes. Alternatively, a shift in family circumstances or in the makeup of a household can pose labor constraints.

This is reflected in the case of Habiba, who has four children—three boys and one girl. When I was living in Warda in 2007–8, Habiba used to bake regularly; this was the bread that her family ate. At that stage, her teenage daughter still lived at home and her eldest son was married. Her son and his wife lived in a separate apartment across a dirt road but they still ate together, and his wife contributed her labor to the household. So Habiba had a daughter and a daughter-in-law to help her bake.

Things had changed, though, when I returned in 2015, just before Eid al-Adha, one of the main Muslim festivals. Although the family had saved 10 ardab of their annual wheat harvest for household use, when I asked Habiba if she would be making bread for the upcoming holiday, she responded that she was not baking much. "We don't have time," she said. Her daughter had married and moved out, and her first son's wife was in her eighth month of pregnancy, tired and weak. With numerous household tasks that she had to do on her own and some health problems, Habiba was not able to bake regularly. Sometimes, she said, she would get together to bake bread with her neighbors, indicating the possibility of sharing labor beyond household boundaries. But mostly, they had started buying baladi bread. One night, over a dinner of various vegetable dishes served with baladi bread, her husband Khaled explained to me, "The bread of the home is better. . . . But you have seen Habiba, you know she is ill, so we have decided to bear this bread for this year." He pointed to the baladi bread on the table as he spoke. That Khaled used the verb *to bear* (tahamil) speaks to his sense of sacrifice. For him, having to buy bread in some ways compromised the status of the household. Yet it was a sacrifice that he understood had to be made in the absence of labor to produce bread in the home.

The following year, when I returned to Warda, the family's second son had married and the first son's wife was in better health after having her baby. Habiba was now baking again. I asked Habiba what she thought about having her second son's wife in the home and whether she helped her. "Yes," she responded, "she kneads and bakes and everything." Her wording illustrated the primacy of baking labor in the ranking of household tasks. With homemade bread once again in the house, the sense of normalcy had returned.

When it comes to sourcing labor for baking bread, what is needed is not just more hands but more trained hands. Some parts of the baking process—such as the expansion of dough into a perfect circle on the matrah—require considerable skill. Around the oven, there is a clear hierarchy of expertise between the older, more experienced women, who take on the harder tasks and oversee the whole process, and the younger women, whose roles are more menial. At the same time, there is also an ongoing process of skill transfer as the older women help train their younger counterparts. For example, when Khadiga, Salma, and Magda were almost finished, they let the three girls who had been helping, all in their early teens, have a turn. Each girl sat in front of the oven, putting in loaves, moving them around, and taking them out, as the women provided a running commentary. Put it in the oven this way. Rotate it now. Don't take it out yet. Wait. Through such supervised labor, the girls hone their skills so that they are better able to help and, once they marry, are ready to take responsibility for bread production. Teaching younger women to bake is a way to ensure that they can meet gendered labor expectations and not disrupt associated relations of power within their marital households. It is also a way of securing the continuous supply of quality bread into the future, not just for this household but for the households into which the girls will marry.[6]

The stakes of home baking are evident in the careful way in which the women work. As Khadiga and her relatives came toward the end of the dough, I accompanied Salma into another room to watch her prepare the next batch. She dipped her hands into a small dish of water and scooped up handfuls of dough, each one almost exactly the same size. She threw the dough from hand to hand a couple of times before placing it on the mat, pressing down lightly with her outstretched palm (figure 5.3). As she left the dough to rest, a few of the mounds merged into each other. Rather than pulling them apart, the girls helping her meticulously sprinkled bran on the joined part and then carefully used a knife to separate them, so as not to interfere with the integrity of the risen dough. When it came time to pick up each piece, the girls gradually edged their two hands under it until the dough was safely and evenly balanced across them—almost as one would cradle an infant, supporting the head—before lifting and placing it gently on the matrah to carry to the oven room. Producing bread in this way is not something the women take lightly.

This care was evident, also, in the ways in which the women responded to rare mistakes. Just one time when Magda put a new loaf into the oven, it hit a loaf that was already cooked and was cooling on the lip of the oven. Rather than discarding the damaged loaf, though, she painstakingly picked individual pieces of uncooked dough off the loaf before putting it back in the oven to

FIGURE 5.3. Dough resting. Photograph by the author.

brown again. It was clear that the women were keen not to waste anything. On another occasion, when I was watching Marwa bake with her thirteen-year-old daughter, the daughter made a mistake. She was tossing the matrah in the air, trying to expand the loaf to fill the round circle, when the loaf folded over on itself. "It's ruined," said Marwa. Setting the dough aside, she said that she would have to give it to their chickens. After that, it seemed that her interest in giving her daughter a chance to practice was outweighed by the risk of another mistake; she limited her daughter's contribution to just covering the matrah with bran, putting the dough on top, and then passing it back to Marwa to expand.

In this context, therefore, the sharing of skilled labor is a device of staple security—a mechanism for ensuring that family members can eat their desired staple. Baking and gifting homemade bread is also a way of maintaining social networks within and between families—the relationship with a mother-in-law, for instance, or with neighboring households. The taste of a staple encompasses not just flavor and nutritional composition but the social relations of its production. These social relations of production are contingent, though, on the women having something to turn into bread. Some of these inputs, like the labor, have no monetary cost; others have to be paid for.

Accessing Inputs

The homemade bread that women bake in Fayoum, like baladi bread, has only four ingredients—flour, yeast, salt, and water.[7] The latter three of these ingredients seldom enter discussions about bread or baking. Most women use instant yeast, purchased in small quantities from the market or from one of the small stores in the village—a point of contrast with other home-baking traditions where sourdough cultures are highly valued and exchanged between neighbors and across generations (Kanafani-Zahar 1997, [Jessica] Lee 2011). Neither the raising agent nor the salt or water are in short supply or considered key determinants of the bread's taste. Flour, therefore, is the ingredient that shapes both the ability to make bread and its flavor.

Wheat flour is the primary constituent of most Egyptian breads, although some of the regional specialty breads (discussed later in the chapter) include other kinds of flour. A few families in Warda still bake a bread known as bitau, which is a smaller bread, around seven inches in diameter, made from a mix of wheat, sorghum, and sometimes maize flour, flavored with fenugreek. But this is less common than it used to be. People in Warda told me that the reason for this decline is partly because the younger generation of women do not know how to make bitau and partly because it requires a wood oven, which not everyone has. Such explanations underscore the significance of both skilled labor and fuel to the maintenance of a staple. They also speak to the continuities and shifts in rural households' staple food practices.

The type of homemade bread prevalent in Fayoum today is a large round loaf, roughly fifteen inches in diameter (figure 5.2). Since this bread is made entirely from wheat flour, obtaining wheat is just as important to women baking homemade bread as it is to the government officials managing the baladi bread program. In addition, the taste of homemade bread is affected by the level of refinement of the flour from which it is made, just like with the changing government specifications for baladi bread (chapter 1).[8]

In Warda, women use three kinds of flour for baking bread. The first they refer to as qamh, which means, literally, wheat. This is typically sourced from grain that a household grows itself and takes to the village mill to be ground into a dark, unrefined flour. People in the village do not talk in terms of extraction rates, but qamh is darker than other flours. Sometimes policy reports describe qamh as having a 100 percent extraction rate, but since women often sift the flour once they bring it home (removing some of the coarser bran and germ particles), the extraction rate is probably slightly lower. The second kind of flour is known as daqiq baladi, *daqiq* meaning flour and *baladi*, in this context, meaning local. Baladi flour is an 82 percent extraction flour, meaning that the removal of bran and germ during the milling process reduces the weight of flour produced from a given quantity of grain by 18 percent. It is the same as the flour used for baladi bread, produced in both government-owned mills and government-contracted private mills from a mix of domestic and imported grain. The third kind of flour is known as zero. This is a more refined, whiter flour, in which even more of the bran and germ have been removed, resulting in an extraction rate of 72 percent. It is produced in privately owned mills from imported grain.

The ratio between these flours is significant because it shapes the quality of the bread. One time I watched two women in the village kneading, working with a huge vat of dough. With their hands immersed in the dough, twisting and pummeling it with force, it became clear that they were unhappy with the consistency. To me it looked a bit watery, but they said that the problem was the type of flour they had used. They sent their mother to buy some zero to add in. On another occasion, while watching Marwa bake, I asked her why she added zero to the dough. She replied, "So that the bread is good [hilu], clean [nidif]." That day she was making less bread than she normally does. She had mixed 6 kg of baladi flour (purchased because the flour from her homegrown wheat had become contaminated with insects) and 2 kg of zero. When it came to making the first dough rounds on her matrah, they did not spread out very easily. She commented that the refined flour makes the dough tough (gamid). Nonetheless, what she perceived as being a better taste clearly offset the added difficulty of working with such dough. Sometimes those eating the bread also comment on the ratio of refined to unrefined flour. One time, while eating a meal at my neighbor's house, Khadiga's husband said that he did not like the bread they had made with that year's wheat harvest. It was a bit crumbly, he thought. "It's not good with the homegrown wheat [qamh]," he told Khadiga. "It must have the more refined flour [daqiq]."

So the choice of which flour to bake with affects the quality of the home-made bread. But given that these flours come from different sources, this choice also has ramifications for the ability to make homemade bread. In the case of qamh, this flour is usually produced from the portion of a wheat harvest that farmers save for their own use. Farming households like Habiba's and Marwa's store this wheat as grain in the home, since fumigated grain is less likely to mold or rot than flour; then, as the need arises, they take it to the village mill to be ground into qamh. Once the wheat has been harvested and stored, the only payment associated with using qamh is the small milling fee of 3EGP per keila (an old measurement of weight, still commonly used in rural

Egypt, equivalent to 12 kg). But women who do not grow wheat, like Khadiga, Magda, and Leila, do not have ready access to qamh. When I first got to know the family, the matriarch of the household was still alive and the extended family cooked and ate communally, baking bread with the wheat her husband produced. After she died, though, each son began to eat separately with his family, leaving only the father's new wife and the wife of the one son who works in the fields, Salma, with their own supplies of qamh. Sometimes the women exchange with one another. Leila told me how she might swap a metal cooking dish with Salma for a bag of qamh, for example. Occasionally, families who do not have homegrown wheat buy grain from other farmers in the village to mill locally. This is what Habiba's family decided to do in 2019 when they scaled back their cultivation and did not plant any wheat (see chapter 2). But typically, qamh does not change hands by money. Access to this form of flour is thus not usually mediated by cost and cash availability but by land ownership and the decision to grow wheat.

For the other kinds of flour, by contrast, monetary payments are the medium of exchange. People purchase zero flour from the little stores in the village. It is expensive, but they buy it in small quantities, in plastic bags by the kilo rather than in sacks by the tens of kilos. It is a supplement that women add to alter the quality of the bread but not a necessity.[9] I have never heard a woman talk about the price of this refined flour as being a constraint on her ability to bake. For families that do not have access to qamh, on the other hand, the cost of baladi flour, which can be used as the primary component of the bread, is another matter. Baladi flour is sold from the bakeries that make baladi bread, as well as from small stores in the village. When I was living in Warda in 2007–8, there were frequent complaints about the spiraling cost of this flour. The phrase "flour is now for"—followed by a figure—was a recurrent theme in my fieldnotes, with no need to specify the quantity (a 50-kg sack) or quality (82 percent extraction) of flour in question, because those were taken as a given. Over the course of the year, the price ticked up from what women recalled at an unspecified point of time "in the past" as 40EGP to 90EGP, then 134EGP, then 140EGP. A number of people commented that they could not afford to buy flour to bake. It was cheaper for them to buy baladi bread. Their supply of a quality staple was limited, therefore, by the high price of the key input.

In 2014, as part of the government's broader reforms to its subsidy program (discussed in chapter 4), the government addressed the issue of flour prices. Recognizing that a number of the country's rural poor bake their own bread, government officials understood that, to these constituents, especially among those who do not grow wheat, the availability of affordable flour is more important than the availability of affordable bread. So the Ministry of Supply introduced a measure whereby people living in one of thirteen governorates where home baking is prevalent could use their smart cards to obtain baladi flour—instead of baladi bread—at a subsidized price (Abdalla and Al-Shawarby 2017). Individuals are entitled to 10 kg of subsidized flour per month at a substantially reduced price: in 2018, 50 kg of subsidized flour cost 40EGP (compared to a market price of 200EGP).

On my visits to Warda since these reforms, most of the families who have smart cards have told me that they use them to get baladi flour instead of baladi bread. "It's better to get flour from the tamwin [literally, "supply," shorthand for the Ministry of Supply or the subsidy program it operates] and then bake bread at home," one man told me. Not only does this mean that a family knows where its bread comes from, but homemade bread tastes quite different to baladi bread, even when it is made with the same baladi flour. Those who grow their own wheat also sometimes use their cards to get baladi flour to supplement their qamh. Take Salma, for instance. The wheat her husband grows is not sufficient for her to bake bread year round for her family of seven. When I asked Salma's sister-in-law Leila how Salma is able to provide bread for her family given her limited harvest, she responded, "It's the subsidized flour that makes it possible." Thus it is the ownership of a smart card and access to cheap flour that enables Salma to produce the kind of bread her family likes to eat. In addition, baladi flour can provide a useful backup in times of need, such as the occasion described above when Marwa's qamh became contaminated by insects.

The other key input to bread production is fuel. Whereas my former neighbors were using a wood-fired oven (furn baladi) to bake on the morning described at the start of the chapter, most people now use gas ovens (furn ifrangi) (figure 5.4). These ovens are a part of the trousseau that families in the village provide to their daughters when furnishing the marital home. Each woman in my neighbor's household, for instance, has her own gas oven in her family's set of rooms. When I visited the village in 2018, the roof of the shed that had housed the baladi oven had collapsed, and the oven was unusable. They were hoping to build a new one but, in the meantime, were using their gas ovens. Cooking on gas is less labor-intensive. Without needing one person to stoke the fire and manage the temperature while another places the dough in the oven, it is easier for a woman to bake on her own. But whereas women can gather the dried stalks, straw, and wood that fuel the baladi ovens from the surrounding countryside, they have to buy the gas canisters that fuel the gas

FIGURE 5.4. Baking bread in a gas oven. Photograph by the author.

ovens (there is no piped gas supply in the village). In the past, they could get a certain number of gas canisters at a subsidized price on their ration cards, but in 2016 the government stopped its fuel subsidies.

The price and availability of gas can therefore prove a constraint on home baking. When I visited Warda in 2019, the women in Khadiga's household complained about the high cost of gas. They were keen to rebuild the baladi oven but were not sure where it could go now that its courtyard space had been turned into a coop for chicks and ducks. Salma told me that delivery of a new gas canister costs 85EGP. "So from one hundred that leaves fifteen," she added, revealing the small denominations in which she calculates her expenses and the burden this expenditure places on her. If they only use the canister to fire the burners on which they do most of their cooking, it lasts twenty days. If they use it to fuel their gas oven so as to bake, it does not last that long.

The potential constraint to home baking posed by accessing the necessary fuel was apparent in another conversation with a woman in a household that has both a wood-fired baladi oven and a gas oven. "We use the baladi oven more in the winter days," she said, "when there are problems with the gas supply and often you can't find gas anywhere." According to her, the use of these traditional ovens "is becoming less and less common, even in the countryside." She added, however, "People return to it in times of need. Because when you can't find the gas cylinders, how else are you going to eat?" Her words highlighted the centrality of fuel to baking. They also highlighted the fact that, to her, to eat means to eat bread. Although she could always purchase bread, for her and for families like hers, homemade bread is the only satisfactory choice.

Preserving Loaves

Given the work and the time required to bake a bread that must be left to rise before being carefully shaped into loaves, women do not bake every day. Rather, they bake larger quantities every few weeks or so.[10] There is, however, another kind of daily labor required to ensure that their families have good homemade bread to eat. This is the labor of managing bread within the home. These tasks may be small, like those of handling baladi bread at the bakery (chapter 4), but they are equally significant for ensuring that people have a satisfactory staple at each meal. These practices are shaped by the material characteristics of the bread—its propensity to go stale, harden, or mold— just like the practices of handling baladi bread are shaped by that bread's tendency to go soggy, fold, or tear. But they are practices designed not to maintain quality during conveyance, since this bread is seldom transported far, but to preserve in place.

Like baladi bread, homemade bread does not have any preservatives in it beyond the salt.[11] But while this is not so much of a concern with the former, since many people buy baladi bread on a daily basis, it matters when bread is being produced only every few weeks. To ensure that homemade bread remains palatable over this period requires careful management. Women in Warda employ two preservation techniques: freezing and drying.

At the end of a baking session, women cut their freshly baked loaves into quarters and divide them into two piles. The first pile they keep as what they call fresh bread, 'aish tari (figure 5.5). They leave some of this bread out for eating over the next day or two, either on a tray, perhaps covered by a cloth to keep the flies off, or in the fridge. The remainder of the fresh bread, they freeze. This preservation option is only available to those who have freezers, but most households have fridge-top freezer compartments (chest freezers are uncommon except among the wealthiest). Freezing halts the bread's deterioration into mold; it offers a freezer-maintained freshness.[12] When it comes time to eat, a particular kind of care work is required to transform these frozen loaves into desirable bread.

On a winter evening, just after sunset, two teenage girls—Khadiga's daughter and her new daughter-in-law—are in the courtyard of the home. The

FIGURE 5.5. Fresh bread. Photograph by the author.

stars are coming out in the clear dark sky and there is a chill in the air. The girls are crouched beside a metal bowl full of hot coals. One by one, they take loaves from the pile beside them and lay them on the flames. They watch the ice crystals disappear as the loaves transform from stiff to flexible. They turn each quarter over once or twice to make sure that the thicker part of the loaf, around the edge, defrosts, as well as the thinner middle part. They take the bread off the flames before it changes color. They want to thaw it from its frozen state, not toast it to a crisp. Once they have worked their way through the pile of twenty or so quarters, they wrap the bread in a cloth and bring it through to the table, ready as dinner is served.

These practices of freezing and heating are quotidian practices of producing good homemade bread.[13] Small fires, like the one the girls are using, are commonly used in the winter, also providing a valued source of warmth on cold evenings in poorly insulated homes. As the sun starts going down and evening closes in, bright flames appear throughout the village as people build fires in metal bowls outside their doorways to prepare bread for the evening meal. For meals earlier in the day, and at times of year when the intense heat of an open fire renders it unappealing, women heat the bread on their gas burners.

Fresh bread is not, however, the only kind of homemade bread that people value. On baking days, the second pile of bread is for what the women call dry bread, ʿaish nashif. This is not the dryness of staleness; it is a specifically produced dryness designed to prolong the bread's life (figure 5.6).

Marwa has just finished baking. Her bread is piled on a low table. She takes a knife and, before she starts cutting, says, "bismilah [in the name of God]." Marwa is pious; her day is punctuated by such invocations. She starts cutting the loaves into quarters, examining each one as she does so. She looks at the loaves' thickness and color. Sometimes she tries to open them to see if they will part, like a pita bread, or if their top and bottom layers are welded together. She places the loaves that she will be keeping as fresh bread on a metal tray, covered in a galabiya; the rest she piles onto a matrah. "The thin and soft ones, we eat fresh," she says. "The rest, we dry." She turns down the heat of the gas oven, which she has been using for baking, and starts drying the bread. For the first ten or so quarters, she says, "bismilah," before placing each one back in the oven; after that, she continues in silence. She carefully moves the bread quarters around different parts of the oven to ensure that they are properly dried. She takes them out every so often and feels them, squeezing the thicker parts to see if they have any remaining softness. She stands the loaves on their sides near the mouth of the oven to dry out their last side. When the bread is finally fully dry, she lays it carefully on a large metal dish, not overlapping and neatly arranged in a circle.

This is the labor of making bread dry. Once in this state, the bread can last two months without any need for wrapping or covering. When I visited one woman in the village, she showed me an open cardboard box in the corner of her living room, which was full of dry bread. She explained how she only bakes every two months or so and dries all the loaves. I asked whether she preferred dry bread to fresh. "It's not a matter of preference," she responded, "it's the circumstances." She does not have enough room in her fridge-top freezer for bread, she said. She would love a chest freezer, where she could put bread and other cooked items and they would not get all squashed and stick together. But not very many people in the village have freezers like this, due to their cost (around 8,000EGP). So, the choice of preservation technique depends in part on access to freezing infrastructure. It also depends on the time of year. Drying bread is more common in the hot summer months. In the winter, when the higher humidity means that dry bread does not stay dry so long, women more commonly freeze their loaves.

When it comes time to eat dry bread, sometimes women moisten the bread—a practice not as laborious as the heating of the frozen bread, involving

FIGURE 5.6. Dry bread. Photograph by the author.

either sprinkling with water, or briefly immersing each loaf in a bowl of water. This does not make the bread soft, like fresh bread, but makes it less stiff, more pliable, and to some, more pleasing. Often, though, people eat the dry bread as it is. Dry bread cannot be folded to scoop up a stew, but it can be dipped, a bit like a cracker. Marwa says she likes to eat it dry. She feels that with dry bread she eats less, and she is always longing to be thinner (she is one of only a couple of women I have heard talk about bread consumption and their weight).

In addition to these quotidian practices of maintaining the quality of home-made bread, there are practices of not wasting bread.[14] At the end of a meal, for instance, there is typically bread left over, since it is customary for women to place more on the table than they anticipate their family will eat. As one of the women or girls in the family clears the table, she will pick up the bread remainders left in the place where each person was sitting (figure 5.7). If they are small pieces or crumbs, she may wipe them into a dish with other leftovers, to be fed to the household poultry. But any pieces that are still substantially whole, she will dust off, pat clean, and place to the side to serve at the next meal. This is in part because there is a cultural norm that it is wrong (haram) to throw away bread (see Stamatopoulou-Robbins 2019, chapter 4). But it is also

FIGURE 5.7. After a meal. Photograph by Mariam Taher.

because people have an interest in not wasting a staple food that they value and have invested in producing.

These everyday practices of baking and preserving bread are practices of staple security for rural households. The loaves piled high at the end of a baking session capture a moment of security, the knowledge that a family will have good bread to eat for the next few weeks. However, such a moment is transient. The work continues, drying or freezing loaves so that they stay palatable, baking another batch once the pile is consumed.

A quality staple is not the only thing being produced in these moments. Social relations within and beyond the household are also produced through the shared acts of baking bread and feeding others. The value of approaching these practices through the lens of staple security is that it helps connect them to others seemingly so different—like Fayza standing in line to get a smart card (chapter 4). In doing so, it reveals the contrasting logics, relationships, and temporalities that underpin varied efforts to secure a quality staple food. The same household may move from one form of practice to another if their situation changes. If, for instance, a family does not have enough labor to bake bread, or cannot afford the flour, it will resort to the practices documented in the previous chapter—a family member going to a bakery, using a smart card if they have one, and buying bread. There is also a spatial pattern to these varied forms of staple security. The practices documented in this chapter are more common in rural areas where people grow wheat and have the space for large ovens, as well as in contexts where women do not work outside the home. But homemade bread does enter into and move through urban areas. I turn now to Cairo to explore how urban residents who eat homemade bread—but do not bake—secure its supply.

In the City

A woman is sitting on the sidewalk of a busy Cairo street. In front of her is a small basket full of eggs, a plastic bucket with homemade cheese, and a bag of dried sour milk balls. To one side of her is a bundle of cloths. Hidden within those cloths is a stack of bread known as ʿaish beiti. Despite its generic name—ʿaish beiti means homemade bread—this is a specific kind of bread: a round, flat bread like baladi bread but slightly larger in diameter and lighter in color (figure 5.8). On other streets, women are selling similar wares but the bread wrapped within their cloths or protected by plastic sheets is different. Instead of ʿaish beiti they may be selling the fenugreek-flavored bitau bread or the hard cracker-like roqaq. That bread is being sold on the streets is not, in itself, surprising. It is common to see men and women selling loaves of bread, packaged in plastic bags or laid out loose in rows, on makeshift tables fashioned out of crates or trays balanced on stands. But what makes these women's breads distinct is the fact that they are homemade.

In an urban landscape full of bread-buying options, the presence of these vendors indicates that there is a market in Cairo for breads made in the home. It is a market that exists even though these homemade breads are significantly more expensive than baladi bread—up to thirty times the price, between 0.75EGP and 1.5EGP a loaf. Yet these are not elite breads. Indeed, most upper-class Cairenes would be unlikely to buy bread from a street-side vendor (they are more likely to buy bread from grocery stores or specialized bakeries). The fact that even quite poor people are willing on occasion to pay for this bread signals the value it holds for them.

Cairo residents who choose to buy homemade bread tend to articulate its value in general terms of this bread being good (hilu) or better (ahsan). Fayza,

FIGURE 5.8. Baladi bread (*left*) and ʿaish beiti (*right*). Photograph by Mariam Taher.

for instance, whose travails with her smart card were documented in the previous chapter, sometimes buys ʿaish beiti for special occasions. She says, "The ʿaish beiti is good bread. It's from our wheat, watered with beautiful and nourishing Nile water." She speaks these words with a certain vehemence, emphasizing the adjectives. She knows that ʿaish beiti is made with both baladi and zero flour, but perhaps does not realize that the more refined flour, by law, has to be made from imported, non-Egyptian wheat. Nonetheless, the truth of her claim is of less significance than the fact that, to her, part of the perceived quality of homemade bread lies in its local origins. There is a parallel here with the "ours"/"not ours" dichotomy used in postsocialist Moscow to describe Russian foods as superior to foreign foods in taste, quality, and healthiness (Caldwell 2002). But in this case, the other breads to which Fayza compares ʿaish beiti are also produced locally and with largely local ingredients, as opposed to being imported from multinational baking companies. It is notable, therefore, that Fayza sees homemade bread as being somehow *more* local.

The local identity of homemade bread is tied to a sense of rurality, even though, as I discuss below, this bread can be produced in urban areas. For people who grew up in the countryside but now live in the city, homemade bread carries associations of rural childhoods and a sense of security tied to memories of home. The nostalgia around homemade bread is reflected in the comments of one man who was born in the Nile Delta and now lives in Cairo. He talked about "the old days, in the countryside" when "things tasted different." His memories of homemade bread are intertwined with those of other tasty foods he used to eat for breakfast. "If someone had chickens, these eggs would really be fresh, or if they had a cow or a water buffalo, they would make milk and butter, and everything would be fresh and the bread would be fresh." In these golden days, "It was shameful for someone to actually buy bread. Every home had its own bread, every household would produce its bread." Thus consuming homemade bread is a way of connecting with an idealized agrarian past. Fayza, who grew up in a village south of Cairo and moved to the city when she got married, often speaks romantically about life in the village. She reminisces about how things used to be, when food was better, higher in quality, not like today. "I don't know why," she says one day, "but this bread from the countryside, it just tastes better."

Since few urban residents bake themselves, most of those who want to eat homemade bread depend on others baking it for them. Their ability to secure this bread is subject, therefore, to the same constraints discussed in the first part of the chapter, namely, those home bakers' access to flour, fuel, and labor. It is dependent, also, on their ability to obtain that bread once it is made. Practices of accessing homemade bread in the city take on three forms.

The first option is to purchase bread from one of the street-side vendors, like those described above, who sell the outputs of their baking in Cairo apartments or homes in rural villages nearby. Yet just as going to a bakery to get baladi bread is not as straightforward as it may seem, neither is going to get homemade bread. These breads are not available in every neighborhood; they are more commonly found in poorer areas than in more affluent ones. Their availability is also not consistent. Walking along a familiar route through the city, sometimes a woman may be in a particular space along the sidewalk; other times the same space will be vacant. One day she may be there, the next day not, or she may be there early in the day but not later. As one Cairo resident explained, "These women, they are less reliable. They are not always there. They bake small amounts of bread, as much as they can manage, not like the big oven of a bakery, and then, when it is sold, that is it." These words came from a man who says that he only eats baladi bread and does not buy homemade. Thus what to him seems like a lack of reliability may, rather, reflect his lack of understanding of these vendors' spatial and temporal patterns. Locating homemade bread vendors requires a particular kind of expertise.

Homemade bread cannot typically be identified by sight, since it is often not clearly displayed, wrapped instead within a cloth bundle or under a piece of thick plastic. Finding it therefore depends on a close knowledge of the neighborhood and the vendors who inhabit its sidewalks. When my research assistant Mariam asks a woman at a vegetable stand about ʿaish beiti in her neighborhood, the response she receives is illustrative. "If it's beiti you want," the woman says, "go this way." She points. "You will find a man selling tomatoes and a few other things on the left side of the road. Next to him, there is a woman selling ʿaish beiti." The coordinates by which this woman knows the city are the vendors who populate its streets, whose positioning and wares she knows intimately.

Talking with Fayza in her home, her description of the landscape of homemade bread vendors is telling in a different way. "ʿAish beiti is widely available," she says. "Why, in Maʿadi alone, there is who? Om Amir in Fayda Kamel; Om, what was it? Om Zeinab; and another one called Om Hanan. Every neighborhood has about two or three selling this bread. . . . Oh, and there is another girl, called Fatma, and there is also Om Oweis." It is notable that she refers to each seller by name, mostly using the mother-of designation (Om Amir, mother of Amir), a respectful way of speaking about a woman of childbearing age. This suggests the personalized nature of the relationship through which this commercial exchange takes place. It is trust in the seller and knowledge of her established reputation as a good baker that leads a customer to buy homemade bread from her.

An alternative practice of getting homemade bread in the city is through informal buying arrangements. One middle-aged Egyptian woman who lives in Cairo and is working on her PhD in politics told me how she gets bread from a friend who buys bread from a woman who bakes in her Cairo home. The friend buys five kilos at a time and puts it in her freezer until she is ready to eat it. Her friend will then trade with her, perhaps some good cheese in return for loaves of bread. Less elite urban residents also set up similar arrangements. Two brothers who live in Fayoum city, for example, one of whom works as a driver, the other as an agricultural specialist for a development project, told me about an agreement they have with a woman who lives in a rural area just outside the city. She makes a large, round homemade bread, similar to what women in Warda bake. They buy ten kilos of bread at a time.

Fayza describes how this practice works in her neighborhood, giving the example of one woman who is from the outskirts of Cairo. This woman comes to Fayza's neighborhood every Thursday through Saturday. She bakes bread—mostly ʿaish beiti, but sometimes bitau—and also sells eggs, homemade cheese, butter, fermented milk, and garlic. "People give her their orders on Saturday," Fayza explains. "They say they want, for example, twenty loaves, thirty, or ten. She makes bread to these orders and returns and distributes. Anyone can order for their household use, but especially if, for example, someone has a special occasion, they will place an order." Such informal buying arrangements can also facilitate on-street access. As Fayza says, this woman "always bakes some extra, in addition to the order, for someone passing by who sees her bread and likes it or wants to buy some. Or if some bread is left over, she will stay and sit with it in the street."

The third option for accessing homemade bread in the city is through networks of exchange with rural areas.[15] Many Cairo residents have familial connections in villages and bring bread back with them when they return from visiting their families. As one woman explained, "When we go to the countryside, we bake bread with our relatives. Usually, we end up taking a lot of bread back with us. If we get bread from the various families there, we take home a large amount and we freeze it and use it for a long time. They give us shamsi bread [a bread common in Upper Egypt]." Another man from a rural village in Tanta who lives and works in Cairo with his brother described how they always bring the thin and crispy roqaq bread back from the village when they go to see their families over the weekend. While they also eat baladi bread, they have to pay the nonsubsidized price for it, as their wives keep their smart cards to use for their families back home. Thus the roqaq from the village is one less thing they have to purchase. They eat the bread with cheese, pickled vegetables, or yogurt for breakfast, and with falafel and maybe greens for lunch, forgoing dinner. "It serves us well, the bread we bring with us," the man said. "Yes, it makes a difference, it supports us."

Families in rural areas sometimes send bread to relatives living in the city. One day Fayza's brother, who still lives in the village, sent her a package of eggplant, eggs, tomatoes, grapes, butter, jute mallow, and beans, along with some homemade bread. The package was delivered by another relative who was making a trip to the city. When Khadiga's husband was living away from home for a few months, working on a building project in one of the oasis towns in the Western Desert, Khadiga and her sisters-in-law would bake a batch of bread every few weeks and send it to him—some 350 miles away—via a bus. Sometimes these networks of exchange extend beyond the family, people bringing back bread from the countryside for their friends, neighbors, or colleagues. Typically, no money will change hands for this bread. As Fayza explains, "If someone is bringing bread from their village, it is a gift, of course—there is no money paid for this. If I ask so-and-so to bring me shamsi bread, he will not take money for it." Yet there are other ways of reciprocating. Fayza continues, "I can, when he is leaving again, send something with him. If I know he has a son, I could send him with a sweatsuit or some sneakers, or I can give him a headscarf for his wife. I can return the favor but without money entering the picture."

When Mariam traveled to see her sister and mother in Germany, Fayza gave her a series of gifts to take for them. Among these gifts were a pink galabiya, brought back from Saudi Arabia by her sister when she went on a pilgrimage; boxes of cooked jute mallow, rice and chicken, and stuffed cabbage leaves; and two loaves of shamsi bread. Handing Mariam the loaves from her freezer to pack in her suitcase, Fayza noted that this bread was "the nice one, from the countryside."

The giving of bread as a gift underscores the value attached to a staple food with homemade characteristics. It shows how even if a food is eaten every day, three times a day, that food does not fade into the background of mundanity; its taste is important. Thus these seemingly small practices—navigating sidewalks to locate vendors, making informal buying arrangements with home bakers, or bringing bread from the countryside—are practices of staple security in that they are efforts to secure the kind of bread people like to eat. Unlike going to buy baladi bread, these are not daily practices. They are irregular efforts to obtain a favored bread, which rest on social relationships that are not essential to the transactions at baladi bread bakeries. Moreover, they are motivated by particular quality ideals—a yearning for a bread that carries the taste of childhood, or valuing of the bodily labor that goes into that bread's production—rather than driven by the fear of scarcity. In the next section, I explore how Egypt's homemade breads are present in other ways in the capital city and beyond.

In the Nation

The Agricultural Museum in Cairo occupies what was once the palace of the daughter of Khedive Ismail, ruler of Egypt and Sudan in the mid-nineteenth century. Surrounded by beautiful gardens, the museum offers welcome respite from the bustle, noise, and dirt of the city's traffic-filled streets. Yet the buildings are crumbling, the exhibits fading, and the visitors few and far between. The space exudes an air of abandonment, broken only by the noise of intermittent groups of schoolchildren passing through. I visited during my first period of fieldwork in Egypt, back in 2007. Feeling slightly uncomfortable on my own, with a rather creepy security guard trailing me, I walked through the near-empty buildings of the Plant Wealth collection. The dusty rooms smelled strongly of mothballs, reminding me of my grandmother's home. In among the exhibits of the wheat and barley section, I came across a number of display cases full of bread. Wax models of different shapes and sizes lined the shelves of glass cabinets, accompanied by handwritten labels in Arabic and English. The models of these diverse, regional breads embody practices of home baking, which take on different forms in different parts of the country. My fieldnote entry for that day reads, "INTERESTING"—with capital letters to ensure I did not forget it. "Indicative of the centrality of bread that they have a section of the museum devoted to it!" At the time I was surprised, hence the exclamation point. But the exhibit is not all that surprising given the role bread plays as Egypt's staple food.

Seven years after this visit, I met with the daughter of the man who curated the museum's bread exhibit. Hana is a nutritionist, originally trained as a pediatrician, now elderly but still spirited. Sitting in a smoky café in an upscale neighborhood of Cairo on plush red sofas, drinking lattes, she told me that the exhibition stemmed from a survey of bread that her father, who was a doctor, did in the 1940s. Traveling around the country, he collected recipes for various kinds of breads that were being baked in different regions. She still has his handwritten notes. She can remember how particular he was as he put together the bread exhibition, wanting to have an artist create very accurate wax models of each type. The models crystallize multiple temporalities—homemade bread as a thing of the past, a source of contemporary value, and a reason for future alarm.

Hana pulled out her MacBook Air and brought up the website of a virtual exhibition from France's Agropolis-Museum on the "traditional breads in the Egyptian countryside." The exhibition invites the viewer to "discover traditional bread making techniques in Egypt that have remained virtually unchanged for centuries."[16] A link leads the viewer to a page on the "traditional breads of the Cairo Agricultural Museum," where photographs of the wax models I witnessed in person are displayed in a table, alongside a map indicating the governorate where that bread is found, the name in French, and the name in Arabic. Clicking on any row in the table brings a close-up image of the bread—or rather the model of the bread, the sheen of the wax disclosing its unreal nature—and a few sentences describing its size and composition. Captured in wax, the models are static, a notable contrast with the dynamism of the breads they are meant to represent. As Hana clicked through the eleven breads in turn, she provided a running commentary on each bread's notable characteristics. One of the breads, named khubz baladi tari (local fresh bread), is similar to the kind that women are baking in Warda, although this is not the term they use to describe it.

Hana's performance of Egypt's bread bounty, using the website as a prop, resonated with a narrative I heard from a number of elite Cairo residents. This is a class-based narrative that values Egypt's bread multiplicity not in terms of quotidian consumption but as a cultural object. Those who celebrate these breads are unlikely to buy them off the streets or to live in villages where people are baking them. They may enjoy eating them on occasion, during their travels or as gifts from people who work for them, but they do not consider these breads staples. Rather, they appreciate diverse homemade breads because they see them as part of their heritage, a heritage rooted in the longevity of bread baking and consumption in Egypt. As one policy report notes, "This traditional way of baking has been passed down over many generations going back to Egypt's ancient civilization."[17] The evocation of ancient times is a common way of signaling value and legitimacy in Egypt; indeed, the conversation with Hana was peppered with references to pharaonic times. Thus homemade breads carry historical and cultural weight.

Among these Cairo elites, the concern is therefore to ensure that these diverse breads do not die out. This concern is premised on a narrative of decline—a sense that practices of home baking are disappearing and that the diversity of bread types, so vital to Egypt's cultural heritage, is at risk.[18] One Egyptian activist who is engaged in the Slow Food movement described this as a state of "decay," with things "falling apart, going to waste, being lost." Despite Egypt having a "long tradition connected to bread," she worries that bread has become "devalued." While such a descriptor seems ironic, given the huge amount of money and effort that goes into procuring wheat and producing subsidized bread, as discussed in earlier chapters of this book, to her baladi bread holds little value. It is not something that she eats, nor is it something that she considers worthy of celebration. To her, the only breads that uphold Egypt's long tradition of bread baking are the rarer regional breads to which she assigns a fetishized quality.

While women in Warda often comment that "everyone" bakes, urban commentators often comment that "nobody" bakes. The people putting forward this latter narrative tend not to be closely connected to rural livelihoods and so are perhaps unaware that small-scale farmers save much of their wheat for household use (chapter 2). They also tend not to be people who formerly baked themselves. Their concern thus centers on the figure of the anonymous rural woman who used to bake but no longer does and, by not doing so, jeopardizes

Egypt's cultural wealth. As Hana recounted, "A lot of bread making went down. . . . Modern girls have fancy nails, are educated, wear elasticated jeans. They wouldn't sit on the floor in front of the oven, the oven room is hot." She places a purified agrarian past in contrast with the dubious aesthetic of the modern present. Although bread-baking practices have evolved significantly over the years, incorporating the use of gas ovens, for instance, and forms of instant yeast, in Hana's vision homemade bread is firmly lodged in a nonmodern, traditional domain.

In one conversation with Hisham, who works as a driver in Cairo, he stated with a degree of certitude, "No people bake bread. Even in the village, no one is free to make the dough and bake." His reference to people's lack of availability pointed to his sense that people are struggling to get by—a precarity that he shares—and a context in which homemade bread becomes a luxury. Another man placed the blame not on people's busy lives but on their questionable character saying, "Now everyone is lazy, nobody bakes bread anymore." While he worded his comment in general terms, the gender connotations were implicit; since home baking is a female domain, those charged with laziness must be women. In his framing, women have stopped baking not because they have chosen to do other things, or are rejecting gendered expectations within the home, but because they cannot be bothered. Others attribute the decline in baking to the increasing availability of baladi bread in rural areas. This is something that officials from the Ministry of Supply claim to be the case and is also a trend that I have observed to a certain degree in Warda since 2007.[19]

National surveys and statistics are one way of making sense of these competing claims of "everyone" versus "nobody" baking. They offer a way to move from the particularity of a single village in Fayoum or individual conversations with people who eat homemade bread in Cairo to gain insight into broader patterns. Yet the picture from such statistics is partial and contradictory. According to national food consumption surveys conducted by the government in 1981 and 1998, the proportion of households consuming homemade bread declined from 55.9 percent to 17.5 percent over this period (Galal 2002: 144). But with no repeat survey since then, it is impossible to perceive a long-term trend. Other data published by the government in 2010 suggests that homemade bread consumption might be more prevalent. According to the government's Information and Decision Support Center, 42 percent of the population eats homemade bread, with consumption rates ranging from 55 percent in the rural governorates of Upper Egypt to 5.9 percent in urban governorates (Hassan-Wassef 2012: 11–13). But with no details about the methodological basis for reaching these figures, and the unit being the population rather than households, they cannot be directly compared with the earlier survey results. The only thing known with some certainty, therefore, is that much of the domestic wheat harvest is not being sold (chapter 2). Given that the use of grain as seed or feed is limited, this, in itself, is evidence that home baking must be going on.

Despite the questionable veracity of the narrative of bread baking's demise, the threat is stimulating various forms of action. Among those who consider the diversity of a staple to be part of its quality, staple security means ensuring that these varied homemade breads do not become extinct. Their mechanism for doing this is documentation. By logging these diverse breads in various fora, bread-concerned elites seek to ensure that the knowledge of what these breads are and how they are made is not lost.

The first way of rendering these breads legible is through writing. This practice builds on earlier efforts to document regional varieties, including the study done by Hana's father in the 1940s, as well as a survey of village breads conducted in conjunction with a USAID project in the 1980s (Davis 1985). Gamal, the former government official who shared his opinions on the subsidy program (in chapter 4), also lamented the "vanishing" of "over four hundred types of bread," a shift he described as a "high cultural cost." He told me about an encyclopedia of bread in Egypt, plucking a hardback volume off the bookshelf in his home office where we were meeting. The thick layer of dust on the cover suggested infrequent perusal, yet what was important to him was not the regular engagement with these breads but rather the fact that they were recorded in print. I flicked through the volume, titled the *Atlas of Folk Heritage* and published by the Ministry of Culture (Wizarat Al-Thaqafa 2006). That the atlas originated with this government agency rather than with the Ministry of Agriculture, which oversees the production of the grains that go into these breads, or the Ministry of Supply, which manages the food subsidy program, is indicative of how the government values these diverse breads. From the government's perspective, Egypt's varied homemade breads hold value as artifacts, not as staples for daily consumption like baladi bread. Its concern, therefore, is just to ensure that they are not forgotten, recorded in an atlas containing information about the breads baked in different parts of the country, contrasting ways of storing bread, and various maps. As I left, Gamal urged me to buy a copy.

Yet paper records can only reach a limited audience. Other efforts to document Egypt's plurality of breads have sought to speak to wider audiences through online fora. The Ministry of Culture has created a website that celebrates bread as a core aspect of Egyptian culture, alongside musical instruments, clothing, and pottery.[20] The website presents information gathered in a 1998 survey on a range of bread-related themes, including grain storage, baking, and different kinds of bread. One heading leads the reader to information on "bread types and appearance." The page lists sixteen breads but notes that there may be many other types of breads, some used on a daily basis for dipping—a central component of eating in Egypt—and others just for special occasions. That the website text is all in Arabic is suggestive of its desired audience.

Another online repository of bread information is the Ark of Taste, managed by the Slow Food Foundation, an organization based in Italy. The website's stated goal is to document "traditional products, local breeds, and know-how" so as to "point out the existence of these products, draw attention to the risk of their extinction within a few generations, [and] invite everyone to take action to help protect them."[21] The contents of the "ark" are determined by a nomination process. Anyone can go to the foundation's website, fill in an on-line form, and nominate a product for inclusion in the database. So far, the six breads logged for Egypt are all breads that have something of particular note in terms of their ingredients or mode of preparation. They include farashih, a bread cooked on a rounded iron plate over wood-fired flames by Bedouin in Sinai; fayish bread, which is leavened with fermented chickpeas or lentils; and shamsi, a thick sourdough bread. Breads of less obvious uniqueness—such as the one baked by women in Warda, which has similar ingredients to the widely eaten baladi bread though a different size and mode of preparation—do not feature. The potentially endangered status of these breads is a central thread in the information displayed about each bread. As the product description for the shamsi bread notes, "It is now easier for people to purchase pre-made bread or work with instant yeasts instead of sourdough starters to make traditional breads. Therefore, the tradition of making shamsi bread may be lost among younger generations." As the name of the project and its stated rationale indicate, the imperative to document these breads, to bring them into the ark, is tied to a fear of their demise.

These cataloging efforts, from museum exhibitions to websites and ency-clopedia entries, seek to record a quality staple, in this case understood as a re-gionally diverse staple. The metric of such efforts' success is presence, whether on a page or in an exhibit. While the audience for these representations and the impact they have on their viewers may be unclear, they are telling of a particular valuation of bread as a cultural object. This mode of engagement is divorced from the physical acts of kneading dough or eating bread. The breads live on in wax and text.

Conclusion

The practices—of baking, consuming, and seeking to conserve various forms of homemade bread—discussed in this chapter underscore the significance of staple quality. The production of homemade bread is integrally tied to the flows of wheat through the country. It depends on farming households growing wheat and choosing to save rather than sell their grain, or having access to the baladi flour that is used in the subsidized bread program. But it is also tied to taste preferences, cultural associations, and social relations. For those to whom a quality staple is a homemade staple, staple security may encompass such disparate realms of action as baking bread, heating a frozen loaf, navigating a landscape of informal street vendors, or curating museum exhibits.

This focus on bread made in a home highlights how staple security is not just about ensuring that a population, household, or individual has enough bread to avoid hunger. It is about securing a bread that is perceived as being tasty, even if that bread might be more expensive and even among those with limited means. For only good bread befits the role of a staple.

CONCLUSION

Staple foods play a key role in social and political life. They are foods that an-
chor everyday meals, woven into the tapestry of familial interactions through
the most fundamental of social processes, nourishment. They are foods whose
presence provides reassurance, whether at the level of the nation (as cheap,
filling foodstuffs that prevent widespread hunger), within a home (as indicators that family food needs are being met), or on an individual basis (in the
sensorial experience of consumption). They are foods that are varied in their
manifestations and highly distinguishable by taste but act as a simple backdrop
to the dishes they accompany. Drawing on deep historical roots and cultural

---

A STAPLE MEAL. *Photograph by Mariam Taher.*

symbolism, they are foods whose significance extends beyond the calories they provide, positioning them as a matter of concern not just for individuals but also for governing authorities.

The case of China, where in 2015 the government launched a strategy to make a new national staple—the potato—offers an interesting comparative example. Potatoes, in contrast with China's other staples of rice, wheat, and corn, are less water-intensive and provide more nutrition, in terms of calories and vitamins, per unit of land under cultivation. Potatoes are also a crop for which there is considerable potential for increasing current yields (Su and Wang 2019). These are key characteristics given the limited potential for increasing the production of rice, wheat, and corn. For decades, the Chinese government has striven for self-sufficiency in these staple crops, so as to be free from the vulnerabilities associated with reliance on imports. Yet in recent years, the elusiveness of this target has become apparent, leading the government to reorient its approach to securing the nation's food supply (Zhang 2019).

This is the context in which the potato holds promise, as a homegrown, calorie-rich, nutritious food. The problem, though, is that the Chinese do not like to eat potatoes all that much. While popular as a snack or side dish, potatoes are not widely seen as something that would be the center of a meal. Even in the potato-growing inland regions where the vegetable is more integrated into the regional cuisine, the potato has a low status, associated with lack, as it was one of the few foods available in the past during famines. The government has hence embarked on a campaign to promote the potato, sponsoring potato cookbooks, exhibitions, and a television documentary (Klein 2020). But officials are aware that their efforts to convince the population that the potato is a healthy, filling food are unlikely to lead to the tuber's widespread adoption. Their strategy has thus focused, also, on how to shape the potato into the kind of foods that Chinese households do see as staples. Research is underway to incorporate potato flour into steamed buns, noodles, and a rice substitute, and the government has begun promoting a suite of these so-called potato staple foods (Zhang et al. 2017). This approach seeks to make the potato more palatable by concealing not just its taste but its association with backwardness (Klein 2020). Through such activities, the government's hope is that the potato will become part of households' daily consumption patterns.

While the efficacy of this attempt to promote a new staple remains in question, the case demonstrates how staple foods can be objects of political concern.[1] This concern is partly one of national food production. The Chinese government's interest in increasing the consumption of potatoes stems from its anxieties over the limits to increasing the production of other staples, namely rice, wheat, and corn. Its strategy exemplifies the ways in which governments may intervene in the domestic production of staples, whether by promoting their consumption or through other mechanisms, such as the development of higher-yielding, disease-resistant seeds or subsidies on production.[2] The case is a reminder of how—even in a globalized food system, in which all countries source at least some of their foods from beyond their borders—the importing of staples may be perceived as a point of political vulnerability. The lengths to which the Chinese authorities are going to try and embed the potato in family consumption habits speaks to the fact that the taste of a staple matters. The example illustrates how everyday meals within the home can take on political significance and be a site of government intervention.

Staples and Security

These questions around production, trade, and consumption underscore how staple foods are deeply entwined with notions of security, in the sense of both the existential threat tied to the possibility of their absence or low quality, and the practices designed to secure their presence and good quality. Such questions resonate widely because staples are everywhere. Although their prominence varies across culture and class, space and time, staples are not just foods for the poor but the foundations of cuisines. From rice in Japan to fufu in Ghana, tortillas in Mexico to bread in France, most countries have a food, or sometimes multiple region- or class-specific foods, that are understood as being central to a meal. These staples are foods that people expect to be available and to taste decent. Consequently, they are foods around which multiple parties tend to mobilize, from governments, which are often involved in planning for their production and trade, to individuals, who plan for their purchase and preparation.

The concept of staple security that I introduce in this book is useful, therefore, to thinking about staples beyond bread and beyond Egypt. It is helpful, first, because it highlights the affective valence of staple foods. In bringing together the word *staple* with the word *security*, the concept foregrounds the sense of threat attached to the possibility of a palatable staple not being available. This threat is not a casual one, the kind of mild inconvenience that may come from not being able to eat what you would like to. Rather, owing to the nature of a staple, it is a threat to one's very being—to an individual's sense of self and to a nation's political stability. This was brought to international attention in August of 2020 when a warehouse explosion rocked Beirut's port, damaging Lebanon's main grain storage facility. As news filtered out that the damage had left the country with less than a month's grain reserves, the Lebanese Minister of Economy issued a statement that there was "no bread or flour crisis." Ships were on their way, he reassured the population, carrying the grain necessary to cover the country's long-term needs.[3] While the concern, in this case, was about running out of bread, the anxiety that surrounds staple foods is not just about absolute lack. Taste is also important when a food is the center of a meal eaten every day, sometimes multiple times a day. Staple security is as much about the desire for a decent staple as it is about the fear of no staple.

The sense of staple threat pervades the work of government officials who are charged with national planning for strategic crops. The Egyptian government's anxiety over the nation's wheat supply, grain storage, and bread availability parallels that of the Chinese government's over its supply of rice, wheat, and corn (Zhang 2019). It resonates with concerns in Mexico, where increasing reliance on US corn since the signing of the North American Free Trade Agreement has undermined small-scale farmers, agrobiodiversity, and domestic corn production (Gálvez 2018)—a dynamic that is unlikely to change under the renegotiated USMCA agreement.[4] It bears similarities to the case of countries that are grappling with the impact of climate change on their agricultural sector, like Malawi, where domestic production of its staple crop, corn—which provides over half the national caloric intake—is projected to decline by up to a third under increasing temperatures and changes in precipitation (Msowoya et al. 2016). Likewise, the Egyptian government's disquiet over ergot in imported wheat reflects the unease that many countries have about contaminated imports. Even within the United States, whose status as a major agricultural producer and exporter shields it from many of the vulnerabilities that other countries face in terms of their staple supply, government officials consider the prevention of diseased or pest-ridden food from entering the country to be a matter of national security.[5]

The fear of lacking access to a staple, and the wish to eat a tasty staple, also shape the daily lives of individuals within their homes. In these spaces, people may not use the language of threat but the sense of threat is an undercurrent to their days. Just as the Egyptian father in Cairo worries about shortages of baladi bread at the bakeries, a Vietnamese family in Ho Chi Minh City worries about shortages of rice at the grocery store (Gorman 2019), and a Chinese villager carries memories of eating steamed buns made from the indigestible husks of rice during the famine of her childhood (Oxfeld 2017). The woman in rural Egypt who does not have flour to bake and the French villager who sees his local bakery closing share a longing for a particular kind of preferred bread that they can no longer access.[6] The fear of contaminated bread for an Egyptian consumer echoes the fear of contaminated milk for an American consumer (Freidberg 2009, chapter 6). Staple security offers a conceptual foundation for recognizing these varied experiences of anxiety and yearning on the one hand and, on the other, the comfort that comes from having a good staple to eat—and for understanding their significance.

The second reason why staple security is helpful for thinking about staples beyond bread and wheat in Egypt is that, in evoking security as a practice of guarding against threat, it illuminates the multiple actions that are enrolled in ensuring the presence of a decent staple. These actions may complement or counter one another, as the varied acts of plant breeders, farmers, government officials, grain traders, and home bakers documented in this book have demonstrated. The practice of security is, after all, distinct depending on who is at the center of frame. Staple security can thus be a useful concept for understanding government efforts to promote a new staple, like potatoes in China (Klein 2020), or to increase the production of existing staple, as in the investment in cassava in Nigeria (Donkor et al. 2017) or the assistance to rice farmers in Thailand (Laiprakobsup 2019). It also sheds light on government efforts to improve the taste or nutritional quality of a staple, such as Indonesia's wheat flour fortification program (Kimura 2013), or to facilitate access to staple grains through subsidies, as with India's large public distribution system (Bhattacharya, Falco, and Puri 2018).

At the same time, staple security is an entry point for understanding the lived experience of provisioning a good staple within the home. It shows how a small gesture might have large implications as, for instance, in the case of the Cairo resident who airs his baladi bread before packing it to take home, the woman in rural Egypt who heats loaves of homemade bread before serving, or the farmer who fumigates his sacks of harvested grain so that they will last throughout the year. These are all efforts to ensure that families have a palatable staple to eat, just like the people standing in line for hours in Ceaușescu's Romania to obtain key foods (Verdery 1996), the Mexican farmer planting maize so that even when money is short his children will have tortillas to eat (Appendini and Quijada 2016: 445), the Liberian refugees removing dried vegetables and soy protein from donated rice to make it more pleasing to them (Trapp 2016), and the rural households in Singada, Tanzania, planting millet, sorghum, and corn so that they can make the ugali that forms the crux of their diet (Phillips 2018). Those performing these tasks may not articulate their work in terms of security, but it is the anxiety surrounding staple absence and the desire for staple quality that underpin their everyday labors.

Hence staple security is a framework for considering the varied and sometimes contradictory practices of securing staples, whether for a family or nation. It brings together the global dynamics of the international grain trade and scientists working with germplasm from around the world to develop new seeds; the national politics of a huge subsidy program and government efforts to procure and store wheat; and individuals going about their day-to-day business, standing in line at bureaucratic offices, buying loaves at bakeries, and kneading vats of dough. Only by looking at all these pieces in tandem—placing international geopolitics alongside cultural perceptions of what constitutes good bread, a government's fears of bread riots alongside household dynamics of feeding and eating—can the most mundane of Egyptian occurrences, the serving of loaves of bread with a meal, really be understood.

Resources and Security

As well as furthering understandings of food politics, staple security calls for a reconsideration of other kinds of securities that have proliferated across policy, academic, and popular discussions about the environment.[7] In some resource-security couplings, the modifier designates the realm in which security concerns are generated. The term *environmental security*, for instance, captures the instability and conflict that can be associated with resource scarcity (or abundance) and with environmental change (Barnett 2001, Dalby 2009). The prefix *bio-*, in the case of *biosecurity*, relates security to life, in the sense of health, encompassing a range of health-related threats, from disease outbreaks to new biotechnologies, as well as the efforts to counter them (Collier and Lakoff 2012). Climate security pertains to threats associated with climatic conditions, or more specifically, those related to climate change (McDonald 2013). In the case of other resource-security dyads, the modifier indicates more directly the thing that is being secured. Energy security, water security, and food security, for instance, are all about securing things essential to life.[8] It is in the discourse around this latter group of resource securities that staple security has a particular intervention to make.

First, staple security highlights the need to unpack the "security" half of these dyads. In definitions of food, water, and energy security that are commonly cited by scholars and practitioners (box C.1), resource security is a descriptor of a particular condition: a condition in which the resource is not only present but accessible and affordable; a condition that is ongoing rather than temporary; and which is as much about resource quality as it is quantity. *Secu-*

BOX C.1
Defining Resource Security

Food security exists when all people, at all times, have physical and economic access to sufficient, safe and nutritious food to meet their dietary needs and food preferences for an active and healthy life.
    —World Food Summit (FAO 1996)

Water security at any level from the household to the global means that every person has access to enough safe water at affordable cost to lead a clean, healthy and productive life, while ensuring that the natural environment is protected and enhanced.
    —Global Water Partnership (GWP 2000)

Energy security is . . . the availability of energy at all times in various forms, in sufficient quantities, and at affordable prices, without unacceptable or irreversible impact on the environment.
    —World Energy Assessment (UNDP 2004)

Note: There are multiple definitions for each of these concepts, but it is striking how certain definitions developed in international fora have come to dominate the debates, as in the case of the World Food Summit's definition of food security and the Global Water Partnership's definition of water security (Cook and Bakker 2012), both of which are still commonly cited by scholars and policy makers, despite their age. This is not to say, however, that understandings of these concepts are static. In 2013, for instance, UN-Water, an interagency mechanism that coordinates the efforts of United Nations and international organizations working on water issues, began trying to get international parties to sign on to a shared definition of water security that differed in a number of ways from that of the Global Water Partnership. While the success of these efforts remains to be seen, it is a reminder of the dynamism of these concepts, which the fixedness of a written definition obscures. There is, on the other hand, less coherence with regard to energy security. I cite here a prominent definition from an international agency as a point of comparison, but there are numerous contrasting definitions of energy security in use; by some counts, as many as forty-five (Sovacool 2011).

rity, therefore, is a descriptor for something that a household, nation, or energy system has when all those criteria are fulfilled.

This is a very different conceptualization of security from that which has emerged in the literature within anthropology and related fields. In this work, security is understood as both an affectively charged state of being and a set of material actions taken to guard against perceived threats (Low and Maguire 2019). Building on this scholarship, my concept of staple security departs from work on food security to approach the securing of a staple food as a form of everyday action, underpinned by deeply held anxieties and desires. There may be moments when staple security is experienced as a state—when the national silos are full of wheat, a farming household has sacks of grain sufficient for a year's bread supply, a father brings home a large pile of fresh, tasty baladi bread, or a woman finishes baking enough bread to last a month. But such moments are fleeting: the grain is milled into flour and the loaves are eaten. Hence the work to secure good bread must continue, whether at the scale of the nation, sourcing wheat for the next few months of baladi bread production, or at the scale of a household, returning the next day to the bakery.

In foregrounding security as affect and practice, staple security shifts the focus beyond the policy realm to think through the ways security permeates lived experience. To the wider scholarship, therefore, this book raises questions about what it might mean to approach other forms of resource security, like energy security or water security, less as a goal that can be achieved and more as a mode of action. Such efforts to secure resources are intimately tied to historically rooted anxieties and desires, political relations, and everyday labor.

Certainly, the imaginary of an existential threat associated with the possibility of scarcity is something that links food, energy, and water. Just as the Egyptian government is concerned about disruption in the supply of wheat, the UK government is concerned about disruption in the supply of oil and gas (Bridge 2015). A disruption in the supply of water, too, can be a matter of concern for countries reliant on transboundary waters, as is also the case for Egypt, which depends on the Nile for almost all of the nation's water—a situation causing many Egyptians to worry about the dam that Ethiopia is near to completing across the river's upper reaches. In Pakistan, a country also reliant on water from outside its borders, the frequently cited number of days' supply of water in its reservoirs (Hayat 2019) signals potential danger just like the number of days' supply of grain in Egypt's silos. These anxieties show how, even in a world of globally interconnected trade relationships, dependence on another country for basic needs can be understood as a security threat.

This threat is shaped by climate futures and worries about how climate change will affect food production (Asseng et al. 2015, Campbell et al. 2016), energy needs (King and Gulledge 2014, Larcom, She, and van Gevelt 2019), and water supplies (Barnes 2016b, Link, Scheffran, and Ide 2016). It is also steeped in historical experience. Concerns about the supply of staple foods are rooted in memories of famine in China (Zhang 2019), or of times when food was used as a political weapon, as in the 1970s when the United States halted flows of subsidized wheat to Egypt (Mitchell 2002) or the 1990s when the UN embargo cut off Iraq's food imports (Woertz 2013). Anxieties about energy security are shaped by memories of past scarcities, such as those experienced by the OECD countries during the 1970s oil crises, by the Soviet Union during the Second World War, and China in the 1960s (Bridge 2015). Fears about a reliance on transboundary water sources are founded upon those moments when upstream riparians exerted their power, like in 1990 when Turkey stopped the flow of the Euphrates River for a month to fill the reservoir behind the Ataturk Dam (Warner 2012), or in 1948 when the government of India's East Punjab blocked water from flowing into Pakistan's West Punjab, leaving a major canal without water for five weeks (Gilmartin 2015).

The threat that surrounds these fundamental resources is not just the threat of that resource being unavailable but also of its quality being insufficient. Like the Egyptians who care not only about having bread but having bread that they consider palatable, residents of colonias (rural subdivisions) in South Texas care not only about having water but having water that is safe and tastes good, many choosing to source drinking water from vending machines despite having tap water in their homes (Jepson and Brown 2014). Similarly, there is a parallel between the rural Egyptian household that prefers homemade bread and bakes its own, even though cheap subsidized bread is available, and the affluent Mozambican family that prefers the taste of food prepared on an open fire and so continues to use charcoal for cooking, even though electricity is available (Broto, Fátima, and Guibrunet 2020). Security has a taste and texture.

Yet the common definitions of food, water, and energy security give little sense of these historically rooted desires and anxieties or how they thread through everyday experience. The only place where these affective registers come through is in work on *in*security. Scholars have tended, though, to approach this as security's converse state. An individual, household, or nation is secure if the conditions of reliable, affordable access to sufficient, safe food, water, and energy are met; otherwise, it is insecure. If security is seen more as a practice than an achieved status, however, insecurity cannot be parceled off as a distinct form of experience. For it is the sense of threat that is produced by conditions of insecurity that shapes the practice of security. To understand this threat, there is a need to appreciate how it is manifest in the day-to-day. What does it mean, as a farmer, not to know if you will have water in your irrigation canal in the coming year? How does a policy maker feel when a violent conflict breaks out along a key supply pipeline if their job is to ensure a nation's energy supply? What is it like as a parent to worry about your children getting sick if you cannot afford to heat your home? How do recollections of past water crises affect government officials' attitudes toward shared water resources? What does it feel like not to trust that the water coming out of your tap is safe to drink?

My work calls for an interrogation of these affective dimensions not only because they impact people's lives but also because they generate particular forms of response. Approaching security as a practice of responding to an existential threat shows how resource securities are in a constant process of production and negotiation. It brings together varied actions taking place across scales, underpinned by contrasting logics, engaging multiple temporalities, deploying various devices, and evaluated by different metrics, from ambitious national policy initiatives to mundane practices within the home. Rather than seeing a community as water-secure, for instance, this means understanding the practices through which different actors seek to obtain sufficient, good-quality water. These might include actions as disparate as politicians negotiating transboundary water agreements, engineers managing water distribution infrastructures, governments building reservoirs, or individuals storing water within their homes. Rather than classifying an energy system as secure, the notion of energy security as a practice prompts consideration of the ongoing material and social interactions that produce the situation of suitable, affordable, sufficient energy being available at all times.

These are not new subjects of discussion. What is new, though, is bringing them together for analysis through the common lens of security—a lens that shapes the actions of those who supply as well as those who consume. Staple security matters not only to those eating bread but to those providing it, be they government officials running a subsidy program or a mother feeding her family. Energy security matters not only to those who use energy to cook and heat but to government institutions charged with securing national energy supplies or a father who wants to keep his children warm. Yet these interests and practices do not always align. A reenvisioning of water security and energy security hence offers a framework for understanding the many ways in which different actors go about securing core needs, sometimes at the expense of others. It also underscores their stakes.

Second, just as staple security calls for an unpacking of the security half of such dyads, it also calls for a rethinking of the resource component. In departing from work on food security to mark out a distinct domain of staple security, this book disaggregates the category of food. Disaggregation matters due to the particular nature of staple foods, their centrality in people's diets, and their symbolic resonance—and as a result, the deeper sense of threat that surrounds them. This invites reflection on whether insights might be gained by dismantling the "water" or "energy" parts of water and energy security.

This could mean, for instance, thinking about the security ramifications surrounding different kinds of water use—domestic, agricultural, and industrial. Notably, the commonly cited Global Water Partnership definition focuses only on the first of these, defining water security based on a person having access to the water they need for a healthy life: for drinking, cooking, and cleaning (with acknowledgment of broader ecosystem needs) (box C.1).[9] But the amount of water to which a person has access for domestic use is directly tied to the amount of water that is used in agriculture and, to a lesser extent, industry. In defining water security in terms of domestic uses alone, there is a risk of playing into Malthusian narratives in which threat is framed in terms of a growing population and limited water supply, ignoring the fact that the vast majority of water resources are consumed by crops, not people. Reframing this as domestic water security, on the other hand, and looking at it in parallel with agricultural and industrial water securities might open up space for understanding some of the trade-offs among efforts to secure water for different purposes. If, for instance, a government constructs a new canal from a reservoir, this might help provide a consistent source of water for farmers, ensuring their agricultural water security, but at the same time undermine the domestic water security of residents of a local town, who would see water levels in their supply reservoir drop. The value of disaggregating the resource in this instance is not to identify a particular form of the resource that is more interwoven with security than others (as in the case of staples compared to other foods), but rather to recognize the varied actors who have an interest in securing access to this shared resource for contrasting purposes.

In terms of energy security, opening up the word *energy* could also lead in some thought-provoking directions. The definition cited above acknowledges the "various forms" that energy may take. Indeed, the state of energy security rests on this diverse portfolio of energy sources. However, in clustering together such disparate things, important distinctions are lost. As Bridge (2015) writes, "Wind, water, biomass, fossil fuels are all made equivalent under the banner of 'energy,' ignoring the different affordances that each of these distinctive materializations of energy provides" (33). It could be helpful, therefore, to think through the contrasting threats attached to different forms of energy: nuclear versus wind, for instance, or fossil fuels versus hydropower. So, too, closer attention to these energy sources' material differences might lend insight into the different parties involved in securing them and how they go about doing so.

Given that security is present in the lexicon of thinking about environments and resources, there is a need for a more explicit engagement with theorizations of security and how they shape people's engagement with the worlds around them. This book shows how security is an important thing to think about for scholars in anthropology, geography, and related disciplines who are interested in society-environment interactions, and it offers a way in which to do so. What is ultimately at stake here is the quality and experience of everyday life—arriving at a bakery and finding affordable, freshly baked bread; being able to produce a bread that your household prefers; and sitting down for a family meal with bread that is soft and flavorful.

Bread as Life

During my visit to Warda in late 2019, I went to visit Habiba. I traced a path now familiar to me, through the village, past the mosque, down the alleyway, and up the steps to her open doorway. Slipping off my shoes, I called out, "Al-salamu ʿalaikum," a greeting to announce my presence. "Ahlan," welcome, came the voices from inside. As my eyes adjusted to the dim interior, I found Habiba sitting on the floor with her two daughters-in-law and grandchildren, looking up, smiling. They were cross-legged around a low, round table, eating lunch. The men of the family were in the fields, transplanting onion seedlings that day.

This was the home in which I first tried homemade bread in Egypt. Shortly after I arrived in Warda to begin my doctoral fieldwork in 2007, Habiba's husband Khaled invited me to meet his family. Habiba welcomed me into their room for receiving guests, a small room with peeling blue paint, a bed in one corner, and a mat on the cement floor. We sat on the floor, firm cushions behind our backs, drinking tea and doing our best to converse as I struggled to understand their unfamiliar accents and they struggled to understand my imperfect Egyptian dialect. They insisted I stay for lunch and brought in a tray with bowls of cheese, chopped tomatoes, boiled eggs drizzled in oil, melon, and warm homemade bread. Thinking I would be more comfortable eating unaccompanied, they left me with the food, alone save two wild cats hissing at each other and flies buzzing around. This was my first taste of the large, round loaves that are made by rural women in this part of Egypt. They were delicious.

Much has changed since then. Khaled has died, a sad loss following brain injuries sustained after an accident in an auto rickshaw. Their only daughter has married and left home. Their second son has married, his wife joining the wife of the first son as an integral part of the family and its labor structure. The household has expanded with the addition of six grandchildren. The single-story home has been replaced by a new house of the style that indexes wealth

FIGURE C.1. A lunch in Warda. Photograph by the author.

in the village, with a painted façade, tiled balcony, frontal pillars, separate space for livestock, and a second-floor apartment for the second son.

Yet despite the changes, bread remains central to their family sustenance and a key part of daily life. On this morning, the family were eating fermented cheese and chunks of pickled turnips from several small bowls. Around the table, there were piles of baladi bread. The women in this family still bake their own bread, but ever since they obtained a smart card and baladi bread had become more readily available in the village, they have supplemented their homemade bread with this cheap and convenient alternative.

As she had twelve years previously, Habiba insisted that I stay for lunch. Despite my protestations that what they were eating would be plenty, she instructed one of her daughters-in-law to fry a few eggs, make a salad of tomatoes and dill, and buy some falafel from a stand nearby. She also asked her to heat some homemade bread from the freezer. This is the bread that Habiba sees as superior, even though she eats baladi bread and feeds it to her family, and hence it was the bread she wanted to serve to me as a guest. When the daughter-in-law placed the additional food on the table, Habiba asked why she had only brought me one piece of a bread. A quarter of these huge flat loaves is enough for most people, but to offer a single piece of bread rather than a pile of loaves goes against the norms of hospitality. The daughter-in-law responded that this was all they had left. She placed a couple of loaves of baladi bread in a small stack in front of me, just in case I wanted more after I finished the homemade loaf.

We chatted as we ate, our attention occasionally diverted to the toddler twins wandering unsteadily around the room. The conversation ranged from village gossip to agricultural production, family health problems to national politics. Bread was not something that we were talking about, so I was slightly surprised when Habiba pointed at the baladi bread on the table and said, "This is Sisi's bread." It was not clear whether she meant this reference to Egypt's head of state in a positive or negative fashion, nor what the other women around the table thought, although they did note that this bread preceded the current president. Still, Habiba's words hung in the air. They spoke to the presence of Sisi, and of the revolution that brought him to power, at the table, in the meal, in this constitutive moment of family life. The loaves of baladi bread in front of us were an embodiment of the state—a state that sources wheat from Egyptian and foreign fields, manages its circulation and storage, controls the taste and price of that bread, and has done so across successive political regimes. Sitting alongside the baladi loaves, the homemade bread was an embodiment of the women's skilled labor and their efforts to shape loaves to meet their family's taste preferences. The sacks of wheat piled in the neighboring room, just visible through an open doorway, were an embodiment of the men in this family's work in the fields the previous year, and their laboring with seeds, agrochemicals, soil, and irrigation water to produce grain for the household's bread.

This quotidian moment, eating lunch within a home, captures the connections of staple security. It is this amalgam of material and social relationships that shapes whether or not Egyptians have bread from one day to the next—not just enough bread to not go hungry, but enough bread that they deem decent, fitting to the central position that this food plays in their diets. While in some contexts these security connections are explicit, often they go unspoken, embedded in everyday gestures and interactions. Habiba felt no need to say any more. She paused, quiet. Then tore off a piece of bread and continued to eat.

PREFACE

1   The name of this village is a pseudonym.

2   At the time there was a cooperative system through which some households in the village purchased bread, but I never fully understood how it operated and it was clear that it was not open to me as a foreigner.

3   This is not to say that bread has received no attention at all in scholarship on Egypt. There are some notable discussions of bread in Mitchell's *Rule of Experts* (2002), for instance, and there have been a number of studies of Egypt's bread subsidy (e.g., Coelli 2010, Kamal 2015, Abdalla and Al-Shawarby 2017). There have also been several surveys of Egypt's regional breads and their modes of preparation, written in both Arabic (Sha'lan 2002) and English (Davis 1985).

4   In structuring the book in this way, I build on the rich literature on commodity chains, which has demonstrated the value of linking sites of agricultural production and food consumption (e.g., Mintz 1985, Freidberg 2004, West 2012, Tsing 2015).

INTRODUCTION

1   For Egypt's authoritarian regime, protests spark a fear of escalation. Thus, while various forms of public mobilization have increased since the 1990s, so have the state's repressive responses. The Egyptian government's efforts to control protests, through its deployment of the security forces, plainclothes policemen, and hired thugs, speak to its perception of the associated risks (Vairel 2013, Beinin 2015).

2   Security is certainly something that Egyptians discuss on a household or individual basis. The poor and middle-class rural and urban residents with whom I interact talk about security as something that is desirable and that they want from their president. They do not use this terminology, though, when talking about bread.

3   The feddan is the Egyptian measure of area. One feddan is equivalent to 1.04 acres, or 0.42 hectares.

4 Despite its cultivation during the winter, Egyptian farmers grow what is known as spring wheat. Spring wheat varieties, unlike winter wheat varieties, do not require vernalization (a period of sustained cold temperatures) before the head develops. Due to the mild winters in Egypt, these spring varieties can be planted in the fall and harvested in the spring (the same timeframe for the planting of winter wheat in North America, for instance).

5 These statistics are approximations, as there is limited farm-level data collection in Egypt, but they offer a sense of the small-scale nature of most farms in Egypt. Almost all farms in Egypt are irrigated; only along the Mediterranean Coast is rainfall sufficient to support rainfed cultivation.

6 By modern varieties, I mean cultivars developed through scientific breeding over the course of the last century as opposed to varieties developed over centuries through farmer selection, which are known as landraces. According to Egyptian crop scientists, there are no landraces of bread wheat still being cultivated in Egypt. The Agricultural Research Center has samples of thirty-two landraces, though, which government scientists gathered during collection trips in the late 1980s and 1990s and which it is currently examining for potential use in its breeding program (Gharib et al. 2021).

7 Area figures from McGill et al. (2015: 14). Large wheat farms on reclaimed land likely contribute more than 11 percent of production and procurement totals, given their high levels of capital input and lack of losses to consumption.

8 Mitchell (2002) argues that increasing reliance on imported wheat was tied to shifting consumption patterns within Egypt. With growing demand for meat among the more affluent, Egyptian farmers diverted crops they had previously consumed themselves (maize, barley, sorghum) to fodder use, leaving them dependent on wheat bread, demand for which was met, increasingly, through imported wheat (Mitchell 2002: 215–16).

9 The wheat grain has three edible parts—bran (the multilayered skin of the kernel), germ (the embryo), and endosperm (the starchy portion).

10 In 2019, for instance, Egypt's imports of wheat exceeded those of its next largest import, maize, by 29 percent in quantity, 57 percent in expenditure. Food and Agriculture Organization of the United Nations, FAOSTAT database, accessed June 21, 2021, http://www.fao.org/faostat.

11 The General Authority for Supply Commodities (GASC) was established in 1968, in the aftermath of the United States suspending flows of subsidized wheat to Egypt through the PL480 program and subsequent shortages (see chapter 3). The creation of a public authority to procure strategic commodities for the state was part of a broader shift under President Nasser, during the 1950s and 1960s, from a predominantly free market system to a planned economy. At the most expansive point in the food subsidy program in the 1970s, GASC was responsible for buying fifty commodities. During the neoliberal reforms of the 1980s and 1990s, Mubarak's government excluded GASC (along with a number of other economic authorities) from its privatization program in an effort to reassure the public that the country's key assets were not going to be turned into private monopolies (Ikram 2007: 62). Today, GASC remains an example of centralized control within

Egypt's economy, but the government has narrowed its remit; it focuses now only on the procurement of wheat and a few other strategic commodities.

12 For insight into the workings of maritime trade and the infrastructures, legal frameworks, and labor relations that constitute ports (which I touch on only briefly in chapter 3), see Khalili 2020.

13 This family, as with many families in the village, seldom eats meat on other days of the week. Since they use meat broth to cook the rice, they typically do not eat rice on other days either.

14 The scene I describe here takes place in a rural context, but although the bread is different from that eaten in urban areas, the ways of eating it are not.

15 There is a technique to tearing off a piece of bread, folding it into a shape that people sometimes describe as "the ear of a cat," and then using it to pick up the food (Naguib 2015: 114).

16 Ta'miya is an Egyptian food similar to falafel but made with ground fava beans rather than chickpeas. Given that *falafel* is a more familiar term, this is the word I use to describe ta'miya in the remainder of the book.

17 Egyptians often refer to the long history of bread consumption, dating back to pharaonic times (see chapter 1). Of course, consumption patterns have not been static over the intervening millennia, but it is difficult to ascertain from the available data how exactly bread consumption has fluctuated. One notable transition, though, is the increasing consumption of wheat bread in the latter half of the twentieth century as farmers increasingly diverted other grains previously used in bread making (maize, barley, sorghum) to fodder usage (Mitchell 2002: 215). Reflecting this shift, per capita wheat consumption (primarily as bread) increased from 112 kg/year in 1970 to 185 kg/year in 1983 (Dethier and Funk 1987).

18 The Egyptian currency is the Egyptian pound, EGP, which is made up of 100 piasters. At the time of writing, in December 2021, 1EGP = $0.06.

19 There are some larger-scale bakeries run by the government and military that produce baladi bread, but the majority (88 percent) of the country's baladi bread is produced in small-scale, privately owned bakeries, which are licensed by the Ministry of Supply (McGill et al. 2015: 60). Some studies of Egypt's bread supply chain have noted that larger bakery operations would bring economies of scale and cost savings to the government (e.g., WFP 2012). The recommended shift toward large-scale production has not been manifest, though, perhaps due to the dense nature of Egypt's urban space and the common practice of daily (or near daily) bread collection on foot, which are better accommodated by smaller and more widely distributed production and sales points.

20 According to Abdalla and Al-Shawarby (2017: 111), the beneficiaries of the baladi bread program represent 85 percent of the total population. This figure declined, however, after the government introduced measures in 2019 to reduce the number of beneficiaries. In 2020, the Minister of Supply announced that 70 million people, or roughly 70 percent of the population, were eligible for subsidized bread ("5 Miliarat EGP taufir ba'd hadhf 10 malayin muwatin min da'm al-khubz," 2020, *Mada Masr*, April 15). As I discuss in chapter 4, though, there are some people outside the system, without working ration cards, who are still reliant on subsidized bread.

21 These poverty and urbanization figures from Dang and Ianchovichina (2016: 44) and David, El-Mallakh, and Wahba (2019: 16) provide useful indications of general patterns but are shaped by the underlying definitions of poverty levels and urban areas—both of which are matters of considerable controversy in the case of Egypt.

22 This sense of a right to cheap, decent bread resonates with work that has conceptualized such material expectations in terms of citizenship, from Graf's (2018) analysis of poor, recently urbanized Moroccans as "cereal citizens," crafting bread from subsidized flour as a way of creating a sense of belonging, to Anand's (2017) analysis of Mumbai residents and the ways in which they forge "hydraulic citizenship" through their efforts to connect to the city's water supply. Indeed, there is a close parallel between the common discourses of "bread as life" (discussed later in this chapter) and "water as life." Just as Anand shows how water services are one mechanism through which people see the state, so too is the provision of a subsidized staple; the practices he documents through which individuals seek to attain those services in some ways mirror those through which Egyptians seek to attain their bread.

23 A recording of this press conference, given March 7, 2017, is available at eXtra News, "Mu'tamar sahafi li-wazir al-tamwin Dr. Ali Al-Moselhy," video, posted March 7, 2017, accessed June 21, 2021, https://www.youtube.com/watch?v =toyhWkFi8SQ.

24 Egyptian Arabic is not the only language in which there is a link between the words for bread, sustenance, and life (Waines 1987).

25 Just as Davidson (2015) argues in the case of rice, bread could be considered what Mauss (2001) termed a "total social fact" in that it is a phenomenon that cuts across society, connecting social, moral, economic, political, legal, and religious domains (see also Counihan 1984).

26 Another indicator of the symbolic resonance of bread is its positioning within a variety of proverbs. In Egypt, "a bite of bread" (luqmit 'aish) is a livelihood, "eating bread is bitter" (akl al-'aish mur) is a reference to life being tough, and the pairing of "bread and salt" ('aish wa malh) represents friendship. Similarly, in Lebanese Arabic dialect, there are numerous proverbs about bread, such as: "He who eats bread is healthy," "The hungry one thinks above all about bread," "A face that does not smile at freshly baked bread" (to describe an aggressive individual), and "He who eats your bread and steps on your foot" (to describe an ungrateful person) (Kanafani-Zaher 1997). In France, a boring experience is "as long as a day without bread"; a person who generates unrealistic expectations "promises more butter than bread" (Kaplan 1997).

27 This mode of interaction has a sacred element both for Muslims, who constitute the majority of the Egyptian population, and Christians, who constitute an estimated 10 percent.

28 There are some sliced breads that are sold in grocery stores, prepackaged and with preservatives, but these are expensive and not widely eaten.

29 It is difficult to make broad statements about American food consumption practices, given the regional variability and differences across social groupings. Beoku-Betts's (1995) study of food preparation and dietary patterns among the

Gullah people of coastal South Carolina and Georgia, for example, contains several striking articulations of rice as a staple within this community. She cites one woman as saying, for instance, "Many people feel that if rice isn't cooked, they haven't eaten." Another explains: "Rice is security. If you have some rice, you'll never starve. It's a bellyful. You should never find a cupboard without it" (Beoku-Betts 1995: 543).

30 Despite the extensive discussion of security in anthropology, geography, and related fields, there has been less among scholars specifically engaging with environmental themes. Within the subdiscipline of environmental anthropology, for example, security has not been a dominant topic of inquiry.

31 For more on the conditions of precarity and forms of dispossession that emerged in Egypt following the expansion of neoliberal markets in the 1980s and 1990s, see Elyachar 2005.

32 Notable exceptions and more nuanced explorations of security in Egypt include Amar's (2013) work on the "human security state" and Grove's (2015) analysis of gendered security and insecurity in Cairo.

33 That is not to say that wheat and bread are the only things Egyptians worry about. They, too, worry about gas prices going up, which affects the cost of fuel for cooking, other market goods, and public transportation.

34 Methodological approaches for studying affect are one of a number of controversies that have emerged in the growing body of work on affect within anthropology and related disciplines. The term itself remains slippery, the distinction between affect and emotion difficult to pin down, and to some, affect represents merely a seductive new framing of old questions. Delving into these theoretical debates is beyond the scope of this book, but for helpful overviews see Skoggard and Waterston 2015, Rutherford 2016.

35 While the 1974 World Food Conference resulted in the first effort by the international aid community to articulate food security as a concept, this work has a longer history, dating back to the 1943 United Nations Conference on Food and Agriculture in Hot Springs, Virginia, which defined "freedom from want" as meaning "a *secure*, an adequate, and a suitable supply of food for every man, woman and child" (Shaw 2007: 3, emphasis added).

36 In the glossary of its *State of Food Insecurity 2001* report, the FAO modified this definition, adding the word *social* to describe a third aspect of access (FAO 2001). Some contemporary analyses, but not all, include this addition in their definition of the concept.

37 A group of urban activists was successful in campaigning for explicit mention of food sovereignty in the new constitution, which was drafted in 2014. According to Article 79 of the constitution: "Each citizen has the right to healthy and sufficient food and clean water. The State shall ensure food resources to all citizens. The State shall also ensure sustainable *food sovereignty* and maintain agricultural biological diversity and types of local plants in order to safeguard the rights of future generations" (Government of Egypt 2014, emphasis added).

38 An article in the state-affiliated newspaper noted, for instance, how "the president has assured numerous times that the loaf of bread is a red line, from the first

moment in which he accepted the responsibility, when security was weak, chaos ruled the streets, and terrorism was hitting us here and there" (Mursi ʿAtallah, 2017, "Kull youm al-khubz khat ahmar!" *Al-Ahram*, March 11).

39 The term *intifada* means, literally, *tremor* or *shaking off*, but in close association with the Palestinian intifadas, it has come to denote a popular uprising against an oppressive regime.

40 Individual efforts to obtain staples are not separate from the geopolitical histories, military regimes, and global trade relations that have shaped and continue to shape nations' food supplies and agricultural production possibilities. Indeed, it is notable that the three examples in this paragraph come from Cuba, Vietnam, and Russia.

41 Sarah McFarlane, 2013, "Egypt's Wheat Problem: How Mursi Jeopardized the Bread Supply," Reuters, July 25.

42 In her discussion of postcolonial political rule in Egypt through to the 2011 revolution, Salem (2020) argues that the distinct feature of Nasser's hegemonic project was that he built sufficient consent to justify the coercive nature of his regime, in part through key interventions in social welfare. While Sadat and Mubarak eroded much of this consent as they introduced neoliberal reforms, the bread subsidy is one consent-building policy that these subsequent regimes sustained.

43 Officials often cite the five-piaster price per loaf, unchanged since 1989, as evidence of their efforts to maintain the bread subsidy even in the face of other expenditure cuts. Yet as I discuss further in chapters 1 and 4, the government has curtailed the program through other means, including reducing the size of the loaf and limiting who is eligible to receive this bread. In August 2021, during the opening of a food production plant, President al-Sisi said that he thought it was time to increase the price of the five-piaster loaf. Despite the flurry of media coverage that this statement generated, as of December 2021 there has been no change. When the Minister of Supply gave a press conference in October 2021 to announce an increase in the price of vegetable oil—the second raise in a year—he allayed fears of any imminent change in bread prices, saying that it would take some time for the government to research and decide a new price for subsidized bread (Omar Fahmy, 2021, "Egypt's Sisi Calls for First Bread Price Rise in Decades," Reuters, August 3; Sarah El Safty, 2021, "Egypt's New Price for Bread Will 'Take Time,' Supply Minister Says," Reuters, October 28).

44 I use pseudonyms for my research site and participants. While the respectful way of addressing someone who is older, particularly in rural areas or in more working-class urban neighborhoods, is in relation to their oldest child (addressing, for example, the mother or father of Ayman as Om Ayman or Abu Ayman), for simplicity's sake, I use first name pseudonyms. For consistency I also omit titles, although the respectful way of addressing experts is with their title and first name (for example, addressing a woman with a PhD, or one trained as an engineer, as Dr. or Engineer Nagwa).

45 This speaks to a broader body of work that has sought new methodological approaches to address the unequal relations of gender, race, and class that shape ethnographic fieldwork (e.g., Berry et al. 2017).

46 The bulk of my research for this book took place after President al-Sisi came to power. Many critics have highlighted the authoritarian nature of Sisi's regime, its failure to bring about an improvement in most Egyptians' quality of life, and the unfulfilled dreams of the 2011 revolution. Such critiques are not central themes of this book, however, for two reasons. The first is because they did not feature prominently in my data, perhaps because subsidized bread—and the wheat procurement required to sustain it—is one of the few forms of social support that Sisi's government has not rolled back significantly. The second reason relates to the current political moment and risks associated with open political critique (for more on this, see Malström 2019). The political climate no doubt shaped the perspectives that people were willing to share with me, particularly those with whom I do not have longstanding relationships. Moreover, I am reluctant to write about the few occasions when people did openly criticize the regime in our conversations, given the risk this could pose to them, were they to be identified, and to me, since I hope to continue working in Egypt.

47 My research approach of combining short-term field visits with other sources of data exemplifies the "patchwork ethnography" that Günel, Varma, and Watanabe (2020) call for in recognition of the fact that researchers' lives and personal and professional commitments inevitably shape their ethnographic practice. This methodological approach was contingent on a research budget that could cover multiple airfares to Egypt. I was fortunate to receive generous support from the American Council of Learned Societies, the George A. and Eliza Gardner Howard Foundation, and the University of South Carolina.

48 For a vivid account of the political challenges of conducting fieldwork in Egypt in recent years, see Malström 2019.

49 Readers familiar with Cairo might think of Maʿadi as an upscale neighborhood, popular with expatriates and affluent Cairenes. It is a neighborhood that has tree-lined streets with large villas, expensive apartment blocks with swimming pools, as well as a commercial district dominated by the kinds of Western coffee shops, bars, and interior design stores that characterize wealthy parts of the city. Yet the nature of the neighborhood changes rapidly toward the west, over the train tracks, and north beyond the main commercial district. These more working-class neighborhoods, which are also technically part of Maʿadi district, are where Mariam and I conducted our research.

50 The newspapers we selected were *Al-Ahram, Al-Badil, Al-Tahrir, Al-Wafd, Al-Youm al-Sabiʿ, Al-Masry al-Youm,* and *Rosa el-Youssef.*

51 For wheat, we searched under qamh (wheat). For bread, we searched under ʿaish (the colloquial term for bread), khubz (bread), and al-khubz al-mudaʿam (subsidized bread). We also searched under al-amn al-ghidhaʾi (food security) and al-iktifaʾ al-dhati (self-sufficiency). In addition to our focused study of the period 2015–18, we did some limited searches of coverage from 2019 and 2020 to check for emerging themes and see if the patterns we had noted from the earlier period were still evident.

CHAPTER 1: STAPLE BECOMINGS

1   Wheat harvesting in many parts of Egypt is now mechanized, but manual harvesting remains common in some areas.

2   The average height of an adult male Egyptian today is 169.3 cm (El-Zanaty and Way 2009: 194), compared with 165.7 cm in Ancient Egypt (Habicht et al. 2015: 520). The wheat in these two images is also most likely of different species. In Ancient Egypt, emmer (*Triticum dicoccon*) and durum wheat (*Triticum durum*) were commonly cultivated, whereas today, almost all the wheat grown in Egypt is bread wheat (*Triticum aestivum*). However, this is not what explains the height difference. The taller height of wheat historically, evident in a range of depictions of the crop from Ancient Egyptian tombs to medieval paintings, is due to the inclusion of dwarf traits in mid-twentieth-century wheat breeding programs (Vergauwen and De Smet 2017).

3   The presentation was posted on the website of the organization that facilitated this networking event for grain professionals, allowing the PowerPoint slides to live on beyond their fleeting presence in a Swiss conference room (Fakhry 2013).

4   Fullilove's (2017) account of the global origins of US wheat and of how the crop was molded by immigrant farmers, as well as McCann's (2007) analysis of the introduction and transformation of maize in the African continent, provide further illustration of how seeds are far from stable objects. The notion of *wheat becoming* speaks to a broader body of scholarship on resource becoming; see, for example, Richardson and Weszkalnys 2014, Kneas 2020.

5   The three archives referenced in this chapter are the National Archives and Records Administration, College Park, Maryland (NARA); the Food and Agricultural Organization of the United Nations Archives, Rome (FAO); and the Rockefeller Foundation Archive Center in Sleepy Hollow, New York (RAC). I refer to the archival citations by record group (RG) and, where applicable, by series (S), box (B), and folder (F). The Foreign Agricultural Service (FAS) reports for Egypt since 1995 are available online through the Global Agricultural Information Network database (https://gain.fas.usda.gov); reports from prior years I located in the US National Archives. I also draw on material collected from the main FAO library in Rome and the library of the FAO regional office in Cairo, as well as documents sourced from online archives of USAID's Development Experience Clearinghouse (https://dec.usaid.gov) and CIMMYT (https://repository.cimmyt.org).

6   My ethnography does not extend to an analysis of wheat breeding today because I have been unable to access these sites of scientific research due to security restrictions (see introduction). While my analysis is unable to offer the insights that ethnographies of seed breeding have provided (Kortright 2013, Hartigan 2017), the absence of such a dimension in this book is in itself indicative of how in Egypt breeding wheat, like baking bread, is a matter of security.

7   The political and social relations that have both shaped and been shaped by transnational seed transfers have been the focus of a rich body of scholarship, from the seminal works of Crosby (1972) and Carney (2002) to more recent explorations of the geopolitical underpinnings of the Green Revolution (Cullather 2013) and a notable study of wheat variety development in the Middle East (Tesdell 2017).

8   State Information Service, 2016, "Sisi Gives Go-Ahead for Wheat Harvest in 1.5-Million-Feddan Project," Egypt State Information Service, May 6, accessed March 18, 2019, https://www.sis.gov.eg/Story/101251.

9   Amani Subhi, 2016, "Shahid . . . Makinat al-hasad tahsud al-qamh fi mashruʿ al-milion wa nisf feddan," *Al-Wafd*, May 5.

10 Whereas in other agriculture-related contexts, officials and scientists typically use the Egyptian area measurement, the feddan, when addressing yields they often talk in terms of hectares, so as to facilitate international comparisons.

11 According to data from the FAO, wheat yields in Egypt are the seventh highest in the world (in this listing, Chile and South Africa are ranked eleventh and thirty-seventh, respectively): data for the year 2018, accessed April 1, 2020, http://www.fao.org/faostat.

12 Egypt has the highest rate of nitrogenous fertilizer applications in the world (data accessed March 31, 2020, http://www.fao.org/faostat). Reliance on such a high level of agricultural inputs has had problematic environmental and social impacts, as a number of studies of the Green Revolution have shown (Lipton and Longhurst 1989, Shiva 1991, Dove and Kammen 1997). High fertilizer use, for instance, has contributed to a degradation of water quality in the River Nile, Egypt's primary water source (Wahaab and Badawy 2004). However, while agricultural and water management professionals are aware of water quality problems, this is not a dominant concern. It is not, for example, something that they talk about as a threat to domestic wheat production. Furthermore, in Egypt the benefits of the Green Revolution have not only accrued to large farmers who can afford expensive inputs, as they have in some other countries (although there are inequalities, as I discuss later in the chapter). This is partly due to the fact that the government has maintained tight control over seed development and distribution (it also controlled fertilizer prices for many years), so as to get these inputs to the smallholders who comprise the majority of Egypt's farmers, rather than letting profit-driven corporations control the process.

13 I focus here on the breeding of the widely cultivated bread wheat varieties, but breeders have also sought to increase the yield and resistance of the durum wheat varieties that are grown in parts of southern Egypt, for use in the pasta industry as well as in bread production (Abdelmageed et al. 2019).

14 Agricultural Research Center of the Egyptian Ministry of Agriculture (ARC) YEAR, "Highlight's of ARC Activities, 1980–1990," cited in York et al. 1994: 11.

15 Hosni Mohamed, 1967, "Wheat Production in the United Arab Republic," *NEWBPIB* [*Near East Wheat and Barley Project Information Bulletin*] 4, no. 2: 1–8, FAO library, Rome.

16 Historical records reveal the severe impact of intermittent rust epidemics on harvests in wheat-producing countries throughout history. The threat of rust is thus not new, and neither are the efforts to counter that threat, although the mechanisms of doing so have changed over time. Staple security has a long history. Texts from Ancient Rome, for instance, refer to rust as a deity to be feared and describe protecting the crop through feasts, processions, and sacrifices to appease the deity (Zadoks 2008). Other wheat diseases that have been sources of concern in Egypt,

but that have not resulted in the same degree of damage as rust, include those caused by fungi known as smut (loose smut, bunt, and flag smut), nematodes, bacteria, and viruses (Haggag 2013).

17 W. M. Tahir, 1969, "Reorientation of Breeding and Testing Programs to Meet Present and Future Needs," *NEWBPIB* 6, no. 3: 1–6, FAO library, Rome, 4.

18 Abdul Hafiz, 1972, "How Can Cereal Rust Studies Be Made More Relevant and Productive?," *NEWBPIB* 9, no. 2: 12–15, FAO library, Rome, 12.

19 Said Dessouki, 1964, "A Review of Wheat and Barley Breeding in the U.A.R.," *NEWBPIB* 1, no. 1: 11–12, FAO library, Rome, 12.

20 The first Near East rust (and bunt) nursery organized by the FAO was distributed in 1952. Other nurseries focused on yield development.

21 The United Arab Republic (UAR) was a political union between Egypt and Syria between 1958 and 1961; Egypt continued to be officially known as the UAR until 1971. K. Thielebein, 1968, "High Yielding Varieties of Food Crops," May 2, Working Party on High Yielding Varieties, PR4/27, AGP, RGIO, FAO, iii.

22 W. M. Tahir, "Report on Duty Trip to the Near East: 27 April to 6 June 1969," Trips and Tours by Staff S–Z, PL6/1, AGP, RGIO, FAO.

23 John Gibler to Norman Borlaug, 1966, "Wheat Improvement 1966," December 28, B2002, S105, RGI.9–1.15, RAC.

24 Samar Samir, 2016, "Al-hukuma tukhasis 50% min mashruʿ al-1.5 milion feddan lil-iktifaʾ al-dhati min al-qamh," *Al-Youm al-Sabiʿ*, January 21.

25 See, for instance, Bret Tate, 2016, "Egyptian Land Reclamation Efforts," GAIN Report, May 16, USDA Foreign Agricultural Service.

26 While these dwarf varieties (sometimes referred to as semidwarf varieties) are commonly associated with Mexico, they have a longer and more complex origin story that reflects longstanding global patterns of seed exchange. This story is centered on a variety called Norin 10, which was the carrier of these dwarf characteristics. US scientists first became familiar with the potential of dwarf varieties in 1946 when a USDA official was sent to Japan to help with reconstruction under the US occupation and was struck by the success of the short-statured variety, Norin 10, which he saw under cultivation. Norin 10 had been developed by Japanese scientists in the 1920s from the crossing of a native Japanese wheat variety (Daruma) with two American varieties (Fultz and Turkey Red) (Reitz and Salmon 1968). The US official coordinated a shipment of Norin 10 seed back to the United States. At a breeding station in Washington, the American scientist Orville Vogel crossed Norin 10 with locally adapted varieties to develop a variety known as Gaines, which produced yields up to 50 percent higher than other varieties then in use. Borlaug heard about this and wrote to Vogel requesting some seed samples, which Vogel duly sent. These seeds, which Borlaug and his colleagues then crossed with Mexican varieties, were the foundation of Green Revolution wheat (Perkins 1997).

27 The FAO established the Near East Wheat and Barley Breeding Project in 1952; in 1961, the project was renamed the Near East Wheat and Barley Improvement and Production Project; and in 1971, it was extended to encompass a number of other crops and renamed the Cereal Improvement and Production Project.

28 Charles Krull Diary, Near East and Middle East Trip, April–May 1966, B250, RG12, RAC, 2–3.

29 Norman Borlaug, Oral History, B15, RG13, RAC, 22.

30 Borlaug Oral History, 255–56.

31 Krull Diary, 2.

32 Charles Krull to Jocko Roberts, September 5, 1966, F4, B1, S812, RG1.2, RAC.

33 Krull to Roberts, September 5, 1966.

34 John J. McKelvey, Officer Diary, Trip to Egypt, December 1968, Reel 68 1968, RG2, RAC.

35 Borlaug Oral History, 25.

36 Elvin Stakman, Oral History, B24, RG13, RAC, 249.

37 Said Dessouki, 1969, "Egypt Country Report," Ninth Ad Hoc Conference on Wheat and Barley Improvement and Production in the Near East, Beirut, October, FAO library, Cairo.

38 Tahir, "Reorientation of Breeding and Testing Programs," 1.

39 American Embassy Cairo, 1982, "Annual Grain and Feed Report," B107, Agricultural Attaché and Counselor Reports 1971–84, RG166, NARA, 4.

40 Abdul Hafiz, 1973, "Impact, Problems, and Potential of the Green Revolution," NEWBPIB 10, nos. 1–2: 10–20, 13; and Abdul Hafiz, 1972, "How Can Cereal Rust Studies be Made More Relevant?," NEWBPIB 9, nos. 2–3: 12–15, 13, FAO library, Rome.

41 Indicative of how Egypt's breeding program has drawn on germplasm from around the world, one group of researchers examined the origin of thirty-three Egyptian wheat cultivars released between 1947 and 2004. They traced the ancestral parents of these cultivars back to thirty-one different countries. While 16 percent of the wheat gene pool was domestic in origin, the remainder came from overseas, with the US, Kenya, and Ukraine contributing the largest amounts. The signature of CIMMYT-developed high-yielding dwarf varieties, derived from Japanese ancestors, was prominent in Egyptian cultivars released after 1970s (Basnet et al. 2011).

42 The potential disjunction between farmers' and breeders' interests has been highlighted in scholarship on farmer seed selection practices. See, for example, Glover, Kim, and Stone's (2020) study of Filipino farmers' ambivalence over golden rice—a genetically modified variety that many scientists think holds great promise as a quality, nutritious staple.

43 Abdel Sidky, 1953, "Proposals to Reorient Egypt's Agricultural Policies," July 11, Egypt Agriculture, B133, FAS Narrative Reports 1950–54, RG166, NARA.

44 American Embassy Cairo, 1961, "Agricultural Policy Report," June 17, Egypt Agricultural Policy, B255, FAS Narrative Reports 1955–61, RG166, NARA.

45 J. Harrington, José Vallega, and Norman Borlaug, 1960, "The 1961–65 Program of the Near East Wheat and Barley Improvement and Production Project," Report F-4556, June 23, FAO library, Cairo, 6.

46 Abdul Hafiz, 1964, "Report on Wheat and Barley Improvement and Production in the Near East Countries," Near East Regional Office of the FAO, Cairo, 122.

47 Reiter Webb, 1978, "Egypt: June Agricultural Highlights," August 3, EGY1978, B76, FAS Agricultural Attaché and Counsellor Reports 1971–84, RG166, NARA.

48 Abdel-Mawla Basheer, 1982, "Wheat Economics in Egypt," Research Report, EMCIP Publication No. 40, Egypt Major Cereals Improvement Project, USAID, USAID Development Experience Clearinghouse, 24.

49 Notably, there was also resistance among Mexican farmers when these varieties were first distributed there. Borlaug recounts: "In the early years, when we first started to try to distribute new [dwarf] varieties, it was a tremendous job. All the good farmers always had seed that was better than yours. And they made no bones about telling you about it. . . . You had to do a real job of salesmanship before you could even get them to try it on their own farms." Borlaug Oral History, 212–13.

50 Basheer, "Wheat Economics in Egypt," 5.

51 Although government controls on fertilizer prices penalized farmers between 1965 and 1973, as the price was set high compared to world market prices, after 1973, as world fertilizer prices soared, the fixed government price became a substantial subsidy (Adams 1986: 53). During the neoliberal government reforms of the early 1990s, the government removed these price controls. Today, farmers frequently comment about how expensive agricultural inputs have become since the government lifted its supports.

52 Gibler to Borlaug, "Wheat Improvement 1966."

53 American Embassy Cairo, 1982 "Annual Grain and Feed Report," 4.

54 American Embassy Cairo, 1980, "Egypt Agricultural Situation Report," January 3, 10, Egypt 1980, B90, Agricultural Attaché and Counselor Reports 1971–84, RG166, NARA.

55 Salah Mansour, 1995, *Egypt Grain and Feed Annual*, Report EG5006, USDA Foreign Agricultural Service, 5. The titles of more recent grain and feed reports that I downloaded from the Foreign Agricultural Service website are italicized, while the titles of older reports, which I obtained from the archives, are in quotation marks.

56 American Embassy Cairo, 1982 "Annual Grain and Feed Report."

57 Hassan Ahmed and Sherif Ibrahim, 1998, *Egypt Grain and Feed Annual*, Report EG8007, USDA Foreign Agricultural Service, 2.

58 According to Egyptian agricultural experts, there are no landraces of bread wheat still being cultivated within the country (see n. 6 in the introduction).

59 The deterioration in outcomes when wheat seeds are replanted is not as significant as it is for hybrid crops. Nor is it a matter of seeds becoming sterile, as in the widespread concerns (to date, unfounded) over genetically modified seeds and "terminator genes" (Stone 2002). Rather, it is a more gradual process, but one that ultimately disadvantages those farmers who are unable to access new seeds and subsequently find that their fields produce steadily less.

60 The ministry produces multiple varieties to accommodate the varied production conditions around the country. The varieties it recommends for the south, for instance, are those that can withstand higher temperatures. In addition, the seeds produced by the ministry include not only bread wheat varieties but also varieties of durum wheat, which are planted in some southern regions. ʿAz Al-Nubi, 2015, "Al-ziraʿa: Intag 18 sanf taqawi qamh wa ziadat 80,000 ardab ʿan al-ʿam al-madi," *Al-Youm al-Sabiʿ*, October 13.

61 Marwa Ahmed, 2015, "Al-zira'a tu'lin taufir 70% min taqawi al-qamh . . . wa khubara': 40% faqat," *Al-Badil*, October 28.

62 Borlaug Global Rust Initiative, "About BGRI," accessed June 22, 2021, http://www .globalrust.org/about-bgri.

63 Salah Mansour, 2012, *Egypt Grain and Feed Update*, July 4, USDA Foreign Agricultural Service, 2.

64 In addition, Egyptian scientists are concerned that increasing temperatures could compound the threat of other diseases. Studies have shown, for instance, that stem rust–resistant genes are temperature-sensitive; under higher temperatures, some varieties that were formerly resistant to stem rust were found to be susceptible (Abdelkader 2015).

65 This goal is one expressed by experts in the ministry's Agricultural Research Center. It is not a formal policy target tied to a specific time horizon. Mohamed Hamza and Mariano Beillard, 2013, *Egypt Grain and Feed Annual*, April 14, USDA Foreign Agricultural Service, 6.

66 The dissemination of this technology was supported by a donor-funded initiative— the Enhancing Food Security in Arab Countries Project. The goal of this project is to "raise wheat production and reduce the Arab World's growing dependence on costly wheat imports." The project was launched in 2011 and funded by the Arab Fund for Economic and Social Development, the Kuwait Fund for Arab Economic Development, the Islamic Development Bank, the OPEC Fund for International Development, the Bill and Melinda Gates Foundation, and the International Center for Agricultural Research in Dryland Areas. In 2018, funding was renewed for the project's third phase. Communication Team ICARDA, 2018, *Enhancing Food Security in Arab Countries*, International Center for Agricultural Research in the Dry Areas, October 9, accessed November 17, 2021, https://www.icarda.org/media /news/enhancing-food-security-arab-countries.

67 While a number of scholars have shown that bread riots are seldom about bread alone (Thompson 1971, Sadiki 2000), references to the so-called bread riots that took place in Egypt in 1977, and the need to mitigate the possibility of such riots happening again, continue to circulate widely in policy discussions.

68 The link between bread and national security is not just an Egyptian story. In relation to the US National Food Administration, for instance, which was created in 1917 and led by Herbert Hoover, Cullather (2013: 20–21) writes, "Riots in American cities and Hoover's own experience in Belgium [where he organized a relief program] confirmed that bread shortages led to unrest." Hoover was aware, Cullather explains, that "bread affects the morale of a people more quickly than any other food." He elaborates, "European governments had long recognized this requirement for domestic order, but Hoover stressed its symbolic and practical ramifications for U.S. strategy. In the midst of war, he told his staff, 'the wheat loaf has ascended in the imagination of men, women, and children as the emblem of national survival and national tranquility.'"

69 The ministry revises its reimbursement according to the changing costs of production. Prior to the 2016 currency devaluation, the reimbursement was 30 piasters/loaf.

70 Ahmed Wally and Olutayo Akingbe, 2020, *Grain and Feed Annual*, Report EG2020-0005, USDA Foreign Agricultural Service, 4.

71 Carroll Conover, 1953, "Foreign Service Dispatch No. 1683, Subject: Egypt Increases Wheat Extraction Rate to 93.3 Percent," February 20, Egyptian Agricultural Policy-Breadstuffs, B133, FAS Narrative Reports 1950–54, RG166, NARA.

72 Carroll Conover, 1953, "Embassy Dispatch No. 24, Subject: Egyptian Breads," July 2, Egyptian Agricultural Policy-Breadstuffs, B133, FAS Narrative Reports 1950–54, RG166, NARA.

73 American Embassy Cairo, 1980, "Annual Grain and Feed Report," August 31, Egypt 1980, B90, Agricultural Attaché and Counselor Reports 1971–84, RG166, NARA.

74 Agricultural Attaché, Cairo, 1978, "Egypt: April Agricultural Highlights," May 16, EGY1978, B76, FAS Agricultural Attaché and Counsellor Reports 1971–84, RG166, NARA.

75 James Ross, 1979, "July Agricultural Highlights," August 2, Egypt 1979, B76, Agricultural Attaché and Counsellor Reports 1971–84, RG166, NARA.

76 This was similar to one of the options that the committee investigated, which was to increase the price to one piaster and the size to 160 g, with an estimated savings of 130.3 million EGP.

77 Agricultural Counsellor, Cairo, 1984, "Egypt Grain and Feed Annual," EGY1984, B122, FAS Agricultural Attaché and Counsellor Reports 1971–84, RG166, NARA.

78 There were some periods when the ministry maintained two sizes of subsidized bread. When, for instance, it doubled the price of baladi bread to two piasters in 1984, it kept a smaller one-piaster loaf. Four years later, when the public had perhaps become accustomed to the two-piaster loaf, the ministry phased out this one-piaster option.

79 How these changes were perceived by the general population is difficult to ascertain from the available sources. Certainly, the absence of protest may have been more a reflection of the authoritarian political context and limits on free expression than an indicator that people were satisfied with the changes.

80 For more on the eligibility criteria and who has access to subsidized bread, see chapter 4.

81 Othman Al-Shernubi, 2017, "Ma yagib an taʿrifahu ʿan daʿam al-khubz," *Mada Masr*, March 19.

82 "As Unemployment Rises, Government Hikes Metro Prices and Reduces Bread Subsidy," 2020, *Mada Masr*, August 19.

83 Omar Fahmy, 2021, "Egypt's Sisi Calls for First Bread Price Rise in Decades," Reuters, August 3.

84 Mohamed Zaki, 2017, "Shakua min suʾ halat wa sughr hagm raghif al-ʿaish fi makhabiz al-Zeitun bil-Qahira," *Al-Youm al-Sabiʿ*, August 4.

85 Throughout history, not just in Egypt but in other bread-eating countries, there have been suspicions that bakers replace flour with other lesser ingredients, or use devious means to inflate the size of their bread (Jacob [1944] 2014).

86 Agricultural Attaché, Cairo, 1978, "Egypt: April Agricultural Highlights."

87 Medhat Wahba, 2015, "Bil-Suar . . . Wazir al-tamwin yazin al-khubz al-muda'am bi-Qena lil-ta'akud min 'adam al-tala'ub bil-wazn," *Al-Youm al-Sabi'*, June 1.

88 There are also dimensions of bread quality that have no taste. In line with the focus on micronutrients in the international development community (Kimura 2013), there have been several internationally sponsored programs to fortify baladi bread with iron and folic acid (Elhakim et al. 2012). Those who eat baladi bread, though, do not typically evaluate it in terms of its vitamin or mineral content, beyond general comments about it being "healthy." Even among consumers who might be interested in nutritional value, this information is not readily available, since the bread is sold unpackaged and without labeling. The widespread expectation for good bread is thus not a widespread expectation for nutrient-fortified bread. So when the international program funding fortification came to an end in 2013 and the government decided not to continue procuring the fortification premix, there was no public outcry. This may have been because the general public were not aware that the quality of their bread was different (indeed, during interviews that Mariam and I conducted in 2015–18, a number of people still referred to baladi bread as having vitamins added to it), or because this was not a matter of concern to them. Either way, this shows how micronutrient content does not carry the same security ramifications as other aspects of bread composition.

89 Most bakers in Egypt, in both bakeries and homes, use instant yeast. The taste of the bread is thus not linked to variations in rising agent, unlike in other parts of the world where, for instance, people bake with sourdough starters ([Jessica] Lee 2011). Hence, whereas flour has been a focus of government policy making, yeast has not.

90 In contrast, Graf (2018) describes urban women in Morocco as paying close attention to the origins and quality of the grain that they buy to turn into flour for making bread—distinctions that may well map onto different wheat varieties, even if they do not articulate them as such. The fact that both the bakeries that produce baladi bread and many of those who bake their own bread (see chapter 5) source wheat as flour, which in turn comes from mills that mix multiple varieties of grain, is perhaps one reason why people do not distinguish between varieties by taste. Even among those who grow their own wheat for home baking, I have not heard farmers talking of choosing to plant a particular variety because of its flavor.

91 Conover, "Embassy Dispatch No. 24."

92 Sherif Ibrahim, 1996, *Egypt Grain and Feed Annual*, Report EG6007, USDA Foreign Agricultural Service, 9.

93 Hassan Ahmed and Sherif Ibrahim, 1997, *Egypt Grain and Feed Annual*, Report EG7002, USDA Foreign Agricultural Service, 2.

94 Ahmed and Ibrahim, 1998, *Egypt Grain and Feed Annual*, 4.

95 Hamza and Beillard, 2013, *Egypt Grain and Feed Annual*, 7.

96 Bobrow-Strain (2012) offers an interesting contrasting analysis of how dark and white breads have, at different points in time and by different groups, variably been seen as preferable to one another in the United States.

97 Conover, "Foreign Service Dispatch No. 1683."

98   J. A. Hutchins, 1967, "Telegram Cairo Embassy to Secretary of State in Washington DC, Subject: Pass Agriculture," June 6, UAR Vegetables, B31, Security Classified Narrative Reports, RG166, NARA.

99   American Embassy Cairo, 1980, "Annual Grain and Feed Report."

100   Shehata (2009) offers a fascinating insight into the broader social contexts in which these breads are eaten. In his ethnography of a textile factory in Alexandria, he describes how in the early years of the factory's operation the management was dissatisfied when workers, who mostly came from nearby rural areas, ate together, sitting on the factory floor, eating communally from shared dishes using homemade peasant bread ('aish falahi). To the managers, such behavior was inefficient. After they banned collective meals, workers shifted to bringing sandwiches made of fino bread, which they could eat on their own as they stood next to their machines (Shehata 2009: 123–24).

101   Mansour, 1995, *Egypt Grain and Feed Annual*, 8.

CHAPTER 2: GOLD OF THE LAND

1   Quoted in Nadine Awadalla, 2020, "Unfazed by Coronavirus, Egyptian Farmers Harvest Their Wheat," Reuters, April 30.

2   According to data from the Ministry of Agriculture, wheat is grown on 4.3 of Egypt's 4.6 million landholdings; 63 percent of Egypt's farms are smaller than a feddan and 95 percent are smaller than 5 feddans (McGill et al. 2015: 2, 12).

3   Fayoum has the fifth highest poverty rate among Egypt's twenty-seven governorates (WFP 2013: 15).

4   According to a national survey conducted in 2016, 8 percent of Egyptians read newspapers daily and 28 percent check the news online every day (Dennis, Martin, and Wood 2016).

5   Eman Muhana, 2015, "Al-zira'a al-Sharqiya: 433 alf feddan munzari'a qamh bi-ziadat 10 alaf 'an al-'am al-madi," *Al-Youm al-Sabi'*, January 11; Mustafa Adel, 2015, "Zira'at 150 alf feddan qamh hadha al-'am bil-Gharbiya," *Al-Youm al-Sabi'*, January 13; Hani Fathi, 2015, "Zira'at 143 alf feddan qamh bi-Beni Sueif bi-ziadat 23 alf feddan 'an al-mustahdaf," *Al-Youm al-Sabi'*, January 27.

6   That newspaper stories can generate particular forms of affect is evident in Allison's book *Precarious Japan* (2013), in which she draws on newspaper articles to show how they contribute to the production of a prevalent sense of hopelessness, despair, and insecurity in contemporary Japan.

7   Mohamed Hamdi, 2015, "Qena tughani lil-hasad: Ya qamh sha'rak 'agabni wa khairak haimla hawasli," *Al Masry al-Youm*, May 24.

8   Salah Hilal, 2015, "Wazir al-zira'a yaktub: Al-qamh . . . qadiat amn qawmi," *Al-Masry al-Youm*, April 24.

9   Haitham Al-Badri and Daha Salih, 2015, "Zira'at Asyut tu'lin hasad 850 fedan qamh wa taurid 399 ton lil-sawami'," *Al-Youm al-Sabi'*, April 22; Mohamed Fathi, 2015, "Hasad 60 alf feddan min al-qamh fi al-Munufiya," *Al-Youm al-Sabi'*, May 3; Amru Khalaf, 2015, "'Zira'at Sohag': Hasad 191 alf feddan min mahsul al-qamh," *Al-Youm al-Sabi'*, May 26.

10 There is a parallel here with China's system of identifying "major" and "super" grain producing counties (Zhang 2017), although unlike in the Chinese case, the designator of top wheat-producing governorate does not bring a package of financial rewards.

11 Medhat Wahba, 2015, "Wazir al-tamwin: Istislam 750 alf ton qamh mahali min al-muzari ʿin mundhu muntasaf Abril," *Al-Youm al-Sabi*ʿ, May 1; ʿAz Al-Nubi, 2015, "Al-ziraʿa: Istislam 3.7 milion ton qamh al-musim al-gadid wa hasad 3 milion feddan," *Al-Youm al-Sabi*ʿ, May 20; Jacqueline Munir, 2015, "Wazir al-tamwin: Haqaqna tarfa bi-istislam 5.3 milion ton qamh bi-musim al-hasad al-akhir," *Al-Youm al-Sabi*ʿ, June 20.

12 Marwa was part of a cooperative from which she would sometimes get fresh bread, which otherwise, as I discuss in the preface, was not at this time readily available for purchase in Warda.

13 Indeed, all crops have a temporality that shapes rhythms of agricultural life, seasonal labor requirements, and patterns of social interaction (Brice 2014).

14 Water is allocated on a rotation system in this part of the country, but whereas in the summer farmers closely adhere to the rotation, in the winter when the water supply is less scarce, farmers have more freedom to choose when they irrigate (Barnes 2014).

15 While ration card holders are now able to get subsidized flour in place of bread, back in 2007 this was not an option (see chapter 4). Hence, if a woman wanted to bake, unless she had grain stored in the home, she had to buy flour at market prices (or buy grain and process it at the village mill).

16 In Fayoum, most people harvest by hand using scythes rather than with mechanical harvesters. Mechanization is more common in the Nile Delta than in the area south of Cairo known as Upper Egypt.

17 I discuss grain storage further in chapter 3.

18 Marwa's yield per feddan is equivalent to 4.3 tons/ha, compared with the national average of 6.8 tons/ha (see chapter 1).

19 In my analysis of the wheat procurement price, I build on a large body of scholarship on the sociology of markets and valuation studies, which has shown how prices do not emerge through the seamless magic of supply and demand. Rather they are produced, in varied forms, through the labors of multiple market agents, operating in a space of uneven and contested relations of power (Çalişkan 2010). Moreover, far from being abstract numbers, prices convey meanings, carry moral significance, and constitute a symbolic system (Velthuis 2007).

20 The 60–70 percent of the harvest that farmers keep is not only used for bread production. Farmers also save grain for use as seed and livestock feed. However, statistics from the Ministry of Agriculture—estimating 65 percent use for bread, 30 percent for feed, and 5 percent for seed—indicate that bread is the major consumptive use (McGill et al. 2015: 6). Khaled told me that some farmers in Warda keep about 10 percent of their grain to reuse as seed, but I have never heard anyone in the village talk about feeding wheat grain to their animals.

21 For more on Egypt's agricultural reform process, see Fletcher 1996.

22 I refer to a singular procurement price here, since that is how it is typically referred to in policy discussions, but the price government agencies pay for farmers' wheat varies slightly depending on their evaluation of its quality, measured in terms of qirat (see chapter 3). In 2015–16, for instance, the government paid 410EGP/ardab for the lowest-quality (22.5 qirat) wheat, and 5EGP and 10EGP more per ardab for wheat with cleanliness levels of 23 and 23.5 qirat, respectively.

23 Other countries have also used the procurement price as a way to incentivize the cultivation of particular crops. In India, for instance, the government set a high procurement price as part of its efforts to attain self-sufficiency in wheat (Cullather 2013).

24 Although the "world price" circulates as an apparent thing, Çalişkan (2010) demonstrates in his analysis of the cotton trade that global markets are made up of multiple regionally specific processes of price realization.

25 One indicator for evaluating the prices offered to farmers is the net nominal protection coefficient (NPC), which is the domestic price divided by the border price of wheat. If the NPC is more than one, it indicates that producers are receiving higher prices than they would if they could sell their product to open markets. If the NPC is below one, it indicates discrimination against producers. From 1971 to 1987, the NPC averaged 0.68; between 1987 and 1995, it averaged 1.05 (Kherallah et al. 2000: 8).

26 The US Foreign Agricultural Service's *Egypt Grain and Feed Annual* reports record these procurement prices, always placing them in comparison with world prices. There were only three years over this period—2003, 2004, and 2007—when the fixed procurement prices ended up lower than world prices at the time of harvest.

27 Given that the procurement price was fixed in advance, the opposite scenario, in which the government ended up paying below market prices for Egyptian wheat, was also a possibility. During the global food crisis in 2007–8, for instance, world prices increased over the growing season while the procurement price remained fixed, meaning that farmers received much less for their wheat at harvest time than they would have if they had been able to sell to open markets.

28 Ahmed Wally, 2016, *Egypt Grain and Feed Annual*, USDA Foreign Agricultural Service.

29 Ahmed Wally, 2017, "Egypt's Local Wheat Procurement Policy Increases Farmers' Profits," GAIN report, February 2, USDA Foreign Agricultural Service.

30 Mona El-Fiqi, 2018, "Disappointments on Wheat," *Al-Ahram Weekly*, July 12.

31 Eric Knecht, 2018, "Egypt Local Wheat Harvest Ends with Sharply Lower Figure," Reuters, June 27.

32 Notably, farming organizations' calls for higher procurement prices went against studies suggesting that, while the removal of fuel subsidies in November 2016 increased farmers' costs (for tractors, pumps, and fertilizers, for instance), the increase in procurement price (in Egyptian currency) more than outweighed this, raising farmers' incomes by 25 percent. Wally, "Egypt's Local Wheat Procurement Policy Increases Farmers' Profits."

33 Cited in El-Fiqi, "Disappointments on Wheat."

34 Wally, 2016, *Egypt Grain and Feed Annual*.

35 A larger body of scholarship in agrarian studies and agricultural economics has highlighted how smallholders react in different ways to price changes, not necessarily increasing production of a crop for sale in response to high prices, depending on their particular circumstances (Barrett 2008, Dove 2011). This work underscores the fact that farming decisions are about much more than economic calculations alone.

36 Data from the Ministry of Agriculture, cited in Mohamed Hamza, 2016, "Nile Nuggets for March 2016," GAIN report, April 5, USDA Foreign Agricultural Service.

37 In the past, the price of clover (barsim) has sometimes been sufficiently high as to encourage farmers to invest their land in clover as a cash crop. During the years I conducted fieldwork in Warda, though, the farmers I knew used their clover primarily for feeding household livestock.

38 The comparison between wheat and onions resonates with a long tradition of scholarship within agrarian studies that has examined the relationship between subsistence and market-oriented production and the reasons why small-scale farmers shift from subsistence to cash crops (Gudeman 1978, Finnis 2006, Li 2014). Yet while some farmers in Warda now plant onions on land where they previously grew wheat, most of those who plant onions maintain at least some area of wheat cultivation. This, therefore, is more a story of subsistence and market realms working in a complementary fashion (see Dove 2011, chapter 6)—farmers growing wheat for household use and onions to make money—than a subsistence crop being displaced by a cash crop. Furthermore, as the discussion of procurement earlier in this chapter underscores, wheat is not only a subsistence crop, even if the government-controlled market in which it operates means that small-scale farmers do not typically associate it with the potential for high profits.

39 Russia and Saudi Arabia were the major markets for Egyptian onions at this point, but since 2019 there has been some diversification into Asian markets.

40 Unlike raised-bed cultivation of wheat, which has yet to be introduced in this part of Fayoum, farmers have long planted vegetable crops like onions in raised beds.

41 The expression he used was "hayikhrib beitna," which means "it will ruin our house." This expression is commonly used to refer to the impact that bad prices will have on a household's fortunes.

CHAPTER 3: GRAIN ON THE MOVE

1 My interviewees' knowledge of Egypt's grain trade came from a number of different perspectives, including people who had worked in grain marketing and trading, agricultural experts who specialized in grain, and journalists who covered commodity trading.

2 Head, Atchison, and Gates offer a fascinating analysis of the same three themes that I address in this chapter—the dynamics of the international wheat trade, quality assessments, and grain storage—based on their research in Australia, providing an interesting point of comparison to this Egyptian case (2012, chapter 6).

3 Analysis of articles on the government's wheat procurement cannot provide insights into how this information is received by those who read the newspapers

4   (a relatively small proportion of the population) or who click through their online versions (limited to those with internet access). It does, however, shed light on the public message the government is seeking to curate through its press releases.

4   It is difficult to get precise figures for the flour needs of the baladi bread program, given the lack of clarity on exactly how many people the program reaches (see chapter 4). This figure comes from "Al-tamwin: Al-misriun yastahlikun 800 alf ton qamh shahriyan li-sina'at al-khubz al-muda'am," 2020, *Al-Bursa*, February 19.

5   The ministry used to sell this flour to the bakeries at a subsidized price, but since the 2014 subsidy reforms it has supplied the flour at market prices and reimbursed the bakeries according to the number of loaves sold (see chapter 4).

6   Nadine Awadalla and Maha El Dahan, 2018, "Traders Say Egypt Delays Wheat Payment Guarantees, Ministry Dismisses Criticism," Reuters, December 5.

7   The first of these two acronyms—CIF and FOB—refer to different types of international shipping agreements. For CIF (cost insurance and freight) wheat, the seller takes on the costs of delivering the wheat to the port destination. In the case of FOB (free on board) wheat, the buyer assumes all liability and delivery costs from the moment when the wheat is loaded into the vessel. The latter two acronyms—SRW and HRS—refer to different kinds of wheat, soft red winter wheat and hard red spring wheat. These acronyms cover the three binary distinctions—winter/spring, soft/hard, and red/white—that agronomists and farmers in many countries (although not in Egypt) use to classify wheat. They are classifications based on growth patterns, protein content, and the resinous content in the seed coating (Barnes 2016a).

8   There is a parallel between such concerns about reliance on foreign wheat in Egypt and concerns about reliance on foreign oil in the United States (Huber 2009). I discuss these points of comparison between staple security and energy security further in the conclusion.

9   Iman Al-Gindi, 2016, "Al-qamh nuqtat di'f al-falah al-misri," *Al-Wafd*, March 6.

10   Drawing on a similar rhetorical strategy, a journalist writing about the Mubarak era noted how, at that time, "America supplied to the Egyptian people three out of every five loaves the Egyptian citizen would eat"—a state of affairs that he felt "put us to shame." Al-Shaf'i Bashir, 2016, "Ayuha al-ghashashun afsadtum farhatina bi-'id al-qamh," *Al-Wafd*, July 30. There is an interesting parallel in this linking of the grain trade and bread consumption with the way the Indian government sought to reduce its reliance on wheat imports back in the 1960s, not by substituting with domestically produced wheat but by reducing consumption. The posters of its publicity campaign showed three chapatis, the third separated from the first two, with the statement: "Every third chapati you eat is made from imported wheat, let's not eat it" (Siegel 2018: 116).

11   Mervat Al-Said, 2016, "Qamh 'ala waraq," *Al-Wafd*, July 16.

12   For more on this macroeconomic context, which resulted in Egypt taking out loans from the International Monetary Fund in 1987 and 1991, see Richards 1991. The conditions of structural adjustment tied to these loans led to cuts in the bread subsidy program (see chapter 1) and neoliberal reforms of the wheat sector (see chapter 2) during the late 1980s and early 1990s.

13 E. A. Abusineina, 1988, "Egypt: FAO Representative's Annual Report for January/December 1987," March 21, Egypt 1984–90, CO, RG8, FAO. For details regarding my archival sources, see n. 5 in chapter 1.

14 Awadalla and El Dahan, "Traders Say Egypt Delays Wheat Payment Guarantees."

15 I write about international market prices here, since they are commonly used as a reference point for evaluating Egypt's position as a major importer. Yet as Çalişkan (2010) shows in his analysis of the cotton trade, the singularity of a world price belies the complexity of multiple processes of price realization that actually constitute global markets.

16 This increase in budget also reflected the fact that the government imported considerably more wheat that year than it did the previous year, due to low domestic procurement and increased bread demand. Data from Chris Rittgers and Sherif Ibrahim, 2008, *Egypt Grain and Feed Annual*, Report EG8003, USDA Foreign Agricultural Service, 4; Cynthia Guven and Sherif Ibrahim, 2009, *Egypt Grain and Feed Annual*, Report EG9002, USDA Foreign Agricultural Service, 4.

17 "Itifaq bain al-zira'a wa al-FAO li-muwagahat al-ghala' fi Misr," 2009, *Al-Youm al-Sabi'*, August 5.

18 Hisham Yassin, 2010, "Al-bank al-dauli yuhadhir Misr min ta'thir irtifa' faturat istirad al-qamh 'ala al-iqtisad al-qaumi," *Al-Masry al-Youm*, October 15; Ashraf Fakri, 2010, "Al-hukuma tu'akid tawafur qamh yakfi 'tafadi a'mal shaghab' haul raghif al-khubz," *Al-Masry al-Youm*, September 18.

19 American Embassy Cairo to Secretary of State, 1966, "Nasser Speech," telegram dated December 23, B34, Security Classified Reports 1966, RG166, NARA.

20 American Embassy Cairo to Secretary of State, 1967, "Ahram Report on Nasser Meeting with US Ambassador," memo, March 20, UAR Cotton-Fairs 1967, B63, FAS Narrative Reports 1967, RG166, NARA.

21 UAR Agricultural-Attaché Services, 1967, "UAR Agricultural Situation Report October 1967," October 18, B63, FAS Narrative Reports 1967, NARA.

22 Vivian Lee and Aida Alami, 2022, "In North Africa, Ukraine War Strains Economies Weakened by Pandemic." *The New York Times*, February 25.

23 For more on how the United States came to be a major source of wheat for Egypt and on the links between these flows of wheat and geopolitical relations, see Mitchell 2002, Iyer 2014.

24 Mutawalli Salem, 2015, "Khubara' yagibuna 'an al-su'al al-sa'b: Hal tangah Misr fi 'ikhtibar al-iktifa' al-dhati'?" *Al-Masry al-Youm*, April 24.

25 Salah Mansour, 2010, "Impact of Russian Wheat Export Ban," GAIN report, August 9, USDA Foreign Agricultural Service; Mohamed Abu Zaid, 2022, "Egypt Issues Wheat Tender as Ukraine War Threatens Supply," *Arab News*, February 27.

26 Concerns about contaminated bread have a long history in many bread-eating countries around the world (Jacob [1944] 2014, Thompson 1971, Bobrow-Strain 2008, Bobrow-Strain 2011).

27 Al-Gindi, "Al-qamh nuqtat di'f al-falah al-misri."

28 This is one of several agriculture-related measurements that is based on the number twelve, not to be confused with the qirat area measurement (one-twenty-fourth of a feddan).

29 Graf (2018) describes a similar dynamic in the case of urban Moroccans' perception of imported versus locally produced wheat. There is also a parallel here with the "ours"/"not ours" dichotomy common in postsocialist Moscow, which positions local goods as superior to foreign goods in taste, quality, and healthiness (Caldwell 2002), and the prevailing sense in Japan that foreign foods are inferior to domestically harvested or produced foods (Bestor 2004: 146).

30 Abdelrahman Fahmi, 2016, "Al-harb asbahat iqtisadiya matlub hukumat iqtisad," *Al-Wafd*, August 3.

31 For an interesting account of how particular grain qualities come to be seen as dominant, see Varty's (2004) analysis of the debates in Canada during the 1920s over whether protein levels should be included in the wheat grading system. Varty demonstrates how the (ultimately failed) proposition that this invisible constituent should become a marker of quality was underpinned not only by a desire to market Canadian wheat's especially high protein content but also by an assumption that this wheat would be used for a particular end product—bread. Moreover, the claim that high protein meant high quality was founded on the notion that this bread would be of a specific type, the "ideal" risen loaf, and produced in a distinct fashion, in mechanized bakeries.

32 Eric Knecht and Maha El Dahan, 2018, "Egypt's GASC Sets New Wheat Terms after Dispute over Fees," Reuters, February 2.

33 The background information in this paragraph is sourced from *Discussion Paper on an Annex for Ergot and Ergot Alkaloids to the Code of Practice for the Prevention and Reduction of Mycotoxin Contamination in Cereals*, 2016, Joint FAO/WHO Food Standards Programme Codex Committee on Contaminants in Foods, 10th session, April 4–8, Rotterdam, The Netherlands.

34 Contrasting views on the safety of contaminated grain are not surprising given that, as a large body of scholarship has demonstrated, safety is a constructed concept and risk a matter of perception, both deeply embedded in politics, science, and socio-technical imaginaries (Beck 2009, Vogel 2013).

35 "Baʿd usbuʿ min al-rafd . . . Misr tataragaʿ wa taqbal istirad qamh yahui tufail al-argot al-musabib lil-ighad wal-saratan," 2016, *Al-Badil*, January 14.

36 The Codex standards are written by the Codex Alimentarius Commission, a body established by the Food and Agricultural Organization of the United Nations and World Health Organization in 1963 that coordinates meetings of 187 member countries to discuss new scientific evidence on food safety issues and to develop or revise international standards accordingly.

37 Cited in Eric Knecht and Maha El Dahan, 2016, "Bureaucrat and Old Fungus Law Hold Egypt's Wheat Supplies Hostage," Reuters, March 5.

38 Cited in Hasan ʿAbd al-Dhahir, 2016, "Nadia Henry: Talauth al-qamh qadiat amn qawmi," *Rosa el-Youssef*, August 18.

39 Khaled Warbi, 2016, "Mustashar ʿal-silaʿ al-tamwiniya' al-asbaq: Al-hukuma tasuru ʿala istirad aqmah mulauatha," *Al-Tahrir*, August 2.

40 Cited in Ibrahim Ramadan, 2016, "Fayed: Lam tadkhul Misr ai habat qamh musaba bil-irgot hata al-an," *Rosa el-Youssef*, July 30.

41   Cited in Eric Knecht, 2016, "Egypt Cancels Zero Ergot Wheat Policy amid Mounting Pressure," Reuters, September 21.

42   Al-Mawaqif al-Masri (The Egyptian Position), 2016, Facebook post dated October 12, accessed May 21, 2020, https://www.facebook.com/almawkef.almasry/posts/892322860867612.

43   For insights into the day-to-day work of port inspection, see Chalfin's analysis of customs officers and their inspection techniques at a Ghanaian port (2010, chapter 6).

44   Eric Knecht and Maha El Dahan, 2017, "Inspection Battle Threatens Egypt's Wheat Supply," Reuters, October 17.

45   Ministry of Agriculture and Land Reclamation Decree No. 562/2019, issued September 2019. Unofficial translation provided in Mariano Beillard and Shaza Omar, 2020, "Egypt Reintroduces Government Pre Shipment Inspections for Grain Imports," GAIN report, February 11, USDA Foreign Agricultural Service.

46   Interview recorded during the Public-Private Dialogue in the Egyptian Grain Sector Workshop, May 2018, accessed February 20, 2019, https://vimeo.com/285837372.

47   Maha El Dahan et al., 2018, "Egypt's Rejection of Russian Wheat over Ergot Creates Latest Supply Snag," Reuters, May 31.

48   Momen Atallah and Maha El Dahan, 2018, "Egypt to Allow Entry of Russian Wheat Cargo Halted for Ergot," Reuters, June 3.

49   Momen Atallah, 2019, "Egypt Accepts French Cargo after Re-testing," Reuters, April 13.

50   The role of such intermediaries has been a key theme in some notable works of food scholarship. Besky (2020), for instance, offers an in-depth look at the work of tasters, auctioneers, blenders, traders, and scientists in the tea commodity chain, clearly illustrating how quality is something that is always in production, with profound social, political, and economic consequences. Bestor's (2004) examination of the Tsukiji market in Tokyo provides a rich portrait of regulators, shippers, auctioneers, traders, brokers, and buyers and their roles in shaping the movement of fish through the marketplace.

51   There are also a number of private silos, which store the wheat imported for private sector use in specialty breads, pasta, and baked goods.

52   The ways in which grain becomes abstract when transported and stored in bulk are demonstrated in Cronon's (1991) discussion of grain markets in late nineteenth-century Chicago. The fact that Egyptian-grown wheat is still largely transported in sacks, and stored within shonas in sacks, however, is a point of departure from countries like the United States that have moved wholly to bulk transportation and storage.

53   About 90 percent of wheat is currently transported by truck (Kamal 2015: 40). The government has an initiative underway, though, to expand grain transportation by rail and by barge along the Nile.

54   Traditional storage structures, like these mud bins or conical underground pits, are not common today. Most farmers store their wheat in sacks made of jute or plastic; some use more expensive plastic barrels (McGill et al. 2015: 40).

55   The ardab is a measure of volume rather than weight, related to the size of the sacks in which farmers have traditionally stored their grain. One ardab is roughly equivalent to 150 kg.

56 Throughout history, grain stores have been integral to state making and state power. Some of the earliest administrative tablets from Ancient Mesopotamia, for example, depict supplies in grain storehouses and withdrawals from them (Scott 2017: 142–44), and states have long invested in infrastructures of grain storage (Van Oyen 2020). There is a notable parallel between grain storage and the storage of other key resources and their links with national security. The government's interest in maintaining a sizable store of grain in its silos is similar, for instance, to its interest in maintaining a minimum level of water in its reservoir, Lake Nasser (see Barnes 2014, chapter 2).

57 The government's policy used to be that it would keep two to three months of wheat in storage, but in 1994 an incoming Minister of Supply increased this to five months. Salah Mansour, 1995, *Egypt Grain and Feed Annual*, Report EG5006, USDA Foreign Agricultural Service.

58 Nadine Awadalla and Maha El Dahan, 2020, "Coronavirus Prompts Major Pre-emptive Egyptian Wheat Buying Spree," Reuters, September 15.

59 The relative benefits and costs of wheat storage as a policy option for countries of the Middle East and North Africa has been a matter of debate among a number of economists (see, for example, Wright and Cafiero 2011, Larson et al. 2013, Michaels et al. 2015).

60 Mahmud Ashab, 2015, "Taurid 4 malayin ton qamh mahali, wa al-ihtiati yakfi hata uktuber," *Al-Ahram*, May 23; "Al-ihtiati yakfi li-muntasaf febrayer almuqbil, shara' 175 alf ton qamh rusi li-intag al-khubz al-muda'am," 2015, *Al-Ahram*, July 23; Mahmud Ashab, 2015, "Istirad 240 alf ton qamh wa al-ihtiati yakfi hata abril," *Al-Ahram*, October 17.

61 Ahmed Al-Nagar, 2015, "Al-ihtiati al-istratigi min al-qamh yafuq hudud al-aman," *Al-Ahram*, August 30.

62 Maha El Dahan, 2020, "Egypt's Sisi Says 'No Issue' with Strategic Wheat Reserves," Reuters, April 7.

63 The media linked the depletion of the reserves in early 2015 to an increase in flour consumption after the introduction of the new smart card system for baladi bread (see chapter 4). However, the Minister of Supply maintained that the reduction of wheat reserves was a deliberate effort to clear space in silos for what was expected to be a particularly large harvest. "We are not facing at all a shortage in the reserves," he stated to the press, "The opposite is true." Cited in Eric Knecht, 2016, "Corruption in Egypt: Egypt's Dirty Wheat Problem," Reuters, March 15.

64 Marwa Ahmed, 2015, "Al-makhzun al-istratigi lil-qamh qarib 'ala al-nafadh," *Al-Badil*, April 22.

65 Mohamed Tahir, 2016, "Al-halaqa al-thaniya fi musalsal mu'amara 'ala al-falah 'ya qamh min yishtirik'?," *Al-Wafd*, May 7.

66 Figures from McGill et al. (2015: xii) and from "Egypt to Launch Commodities Exchange Hub by Year End," 2016, *Mada Masr*, February 2.

67 Mohamed Al-Samkuri, 2015, "Shonat Naga' Hamadi al-gadida: Al-qamh min nasib al-fi'ran," *Al-Masry al-Youm*, April 24.

68 India presents an interesting comparable case of wheat storage development. Here, too, the government has put considerable effort into adding wheat storage

capacity since the 1950s. The relative merits of different types of storage has also been a prominent topic of debate (see Khorakiwala 2017, chapters 6–7, Khorakiwala 2022).

69 The interest of the Egyptian government in developing its grain storage infrastructure is not new, nor is the interest of donors in supporting such projects. In the 1980s, for instance, a USAID project funded construction of a 100,000-ton silo complex at Safaga, a port on the Red Sea. Indicative of why such projects might be attractive for donors to fund, a clause in the project agreement noted that in return, the government would open the port to US grain exporters and shippers, expanding their Egyptian market. USAID, 1981, *Safaga Grain Silo Complex: Project Paper*, Washington, DC, USAID, USAID Development Experience Clearinghouse. Likewise, in the early 1990s, the World Bank funded a project to expand and repair Egypt's agricultural storage infrastructure.

70 Al-Safha al-Rasmia li-Wizarat al-Tamwin wa al-Tigara al-Dakhiliya, "Al-mashur' al-qawmi al-sawami' . . . wizarat al-tamwin wa al-tigara al-dakhiliya," video, accessed March 4, 2020, https://www.facebook.com/watch/?v=238397860429730.

71 Sami Salaheldin is the regional director of Cimbria, a leading supplier of grain handling and storage technology. At his request, I use his real name rather than a pseudonym.

72 "Military Man Named Supply Minister for Top Wheat Importer Egypt," 2016, Reuters, September 6.

73 Egyptian Ministry of Supply and Internal Trade, 2016, "Wazir al-tamwin: Al-hamalat 'ala al-sawami' wa al-shoan igra' taqum bihi al-wizara sanawiyan ba'd ghalq musim al-taurid," June 26, accessed November 17, 2016, http://www.msit.gov.eg/ar/index.php/mnews/item/983-2016-06-26-15-55-35.

74 This figure comes from Warbi, "Mustashar 'al-sila' al-tamwiniya' al-asbaq." There was, however, wide variation in the figures cited for the costs of this corruption scandal.

75 Cited in Bahir Al-Qadi, 2016, "Barlamani: Al-hukuma a'tat fursa li-'al-haramiya' liyatala'abu fi luqmat 'aish al-ghalaba," *Al-Tahrir*, July 25.

76 Al-Said, "Qamh 'ala waraq."

77 Cited in "Blumberg Says Its High-Tech Silos Not Used to Store Egyptian Wheat," 2016, Reuters, July 20.

78 Eric Knecht, 2016, "Blumberg's High-Tech Attempt to Ease Egyptian Grain Drain," Reuters, April 7.

CHAPTER 4: SUBSIDIZED BREAD

1 There are also 149 government-owned bakeries and 184 bakeries operated by the police and the military. However, the small-scale private bakeries (of which there were 17,435 in 2013) are responsible for producing 88 percent of the country's baladi bread (McGill et al. 2015: 60).

2 It is illegal to sell government-subsidized bread from anywhere other than the licensed bakeries. Although this sometimes happens, most of the bread for sale on the side of the streets, while it may look like baladi bread, is in fact whiter, made

with a more refined flour and less bran than the government-subsidized bread, often prepackaged in bags of five or ten.

3 The cost of baladi bread has remained stable since 1989, but the cost of other breads depends on market conditions (and has increased significantly since the currency devaluation and removal of fuel subsidies in 2016), so the value of baladi bread relative to other kinds of bread fluctuates. In September 2019, the cost of a nonsubsidized loaf of bread was typically around 1EGP. Those subsidized bread bakeries that were willing to sell to people without ration cards charged around 0.5EGP a loaf.

4 Poverty figures from CAPMAS 2017–18 income and expenditure survey data, based on a national poverty line of 735.7EGP/month, cited in Nehal Samir, 2019, "32.5 Percent of Egypt Population Live in Poverty," *Daily News Egypt*, July 29.

5 Welfare figures vary significantly between studies, depending on data and methodology, yet they present a common picture of precarity as the predominant condition in Egypt (even prior to the 2016 currency devaluation and restructuring, which has exacerbated economic insecurity). One study classifies Egyptians into three groups—the poor (29.2 percent), the vulnerable, defined as those above the poverty line but susceptible to falling into poverty (61.0 percent), and the upper middle class and affluent (9.8 percent) (Dang and Ianchovichina 2016: 44). Another study divides Egypt's population into four categories—the poor (25.2 percent), the vulnerable (23.7 percent), the middle class (44.0 percent), and the affluent (7.1 percent) (Abu-Ismail and Sarangi 2013: 16).

6 Clip included in a video published by the Ministry of Supply in 2015. "Bidaiat mandhumat al-khubz wa al-farq beinha wa bein al-madi wa bidaiat tatwir al-magmu'at," posted June 28, 2015, accessed May 22, 2020, https://www.youtube.com /watch?v=NPsa2e2i6UM.

7 Due to the limited access to bakeries and bakery workers that Mariam and I were able to get, this chapter focuses primarily on the bakeries as sites of sale rather than production.

8 For more on the global food crisis of 2007–8, see Johnston 2010.

9 The estimated production capacity of the military bakeries is only 500,000 loaves a day, which is just a small fraction of the 25 million needed to serve all of Cairo (Kamal 2015: 43).

10 This man's calculation was based on an overestimation of the size of the loaves, which have not been over 140 g for some time (see chapter 1). However, even with a more accurate estimation of a kilogram of baladi bread as comprising around 10 loaves, the cost difference of bread as food for humans (0.5EGP) versus food for animals (up to 4EGP) is significant.

11 While this measure was designed to keep demand in check, reports suggest that baladi bread consumption has actually increased since the reforms, in part due to improvements in the quality of the bread, discussed later in the chapter, and in part due to an increase in the cost of other foods since the 2016 currency devaluation. See Medhat Wahba, 2015, "Wafqan li-tasrihat al-rais al-Sisi, makhzun al-qamh yakfi li-intag al-khubz al-muda'am 25 yauman bi-igmali 800 alf ton qamh,"

*Al-Youm al-Sabi*ʿ, May 13; Eric Knecht and Maha Al-Dahan, 2017, "As Austerity-Hit Egyptians Turn to Bread, Wheat Imports Hit New Highs," Reuters, March 16.

12 The studies of average bread consumption were done by the National Nutrition Institute. A nutritionist I interviewed who works for the institute told me about the results, which were not published. Further corroborating this scale of baladi bread consumption, an Egyptian economist told me that she had analyzed unpublished data from the 2017–18 household budget survey and calculated an average baladi bread consumption of two to three loaves a day.

13 Martínez (2018b) analyzes similar activities among bakers in Jordan but argues that they cannot be simply understood as fraudulent "leaks" that go against the government's interests. Instead, he suggests, they are tactics that are often born of necessity and that frequently entail varied forms of cooperation with government employees.

14 The ministry revises its reimbursement price based on changing costs of production (after the 2016 currency devaluation, for instance, it increased the reimbursement from 30 piasters per loaf to 60 piasters per loaf), but some bakers complain that these revisions are not done frequently enough.

15 Similar associations between bread lines and scarcity are found in other countries as well. In the United States, for instance, *breadline* refers to people waiting for handouts of free food (Poppendieck 2014). The term has also, more broadly, come to be synonymous with the subsistence level.

16 That this economist called on me to "go to any Egyptian village" to check the widespread availability of baladi bread points to the fact that many people beyond Egypt's urban centers depend on this bread. It also reflects an assumption that the supply of baladi bread would be less reliable in rural areas than in cities like Cairo.

17 It is common in Cairo for lines to be informally segregated by gender, whether at a metro ticket booth or bakery outlet, so as to prevent men and women from being in the uncomfortably close proximity of a squashed line.

18 At the height of the bread shortage, for example, in February and March 2008, nine people were killed in fights that broke out in bread lines. See Cynthia Johnston, 2008, "In Egypt, Long Queues for Bread That's Almost Free," Reuters, April 6.

19 Guyer writes about waiting in line for gas in Nigeria at a time of shortages—a similar experience in that it is one permeated with the anxiety of not having access to something that is perceived as a staple for everyday life (2004, chapter 6).

20 "ʿAish al-tamwin," video, posted March 7, 2015, accessed May 20, 2020, https://www.youtube.com/watch?v=BPWsoLVEowA.

21 Ragib talked about dead people as being the focus of the database cleanup, but, as I discuss later in the chapter, the ministry is also seeking to filter out others whom it deems undeserving of subsidized bread.

22 While the receipt, in theory, is a way of people holding bakeries accountable, in practice most baladi bread consumers do not seem all that concerned about receipts. In her twenty-two months of observation, Mariam seldom noted people checking their receipts, no doubt for some because they are unable to read them or could only do so with great difficulty—literacy rates in Egypt are only

71 percent for the adult population. More commonly, people just pocketed the receipts with their card and change, or dropped them on the floor. Nor did Mariam find that people seemed all that bothered when bakeries ran out of paper and so were unable to provide receipts, as happens quite frequently, perhaps because they assume that the calculations will be correct. Literacy data from "Egypt: Education and Literacy," UNESCO Institute for Statistics, accessed June 28, 2021, http://uis .unesco.org/en/country/eg.

23 Studies in other countries have similarly highlighted the role of paperwork within bureaucracies (Hull 2012) and the frustrations associated with completing and filing that paperwork (Graeber 2016). There are parallels, for instance, with Dickinson's accounts of the documentation required to access food stamps in New York City (Dickinson 2016, Dickinson 2020). The notable distinction between the US and Egyptian cases, though, is that, whereas baladi bread is both presented and perceived as a citizen's right, eaten by 70–80 percent of the population, including not just the poor but members of the middle class, food stamps are designed as a form of assistance to the neediest, reaching just 13 percent of the population.

24 According to a government decree issued in 2017 (Ministerial Decree 178), the following groups are eligible for a card: (1) the unemployed, informal sector workers, and part-time employees with incomes less than 800EGP a month; (2) public and private sector employees with incomes less than 1,500EGP a month; (3) pensioners with incomes less than 1,200EGP a month; and (4) the disabled.

25 According to the criteria introduced by the ministry in 2019, anyone who owns a new car (2013 model or later) or owns agricultural land (area greater than 15 feddans), or pays a large phone bill (>800EGP/month), high electricity bill (>1,000 kW/month), or school fees (>50,000EGP/year/child) is not eligible for a smart card.

26 Many government agencies maintain Facebook sites, ostensibly as a way to communicate with the public, roughly 40 percent of whom (39 million) have Facebook accounts. Data from the *State of Social Media 2019* report, produced by Crowd Analyzer, a social media monitoring and analytics firm based in Cairo, accessed December 6, 2021, https://www.crowdanalyzer.com/reports/state-of-social-media -report-2019.

27 The difficulties faced by those without smart cards became front-page news in the spring of 2017 when there were protests after the bread allocation for those who had yet to receive their smart cards was cut. For more on this case, see Ketchley and El-Rayyes 2017.

28 In approaching these practices as forms of maintenance, I build on other scholarship that has drawn attention to the importance of everyday acts of keeping things going, or repairing them when they go wrong, as a realm of action that often goes unseen but which is vital for the ongoing function of various infrastructures (e.g., Graham and Thrift 2007, Anand 2015).

29 Within Islam, the gifting of bread to those in need is seen as an act of virtue. Stamatopoulou-Robbins (2009: 144–45) offers an interesting account of Palestinians donating money for bread to those in need as a way of absolving sin.

30 Nadine Awadalla, 2019, "Big Phone Bill? New Car? Wealthier Egyptians Lose Subsidies, Prompting Complaints," Reuters, March 28.

31 "5 Miliarat EGP taufir ba'd hadhf 10 malayin muwatin min da'm al-khubz," 2020, *Mada Masr*, April 15.

32 *In sha' Allah*, which means "God willing," is a common expression in the Arabic-speaking world used to express hope (as opposed to certainty) that an event will happen in the future.

33 Bisan Kassab, 2019, "La tatama'nou: Al-da'am la yasul li-mustahaqia," *Mada Masr*, September 30.

34 Quoted in Samar Salama, 2017, "Shadia Thabit tutalib bitaghyir sharikat tiba'at kurut al-tamwin bi-sabab al-bitaqat al-talifa," *Al-Youm al-Sabi'*, November 27.

35 Egypt's literacy rate is 71.2 percent for the adult population over the age of 15 (77 percent for men, 66 percent for women). Literacy rates are particularly low among the elderly (43 percent for men over the age of 65, 21 percent for women). Literacy data for the year 2017 from "Egypt: Education and Literacy."

36 The length of military service ranges from one to three years, depending on education level. Those who are only sons, support their parents, have dual nationalities, or face medical problems can be exempt from service.

37 For comparable accounts of how varied tastes shape the experience and practice of eating among those dependent on food assistance, see Rock, McIntyre, and Rondeau 2009, Trapp 2016.

38 In a similar case, Martínez and Sirri (2020) comment on the close association between bakeries that sell subsidized bread in Amman, Jordan, and the state, despite the fact that they are privately owned. Bakeries, they argue, are an important site for quotidian engagement between citizens and the state.

39 There is a longer record of complaints about the quality of baladi bread. In Ghannam's (1995) analysis of food buying practices in a Cairo neighborhood, for example, she wrote about how women considered subsidized bread to be "the worst bread available in the market," due to the fact that it was "below their standards of cleanliness" and often contained "stones, insects, worms, pieces of wood, and other objects" (Ghannam 1995: 132–33).

40 This website, titled "Grievances," is an initiative of the Arabic Network for Human Rights Information, accessed May 20, 2020, http://www.humum.net. Cited quotes are from postings "March 6, 2008," "July 22, 2008," "March 1, 2010," "July 14, 2010," and "October 17, 2010."

41 Mohamed Badawi, 2011, "Ila . . . raghif al-'aish," *Al-Wafd*, November 10.

42 Schielke (2015) offers a notable description of the work of bakery inspection. Referring to one inspector who saw his job of inspecting the sanitary conditions in bakeries as being not only poorly paid but pointless, he writes, "In 2007 his work consisted of going every day to the same state-subsidized bakery, where he, with two other inspectors, wrote 'condition: normal' in the inspection book and signed, no matter what the real condition of the bakery might be" (69).

43 Islam Gamal, 2017, "Bil-suar . . . Qari' ya'thur 'ala burs bi-raghif 'aish fi Helwan," *Al-Youm al-Sabi'*, August 8.

44 Among more elite Egyptians, who do not have ration cards and who seldom or rarely eat this bread, there are contrasting perspectives. Some talk about their love for baladi bread, either based on its taste or how it makes them feel connected

to the masses. Others regard the bread with a contempt that is often tied to their contempt for the ruling regime. "It tastes like government, like paper," one young man from an affluent background commented. Another recounted how in his home baladi bread is referred to as the "dogs' bread," unfit for human consumption.

45 Ministry of Supply, "Bidaiat mandhumat al-khubz wa al-farq beinha wa bein al-madi wa bidaiat tatwir al-magmu ʿat," video, posted June 28, 2015, accessed May 22, 2020, https://www.youtube.com/watch?v=NPsa2e2i6UM.

46 While people sometimes employ similar practices when they handle other kinds of breads, many nonsubsidized breads are sold prepackaged, obviating the need (or potential) for this work of airing, rejecting, stacking, and packing.

47 Some people use other receptacles to transport their bread home, like cardboard boxes or string bags, or they borrow a rack from the bakery. However, plastic bags are the most common medium of conveyance in Cairo, given their convenience for carrying multiple goods and widespread availability. In rural areas, in contrast, it is common for those who buy bread to carry it home on a rack or in a big dish, so airing at the bakery is less important.

CHAPTER 5: HOMEMADE BREAD

1 The importance many people attach to the taste of their staple food is a consistent theme within food scholarship, whether that quality derives from the particular crop variety (González 2001, Temudo 2011, Avieli 2012, Appendini and Quijada 2016, Keleman Saxena 2017) or how it is processed into food (Wynne 2015, Phillips 2018).

2 Unlike baladi bread bakeries in urban areas, which are generally open all day, the baladi bread bakeries in Warda tend to close around 9AM. Due to the different patterning of rural life, however, and the proximity of the bakeries to people's homes, I never heard this as a source of complaint. The bakeries have also set up delivery programs, through which a worker collects bread for a group of smart card holders and brings it to their houses in return for a small fee.

3 In rural Fayoum, people refer to bakeries as al-tabuna rather than al-furn (the oven), as they do in Cairo.

4 Other studies of home baking have also highlighted this practice of giving bread as a gift (Counihan 1984, Kanafani-Zaher 1997).

5 Although polygamy is permitted in Islam, it is not all that common in Fayoum, limited to more affluent men who have the resources to support two wives.

6 Wynne (2015) describes a similar process, through which older women in rural Yucatán teach younger girls how to make tortillas so that they can meet gendered labor expectations.

7 Some of the regional breads discussed later in the chapter include other ingredients, like forms of sweetening, fat, or spice.

8 In contrast with other staples such as rice, where the crop variety is a key determinant of taste (Temudo 2011, Avieli 2012), I have never heard anyone in Egypt talk about the various varieties of wheat as having different tastes. Thus, even

with homemade bread, where there is a direct link between the variety a farmer chooses to grow and the flour from which their family bakes (as opposed to the flour that goes into baladi bread, which is sourced from a range of varieties of domestic and imported grains that are mixed together in silos), people understand taste as being more about the milling process than variety.

9   The only context in which zero flour is a key requirement is when women are making special breads and baked goods for festivals and celebrations. The kahk biscuits that are baked for weddings and the Eid al-Fitr, for instance, as well as the thin roqaq bread that is baked for the Eid al-Adha, are made with only zero flour.

10 This mode of baking is a point of contrast with the daily labor of preparing other staples, like tortillas in rural Yucatán, Mexico (Wynne 2015), or rice in southern China (Oxfeld 2017).

11 The use of instant yeast in both homemade and baladi bread exacerbates their propensity to mold compared to sourdough bread, which typically lasts longer.

12 The freezing of fresh bread, which was not possible before women in the village had access to freezers, is an apt illustration of the shift that Freidberg (2009) documents, from *fresh* as meaning direct from the oven or farm (closeness to nature), to *fresh* as depending on a whole range of technologies (protection from nature).

13 Sometimes people also adopt these practices for baladi bread, even though this bread is readily available for purchase. It is not uncommon for people in both urban and rural areas to buy enough baladi bread for multiple days and then freeze some of the loaves.

14 There is a parallel here with the practice among the Zapotec of not wasting maize, using stale tortillas in other dishes, heating tortillas that are beginning to mold so that the spores can be brushed off, or feeding very old or animal-infested tortillas to livestock and poultry (González 2001: 158).

15 Graf (2018) describes urban-rural linkages in Morocco that similarly sustain access to breads valued for their associations with rural childhoods. Yet in the Moroccan case, urban residents source grain rather than bread from rural kin, which they then bake with—a practice more common in urban Morocco than it is in urban Egypt.

16 Agropolis-Museum, "Les pains traditionnels dans l'Égypte contemporaine," accessed April 2, 2018, http://museum.agropolis.fr/pages/expos/egypte/fr/cuisine/pains/index.htm. The museum has now closed due to insufficient funding but still maintains the online archive of its former exhibitions.

17 Mohamed Hamza and Ahmed Wally, 2015, "Nile Nuggets for August 2015," GAIN report, August 30, USDA Foreign Agricultural Service, 2.

18 There is a parallel here with broader discourses about the value and potential demise of indigenous knowledge, which persist despite the contested the nature of the concept (Dove 2006). Scholars and activists have lamented, for instance, the decline of "traditional food-processing knowledge" in Egypt and loss of "indigenous inputs and breeds" (Pozzi and El-Sayed 2017: 50).

19 See, for instance, Mohamed Omran, 2016, "'Al-tamwin': Istihlak al-usra al-rifiya min al-khubz al-muda'am yafuq al-usra al-hadariya," *Rosa el-Youssef*, August 7.

20 Al-Hai'a al-'Ama li-Qusur al-Thaqafa, "Atlas Al-Khubz," accessed May 20, 2020, http://www.gocp.gov.eg/Atlas/atlas01/index.html.

21 Slow Food Foundation for Biodiversity, "Ark of Taste," accessed May 6, 2020, https://www.fondazioneslowfood.com/en/what-we-do/the-ark-of-taste.

CONCLUSION

1 Representatives of the potato industry in China claim that the government's rhetoric has not translated into sufficient policy support to achieve the hoped-for increases in production and consumption. Abraham Inouye, 2018, "China: Potato and Potato Products," GAIN report CH18066, October 30, USDA Foreign Agricultural Service.

2 The Chinese government's efforts to shape people's staple choice is not unique. Earle (2018) traces, for example, how the potato was also a focus of promotional efforts in eighteenth-century Europe, as statesmen and scientists touted its benefits as a cheap and nourishing food. Siegel (2018) describes how the Indian government sought to reduce the consumption of wheat and rice as staples in the 1950s, in part through the promotion of other "substitute" or "supplementary" foods like sweet potatoes—an effort that ultimately failed.

3 Ellen Francis and Maha El Dahan, 2020, "After Blast, Lebanon Has Less than a Month's Grain Reserves," Reuters, August 5.

4 In 2020, the United States–Mexico–Canada Agreement (USMCA) replaced NAFTA as the agreement governing trade relations between the three countries.

5 The US House Agriculture Committee held a hearing in 2015, for example, on the theme of "US Agriculture and National Security" (November 4, 2015, Serial No. 114-133). In his opening statement, the committee chairman noted, "Agriculture and national security are intertwined . . . whether it is ensuring that food is available to meet nutritional needs . . . or ensuring that food coming into our borders is disease- and pest-free."

6 Norimitsu Onishi, 2019, "French Baguettes from a Vending Machine? 'What a Tragedy,'" *New York Times*, November 10, accessed January 7, 2021, https://www.nytimes.com/2019/11/10/world/europe/france-bakery-closures.html.

7 These are not new concepts, but they are concepts that have come increasingly to the fore of policy, academic, and popular debates over recent years (see Cook and Bakker 2012, Bridge 2015).

8 When Collier and Lakoff (2012) write about biosecurity in terms of securing health, they do so in the sense of securing a condition rather than a material thing. Biosecurity is thus distinct from the concepts of food, water, and energy security, which are more directly comparable.

9 Other scholars have also critiqued the Global Water Partnership's definition on this basis (see, for example, van Hofwegen 2009), and more recent definitions of water security, like that developed by UN-Water in 2013, integrate multiple water uses.

Abboud, Samer, Omar Dahi, Waleed Hazbun, Nicole Sunday Grove, Coralie Pison Hindawi, Jamil Mouawad, and Sami Hermez. 2018. "Towards a Beirut School of Critical Security Studies." *Critical Studies on Security* 6, no. 3: 273–95.

Abdalla, Moustafa, and Sherine Al-Shawarby. 2017. "The Tamween Food Subsidy System in Egypt: Evolution and Recent Implementation Reforms." In *The 1.5 Billion People Question: Food, Vouchers, or Cash Transfers?*, edited by Harold Alderman, Ugo Gentilini, and Ruslan Yemstov, 107–50. Washington, DC: World Bank.

Abdelkader, M. 2015. "Wheat Stem Rust and Climatic Changes in Egypt during the Last Five Years." Paper presented at the Fourth International Conference on Agriculture and Horticulture, July 13–15, Beijing.

Abdelmageed, Kishk, Xu-hong Chang, De-mei Wang, Yan-jie Wang, Yu-shuang Yang, Guang-cai Zhao, and Zhi-qiang Tao. 2019. "Evolution of Varieties and Development of Production Technology in Egypt Wheat: A Review." *Journal of Integrative Agriculture* 18, no. 3: 483–95.

Abu-Ismail, Khalid, and Niranjan Sarangi. 2013. *A New Approach to Measuring the Middle Class: Egypt*. New York: United Nations Economic and Social Commission for Western Asia.

Abul-Magd, Zeinab. 2017. *Militarizing the Nation: The Army, Business, and Revolution in Egypt*. New York: Columbia University Press.

Adams, Richard. 1986. *Development and Social Change in Rural Egypt*. Syracuse, NY: Syracuse University Press.

Ahmed, Akhter, Howarth Bouis, Tamar Gutner, and Hans Lofgren. 2001. *The Egyptian Subsidy System: Structure, Performance and Options for Reform*. IFPRI Research Report No. 119. Washington, DC: International Food Policy Research Institute.

Al-Shawarby, Sherine, and Heba El-Laithy. 2010. *Egypt's Food Subsidies: Benefit Incidence and Leakages*. Washington, DC: World Bank.

Alderman, Harold, and Joachim von Braun. 1986. "Egypt's Food Subsidy Policy: Lessons and Options." *Food Policy* 11, no. 3: 223–37.

Alderman, Harold, Ugo Gentilini, and Ruslan Yemstov, eds. 2018. *The 1.5 Billion People Question: Food, Vouchers, or Cash Transfers?* Washington, DC: World Bank.

Ali, Sonia, and Richard Adams. 1996. "The Egyptian Food Subsidy System: Operation and Effects on Income Distribution." *World Development* 24, no. 11: 1777–91.

Allison, Anne. 1991. "Japanese Mothers and Obentos: The Lunch-Box as Ideological State Apparatus." *Anthropological Quarterly* 64, no. 4: 195–208.

Allison, Anne. 2013. *Precarious Japan*. Durham, NC: Duke University Press.

Alwang, Jeffrey, Samy Sabry, Kamel Shideed, Atef Swelam, and Habib Halila. 2018. "Economic and Food Security Benefits Associated with Raised-Bed Wheat Production in Egypt." *Food Security* 10: 589–601.

Amar, Paul. 2013. *Security Archipelago: Human-Security States, Sexuality Politics, and the End of Neoliberalism*. Durham, NC: Duke University Press.

Anand, Nikhil. 2015. "Leaky States: Water Audits, Ignorance, and the Politics of Infrastructure." *Public Culture* 27: 305–30.

Anand, Nikhil. 2017. *Hydraulic City: Water and the Infrastructures of Citizenship in Mumbai*. Durham, NC: Duke University Press.

Andrae, Gunilla, and Bjorn Beckman. 1985. *The Wheat Trap: Bread and Underdevelopment in Nigeria*. London: Zed Books.

Appendini, Kirsten, and Ma. Guadalupe Quijada. 2016. "Consumption Strategies in Mexican Rural Households: Pursuing Food Security with Quality." *Agriculture and Human Values* 33: 439–54.

Asseng, S., F. Ewert, and P. Martre et al. 2015. "Rising Temperatures Reduce Global Wheat Production." *Nature Climate Change* 5: 143–47.

Asseng, Senthold, Ahmed Kheir, Belay Kassie, Gerrit Hoogenboom, Aly Abdelaal, Dorota Haman, and Alex Ruante. 2018. "Can Egypt Become Self-Sufficient in Wheat?" *Environmental Research Letters* 13, no. 9: 094012.

Avieli, Nir. 2012. *Rice Talks: Food and Community in a Vietnamese Town*. Bloomington: Indiana University Press.

Babar, Zahra, and Suzi Mirgani, eds. 2014. *Food Security in the Middle East*. New York: Oxford University Press.

Barnes, Jessica. 2012. "Expanding the Nile's Watershed: The Science and Politics of Land Reclamation in Egypt." In *Water on Sand: Environmental Histories of the Middle East and North Africa*, edited by Alan Mikhail, 251–72. New York: Oxford University Press.

Barnes, Jessica. 2014. *Cultivating the Nile: The Everyday Politics of Water in Egypt*. Durham, NC: Duke University Press.

Barnes, Jessica. 2016a. "Separating the Wheat from the Chaff: The Social Worlds of Wheat." *Environment and Society: Advances in Research* 7: 89–106.

Barnes, Jessica. 2016b. "Uncertainty in the Signal: Modeling Egypt's Water Futures." *Journal of the Royal Anthropological Institute* 22, no. S1: 46–66.

Barnes, Jessica, and Mariam Taher. 2019. "Care and Conveyance: Buying Baladi Bread in Cairo." *Cultural Anthropology* 34, no. 3: 417–43.

Barnett, Jon. 2001. *The Meaning of Environmental Security: Ecological Politics and Policy in the New Security Era*. London: Zed Books.

Barrett, Christopher. 2008. "Smallholder Market Participation: Concepts and Evidence from Eastern and Southern Africa." *Food Policy* 33: 299–317.

Basnet, Bhoja, Mohamed Ali, Amir Ibrahim, Thomas Payne, and Moussa Mosaad. 2011. "Evaluation of Genetic Bases and Diversity of Egyptian Wheat Cultivars Released during the Last 50 Years Using Coefficient of Parentage." *Communications in Biometry and Crop Science* 6, no. 1: 31–47.

Beck, Ulrich. 2009. *World at Risk*. Cambridge: Polity Press.

Beinin, Joel. 2015. *Workers and Thieves: Labor Movements and Popular Uprisings in Tunisia and Egypt*. Palo Alto, CA: Stanford University Press.

Beoku-Betts, Josephine. 1995. "We Got Our Way of Cooking Things: Women, Food, and Preservation of Cultural Identity among the Gullah." *Gender and Society* 9, no. 5: 535–55.

Berger, Peter. 2018. "Millet, Rice, and the Constitution of Society in Central India." *Paideuma: Mitteilungen zur Kulturkunde* 64: 245–64.

Bergeron, Suzanne. 2005. *Fragments of Development: Nation, Gender, and the Space of Modernity*. Ann Arbor: University of Michigan Press.

Berry, Maya, Claudia Arguelles, Shanya Cordis, Sarah Ihmoud, and Elizabeth Estrada. 2017. "Toward a Fugitive Anthropology: Gender, Race, and Violence in the Field." *Cultural Anthropology* 32, no. 4: 537–65.

Besky, Sarah. 2020. *Tasting Qualities: The Past and Future of Tea*. Oakland: University of California Press.

Besteman, Catherine. 2020. *Militarized Global Apartheid*. Durham, NC: Duke University Press.

Bestor, Theodore. 2004. *Tsukiji: The Fish Market at the Center of the World*. Berkeley: University of California Press.

Bhattacharya, Shrayana, Vanita Leah Falco, and Raghav Puri. 2018. "The Public Distribution System in India: Policy Evolution and Program Delivery Trends." In *The 1.5 Billion People Question: Food, Vouchers, or Cash Transfers?*, edited by Harold Alderman, Ugo Gentilini, and Ruslan Yemstov, 43–101. Washington, DC: World Bank.

Bobrow-Strain, Aaron. 2008. "White Bread Bio-Politics: Purity, Health, and the Triumph of Industrial Baking." *Cultural Geographies* 15: 97–118.

Bobrow-Strain, Aaron. 2011. "Making White Bread by the Bomb's Early Light: Anxiety, Abundance, and Industrial Food Power in the Early Cold War." *Food and Foodways* 19, no. 2: 74–97.

Bobrow-Strain, Aaron. 2012. *White Bread: A Social History of the Store-Bought Loaf*. Boston: Beacon Press.

Bohstedt, John. 2008. "Food Riots and the Politics of Provisions from Early Modern Europe and China to the Food Crisis of 2008." *Journal of Peasant Studies* 43, no. 5: 1035–67.

Breisinger, Clemens, Olivier Ecker, Perrihan Al-Riffai, and Bingxin Yu. 2012. *Beyond the Arab Awakening: Policies and Investments for Poverty Reduction and Food Security*. Washington, DC: International Food Policy Research Institute.

Brice, Jeremy. 2014. "Attending to Grape Vines: Perceptual Practices, Planty Agencies and Multiple Temporalities in Australian Viticulture." *Social and Cultural Geography* 15, no. 8: 942–65.

Bridge, Gavin. 2015. "Energy (In)security: World-Making in an Age of Scarcity." *Geographical Journal* 181, no. 4: 328–39.

Broto, Vanesa, Maria Fátima, and Louise Guibrunet. 2020. "Energy Profiles among Urban Elite Households in Mozambique: Explaining the Persistence of Charcoal in Urban Areas." *Energy Research and Social Science* 65: 101478.

Burns, William. 1985. *Economic Aid and American Foreign Policy toward Egypt, 1955–1981.* Albany: State University of New York Press.

Byerlee, Derek, and Piedad Moya. 1993. *Impacts of International Wheat Breeding Research in the Developing World, 1966–1990.* Mexico City: CIMMYT.

Caldwell, Melissa. 2002. "The Taste of Nationalism: Food Politics in Postsocialist Moscow." *Ethnos* 67, no. 3: 295–319.

Çalişkan, Koray. 2010. *Market Threads: How Cotton Farmers and Traders Create a Global Commodity.* Princeton, NJ: Princeton University Press.

Campbell, Bruce, Sonja Vermeulen, Pramod Aggarwal, Caitlin Corner-Dolloff, Evan Girvetz, Ana Maria Loboguerrero, Julian Ramirez-Villegas, Todd Rosenstock, Leocadio Sebastian, Philip Thornton, and Eva Wollenberg. 2016. "Reducing Risks to Food Security from Climate Change." *Global Food Security* 11: 34–43.

Carney, Judith. 2002. *Black Rice: The African Origins of Rice Cultivation in the Americas.* Cambridge, MA: Harvard University Press.

Cassell, Joan, ed. 1987. *Children in the Field: Anthropological Experiences.* Philadelphia: Temple University Press.

Chalfin, Brenda. 2010. *Neoliberal Frontiers: An Ethnography of Sovereignty in West Africa.* Chicago: University of Chicago Press.

CIMMYT [International Center for Wheat and Maize Improvement]. 1988. *CIMMYT Report on Wheat Improvement 1985–86.* Mexico City: CIMMYT.

Clapp, Jennifer. 2017. "Food Self-Sufficiency: Making Sense of It, and When It Makes Sense." *Food Policy* 66: 88–96.

Coelli, Tim. 2010. *The Cost Efficiency in the Production and Distribution of Subsidized Bread in Egypt.* Washington, DC: World Bank.

Collier, Stephen, and Andrew Lakoff, eds. 2012. *Biosecurity Interventions: Global Health and Security in Question.* New York: Columbia University Press.

Cook, Christina, and Karen Bakker. 2012. "Water Security: Debating an Emerging Paradigm." *Global Environmental Change* 22, no. 1: 94–102.

Cornet, Candice, and Tami Blumenfield, eds. 2016. *Doing Fieldwork in China . . . with Kids! The Dynamics of Accompanied Fieldwork in the People's Republic.* Copenhagen: NIAS Press.

Counihan, Carole. 1984. "Bread as World: Food Habits and Social Relations in Modernizing Sardinia." *Anthropological Quarterly* 57, no. 2: 47–59.

Cowen, Deborah. 2014. *The Deadly Life of Logistics: Mapping Violence in Global Trade.* Minneapolis: University of Minnesota Press.

Crapanzano, Vincent. 1980. *Tuhami: Portrait of a Moroccan.* Chicago: University of Chicago Press.

Cronon, William. 1991. *Nature's Metropolis: Chicago and the Great West.* New York: W. W. Norton.

Croppenstedt, Andre, Maurice Saade, and Gamal Siam. 2006. *Food Security and Wheat Policy in Egypt.* Roles of Agriculture Project Policy Brief No. 2. Rome: FAO.

Crosby, Alfred. 1972. *The Columbian Exchange: Biological and Cultural Consequences of 1492.* Westport, CT: Greenwood Press.

Cullather, Nick. 2013. *The Hungry World: America's Cold War Battle against Poverty in Asia.* Cambridge, MA: Harvard University Press.

Dalby, Simon. 2009. *Security and Environmental Change*. Cambridge: Polity Press.

Dang, Hai-Anh, and Elena Ianchovichina. 2016. *Welfare Dynamics with Synthetic Panels: The Case of the Arab World in Transition*. Development Research Group, Policy Research Working Paper 7595. Washington, DC: World Bank.

David, Anda, Nelly El-Mallakh, and Jackline Wahba. 2019. *Internal versus International Migration in Egypt: Together or Far Apart?* Working Paper 1366. Cairo: Economic Research Forum.

Davidson, Joanna. 2015. *Sacred Rice: An Ethnography of Identity, Environment, and Development in Rural West Africa*. New York: Oxford University Press.

Davis, Karen. 1985. A *Survey of Egyptian Village Breads*. Egyptian Major Cereals Improvement Project Report. Cairo: USAID.

Dennis, E. E., J. D. Martin, and R. Wood. 2016. "Media Use in the Middle East, 2015: A Six-Nation Survey." Northwestern University in Qatar. Accessed June 21, 2021. http://www.mideastmedia.org/survey/2015.

Dethier, Jean-Jacques. 1991. "Egypt." In *The Political Economy of Agricultural Pricing Policy, Volume 3: Africa and the Mediterranean*, edited by Anne Krueger, Maurice Schiff, and Alberto Valdes, 15–78. Baltimore: Johns Hopkins University Press.

Dethier, Jean-Jacques, and Kathy Funk. 1987. "The Language of Food: PL480 in Egypt." *Middle East Report* 145: 22–28.

Dickinson, Maggie. 2016. "Working for Food Stamps: Economic Citizenship and the Post-Fordist Welfare State in New York City." *American Ethnologist* 43, no. 2: 270–81.

Dickinson, Maggie. 2020. *Feeding the Crisis: Care and Abandonment in America's Food Safety Net*. Berkeley: University of California Press.

Diphoorn, Tessa. 2016. *Twilight Policing: Private Security and Violence in Urban South Africa*. Berkeley: University of California Press.

Donkor, Emmanuel, Stephen Onakuse, Joe Bogue, and Igancio Carmenado. 2017. "The Impact of the Presidential Cassava Initiative on Cassava Productivity in Nigeria: Implication for Sustainable Food Supply and Food Security." *Cogent Food and Agriculture* 3, no. 1: 1368857.

Dove, Michael. 2006. "Indigenous People and Environmental Politics." *Annual Review of Anthropology* 35: 191–208.

Dove, Michael. 2011. *The Banana Tree at the Gate: The History of Marginal Peoples and Global Markets in Borneo*. New Haven, CT: Yale University Press.

Dove, Michael, and Daniel Kammen. 1997. "The Epistemology of Sustainable Resource Use: Managing Forest Products, Swiddens, and High-Yielding Variety Crops." *Human Organization* 56, no. 1: 91–101.

Draz, Ibrahim, Mohammed Abou-Elseoud, Abd-Elmageed Karama, Omaima Alla-Eldein, and Ahmed El-Bebany. 2015. "Screening of Wheat Genotypes for Leaf Rust Resistance along with Grain Yield." *Annals of Agricultural Science* 60, no. 1: 29–39.

Du Puis, Melanie. 2002. *Nature's Perfect Food: How Milk Became America's Drink*. New York: New York University Press.

Dwyer, Kevin. 1982. *Moroccan Dialogues: Anthropology in Question*. Baltimore: Johns Hopkins University Press.

Earle, Rebecca. 2018. "Promoting Potatoes in Eighteenth-Century Europe." *Eighteenth-Century Studies* 51, no. 2: 147–62.

Ecker, Olivier, Perrihan Al-Riffai, Clemens Breisinger, and Rawia El-Batrawy. 2016. *Nutrition and Economic Development: Exploring Egypt's Exceptionalism and the Role of Food Subsidies*. Washington, DC: International Food Policy Research Institute.

El Dardiry, Giulia, and Sami Hermez. 2020. "Critical Security and Anthropology from the Middle East." *Cultural Anthropology* 35, no. 2: 197–203.

El-Togby, Hassan, and Elham Talaat. 1971. "Wheat Improvement and Production in Egypt." In *Proceedings of the First Wheat Workshop, El Batan, Mexico*, edited by R. A. Fischer and Dean Bork, 25–27. Mexico City: CIMMYT.

El-Zanaty, Fatma, and Ann Way. 2009. *Egypt Demographic and Healthy Survey 2008*. Cairo: Ministry of Health, El-Zanaty and Associates, and Macro International.

Elhakim, Nadine, Arnaud Laillou, Anwar El Nakeeb, Rukia Yacoub, and Magdy She-hata. 2012. "Fortifying Baladi Bread in Egypt: Reaching More than 50 Million People through the Subsidy." *Food and Nutrition Bulletin* 33, no. S4: S260–S271.

Elyachar, Julia. 2005. *Markets of Dispossession: NGOs, Economic Development, and the State in Cairo*. Durham, NC: Duke University Press.

Engel, Barbara. 1997. "Not by Bread Alone: Subsistence Riots in Russia during World War I." *Journal of Modern History* 69: 696–721.

Erkal, Namik. 2020. "Reserved Abundance: State Granaries of Early Modern Istanbul." *Journal of the Society of Architectural Historians* 79, no. 1: 17–38.

Escobar, Arturo. 1994. *Encountering Development: The Making and Unmaking of the Third World*. Princeton, NJ: Princeton University Press.

Evans-Pritchard, Edward Evan. 1940. *The Nuer: A Description of the Modes of Livelihood and Political Institutions of a Nilotic People*. Oxford: Oxford University Press.

Fakhry, Sherif. 2013. "Grain Importations into Egypt: Overall Situation and a View of Logistics, Quality Requirements, and Risks." Presentation at Global Grain Conference, November 12–14, Geneva.

FAO [Food and Agricultural Organization of the United Nations]. 1996. *Rome Declaration on World Food Security and World Food Summit Plan of Action*. World Food Summit, November 13–17, 1996. Rome: FAO.

FAO [Food and Agricultural Organization of the United Nations]. 2001. *The State of Food Insecurity in the World 2001*. Rome: FAO.

Fassin, Didier. 2013. *Enforcing Order: An Ethnography of Urban Policing*. Cambridge, MA: Polity Press.

Feldman, Gregory. 2011. *The Migration Apparatus: Security, Labor, and Policymaking in the European Union*. Palo Alto, CA: Stanford University Press.

Finnis, Elizabeth. 2006. "Why Grow Cash Crops? Subsistence Farming and Crop Commercialization in the Kolli Hills, South India." *American Anthropologist* 108, no. 2: 363–69.

Fletcher, Lehman, ed. 1996. *Egypt's Agriculture in a Reform Era*. Ames: Iowa State University Press.

Flinn, Juliana, and Leslie Marshall, eds. 1998. *Fieldwork and Families: Constructing New Models for Ethnographic Research*. Honolulu: University of Hawai'i Press.

Fluri, Jennifer. 2011. "Bodies, Bombs and Barricades: Geographies of Conflict and Civilian (In)Security." *Transactions of the Institute of British Geographers* 36, no. 2: 280–96.

Francks, Penelope. 2003. "Rice for the Masses: Food Policy and the Adoption of Imperial Self-Sufficiency in Early Twentieth-Century Japan." *Japan Forum* 15, no. 1: 125–46.

Freidberg, Susanne. 2004. *French Beans and Food Scares: Culture and Commerce in an Anxious Age*. Oxford: Oxford University Press.

Freidberg, Susanne. 2009. *Fresh: A Perishable History*. Cambridge, MA: Harvard University Press.

Frerichs, Sabine. 2016. "Egypt's Neoliberal Reforms and the Moral Economy of Bread: Sadat, Mubarak, Morsi." *Review of Radical Political Economics* 48, no. 4: 610–32.

Fullilove, Courtney. 2017. *The Profit of the Earth: The Global Seeds of American Agriculture*. Chicago: University of Chicago Press.

Galal, Osman. 2002. "The Nutrition Transition in Egypt: Obesity, Undernutrition, and Food Consumption in Context." *Public Health Nutrition* 5, no. 1A: 141–48.

Gálvez, Alyshia. 2018. *Eating NAFTA: Trade, Food Policies, and the Destruction of Mexico*. Berkeley: University of California Press.

Garth, Hanna. 2020. *Food in Cuba: The Pursuit of a Decent Meal*. Stanford, CA: Stanford University Press.

Gertel, Jorg, and Petra Kuppinger. 1994. "Space, Social Reproduction and Food Security in Cairo/Egypt." *GeoJournal* 34, no. 3: 277–86.

Ghanem, E. 1994. "Wheat Improvement in Egypt with Emphasis on Heat Tolerance." In *Wheat in Heat-Stressed Environments: Irrigated, Dry Areas and Rice-Wheat Farming Systems*, edited by David Saunders and Gene Hettel, 12–16. Mexico City: CIMMYT.

Ghannam, Farha. 1995. "Gender and Food in Everyday Life." In *The Metropolitan Food System of Cairo*, edited by Jörg Gertel, 125–40. Saarbrücken, Germany: Verlag für Entwicklungspolitik.

Gharib, Mohammed, Naglaa Qabil, and A. H. Salem et al. 2021. "Characterization of Wheat Landraces and Commercial Cultivars Based on Morpho-phenological and Agronomic Traits." *Cereal Research Communications* 49: 149–59.

Gilmartin, David. 2015. *Blood and Water: The Indus River Basin in Modern History*. Berkeley: University of California Press.

Glover, Dominic, Sung Kyu Kim, and Glenn Stone. 2020. "Golden Rice and Technology Adoption Theory: A Study of Seed Choice Dynamics among Rice Growers in the Philippines." *Technology in Society* 60: 101227.

Glück, Zoltan, and Setha Low. 2017. "A Sociospatial Framework for the Anthropology of Security." *Anthropological Theory* 17, no. 3: 281–96.

Gnaba, Abdu. 2011. *Anthropologie des Mangeurs de Pain*. Paris: L'Harmattan.

Goldstein, Daniel. 2010. "Toward a Critical Anthropology of Security." *Current Anthropology* 51, no. 4: 487–517.

González, Roberto. 2001. *Zapotec Science: Farming and Food in the Northern Sierra of Oaxaca*. Austin: University of Texas Press.

Gorman, Timothy. 2019. "Food Crisis to Agrarian Crisis? Vietnam's Food Security Strategy and the Future of Rural Livelihoods in the Mekong Delta." In *Food Anxiety in Globalizing Vietnam*, edited by Judith Elhert and Nora Faltmann, 235–66. London: Palgrave Macmillan.

Government of Egypt. 2014. *Dustur Gumhuriyat Misr al-'Arabiya*. Cairo: Government of Egypt.

Graeber, David. 2016. *The Utopia of Rules: On Technology, Stupidity, and the Secret Joys of Bureaucracy*. Brooklyn, NY: Melville House.

Graf, Katharina. 2018. "Cereal Citizens: Crafting Bread and Belonging in Urbanising Morocco." *Paideuma: Mitteilungen zur Kulturkunde* 64: 244–77.

Graham, Stephen, and Nigel Thrift. 2007. "Out of Order: Understanding Repair and Maintenance." *Theory, Culture and Society* 24, no. 1: 1–25.

Grove, Nicole. 2015. "The Cartographic Ambiguities of HarassMap: Crowdmapping Security and Sexual Violence in Egypt." *Security Dialogue* 46, no. 4: 345–64.

Gudeman, Stephen. 1978. *The Demise of a Rural Economy*. London: Routledge.

Günel, Gökçe, Saiba Varma, and Chika Watanabe. 2020. "Manifesto for Patchwork Ethnography." Member Voices, *Fieldsights*, June 9. https://culanth.org/fieldsights/a -manifesto-for-patchwork-ethnography.

Gusterson, Hugh, and Catherine Besteman, eds. 2009. *The Insecure American: How We Got Here and What We Should Do about It*. Berkeley: University of California Press.

Gusterson, Hugh, and Catherine Besteman. 2019. "Cultures of Militarism." *Current Anthropology* 60, no. S19: S3–S14.

Gutner, Tammi. 1999. *The Political Economy of Food Subsidy Reform in Egypt*. Food Consumption and Nutrition Division Discussion Paper No. 77. Washington, DC: International Food Policy Research Institute.

Guyer, Jane. 2004. *Marginal Gains: Monetary Transactions in Atlantic Africa*. Chicago: University of Chicago Press.

GWP [Global Water Partnership]. 2000. *Towards Water Security: A Framework for Action*. Stockholm: Global Water Partnership.

Habicht, Michael, Maciej Henneberg, Lena Öhrström, Kaspar Staub, and Frank Rühli. 2015. "Body Height of Mummified Pharaohs Supports Historical Suggestions of Sibling Marriages." *American Journal of Physical Anthropology* 157, no. 3: 519–25.

Hafez, Sabry. 1994. "Food as a Semiotic Code in Arabic Literature." In *Culinary Cultures of the Middle East*, edited by Sami Zubaida and Richard Tapper, 257–80. London: I. B. Tauris.

Haggag, Wafaa. 2013. "Wheat Diseases in Egypt and Its Management." *Journal of Applied Sciences Research* 9, no. 1: 46–50.

Hamdy, Sherine. 2012. *Our Bodies Belong to God: Organ Transplants, Islam, and the Struggle for Human Dignity in Egypt*. Berkeley: University of California Press.

Harrigan, Jane. 2014. *The Political Economy of Arab Food Sovereignty*. London: Palgrave Macmillan.

Harrison, Faye Venetia, ed. 1991. *Decolonizing Anthropology: Moving Further toward an Anthropology for Liberation*. Washington, DC: Association of Black Anthropologists, American Anthropological Association.

Hartigan, John. 2017. *Care of the Species: Races of Corn and the Science of Plant Biodiversity*. Minneapolis: University of Minnesota Press.

Hassan-Wassef, Habiba. 2012. "The Politics of Bread in Egypt." CIHEAM [International Center for Advanced Mediterranean Agronomic Studies] *Watch Letter* 23 (December): 11–14.

Hayat, Maira. 2019. "Security, Storage and Measurement: The Temporal Politics of Accumulating Water in Pakistan." Paper presented at the Annual Meetings of the American Anthropological Association, November 20–24, Vancouver, BC.

Head, Lesley, Jennifer Atchison, and Alison Gates. 2012. *Ingrained: A Human Bio-geography of Wheat*. Farnham, UK: Ashgate.

Headey, Derek. 2010. *Rethinking the Global Food Crisis: The Role of Trade Shocks*: IFPRI Discussion Paper No. 958. Washington, DC: International Food Policy Research Institute.

Heigermoser, Maximilian, Linde Götz, and Miranda Svanidze. 2018. "Egypt's Wheat Tenders: A Public Notice Board for Black Sea Grain Notations?" Lecture for the 58th Annual GEWISOLA Conference (Society for Economic and Social Sciences in Agriculture), "Visions for an Agricultural and Food Policy after 2020" (September 12–14), Kiel, Germany.

Hossain, Naomi, and Patta Scott-Villiers, eds. 2017. *Food Riots, Food Rights and the Politics of Provisions*. New York: Routledge.

Huber, Matthew. 2009. "The Use of Gasoline: Value, Oil, and the 'American Way of Life.'" *Antipode* 41, no. 3: 465–86.

Hull, Matthew. 2012. *Government of Paper: The Materiality of Bureaucracy in Urban Pakistan*. Berkeley: University of California Press.

Ikram, Khaled. 2007. *The Egyptian Economy, 1952–2000: Performance, Policies, and Issues*. London: Routledge.

Iyer, Samantha. 2014. *The Paradox of Poverty and Plenty: Egypt, India, and the Rise of US Food Aid, 1870s to 1950s*. PhD dissertation, University of California, Berkeley.

Jacob, H. [1944] 2014. *Six Thousand Years of Bread: Its Holy and Unholy History*. New York: Skyhorse.

Jarosz, Lucy. 2011. "Defining World Hunger: Scale and Neoliberal Ideology in International Food Security Policy Discourse." *Food, Culture, and Society* 14, no. 1: 117–39.

Jepson, Wendy, and Hannah Lee Brown. 2014. "'If No Gasoline, No Water': Privatizing Drinking Water Quality in South Texas Colonias." *Environment and Planning A* 46: 1032–48.

Johnston, Deborah. 2010. "Introduction to a Symposium on the 2007–8 World Food Crisis." *Journal of Agrarian Change* 10, no. 1: 69–71.

Kamal, Oday. 2015. *Half-Baked, the Other Side of Egypt's Baladi Bread Subsidy: A Study of the Market Intermediaries and Middlemen in the System*. Barcelona: CIDOB [Barcelona Centre for International Affairs].

Kanafani-Zahar, Aida. 1997. "'Whoever Eats You Is No Longer Hungry, Whoever Sees You Becomes Humble': Bread and Identity in Lebanon." *Food and Foodways* 7, no. 1: 45–71.

Kaplan, Steven. 1997. "Breadways." *Food and Foodways* 7, no. 1: 1–44.

Kaplan, Steven. 2006. *Good Bread Is Back: A Contemporary History of French Bread, the Way It Is Made, and the People Who Make It*. Durham, NC: Duke University Press.

Keleman Saxena, Alder. 2017. *Agrobiodiversity, Food Security, and Food Culture in Cochabamba, Bolivia*. PhD dissertation, Yale School of Forestry and Environmental Studies, New Haven, CT.

Ketchley, Neil, and Thoraya El-Rayyes. 2017. "On the Breadline in Sisi's Egypt." *Middle East Report Online*, March 29, 2017. https://merip.org/2017/03/on-the-breadline-in-sisis-egypt.

Khalili, Laleh. 2020. *Sinews of War and Trade: Shipping and Capitalism in the Arabian Peninsula*. London: Verso.

Kherallah, Mylene, Hans Lofgren, Peter Gruhn, and Meyra Reeder. 2000. *Wheat Policy Reform in Egypt: Adjustment of Local Markets and Options for Future Reforms.* IFPRI Research Report No. 115. Washington, DC: International Food Policy Research Institute.

Khorakiwala, Ateya. 2017. *A Well-Fed Subject: Modern Architecture in the Quantitative State, India (1943–1984).* PhD dissertation, Harvard University, Cambridge, MA.

Khorakiwala, Ateya. 2022. "Floors and Ceilings: The Architectonics of Accumulation in the Green Revolution." In *Architecture in Development: Systems and the Emergence of the Global South,* edited by Aggregate Architectural History Collaborative, 343–62. London: Routledge.

Khouri-Dagher, Nadia. 1996. "The State, Urban Households, and Management of Daily Life: Food and Social Order in Cairo." In *Development, Change, and Gender in Cairo,* edited by Diane Singerman and Homa Hoodfar, 110–33. Bloomington: Indiana University Press.

Kimura, Aya. 2013. *Hidden Hunger: Gender and the Politics of Smarter Foods.* Ithaca, NY: Cornell University Press.

King, Marcus, and Jay Gulledge. 2014. "Climate Change and Energy Security: An Analysis of Policy Research." *Climatic Change* 123: 57–68.

Klein, Jakob. 2020. "Eating Potatoes Is Patriotic: State, Market and the Common Good in Contemporary China." *Journal of Current Chinese Affairs* 48, no. 3: 340–59.

Kloppenburg, Jack. 2005. *First the Seed: The Political Economy of Plant Biotechnology.* Madison: University of Wisconsin Press.

Kneas, David. 2020. "Placing Resources: Junior Mining Companies and the Locus of Mineral Potential." *Geoforum* 117: 268–78.

Kortright, Chris. 2013. "On Labor and Creative Transformations in the Experimental Fields of the Philippines." *East Asian Science, Technology and Society* 7, no. 4: 557–78.

Laiprakobsup, Thanapan. 2019. "The Policy Effect of Government Assistance on the Rice Production in Southeast Asia: Comparative Case Studies of Thailand, Vietnam, and the Philippines." *Development Studies Research* 6, no. 1: 1–12.

Larcom, Shaun, Po-Wen She, and Terry van Gevelt. 2019. "The UK Summer Heatwave of 2018 and Public Concern over Energy Security." *Nature Climate Change* 9: 370–73.

Larson, Donald, Julian Lampietti, Christophe Gouel, Carlo Cafiero, and John Roberts. 2013. "Food Security and Storage in the Middle East and North Africa." *World Bank Economic Review* 28, no. 1: 48–73.

Laudan, Rachel. 2013. *Cuisine and Empire: Cooking in World History.* Berkeley: University of California Press.

Lee, Jessica. 2011. "Yeasts Are People Too: Sourdough Fermentation from the Microbe's Point of View." In *Cured, Fermented and Smoked: Proceedings of the Oxford Symposium on Food and Cookery 2010,* 175–88. Totnes, UK: Prospect Books.

Lee, Seung-Joon. 2011. *Gourmets in the Land of Famine: The Culture and Politics of Rice in Modern Canton.* Palo Alto, CA: Stanford University Press.

Lemanski, Charlotte. 2012. "Everyday Human (In)Security: Rescaling for the Southern City." *Security Dialogue* 43, no. 1: 61–78.

Li, Tania. 2014. *Land's End: Capitalist Relations on an Indigenous Frontier.* Durham, NC: Duke University Press.

Link, Michael, Jürgen Scheffran, and Tobias Ide. 2016. "Conflict and Cooperation in the Water-Security Nexus: A Global Comparative Analysis of River Basins under Climate Change." *WIREs Water* 3, no. 4: 495–515.

Lipton, Michael, and Richard Longhurst. 1989. *New Seeds and Poor People*. Baltimore: Johns Hopkins University Press.

Low, Setha. 2003. *Behind the Gates: Life, Security, and the Pursuit of Happiness in Fortress America*. New York: Routledge.

Low, Setha, and Mark Maguire, eds. 2019. *Spaces of Security: Ethnographies of Securityscapes, Surveillance, and Control*. New York: New York University Press.

Lutz, Catherine. 2002. "Making War at Home in the United States: Militarization and the Current Crisis." *American Anthropologist* 104, no. 3: 723–35.

Maguire, Mark, Catarina Frois, and Nils Zurawski, eds. 2014. *The Anthropology of Security: Perspectives from Policing, Counter-terrorism, and Border Control*. London: Pluto Press.

Malström, Maria Frederika. 2019. *The Streets Are Talking to Me: Affective Fragments in Sisi's Egypt*. Berkeley: University of California Press.

Martínez, José. 2017. "Leavening Neoliberalization's Uneven Pathways: Bread, Governance and Political Rationalities in the Hashemite Kingdom of Jordan." *Mediterranean Politics* 22, no. 4: 464–83.

Martínez, José. 2018a. "Leavened Apprehensions: Bread Subsidies and Moral Economies in Hashemite Jordan." *International Journal of Middle East Studies* 50: 173–93.

Martínez, Jose. 2018b. "Site of Resistance or Apparatus of Acquiescence? Tactics at the Bakery." *Middle East Law and Governance* 10: 160–84.

Martínez, José. 2020. "Topological Twists in the Syrian Conflict: Re-thinking Space through Bread." *Review of International Studies* 46, no. 1: 121–36.

Martínez, José, and Brent Eng. 2017. "Struggling to Perform the State: The Politics of Bread in the Syrian Civil War." *International Journal of Political Sociology* 11: 130–47.

Martínez, Jose, and Omar Sirri. 2020. "Of Bakeries and Checkpoints: Stately Affects in Amman and Baghdad." *Environment and Planning D: Society and Space* 38, no. 5: 849–66.

Masco, Joseph. 2014. *The Theater of Operations: National Security Affect from the Cold War to the War on Terror*. Durham, NC: Duke University Press.

Mauss, Marcel. 2001. *The Gift: The Form and Reason for Exchange in Archaic Societies*. 2nd ed. London: Routledge.

Maystadt, Jean-Francois, Jean-Francois Trinh Tah, and Clemens Breisinger. 2012. *Does Food Security Matter for Transition in Arab Countries?* IFPRI Discussion Paper No. 1196. Washington, DC: International Food Policy Research Institute.

McCann, James. 2007. *Maize and Grace: Africa's Encounter with a New World Crop*. Cambridge, MA: Harvard University Press.

McDonald, Matt. 2013. "Discourses of Climate Security." *Political Geography* 33: 42–51.

McFarland, Stephen. 1985. "Anatomy of an Iranian Political Crowd: The Tehran Bread Riot of December 1942." *International Journal of Middle East Studies* 17, no. 1: 51–65.

McGill, Julian, Dmitry Prikhodko, Boris Sterk, and Peter Talks. 2015. *Egypt: Wheat Sector Review*. Rome: FAO.

McLean, Athena, and Annette Leibing, eds. 2007. *The Shadow Side of Fieldwork: Exploring the Blurred Borders between Ethnography and Life*. Malden, MA: Blackwell.

Meyer, Günter. 1998. "Economic Changes in the Newly Reclaimed Lands: From State Farms to Small Holdings and Private Agricultural Enterprises." In *Directions of Change in Rural Egypt*, edited by Nicholas Hopkins and Kirsten Westergaard, 334–57. Cairo: American University in Cairo Press.

Michaels, Sean, Michelle Battat, Dana Erekat, Arnold de Hartog, and Julian Lampietti. 2015. *The Grain Chain: Food Security and Managing Wheat Imports in Arab Countries*. Washington, DC: World Bank and FAO.

Middleton, Townsend, and Jason Cons. 2014. "Coming to Terms: Reinserting Research Assistants into Ethnography's Past and Present." *Ethnography* 15, no. 3: 279–90.

Mikhail, Alan. 2011. *Nature and Empire in Ottoman Egypt: An Environmental History*. Cambridge: Cambridge University Press.

Mintz, Sidney. 1985. *Sweetness and Power: The Place of Sugar in Modern History*. New York: Penguin.

Mitchell, Timothy. 2002. *The Rule of Experts: Egypt, Technopolitics, Modernity*. Berkeley: University of California Press.

Msowoya, Kondwani, Kaveh Madani, Rahman Davtalab, Ali Mirchi, and Jay Lund. 2016. "Climate Change Impacts on Maize Production in the Warm Heart of Africa." *Water Resources Management* 30: 5299–312

Murray, Mary Anne. 2000. "Cereal Production and Processing." In *Ancient Egyptian Materials and Technology*, edited by Paul Nicholson and Ian Shaw, 505–36. Cambridge: Cambridge University Press.

Nagar, Richa. 2014. *Muddying the Waters: Coauthoring Feminisms across Scholarship and Activism*. Urbana: University of Illinois Press.

Naguib, Nefissa. 2015. *Nurturing Masculinities: Men, Food, and Family in Contemporary Egypt*. Austin: University of Texas Press.

Ochs, Juliana. 2013. *Security and Suspicion: An Ethnography of Everyday Life in Israel*. Philadelphia: University of Pennsylvania Press.

Ohnuki-Tierney, Emiko. 1993. *Rice as Self: Japanese Identities through Time*. Princeton, NJ: Princeton University Press.

Orlove, Ben. 1997. "Meat and Strength: The Moral Economy of a Chilean Food Riot." *Cultural Anthropology* 12, no. 2: 234–68.

Owen, Edward Roger John. 1969. *Cotton and the Egyptian Economy, 1820–1914: A Study in Trade and Development*. Oxford: Clarendon Press.

Oxfeld, Ellen. 2017. *Bitter and Sweet: Food, Meaning, and Modernity in Rural China*. Berkeley: University of California Press.

Patel, Raj. 2009. "Food Sovereignty." *Journal of Peasant Studies* 36, no. 3: 663–706.

Patel, Raj, and Philip McMichael. 2009. "A Political Economy of the Food Riot." *Review: A Journal of the Fernand Braudel Center* 32, no. 1: 9–35.

Paxson, Heather. 2013. *The Life of Cheese: Crafting Food and Value in America*. Berkeley: University of California Press.

Perkins, John. 1997. *Geopolitics and the Green Revolution: Wheat, Genes and the Cold War*. New York: Oxford University Press.

Phillips, Kristin. 2018. *An Ethnography of Hunger: Politics, Subsistence, and the Unpredictable Grace of the Sun*. Bloomington: Indiana University Press.

Poppendieck, Janet. 2014. *Breadlines Knee-Deep in Wheat: Food Assistance in the Great Depression*. Berkeley: University of California Press.

Pozzi, Sara, and Sara El-Sayed. 2017. "Where's Our Baladi Food?" In *The Food Question in the Middle East*, edited by Malak Rouchdy and Iman Hamdy, 45–60. Cairo Papers in Social Science 34, no. 4. Cairo: American University in Cairo Press.

Rabinow, Paul. [1977] 2007. *Reflections on Fieldwork in Morocco*. Berkeley: University of California Press.

Reitz, Louis, and S. Salmon. 1968. "Origin, History, and Use of Norin 10 Wheat." *Crop Science* 8, no. 6: 668–89.

Richards, Alan. 1986. *Egypt's Agricultural Development, 1800–1980*. Boulder, CO: Westview Press.

Richards, Alan. 1991. "The Political Economy of Dilatory Reform: Egypt in the 1980s." *World Development* 19, no. 12: 1721–30.

Richards, Audrey. 1932. *Hunger and Work in a Savage Tribe: A Functional Study of Nutrition among the Southern Bantu*. London: Routledge.

Richardson, Tanya, and Gisa Weszkalnys. 2014. "Resource Materialities." *Anthropological Quarterly* 87, no. 1: 5–30.

Ries, Nancy. 2009. "Potato Ontology: Surviving Postsocialism in Russia." *Cultural Anthropology* 24, no. 2: 181–212.

Rock, Melanie, Lynn McIntyre, and Krista Rondeau. 2009. "Discomforting Comfort Foods: Stirring the Pot on Kraft Dinner and Social Inequality in Canada." *Agriculture and Human Values* 26: 167–76.

Rubaii, Kali. 2021. "When States Need Refugees: Iraqi Kurdistan and the Security Alibi." In *Un-settling Middle Eastern Refugees: Regimes of Exclusion and Inclusion in the Middle East*, edited by Marcia C. Inhorn and Lucia Volk, 25–39. New York: Berghahn Books.

Rutherford, Danilyn. 2016. "Affect Theory and the Empirical." *Annual Review of Anthropology* 45: 285–300.

Sadiki, Larbi. 2000. "Popular Uprisings and Arab Democratization." *International Journal of Middle East Studies* 32: 71–95.

Sadowski, Yahya. 1991. *Political Vegetables? Businessman and Bureaucrat in the Development of Egyptian Agriculture*. Washington, DC: Brookings Institution.

Salem, Sara. 2020. *Anticolonial Afterlives in Egypt: The Politics of Hegemony*. Cambridge: Cambridge University Press.

Samimian-Darash, Limor, and Meg Stalcup. 2017. "Anthropology of Security and Security in Anthropology: Cases of Counterterrorism in the United States." *Anthropological Theory* 17, no. 1: 60–87.

Schewe, Eric. 2017. "How War Shaped Egypt's National Bread Loaf." *Comparative Studies of South Asia, Africa and the Middle East* 37, no. 1: 49–63.

Schielke, Samuli. 2015. *Egypt in the Future Tense: Hope, Frustration, and Ambivalence before and after 2011*. Bloomington: Indiana University Press.

Scobie, Grant. 1981. *Government Policy and Food Imports: The Case of Wheat in Egypt*. IFPRI Research Report No. 29. Washington, DC: International Food Policy Research Institute.

Scott, James C. 2017. *Against the Grain: A Deep History of the Earliest States*. New Haven, CT: Yale University Press.

Sen, Amartya. 1983. *Poverty and Famines: An Essay on Entitlement and Deprivation.* Oxford: Oxford University Press.

Shaw, John. 2007. *World Food Security: A History since 1945.* New York: Palgrave Macmillan.

Sha'lan, Samih Abd el-Ghaffar. 2002. *Al-Khubz fi al-Ma'thurat al-Sha'biya: Dirasa fi al-Atalis al-Fulkluriya.* Cairo: 'Ain for Human and Social Studies.

Shehata, Samer. 2009. *Shop Floor Culture and Politics in Egypt.* Albany: State University of New York Press.

Shiva, Vandana. 1991. *The Violence of the Green Revolution: Third World Agriculture, Ecology, and Politics.* London: Zed Books.

Siegel, Ben. 2018. *Hungry Nation: Food, Famine, and the Making of Modern India.* Cambridge: Cambridge University Press.

Skoggard, Ian, and Alisse Waterston. 2015. "Introduction: Toward an Anthropology of Affect and Evocative Ethnography." *Anthropology of Consciousness* 26, no. 2: 109–20.

Sovacool, Benjamin. 2011. "Introduction: Defining, Measuring, and Exploring Energy Security." In *The Routledge Handbook of Energy Security,* edited by Benjamin Sovacool, 1–42. Abingdon, UK: Routledge.

Sowers, Jeannie. 2011. "Remapping the Nation, Critiquing the State: Narrating Land Reclamation for Egypt's 'New Valley.'" In *Environmental Imaginaries of the Middle East,* edited by Diana Davis and Terry Burke, 158–91. Athens: Ohio University Press.

Springborg, Robert. 1979. "Patrimonialism and Policy Making in Egypt: Nasser and Sadat and the Tenure Policy for Reclaimed Lands." *Middle Eastern Studies* 15, no. 1: 49–69.

Srage, Nader. 2014. *Misr al-Thaura wa Shi'arat Shababiha: Dirasa Lisaniya fi 'Afawiyat al-Ta'bir.* Doha: Arab Center for Research and Policy Studies.

Stamatopoulou-Robbins, Sophia. 2019. *Waste Siege: The Life of Infrastructure in Palestine.* Stanford, CA: Stanford University Press.

Stewart, Kathleen. 2007. *Ordinary Affects.* Durham, NC: Duke University Press.

Stone, Glenn. 2002. "Both Sides Now: Fallacies in the Genetic-Modification Wars, Implications for Developing Countries, and Anthropological Perspectives." *Current Anthropology* 43, no. 4: 611–30.

Su, Wang, and Jian Wang. 2019. "Potato and Food Security in China." *American Journal of Potato Research* 96: 100–101.

Temudo, Marina. 2011. "Planting Knowledge, Harvesting Agro-Biodiversity: A Case Study of Southern Guinea-Bissau Rice Farming." *Human Ecology* 39: 309–21.

Tesdell, Omar. 2017. "Wild Wheat to Productive Drylands: Global Scientific Practice and the Agroecological Remaking of Palestine." *Geoforum* 78: 43–51.

Thompson, E. P. 1971. "The Moral Economy of the English Crowd in the Eighteenth Century." *Past and Present* 50: 76–136.

Tilly, Louise. 1971. "The Food Riot as a Form of Political Conflict in France." *Journal of Interdisciplinary History* 2, no. 1: 23–57.

Timmer, Peter, Hastuti Hastuti, and Sudarno Sumarto. 2018. "Evolution and Implementation of the Rastra Program in Indonesia." In *The 1.5 Billion People Question: Food, Vouchers, or Cash Transfers?*, edited by Harold Alderman, Ugo Gentilini, and Ruslan Yemstov, 265–307. Washington, DC: World Bank.

Trapp, Micah. 2016. "You-Will-Kill-Me Beans: Taste and the Politics of Necessity in Humanitarian Aid." *Cultural Anthropology* 31, no. 3: 412–37.

Trego, Rachel. 2011. "The Functioning of the Egyptian Food-Subsidy System during Food-Price Shocks." *Development in Practice* 21, no. 4–5: 666–78.

Tsing, Anna. 2015. *The Mushroom at the End of the World: On the Possibility of Life in Capitalist Ruins*. Princeton, NJ: Princeton University Press.

UNDP [United Nations Development Program]. 2004. *World Energy Assessment Overview: 2004 Update*. New York: UNDP.

Vairel, Frédéric. 2013. "Protesting in Authoritarian Situations: Egypt and Morocco in Comparative Perspective." In *Social Movements, Mobilization, and Contestation in the Middle East and North Africa*, edited by Joel Beinin and Frédéric Vairel, 33–48. Palo Alto, CA: Stanford University Press.

van Hofwegen, Paul. 2009. "Capacity Challenges on the Path towards Water Security." In *Water for a Changing World: Developing Local Knowledge and Capacity*, edited by Guy Alaerts and Nicolas Dickinson, 201–13. Delft, Netherlands: UNESCO-IHE.

Van Oyen, Astrid. 2020. *The Socio-economics of Roman Storage: Agriculture, Trade, and Family*. Cambridge: Cambridge University Press.

Varty, John. 2004. "On Protein, Prairie Wheat, and Good Bread: Rationalizing Technologies and the Canadian State, 1912–1935." *Canadian Historical Review* 85, no. 4: 721–53.

Velthuis, Olav. 2007. *Talking Prices: Symbolic Meanings of Prices on the Market for Contemporary Art*. Princeton, NJ: Princeton University Press.

Verdery, Katherine. 1996. *What Was Socialism and What Comes Next*. Princeton, NJ: Princeton University Press.

Vergauwen, David, and Ive De Smet. 2017. "From Early Farmers to Norman Borlaug— The Making of Modern Wheat." *Current Biology* 27, no. 17: R858–R862.

Vogel, Sarah. 2013. *Is It Safe? BPA and the Struggle to Define the Safety of Chemicals*. Berkeley: University of California Press.

Voll, Sarah. 1980. "Egyptian Land Reclamation since the Revolution." *Middle East Journal* 34, no, 2: 127–48.

Wahaab, Rifaat, and Mohamed Badawy. 2004. "Water Quality Assessment of the River Nile System: An Overview." *Biomedical and Environmental Sciences* 17: 87–100.

Waines, David. 1987. "Bread and Society: An Essay on the Staff of Life in Medieval Iraq." *Journal of Economic and Social History of the Orient* 30, no. 3: 255–85.

Warner, Jeroen. 2012. "The Struggle over Turkey's Ilisu Dam: Domestic and International Security Linkages." *International Environmental Agreements* 12: 231–50.

Weismantel, Mary. 1988. *Food, Gender, and Poverty in the Ecuadorian Andes*. Philadelphia: University of Pennsylvania Press.

Weiss, Brad. 1996. *The Making and Unmaking of the Haya Lived World*. Durham, NC: Duke University Press.

West, Paige. 2012. *From Modern Production to Imagined Primitive: Tracking the Commodity Ecumene for Papua New Guinean Coffee*. Durham, NC: Duke University Press.

WFP [World Food Programme]. 2012. *Optimizing the Baladi Bread Supply Chain: Project Documentation Report*. Food Subsidy Reform Project Report. Cairo: WFP.

WFP [World Food Programme]. 2013. *The Status of Poverty and Food Security in Egypt: Analysis and Policy Recommendations*. Summary Report (May). Cairo: WFP.

Williams-Forson, Psyche. 2010. "Other Women Cooked for My Husband: Negotiating Gender, Food, and Identities in an African American/Ghanaian Household." *Feminist Studies* 36, no. 2: 435–61.

Winter, Yves. 2016. "The Siege of Gaza: Spatial Violence, Humanitarian Strategies, and the Biopolitics of Punishment." *Constellations* 23, no. 2: 308–19.

Wittman, Hannah. 2011. "Food Sovereignty: A New Rights Framework for Food and Nature?" *Environment and Society: Advances in Research* 2: 87–105.

Wizarat Al-Thaqafa [Ministry of Culture]. 2006. *Atlas al-Ma'thurat al-Sha'biya al-Misriya*. vol 1. Cairo: Al-Hai'a al-'Ama li-Qusur al-Thaqafa.

Woertz, Eckart. 2013. *Oil for Food: The Global Food Crisis and the Middle East*. Oxford: Oxford University Press.

Wolford, Wendy, and Ryan Nehring. 2013. "Moral Economies of Food Security and Protest in Latin America." In *Food Security and Sociopolitical Stability*, edited by Christopher Barrett, 303–22. Oxford: Oxford University Press.

Wright, Brian, and Carlo Cafiero. 2011. "Grain Reserves and Food Security in the Middle East and North Africa." *Food Security* 3, no. S1: S61–S76.

Wynne, Lauren. 2015. "'I Hate It': Tortilla-Making, Class, and Women's Tastes in Rural Yucatan, Mexico." *Food and Foodways* 18, no. 3: 379–97.

York, E. T., Jr., Donald Plucknett, Jim Ross, Harold Youngberg, and Leticia Solaún. 1994. *The National Agricultural Research Project's Contributions to Significant Advances in Egyptian Agriculture*. Cairo: USAID and Ministry of Agriculture and Land Reclamation.

Zadoks, Jan. 2008. *On the Political Economy of Plant Disease Epidemics*. Wageningen, Netherlands: Wageningen Academic.

Zhang, Hong, Fen Xu, Yu Wu, Hong-hai Hu, and Xiao-feng Dai. 2017. "Progress of Potato Staple Food Research and Industry Development in China." *Journal of Integrative Agriculture* 16, no. 12: 2924–32.

Zhang, Hongzhou. 2019. *Securing the "Rice Bowl": China and Global Food Security*. Singapore: Palgrave Macmillan.

Zhang, Shaohua. 2017. "Riding on Self-Sufficiency: Grain Policy and the Rise of Agrarian Capital in China." *Journal of Peasant Studies* 54: 151–61.

NEWS SOURCES

Al-Ahram
Al-Badil
Al-Bursa
Al-Masry al-Youm
Al-Tahrir
Al-Wafd
Al-Youm al-Sabi'
Daily News Egypt
Egypt State Information Service
Mada Masr
Reuters
Rosa el-Youssef

ARCHIVES AND SERIALS

CIMMYT Publications Depository (online archive), https://repository.cimmyt.org, International Maize and Wheat Improvement Center (CIMMYT), Mexico City

Egypt Grain and Feed Annual [and other update report series]. Foreign Agricultural Service, Cairo Office, American Embassy, Egypt

Food and Agriculture Organization of the United Nations Archives, Rome

Near East Wheat and Barley Project Information Bulletin, Food and Agriculture Organization of the United Nations, Rome

Rockefeller Foundation Archive Center, Sleepy Hollow, NY

USAID Development Experience Clearinghouse (online archive), https://dec.usaid.gov, US Agency for International Development (USAID), Washington, DC

US National Archives and Records Administration, College Park, MD

Page numbers followed by *f* refer to illustrations.

becoming, process of, 43, 79, 246n4

Beirut port explosion (2020), 227-28

Beoku-Betts, Josephine, 242n29

Besky, Sarah, 261n50

Bestor, Theodore, 261n50

biosecurity, 230, 270n8

bitau bread, 13f, 202, 212, 215

black market, 28, 161, 162

Blumberg Grain, 147, 149-50

Bobrow-Strain, Aaron, 253n96

Borlaug, Norman, 50-53, 59, 248n26, 250n49

bran, 240n9; in baking process, 2, 154, 194, 200; in baladi bread, 12, 63, 73, 74; milling process and, 7, 72-73, 202-3; in other kinds of bread, 13f, 194, 263n2

bread consumption: dry bread, 209-10, 210f; everyday, 10, 18-19, 63, 78, 116, 155, 181, 236-38; fino bread, 76, 254n100; in France, 15, 227, 242n26; frequency and quantity, 10-11, 15-16, 126, 131-32, 241n17, 264n11, 265n12; gender and social norms and, 9-10, 16, 195-96, 210, 237-38; homemade bread, 193, 214, 220-21; incentives to limit, 160; in India, 258n10; low prices and, 66; population growth and, 50; religious and spiritual dimensions, 18, 242n27; served with meals, x, xxiif, 9-10, 10f, 181, 198; as a tool, 9, 17, 241n15. See also taste

bread lines, 156, 157-58, 159-64, 180, 265n18; segregated by gender, 265n17; term usage, 265n15

bread making: cooling and packaging, 2, 184-86, 186f, 268nn46-47; dough preparation and baking, 153-54, 191-92, 200-201, 201f; flour prices and, 91-92, 204-5; ingredients, 70, 202-5, 268n7; labor and social relations of, 196-201; leavening agents, 17, 202, 222, 253n89, 269n11; mechanized vs. manual, 11; mixing of different flours, 71-72, 137, 203; national decline in, 219-22; ovens and fuel, 154, 190f, 192f, 205-7, 206f

bread prices, 3, 21, 27, 74, 264n3; 'aish beiti, 212; baladi, 11, 12, 63, 65-68, 244n43, 252n76, 252n78; shami and fino, 77-78

bread riots, 26-27, 66, 79, 230, 251n67; absence of, 67, 252n79; in American cities, 251n68

bread subsidy. See subsidized bread program

breeding, 47, 101, 240n6. See also wheat breeding

Bridge, Gavin, 235

Bunge, 128, 133

bureaucratic paperwork, 157, 167-69, 172-80, 266n23

Cairo, 33, 35-36, 220, 267n39; access to home-made bread in, 193, 212-16; Agricultural Museum, 217-18; baladi bread bakeries in, 11-12, 153, 156, 161-63, 167, 265nn16-17; breads commonly found in, 13f; Ma'adi neighbor-hood, 36, 183, 215, 245n49

China, 16, 228, 232-33, 255n10; potato cultiva-tion, 226, 229, 270nn1-2

CIMMYT (International Center for Wheat and Maize Improvement), 46, 51, 53, 58, 249n41

citizenship, 242n22

class, 16, 19, 28, 212, 219, 227; baladi bread consumption and, 168, 266n23, 267n44; cat-egories, 264n5; connotations of term baladi, 12. See also elites

climate change, 59, 228, 230, 232, 251n64

clover, 4, 89, 104, 110, 257n37

Codex Alimentarius, 130-31, 260n36

Collier, Stephen, 270n8

commodity chains, 75, 239n4, 261n50

cooperatives: agricultural, 55, 96f; bread, 239n2, 255n12

corn: flour, 13f, 71-72, 76f, 202; tortillas, 15, 16-17, 18, 227, 229, 268n6, 269n14; US exports, 228

coronavirus pandemic, xi, 83, 95, 140, 141

corruption, 99, 124-25, 148-50, 263n74; baladi bread bakeries and, 167

Craigslist, 113-14, 115, 124, 126, 128

Cronon, William, 261n52

cropping patterns or decisions, 56, 86, 100-101, 257n38; government control over, 95, 96f; high procurement prices and, 107, 108, 110; soil type and, 104; staple security and, 110-11

Cuba, 27-28, 244n40

cultural heritage, bread-baking, 193, 219, 221-22

Damietta port, 128-29, 131, 135, 136, 138f

daqiq baladi (baladi flour), 202-3, 204-5, 223

desert reclamation. See land reclamation

Dessouki, Said, 52-53

diet bread, 13f

Mexico, 17, 228, 229; tortillas as a staple, 15, 16, 18, 227, 269n10, 269n14; wheat varieties from, 46, 50–54, 55–57, 248n26, 250n49

miladin bread, 13*f*

military: bakeries, 158, 159, 263n1, 264n9; metaphors, 3, 24, 47; security, 20, 24; service, 110, 180–81, 267n36

millet, 13*f*, 14, 16, 229

mills/milling, 7, 8*f*, 100, 188; extraction rates, 72–73, 74–75, 203; mixing of grain varieties, 71, 253n90; in villages, 94, 102, 136, 203

Ministry of Agriculture, 6–7, 29, 86, 95, 221; ergot study, 132–33; goal to increase wheat production, 59–60, 62, 251n65; scientists, 47, 59; seed production, 55, 57–58, 250n60; support to wheat farmers, 99, 100

Ministry of Culture, 221–22

Ministry of Military Production, 166

Ministry of Supply and Internal Trade, 7, 17, 116, 142, 149; Facebook page, 144, 169; grain storage policy, 140, 262n57, 262n59; improvements to bread quality, 182, 183–84; smart (ration) cards, 166, 168–72; storage infrastructure development, 144, 147; subsidized bread program, 12, 65–69, 71–72, 73–74, 156, 159; wheat procurement policy, 87–88, 96*f*, 99–100; wheat reserves and, 140, 141, 262n63. *See also* General Authority for Supply Commodities (GASC); tamwin offices; tamwin stores

Mintz, Sidney, 19

Mitchell, Timothy, 50, 239n3, 240n8

Morocco, 15, 242n22, 253n90, 260n29, 269n15

Morsi, Mohamed, 29, 30, 45, 159, 182

Mubarak, Hosni, 2, 30, 66, 158, 240n11, 244n42

Nasser, Gamal Abdel, 30, 45, 123, 240n11, 244n42

national security, 21, 26, 31, 86, 228; bread and, 25, 70, 155, 251n68; grain storage and, 139, 227, 262n56; wheat contamination and, 131

neoliberalism, 20; reforms in Egypt, 66, 68, 97, 240n11, 244n42, 250n51, 258n12

newspaper articles: complaints about baladi bread, 69, 70, 181–82; on imported wheat, 24, 116, 121, 122, 125, 258n10; on poor-quality wheat, 126–27, 130, 131–32; as sources, 36, 254n6, 257n3; on subsidized bread program,

179, 243n38; on wheat cultivation, 45, 50, 58, 84, 85–88, 102, 111; on wheat storage, 141, 143, 144, 145

Nile Valley and Delta, 49, 136–37, 145, 255n16; agricultural land, 4, 6*f*

nutrition, 11, 229, 270n5; Ancient Egyptian diet and, 41, 43; baladi bread and, 14, 73, 253n88; food security and, 23, 24, 25; potatoes and, 226

obesity, 11

oil: cooking, 27, 67, 160–61, 172, 178, 244n43; national supply and revenue, 21, 122, 232, 233

1.5 Million Feddans Project, 50

onion cultivation, 82, 89, 257nn39–40; compared to wheat cultivation, 85, 102, 103–4, 105*f*, 106–10, 257n38

Ottoman rule, 4, 29

Pakistan, 232, 233

parenting and fieldwork, 32–37

ports, 8, 31, 136, 138*f*; wheat inspection at, 127, 128–35

potatoes, 14–15, 17, 28; promoted in China, 226, 229, 270nn1–2

poverty rates, 12, 154, 168, 242n21, 264nn4–5; in Fayoum Governorate, 254n3

preserving bread, 18, 207–12, 269n11

prices. *See* bread prices; wheat prices; world market prices

Principal Bank of Development and Agricultural Credit, 8*f*, 136

protests: food riots, 26–27; government efforts to control, 239n1; over bread shortages, x, 1–2, 159, 266n27; over increased bread prices, 3, 66

proverbs, bread, 242n26

qamh flour, 202–4

qirat, grain quality measurement, 127, 259n28

raised-bed cultivation, 59–62, 61*f*, 84, 257n40

ration cards. *See* smart cards

reclamation. *See* land reclamation

refined flour, 7–8, 8*f*, 73, 100; breads made from, 12, 13*f*, 76, 264n2; controls on production and marketing, 96*f*; zero flour as, 203, 204, 213, 269n9